Dorman Bridgman Eaton

**Civil Service in Great Britain**

A History of Abuses and Reforms and their bearing upon American Politics

Dorman Bridgman Eaton

**Civil Service in Great Britain**
*A History of Abuses and Reforms and their bearing upon American Politics*

ISBN/EAN: 9783337079390

Printed in Europe, USA, Canada, Australia, Japan

Cover: Foto ©ninafisch / pixelio.de

More available books at **www.hansebooks.com**

# A HISTORY OF

# ABUSES AND REFORMS

### AND THEIR

# BEARING UPON AMERICAN POLITICS

## By DORMAN B. EATON

*"I think every one, according to the way Providence has placed him
in, is bound to labor for the public good as far as he is able."*
JOHN LOCKE

## NEW YORK
## HARPER & BROTHERS, PUBLISHERS
### FRANKLIN SQUARE
### 1880

# NOTE.

In submitting these pages to the public, it seems proper I should state that the views they express concerning administration in Great Britain are not based solely upon the authorities cited. During a sojourn of more than a year in that country, I had given special attention to the subject. The general studies then made have been recently verified by special inquiries conducted in her principal Executive Departments;* and it is but just to add that these later investigations were undertaken pursuant to the request conveyed to me in the following communication:

DEPARTMENT OF STATE,
WASHINGTON, *June* 25, 1877.

*Honorable* DORMAN B. EATON, *Chairman Civil Service Commission:*

SIR,—*The Act of March* 3, 1871 (*R. S., § 1753), having, in terms, conferred certain authority upon the President for the regulation of the Civil Service, the proper exercise of which may make it desirable that he should possess fuller information concerning the methods of such regulation in countries where that service sustains relations most analogous to those of the Civil Service of the United States, I have been requested by the President to say to you that he hopes you may find it practicable to investigate and make a report to him concerning the action of the English Government in relation to its Civil Service, and the effects of such action since 1850.*

*But I must add that, there not appearing to be any appropriation available for such purpose, you will not be authorized to incur any expense for which the United States is to be held responsible.*

*I have the honor to be, Sir, your obedient servant,*

W. M. EVARTS.

In bringing the substance of the report submitted to the President before the public in this volume, I may be mistaken in the value of the facts it presents as a contribution to the literature of reform; but I cannot be in my painful sense of the many defects in the execution of the work.

D. B. E.

---

* I am much indebted to various British officers and to several other gentlemen for their polite and valuable assistance in aid of my inquiries; and, without mentioning other names, I desire to return my special thanks to Sir Charles Trevelyan, the venerable reformer and statesman, and to Horace Mann, Esq., the efficient and accomplished Secretary of the British Civil Service Commission.

# INTRODUCTION

## BY

## GEORGE WILLIAM CURTIS.

---

THE author of this book, Mr. Dorman B. Eaton, is the chairman of the commission for devising rules and regulations for the purpose of reforming the Civil Service, which was authorized by the Act of Congress approved by President Grant March 4th, 1871. Soon after President Hayes entered upon the duties of his office, he requested Mr. Eaton personally to investigate the operation of the reformed system in England, and to prepare a report upon the results of his observation. Mr. Eaton accepted the invitation of the President, and devoted several months, with characteristic zeal and thoroughness, to an exhaustive inquiry upon the spot into the reasons, methods, and results of the reform. His studies soon showed him that the new system of appointment and the new tenure of place in the Civil Service were but logical steps of progress in the political development of England. The unreformed Civil Service in Great Britain, as in the United States, was founded upon the theory of feudal times, that public offices are the property of the ruler. Upon this theory they were filled for his benefit, and without regard to the fitness of the officer or to the public welfare, and Mr. Eaton well calls the Forty-fifth Article of Magna Charta the first Civil Service Rule.

By that article the king engaged not to "make any justices, constables, sheriffs, or bailiffs but of such as know the law of the realm." This was a declaration that administrative offices should be filled by those who were competent, and not merely by royal favor.

Pursuing his interesting researches from epoch to epoch, Mr. Eaton's report has taken, naturally and fortunately, the form of a history of the development of the Civil Service in England, from the earliest day down to its present efficient and excellent condition. It is a comprehensive manual of information upon the subject, and there is no other work of the kind. It answers the historical, theoretical, and practical questions which are asked by every inquirer, the answers to which have been hitherto very difficult to find. The work, indeed, is a timely and valuable contribution to the literature of the reform, as well as an exceedingly interesting study in a neglected branch of historical and political inquiry. The history of the movement for reform in the United States does not fall within the scope of Mr. Eaton's work, nor could he properly, in this report, express at length his views of the results that have been accomplished under the present administration. Yet he treats fully of those principles of a sound service which are common to both countries, and he presents a complete and well-reasoned argument for their enforcement in the United States. There are few points which any serious thinker upon the subject will find to have escaped Mr. Eaton's attention, while the evidence of care in the preparation of the work is sure to command sympathy and confidence.

The reform movement which ended in the appointment of the commission of which Mr. Eaton is chairman, was begun by Mr. Thomas Allen Jenckes, a representative in Congress from Rhode Island from 1863 until 1871. His attention, and that of many others, had been turned to the subject at the close of the war by the enormous increase of the number of places within the patronage of the Government, and by the new and extraordinary doctrines and practices in regard to their distribution. These doctrines and practices threatened popular government itself. The "spoils" system introduced by President Jackson, which is now stigmatized as the "American system," imperils not only the purity, economy, and efficiency of the administration of the Government, but it destroys confidence in the method of popular government by party. It creates a mercenary political class, an oligarchy of stipendiaries, a bureaucracy of the worst kind, which controls parties with relentless despotism, imposing upon them at the elections issues which are prescribed not by the actual feeling and interest of the country but solely by the necessities and profit of the oligarchy, while, to secure this advantage, party-spirit, the constant and mortal peril of republics, is inflamed to the utmost. It is a system which, by requiring complete servility to the will of the oligarchy, both as the tenure of minor place and as the condition of political promotion, destroys the individual political independence which is the last defence of liberty. An election thus becomes merely the registry of the decree of a cabal. Government by the people, four-fifths of whom simply vote for the ticket or the measures prepared by the oligarchy, sinks practically into the empire of a corrupt ring. In a country where every citizen ought to take an active part in practical politics, this system disgusts with politics, and repels from them good citizens who cannot compete with the professional political class which gives all its time to a pursuit by which it profits. The system necessarily excludes able men from public life, and makes a great many of the conspicuous names in politics little illustrative of the real leadership of American ability, enterprise, and progress. The name of politician and officeholder becomes a byword, and casts ridicule upon the very name of reform. How complete was the subjugation of public sentiment in this country within a few years, and how audacious the effrontery of the spoils system, may be inferred from the deliberate argument of one of Tweed's political attorneys, that such "rings" are inevitable and indispensable in a free country; and from the contemptuous bitterness with which a leader of the party opposed to Tweed echoed the same sentiment, by sneering that when Dr. Johnson described patriotism as the last refuge of a scoundrel, he did not know the infinite possibilities of the word reform. There is no more startling sign of political demoralization than the craft which turns the follies of reformers into blows at reform. This situation has been plainly seen by the most intelligent observers of our politics. In the second volume of his *Constitutional History of the United States*, Von Holst quotes Senator Marcy's notorious declaration that "the politicians of New York * * * see nothing wrong in the rule that to the victor belong the spoils of the enemy;" and adds, "From that hour this maxim has remained an inviolable principle of American politicians, and it is owing only to the astonishing vitality of the people of the United States, and to the altogether unsurpassed and unsurpassable favor of their natural conditions, that the State has not succumbed under the onerous burden of the curse."

Mr. Jenckes began the general discussion of the subject in a report of the Joint Select Committee on Retrenchment, of which he was chairman. It was presented to the House of Representatives on the 25th of May, 1868, and, with its appendix, contains a mass of information which shows how deep was his interest and how careful his investigation. The question of reform had been very fully considered in England for several years when Mr. Jenckes began his inquiries, and he entered into correspondence with Sir Stafford H. Northcote and Sir Charles E. Trevelyan, who wrote the masterly report upon the organization of the Permanent Civil Service in Great Britain, dated November 23d, 1853. This report, with the Blue Book called "Papers relating to the Reorganization of the Civil Service," had opened the whole question in England. The Blue Book contained the elaborate opinions of leading Englishmen in every department of private and public life, and presents completely the argument, the objections, and the refutations. No objection has been suggested in this country which is not satisfactorily answered in this Blue Book. The instructive reports and speeches of Mr. Jenckes, although treated in Congress with little consideration, aroused great interest in the public mind, and led to some discussion in the press. The law of 1871, authorizing the inquiry under which President Grant appointed the commission of which Mr. Eaton is now chairman, was the last public service of Mr. Jenckes; but during the short remainder of his life his interest in the question was unabated. His valuable counsel was sought by the commission in the early days of their labors, and it was most willingly given.

The rules recommended to President Grant, and adopted by him, were never effectively carried into practice at any point of the service. The reasons for this failure were many, and it is not necessary to consider them here. They all served, however, to show more clearly the extent and the power of the evils of the system of patronage in the Civil Service, and the necessity of reform. The subject having attracted public attention, was cautiously mentioned in the platforms of all political parties, but the allusions were evasive, and were evidently intended only to propitiate a desire for reform which the party managers did not believe to be strong or general enough to compel its gratification. The subject, however, is one that necessarily interests intelligent citizens, and, although derided by politicians, it is not surprising that Mr. Hayes, in his letter accepting the nomination for the Presidency, spoke of reform in the Civil Service as one of the questions so important as to demand an expression of his convictions in regard to it. He declared that the resolution upon the subject, in the platform of the Convention that nominated him, was of "paramount interest:" and, after a vigorous expression of his views, he concluded by saying, "The reform should be thorough, radical, and complete. We should return to the principles and practice of the founders of the Government, supplying by legislation, when needed, that which was formerly the established custom. They neither expected nor desired from the public officers any partisan service. They meant that public officers should give their whole service to the Government and to the people. They meant that the officer should be secure in his tenure so long as his personal character remained untarnished and the performance of his duties satisfactory. If elected, I shall conduct the administration of the Government upon these principles, and all constitutional powers vested in the Executive will be employed to establish this reform."

Notwithstanding the strong declarations of the Republican platform and of the candidate upon this subject, the managers of both parties carefully gave the chief prominence during the canvass of 1876 to other questions, and there was no general popular discussion of reform. But in his inaugural address President Hayes unequivocally reaffirmed the views of his letter of acceptance. He said, "I ask the attention of the public to the paramount necessity of reform in the Civil Service—a reform not merely as to certain abuses and practices of so-called official patronage which have come to have the sanction of usage in the several departments of our Government, but a change in the system of appointment itself—a reform that shall be thorough, radical, and complete—a return to the principles and practices of the founders of the Government."

The President gave the most conspicuous proof of his since
ity in selecting for the Secretaryship of the Interior Mr. Carl
Schurz, who is known as a faithful friend of reform.

During the administration of President Hayes, although its
conduct upon this subject has been inexplicably inconsistent,
and although no general and uniform system of determining
minor appointments has been adopted, yet very much more
reform has been accomplished than under any previous administration. The abuse of Congressional dictation of nominations has been in a great degree remedied. The usurpation
of executive power, called the courtesy of the Senate, by which
the Senator or Senators from a State control the confirmation
of all appointments in it, has been in a conspicuous instance
overthrown. The interference, in caucuses and conventions, of
office-holders, with all their patronage to buy votes, has been
prohibited, and had the prohibition been vigorously enforced,
the results would have been very much more favorable to the
rapid progress of reform. The robbery known as political assessments, a tax levied by party committees upon office-holders
as the price of their places—a tax which puts up the public
service at auction, and illustrates the degrading tenure of office
under a system of patronage—has been strictly forbidden;
and so far as the President can defend the incumbents by the
frankest expression of his views, and of his determination that
they shall not suffer for refusing to be robbed, the abuse has
been corrected. There is no doubt that the evil has been very
much lessened, but there is no doubt, also, that there is still
connivance at the practice on the part of many superior officers, and the only really effective remedy lies in the appointment of superior officers who are sincerely resolved to stop it.
Reform thrives upon moral confidence, and nothing would develop faith in it so fully as the knowledge that the offices of
great patronage were filled by men thoroughly persuaded of

the necessity of reform, and courageous enough resolutely to enforce it.

The great measure of reform, however, which has been accomplished under the administration of Mr. Hayes, is the substitution of what Mr. Eaton justly calls the merit system for favoritism in appointment at the New York Custom-house and Post-office, the two chief offices in these departments in the country. The faithful enforcement at these offices of the rule that minor appointments shall be made only upon the proved merit of applicants, in a competitive examination, has shown conclusively the practicability of the system. All applicants have been submitted, without fear or favor, to equal tests, and the selections for appointment have been made in the same way from those who have proved their superiority. The character of the persons so appointed, and the value of their services as compared with those appointed under the old system of political and personal favoritism, are but additional proofs of the excellence of the system. In both of these offices, however, the reform has been applied only to original appointments in certain grades, and to certain promotions. The service in both is full of those who were appointed under the old system of favor and reward, and who naturally cherish its traditions. This does not produce an atmosphere of reform, and it makes abuse easier; but it is incontestable that the simplicity of the method and the great value of the result have been demonstrated at these two chief points. If practicable there, reform is practicable everywhere.

These are results which are due wholly to the sincere conviction and purpose of the President, and, however imperfect and incomplete, they are of great importance and significance. It was in pursuance of his general purpose that he asked Mr. Eaton, as chairman of the Civil Service Commission, personally to conduct the inquiry of which this work is the fruit. Mr.

Eaton's report shows conclusively from the experience of Great Britain how the radical vice of our system of appointment in the Civil Service can be corrected. The modern party patronage system in England began in 1693, and continued until the beginning of the reform in 1853. Instead of the "clean sweep," upon every party success, which is the disgrace of our republic, only certain high officers now go out in England when their party is defeated. "We limit," says Mr. Gladstone, "to a few scores of persons the removals and appointments on these occasions, although our ministers seem to us not infrequently to be more sharply severed from one another in principle and tendency than are the successive Presidents of the Great Union." The legitimate sphere of personal political ambition in a free country is that of competition before the public for posts of legislation and of political administration. But the details of the Civil Service belong to a business, not to a political administration, and the line between proper political and non-political places is perfectly well defined. When King James II. insisted that nobody should have an ale or beer license who did not favor his policy, he was only asserting the modern principle that nobody shall be an inspector in the Custom-house, or shall deliver letters at the Post-office, unless he is a supporter of the dominant party. We denounce, as intolerable tyranny, Cromwell's test of Presbyterianism, and the Test Acts of Charles II., which made religious profession of another kind an essential qualification for holding minor office. But they were no more tyrannical, or intolerable, or absurd than our party tests. Sir Robert Walpole's use of the Secret Service money to buy votes in Parliament was no worse than buying votes with patronage in a Convention. I have known an officer of the customs who intended, as a delegate in a party Convention, to vote against the candidate favored by the collector, who was also a delegate. The collector, learning the intention of his subordinate, gave him the choice of voting as the collector wished, or losing his place. The subordinate had a wife and family dependent upon him, and he yielded. This was Sir Robert Walpole's method, but his bribery was manlier than the collector's.

Reform of the system which necessarily produces such abuses is no more an experiment than the reform of any other evil. The system of civil appointment for the public service by patronage and favoritism, like the Corporation and Test Acts—like all other forms of injustice and abuse—when it is challenged by advancing civilization and greater intelligence, must show why it should not be abolished. The abuses which it is said cannot be reformed are merely surviving forms of old venality and wrong, which have been universally condemned as monstrous and intolerable, and whose gradual disappearance marks the progress of society. The readers of this book will decide whether the abuses of the worst days of English party politics—abuses which the good sense of England has entirely removed—are necessary either for the maintenance of party government or for the promotion of political morality in the United States.

# CONTENTS.

# CIVIL SERVICE

### IN

# GREAT BRITAIN.

---

## INTRODUCTORY.

### CHAPTER I.

The character of our early politics.—The sources of our Constitution.—Administrative abuses little anticipated.—The forecast of Washington.—The changes of a century.—Present views as to reform in this country.—First study of administrative questions in Great Britain.—Reasons why we should consider British precedents.—Attention to Civil Service Reform on the part of the principal nations.—Our neglect of the subject.—Extent of reforms in the leading European States.—The situation in Canada.—Causes of our neglect of administrative questions.—Party despotism.—Different theories as to a reform policy.—The value to us of British experience.—Some of the main questions to be considered, and their bearing on our politics.—No mere imitation of British precedents desirable.—Why we must go back in our inquiry to first principles and to the origin of abuses.—The great variety and extent of British administration.—Administration in India.—Our evils all dealt with in the experience of Great Britain.—The policy on which the leading nations have acted in making reforms.—The exposure of abuses a patriotic duty.

An English historian declares that "no nation ever started on its career with a larger proportion of strong character or a higher sense of moral conviction than the English colonies in America. They almost entirely escaped the corruption that so deeply tainted the government at home." [1]

It is universally admitted that our early leaders in politics embodied, in a remarkable degree, the ability and the high moral tone of their generation. There is, perhaps, no more

Lecky's History of England in the Eighteenth Century, vol. ii., p. 2, herein elsewhere cited as 1 or 2 Lecky.

1

striking proof of their statesmanship than the fact that, when
heated from recent battle-fields and filled with righteous indignation at the injustice of the mother country, they yet
brought to the great work of forming a constitution judgments so calm and unprejudiced that they were able to consider her precedents in the same judicial spirit in which they
considered those of other nations. Men of narrower minds
might have rejected all the political wisdom of their race.
They might have given us a constitution as original and as
disastrous as the constitutions which fell to the lot of France.
We can better appreciate the enlightened spirit which animated our early statesmen, if we consider the narrow prejudices which even now stand in the way of improved methods
which are denounced as of foreign origin.

The authors of our constitution accepted good material
wherever they found it ; but from no quarter did they gather
so much as from the experience of England. The theory of
executive power ; the great divisions of government into
three departments, with well-defined jurisdictions ; two houses
of legislation with the whole body of parliamentary law ; trial
by jury ; the habeas corpus ; the common law, with its vast
stores of wisdom, extending to all business and all personal relations ; the long series of statutes so far as not repugnant to
the new system ; criminal definitions and procedure in all
their larger parts ; the theory of military as subordinate to civil
authority ; the political conception of domestic and individual
rights and duties—all these they drew from the same paternal
source from which had flowed their blood, their language,
and their civilization.

With wise adjustments, they incorporated all these political
elements into their new system of government. That government, however, was not to be a mere imitation, but an original and true Republic. They, therefore, rejected royalty and
primogeniture, the entire feudal theory, all class distinctions,
and all mingling of religion with politics. In their place,
they proclaimed common rights, equality before the law, and
freedom of speech and of worship. The new government, for
the very reason that it discards and rises above mere selfish
interests, more than any that has existed in modern times,

both appeals to and requires general intelligence and public virtue. " In proportion as the structure of a government gives force to public opinion, it is essential that public opinion should be enlightened." [1]

At its creation the greatest dangers, the absorbing questions affecting the new government, concerned rights, liberty, and independence. Corruption bred in the daily work of administration, partisan tyranny and debasement growing out of contentions for patronage, office, and power, were almost unknown, and they were but feebly imagined, in the first generation. It was natural that no very definite provisions should be made against such sources of danger. Washington, apparently, looked upon parties as an evil, and perhaps thought they might be avoided. The great power of removal from office was left to mere inference, and it is, therefore, without expressed limitation or safeguard. But that generation must be counted wise and patriotic which provides a remedy for the evils which it knows. Certainly, statesmen who nobly performed the duties of their own trying times, are not to be complained of because they did not take precautions against abuses which were only to afflict the country in future generations. No nation had, at that time, protected itself against the evils of corrupt patronage and favoritism in bestowing office. In no nation but England was there even freedom enough to enable great parties to exist.

A century has passed, and it has produced great changes in the old country and in the new. In Great Britain, these changes have struck deeper both into social life and into the political system than with us. But in the United States they have long since made administrative abuses a source of solicitude and humiliation. They are now recognized as a grave problem in our public affairs. Recently, and for the first time, these abuses have been brought into the foreground of a presidential contest. The promise of their removal has been made the subject of party pledges before the people. Civil service reform has become an issue in national politics.

Administrative abuses are of a kind that will naturally grow

[1] Washington's Farewell Address.

as wealth accumulates, population becomes more dense, and public affairs increase in volume and complexity. They raise issues in their nature as permanent as the selfishness and partisanship from which they are born, and the government which they threaten. Few thoughtful persons are so blind as not to see that a great reform is essential to avert a great calamity. How to bring it about is the question. There is a profound sense of need to purify public administration, to arrest partisan tyranny, and to bestow office upon men of worth and capacity. But the public mind gropes and hesitates and doubts ; having no clear conception as to what is possible, and no definite method upon which it inclines to act. A few statesmen very early comprehended, and the popular mind is now beginning to comprehend, that, though the forming of a wise and just government is the greatest achievement of a people, its honest and vigorous administration involves perils and difficulties little anticipated in the youth of nations.[1] With astonishment, and a sort of despair, the people of the United States now find—as every older nation has found—that the question of good methods, of honest ways, and of faithful servants, in administration, must take its place among the grave and the permanent problems of statesmanship.

There is nothing more remarkable in the experience of Great Britain, during the past century, than the measures she has taken to reform administrative abuses. What we have most neglected in politics, she has most studied—the science of administration. Chatham and Burke set the example of giving that subject a foremost place in the politics of their country : and during the last fifty years it has commanded the earnest attention of her greatest statesmen. She has brought about changes which have elevated the moral tone of her

[1] Washington's experience in war strongly convinced him of the need of competent officers in the military service. The Academy at West Point has been the result. Simple and easy as civil administration was in his day, seven years in the executive chair caused him to advise even the extreme measure of a national university, " a primary object of which should be the education of our youth in the *science of government*." (Washington's Eighth Annual Message.) In his sixth annual message, President Jefferson suggested an amendment to the Constitution to enable " a national establishment for education" to be created and endowed.

official life—reforms which really constitute an era in her history. They are as a silver edge upon the dark cloud which hangs over British administration in former centuries. While this great work has been going on in the mother country, we have fallen away from the better methods of our early history. We have come upon a period when we mourn over the absence of the political virtues recognized in the past—when not a few good citizens despair of again seeing that purity of official life which prevailed during our first generations. The more thoughtful are asking whether the abuses which have been so rapidly developed are due to our neglects as citizens, or are inevitable under republican institutions. The republican theory is arraigned at the bar of public opinion on charges apparently never imagined by its authors. Seeing how much better and more quietly administration is carried on in Great Britain than in the United States, some gloomy and some aristocratic spirits are ready to despair of the republic. They attribute the obvious superiority to causes original and inevitable in the institutions of their own country. If faith in the republican system has not been impaired, respect for official life has been seriously undermined. Obviously, fundamental principles, not less than grave interests, are involved. Nothing would seem, therefore, to be more appropriate or more in the spirit of the great work of our fathers than to inquire whether, in the later experience of Great Britain— which is only a prolongation of that from which they made such large selections—there may not be something adapted to our system and worthy of our consideration. Are her reforms based on principles of which only a monarchy can take advantage, or are they equally available under republican institutions? Can we remove our abuses without changing the form of our government?

But, were there no suggestions from the highest precedents in our history, it would seem to be but the statesmanship of national interest—at a time when the leading states of the world have made it a national policy to bring into comparison even the works of mechanical industry—to make ourselves acquainted with the measures through which the freest and most enlightened of the great nations of Europe has elevated the character of her public administration. No nation can afford to be ill-informed as to the methods by which other nations advance their strength and prosperity. More and more, in later years, the leading governments have comprehended, and have acted upon the theory, that their peace and prosperity are greatly dependent, not merely on officers in very high positions, but upon the fidelity and ability of those in the public service down to the very lowest places. All the leading nations, except the United States, have recently, and as a matter of policy, made searching investigations not only into their own administrative methods but into the methods of other governments. These inquiries have extended to civil and military administration alike ; and neither prejudice nor partisan interests have been allowed to stand in the way of improvements. Prussia set the example, after her humiliation by Bonaparte in 1815, and her position is the fruit of her policy. The present Emperor of Russia acted in the same spirit when he entered upon the reform policy which has done so much to raise his country from the degradation it had reached under the corrupt civil and military service of former reigns. Great Britain had investigated the excellent methods of France and Prussia, before 1854. In later years, Great Britain has steadily acted upon the principle that her prosperity and safety depend on the character of her administration, and that the surest way to correct its abuses is to investigate and expose them. The United States, on the contrary, have, until very lately, given but little attention to the growing abuses of administration at home ; and they have utterly neglected the methods through which rival nations have brought about great reforms.

This neglect has been the result of no general indifference to foreign matters on the part of the American people. They have rather been conspicuous for the zeal and success with which, in every quarter of the globe, they have sought information concerning productions, business, and every process of science and industry. They are far better informed concerning all the ways of raising crops and all the breeds of cattle, horses, sheep, and swine in Great Britain, than they are concerning the means by which her official life has been raised and her politics purified. Our statesmen are familiar enough with the history of *Magna Carta*, the *Habeas Corpus*, the Bill of Rights, the Act of Settlement, and all the great events which preceded our revolution. But what study have they given to the principles and the carefully matured methods of administration upon which the greatest British statesmen of this century have bent their minds? The history and development of literature, science and art, in every leading European State, have been carefully studied by American scholars, and they are a part of the cherished instruction of our educated classes. But what attention has been bestowed upon those profound and salutary systems of administration which have, during the present century, transformed the politics of Europe and made learning and character the handmaids and strength of governments?

" All the governments of Europe have, in our time, singularly improved the *science of administration*; they do more things, and do every thing with more order, more celerity, and at less expense.'

" During the last three quarters of a century a complete revolution has taken place in the civil service of the principle European States. Rigorous and impartial tests of qualification have been applied; and, where formerly were incompetency, routine, and peculation, are now efficiency and fidelity. *The prosperity of these States is owing, in a great degree, to the character of their civil service;* for it has been instrumental to the development of their resources and to public economy.'' [2]

These great changes—this moral regeneration of official life in the Old World—have all the more significance for us because they have taken place during the period within which, by common consent, we have fallen away from the higher standards of our earlier politics. These reforms are not less worthy our attention for the reason that nowhere have they been more complete and more salutary than in Great Britain (and in her colonies and dependencies), where laws and institutions most analogous to our own prevail.

The spirit of improvement has at last come from abroad

---

[1] " Democracy in America." By De Tocqueville, vol. ii. p. 378.

[2] Mr. Andrews, late Minister to Sweden, to Mr. Fish, *Foreign Relations of the United States*, 1876, p. 553.

upon our own borders. A Governor-General of Canada is able to refer to the prospects of that country in language which we can hardly read without interest, if without self-reproach. "It is necessary that the civil service should be given a *status* regulated by their acquirements, their personal qualifications, their capacity for rendering the country efficient service ; and that neither their original appointments nor their subsequent advancement should, in any way, have to depend upon their political connections or opinions. If you will take my advice, you will never allow the civil service to be degraded into an instrument to subserve the ends of any political party. . . . *Happily both the great political parties in this country have given in their adherence to this principle.* . . . And I have no doubt that the anxiety manifested by our friends across the line to purge their own civil service of its political complexion will confirm every true Canadian in the convictions I have sought to impress upon you."[1]

How are we to explain these contrasts, and this strange neglect of what so gravely concerns our honor and our prosperity ? Has it been because, in our days of inexperience and sparse population, we adopted the theory that public administration was an inferior matter, hardly worthy the thoughts of statesmen, which might be handed over to the management of great parties ? Have we acted under that delusion so long that it requires a greater effort than we have made to see the subject in its true relations ? Whatever the cause, it is plain we have allowed abuses to grow almost without a serious effort to remove them. We have neither traced them to their causes nor comprehended their perils. We have endured them with a sort of fatalistic resignation equally suggestive of indifference and despair. We have been supinely floating on the partisan currents of our politics in whatever direction they have flowed. The caprice of the majority has been accepted as the rule of duty. That majority, until the present decade, at least, has tended more and more to become despotic.[2]

---

[1] Farewell speech of Lord Dufferin, Governor-General of Canada, November, 1878.

[2] "I had remarked during my stay in the United States, that a democratic state of society might offer singular facilities for the establishment of despotism." "Democracy in America," vol. ii. p. 389.

Manly independence in politics has naturally decayed. Absorbed by the current questions of party contests, our great officers and political leaders have, decade after decade, remained inactive in the presence of injustice and corruption in the daily affairs of administration such as have not, for nearly half a century, existed in the government of any other leading nation, except Russia. With many politicians, it has come to be treated as unpatriotic to suggest that our methods of dealing with offices and parties can be improved. To such an extent has the prevalence of a partisan spoils system blinded and perverted the public judgment that we need to go back to the time of Walpole, or at least to the time of George III., to find precedents for the scorn and arrogance with which partisan managers and the dominant majority, in this country, have insulted and defied the higher sentiments of the people.

The more sober and introspective mood which has lately come over the public mind is highly favorable to a reform in our administration, and we may reasonably expect that the influence of the reform sentiment will continue to gain strength. But well defined and consistent views and common methods of action on the part of those who support reform are essential. Such views by no means exist. Some of its friends expect to see a reform brought about by a grand popular effort, which shall at once drive all unworthy men from office and open a new era in our politics. Others look upon reform as a work of enlightenment and purification, to be gradually carried forward, and mainly through methods of its own which, by their salutary effects, will win the support needed to hasten its completion. While a third class believe that no reform is possible which is not carried out through party action alone, and by the ordinary processes of partisan politics. We need to decide which of these theories is correct.

Civil service reform in its true scope includes not merely practical methods in administration, under which worth and capacity may gain what is their due, despite corrupt and partisan influence, but it also embodies great principles which concern the duties of office and the very foundations of parties and government. An essential condition of its support is

a belief that our partisan activity is excessive, and that great
parties would be more salutary if they trusted more to principles and to patriotism, and less to mere interest, patronage, and
spoils. But, on the other hand, there are many who believe
that all such base elements are essential to the vigor, if not
to the existence, of great parties. Ordinary human nature—
man as he is and will be in this country—they hold to be incapable of any thing more patriotic or disinterested. They
maintain that our partisan system of dealing with office and
administration is a natural and *original* growth under our institutions. They assert that every attempt to change it is a
sort of rebellion against the theory of the government and
the conditions of its success. They declare that the British
Government is so different in theory and structure, and that
the relations of parties under it are so diverse from party relations in the United States, that all reasoning from one to
the other is unwarranted and misleading. From these views,
it follows that those who seek a reform in our civil service—
and especially those who hope to aid the work by a study of
British precedents—are commending principles which it is
dangerous to act upon. They are urging standards of duty
and methods of action at once chimerical and impracticable—
the dreams of *doctrinaires*—the ideals of amiable enthusiasts
knowing little of politics or of human nature. It is plain that
the merits of these conflicting views cannot be tested without
an inquiry into the history of civil corruption in Great Britain
and a consideration of the relations which parties there hold to
government and to society. It will certainly not be an un-
profitable inquiry, if we shall find that the abuses, (for which
our corrupt partisans apologize by declaring them to be original and inseparable from party government in a republic,)
were in full vigor under despotic kings two centuries before
this continent was discovered, and four centuries before party
government existed. How can we better determine the comparative relations of parties in the two countries than by showing their origin and growth in Great Britain, their attitude
toward the partisan spoils system which prevailed there for
generations, and the manner in which British parties have
been compelled to accept a reform by which that system

has been exterminated and their own salutary vigor has been strengthened?

When we see something like despair over the evils produced by Congressmen interfering with the appointing power, will it not be useful to consider a grand procession of reform measures, in which the origin, the damaging effects, and the removal of those very evils, are but links in the great chain of events? At a time when demagogues proclaim, and faint-hearted, good men fear that it requires an official virtue far beyond any we should expect in this world, to have appointments made on the basis of merit fairly disclosed by non-partisan tests, will it not be profitable to present the history of the accomplishment of precisely that reform by another government acting upon methods quite available to us?

In tracing the history[1] of abuses and reforms in Great Britain, we shall find ourselves considering no unimportant part of those great influences which have shaped the progress of her civilization. The purposes of this volume, fortunately, do not require any profound treatment of the subject. But I am persuaded that its adequate presentation would show that important events, commonly represented as carried forward by influences much more general and external, have really had their foundation in the interests of officials and the prostitution of the public service. For example, the attitude of Great Britain toward this country during our revolutionary war cannot be fully appreciated without a better understanding, than is usually illustrated by historians, of the influence of a despotic and corrupt civil and military administration in that country, by which that war was at least aggravated and prolonged. It is not easy to estimate the extent to which the morality and the policy of a great nation is moulded by the character and the interests of those who fill its offices, apply its resources, and use its name and authority.

In considering the methods by which the most liberal and commercial nation of the Old World has elevated the charac-

---

[1] "To give a full history of civil service reform in England would require a bulky volume." Pamphlet by E. F. Waters, 1878. This interesting pamphlet, which, unfortunately for me, is of very limited range, is the only writing I have been able to find especially devoted to the subject.

ter of its official life, we need not have any purpose of mere imitation. The question for us, like the question for our early statesmen, is whether, from that quarter, we may gather any thing adapted to our needs, and in harmony with our political and social system. And it is because the subject is so general that it will be necessary to consider it quite beyond its direct bearings upon public administration. How does it stand related to liberty, to equality, to popular education, to equal rights and common justice? Is the spirit which has reformed the civil service of Great Britain a monarchical, aristocratic spirit, or is it a republican, democratic, and liberal spirit?

On reflection, it will excite no surprise that British experience is presented as richer, riper, and more varied, as well as vastly more extensive, than that of the United States. It is such, not merely because England had gathered the administrative wisdom of many centuries before the American nation was born. Eliot and Vane, Chatham and Burke, had so lived and spoken that the greatest reformers may even yet gather inspiration and wisdom from their examples. Statutes had been enacted, in the interest of pure and vigorous administration, to the moral level of which none of our own enactments have yet risen, and without which our courts could not sustain their most salutary rulings. We must also remember that Great Britain has ruled over so many millions of people, over countries so diverse and races so different, and that she has held such supremacy in commerce in all quarters of the globe, that every kind of official authority has been exercised upon a scale with which, in many particulars, nothing analogous in our affairs is comparable. To rule British India alone, with its vast public works, its great army of more than 250,000 men, its 200,000 policemen, its revenues of $250,000,000 a year, its population of more than 190,000,000, of many races and creeds—at once difficult to govern and dangerous to neglect—even for a single year—requires more officials, more responsibility, more efficient methods of administration, and I may almost add more care and capacity, than would have sufficed for good administration in all our territories and Indian affairs during this generation. When to India we add the Australian colonies Tasmania and South Africa, Canada and Jamaica, Ceylon and the many islands and stations under the British flag all round the globe —there is presented a variety of official life and opportunities for corruption under a bad system, such as never before, in ancient or modern times, taxed the administrative wisdom of a nation.

As we have to deal with the claim that some of our principal evils are inevitable accompaniments of the blessings of republican government, we shall need to trace them to their true source in the feudal system. Therein we shall find the origin of the spoils system ; and the partisan theory of official irresponsibility in the use of the appointing power in full practice. From thence, we shall trace the gradual development of the idea of official responsibility up to and through a partisan system of appointments and removals, beyond which we have not yet advanced.[1] It is the need of refuting the false theories referred to which makes a historical treatment of the subject indispensable. The course of history and the results of experience through centuries will be the argument and the refutation. The world takes notice that never before has any nation ruled with such success dependencies so broad or profited by a commerce so extensive as now belong to Great Britain. Is that success more due to the form of her government or to the system of her administration ? We are of the same Anglo-Saxon race as the British people. We have a form of government to which we are devoted, and which we do not intend to abandon. If we are compelled to believe that, under our administrative system, we could not manage the dependencies of Great Britain—or even British India

[1] Exceptions must be made of the civil service reform experiment successfully entered upon and needlessly abandoned under President Grant (see Appendix C) ; and of the reform policy and measures of President Hayes, the admirable spirit, and the effects of which—limited in range as these measures have thus far been—are full of encouragement. The administration of the Department of the Interior and of the New York Post Office has been made to approach closely to the British standards ; and the Custom House, at New York City, is being raised out of the quagmire of partisan politics. Political assessments, official interference with the freedom of elections, and the despotic sway of partisan manipulators, have already received a considerable check from the present administration, which shows how easily a more comprehensive and systematic reform may be carried forward.

alone—for a single decade, are we prepared to assign as the cause either the inherent weakness of our form of government or our own incompetency as administrators? If not, what is the cause?

With so much depending on the fidelity and wisdom of officials, it is no matter of surprise that administrative questions have engaged the serious attention of British statesmen. Public administration, in Great Britain, has, in fact, been reduced to something like a science. It has taken rank with legislation; having its fixed principles, its carefully nurtured methods, its theory of parties, its well-considered tests of capacity and character, its limits of work, recreation, age, and responsibility—of which the British people take notice and from which high officers dare not depart. It is all the more worthy our attention, because it is the experience of a people than whom none are more severely practical and utilitarian—of an empire whose institutions are most free and analogous to our own. It will appear that, either in the home government or in India, substantially all the abuses we have endured, and all the specious arguments by which their continuance has been excused, were familiar to English statesmen long before we began to talk about political corruption. Even our late attempts at the limitation of these abuses are but the reproductions of modes of relief quite familiar in British experience.

If we believe that the great care given to public administration, in the older countries, is by reason of any thing peculiar to monarchies, or is a mere attempt to reconcile them to the more liberal ideas of modern times, I venture to think that our mistake is very great. It is only a counterpart of that we make in supposing that a real reform in the civil service of a great nation can be brought about either in a sweeping and sudden way, or by any partisan method, or without a comprehensive and patriotic policy steadily pursued by the government and intelligently supported by the people. We shall, on the contrary, find reason to believe that the work of administrative reform, in the older countries, has been guided by a sagacious and comprehensive statesmanship, aiming at a greater strength and a larger commerce—a statesmanship by no means untouched by national pride and ambition. It has aimed to increase the power of the nation and the patriotism of the people by bringing superior character and capacity into official places of every grade.

I am not unmindful that there are people who will be ready to denounce as unpatriotic any comparison unfavorable to ourselves. But I can feel no patriotism to be higher than that which arraigns our national vices only in the hope of arresting them. "The most important lessons a nation can learn from its own history are to be found in the exposure of its own errors."[1] In the religious and moral sentiments, broadly developed in the homes of our people, and in general education more and more cherished among them, we may surely find a basis as solid and a potency as great for high national effort as ever existed in the citizenship of any country. But such capacity will be of little avail if a sort of Turkish or Mexican conceit that our methods are perfect, and a false patriotism fatal to self-inspection, shall keep us blind to the peril of a decline in the moral tone of official life, while making us half unconscious of its disgrace. Nor will our virtues much more avail if the voice of truth and patriotism is to be silenced by the domineering spirit of the political majority and the partisan leaders. We need to see ourselves distinctly as we appear in the light of administrative wisdom reflected from the foremost nations of the Old World.

[1] "A History of our Own Times," by McCarthy, vol. i., chap. 8.

# CHAPTER II.

At whatever period, short of going back to feudal times, we investigate British administration with the purpose of embracing in its later history all that is material to our own condition, we find not a little to invite us still further into the past, unless we are willing to overlook the old forms of modern abuses.

But for that reason, it would suffice to state its condition when our constitution was adopted, and from thence to trace its progress to our time. Earlier than that date, however, we shall find that there is much especially worthy our attention.

As we go back over its course, we are struck with the evidence, everywhere presented, that the progress made in civil administration, though having many irregularities and oscillations, has really been a sort of evolution from a narrower to a broader wisdom, from ignorance to intelligence, from injustice to justice, from a lower to a higher public morality, from the lawlessness of official caprice to the sternness of official responsibility—in dealing not only with official duties in the strict sense, but with public affairs altogether ; the ascent, though much affected by the character of the king, generally keeping pace with the rising public intelligence and liberty.

It is not necessary to consider whether it has more frequently happened that government has originated in democratic equality and degenerated into despotism, or in despotism of some sort, and been improved up to free institutions. For it is familiar history, but not less instructive to keep in mind, that we may readily go back upon the course of the British, or indeed of any European government, to that period when power over the civil service (I should rather say the king's service) was arbitrary ; when neither character, nor capacity, nor economy, nor justice, nor duty or responsibility of any sort, was recognized by the ruler, if demanded by the subject, in connection with official appointments or removals. Not only the appointing power, but control in every way, on the part of the king or chieftain, over his subordinates, was arbitrary, universal, and unchallenged—the merest perquisite and appendage of paramount authority.

For a long period after there was regular government, it is familiar knowledge that the three great departments—legislative, executive, and judicial—did not exist ; but the king, or the king with his council, made up of his favorites, was supreme over the whole field of government, and exercised every kind of authority. Government of course had none of the modern limitations in favor of religion or right, humanity or conscience, liberty or justice. It was a long period, also, after there were regular officers and departments, in rudimental form, with duties quite analogous to those now assigned them in all the greatest states of the world, before there was any evidence that rulers or officers, having the power of appointment or supervision for the execution of the laws, recognized any obligation to regard merit, or to consult the interests or comfort of the people. Such a sense of obligation is of later origin and of very slow growth. Long after the time when, to use public money for the private purposes of the king or the great officers of state or of any powerful faction in politics (for parties were a later development) was generally regarded as a crime, and was punished as such, there was no public opinion and much less any law that condemned the use of the appointing power, or of any kind of official influence, for such reprehensible purposes. The theory of the notorious

2

Judge Barnard,¹ that, when he gained an office, he acquired
the right to use its patronage and influence to suit himself
and his friends, was the unchallenged creed of every king
and high officer (with the exception of here and there an
official far in advance of his age), from William the Norman
to William Prince of Orange, except we shall find that Cromwell rose to about the partisan level of General Jackson in
the use of the appointing power.

It needs no reasoning to make it plain that a long period
must have elapsed, after some enlightened spirits first
affirmed the true rule of official duty, before there was any
public opinion in its behalf, that materially checked the haughty
pleasure of the kings, lords, or great officers of an arbitrary
age.

The first instance I have met with of the coercive power of
such a public opinion, was early in the thirteenth century,
when the historian says " the opinion of the nation was strongly
expressed in favor of reform, and the king was *compelled* to
choose his subordinate ministers with some reference to their
capacity for business." ²

In view of the facts that, even in these enlightened times,
it is thought a crime for an officer to apply public money for
the use of himself or his party, but is very generally recognized
as no wrong to use his official influence (to say nothing of his
time needed in the public service, just as selfishly), for the
same purpose, we need not express much surprise that the
coarse and obtuse morality of a rude and uneducated people
passed no condemnation upon bribery or upon the open purchase and sale of office. They long remained too blunt and
reckless to take any notice that there is really the same duty
to use public authority that there is to use public property, only
for public purposes. Such arbitrary and corrupt ways of dealing with office, in the ruder ages of British history, were

¹ When Judge Barnard was asked on his trial to explain his system of appointment, this was his answer :
"Here, counsellor, this is my court ; I have won this office ; this
patronage is mine."—George G. Barnard Impeachment, trial, vol. iii., p.
1941.
² Stubbs' Constitutional History of England, vol. i., p. 355.

nothing exceptional in the affairs of government; . r they are but an example of the manner in which all its powers we prostituted; to extort the earnings and hold down in poverty and ignorance the masses of the people; to fill the treasuries, to minister to the vices and luxuries, and to fight the battles, of kings, lords, and bishops. The pleasure, ambition, and power of the kings, nobles, and great officers were everything; justice and equality, duty and economy, the personal worth of the citizen, and the effect of administration upon the people at large, were nothing with those who controlled the nation; except in the rare instances when a long-outraged people would, in wrath and despair, follow a Jack Cade or a Wat Tyler in bloody assault upon their oppressors.

The reigns of the Plantagenets and the Tudors may be regarded as the palmy days of the despotic-spoils system of office; for everything in government and society was in the same spirit —that crushing spirit of feudal subordination and dependence under which all the public offices and places, and nearly all the land of the kingdom, not in the hands of the Crown, the nobles, or the Church, were held subject to a solemn oath and condition to king or lord " to be a liegeman for life . . . and to keep loyalty to him . . . for life and death." Charters and monopolies, in a fit of good-nature, were tossed by a king to some borough, great officer or favorite that had pleased him; and, in a fit of anger or drunkenness, they were as arbitrarily revoked. When a king could " confer two hundred manors upon a brother," and reward every great baron and favorite with rich estates at his will; when every successful warrior was given not only the spoils of his enemy, but lands and houses arbitrarily taken from citizens at home; when vast spaces could be appropriated to forests and pleasure-grounds by kings and dukes without consent if not without compensation; when from amidst the armed followers who attended their journeys, or from the lofty turrets of their castles and palaces, so many of which have survived the spoils system, of which they were the citadels, the great lords and ecclesiastics could look down in haughty defiance upon a half-enslaved common people—then indeed there is no ground for surprise that offices and places, salaries and sinecures, removals and promotions, were the mere perquisites and playthings of the great and the highborn. But we may well wonder, not merely that the system, but that the smallest example of it, should have survived to these times.

It is an interesting fact that the absence of any controlling sense of duty to bestow office, either with reference to the merit of the officer or the interests of the people, tended to make, and to a large extent did make, offices hereditary. It was natural that ministers and noblemen, having offices for sale, should seek to enhance the market price by strengthening all the guarantees of permanence in tenure. There being no standard of right, except power and influence, for holding an office, those in offices naturally and openly used their authority to extend and transmit their tenure. A statute, enacted in 1452, declares that no officer of the customs shall have any "estate certain in his office;" but, significantly enough, it further provides that this prohibition shall not "prejudice our sovereign lady the Queen, the Prince, or the Duke of Buckingham," or several others named, who of course might continue to demand and receive the full market price for offices and places sold in perpetuity. Hence sprung the spirit which supported a hereditary crown and nobility, as well as some other hereditary offices which still survive, and many that do not. In these facts, we may find the reason why frequent removals from office, even in the worst times, were not so serious abuses in England as they have been with us. By its very magnitude, one great evil put some limits to another.

The offices or dignities that early became hereditary and long continued so were very numerous. Nor was this all; for the right to appoint to office and to sell the appointment openly for money became also and long remained hereditary; sometimes in great families and sometimes in the holder for the time being of the offices themselves.

Mr. Stubbs' speaks of hereditary offices being numerous in the thirteenth century. I believe some of these dignitaries (besides the king and nobility), which I think we should call officers, are yet hereditary.

---

[1] Constitutional History, vol. i., p. 355.

In 1552, in the reign of Edward VI.,[1] a law was enacted prohibiting the sale of offices, but it contained this curious exception, that it shall not apply to the Justices of the Court of King's Bench or Common Pleas, or to the Justices of the Assize ; and therefore those officials were expressly left at liberty to exercise freely the hereditary right of making sale, for their own profit, of offices and places in their own courts. And the act further declares that the " prohibition shall not extend to any sale or bargain, gift, promise, nomination, bond, or covenant for office" to be made before March then next : a proviso equally remarkable as illustrating a well developed machinery for contracting for offices and nominations to be made binding by " bonds and covenants," and as suggesting that not a few votes were probably secured for the act by leaving a free market for official corruption during nine months after its passage ! And the illustration will be the more adequate if I add that, so late as 1825,[2] an act was passed for the purchase by the government, from the hereditary owner, of two public offices, one in the Court of King's Bench, and the other in the Common Pleas, and under this law an appraisement of the money value of each office was actually made, and the government paid the value fixed, and became again the owner and possessor of its own functions which had been merchandise in the market for centuries.

These are but specimens of very many instances of the purchase of civil offices ; to say nothing here of the scandalous and open purchase of offices or places in the army, and in the State Church, a practice only arrested in the army in 1871, but which continues in the State Church to the present time, as I shall more fully explain.

It is hardly worth while even to take a glance back of the Norman Conquest ; and from that date to Cromwell the attitude of the government toward public offices and places was much the same. If not bestowed in the mere wantonness of irresponsible and unlimited power, for the gratification of pride, ambition, and passion, or sold for money, they were used to strengthen the power of the Crown, the nobles, the

---

[1] 6 Edward VI., chap. 15.          [2] 6 George IV., chap. 89.

Church, or the court favorites, who held them as perquisites
or spoils. Not offices and places merely, but salaries without
labor or responsibility; charters, grants, and monopolies;
sentences, pardons, exemption from taxation, and from
services by land and sea—were each and all given, sold, with-
held, or exchanged, in the same venal and arbitrary spirit, and
with like impunity.[1] The common people were substantially
unrepresented when this old spoils system was matured, and a
great proportion of them were in a condition of ignorance and
dependence little above slavery; and power was so concentrated in a ruling class that public opinion, even had it been
far more enlightened, could have put only slight check upon
the arbitrary use of official authority.

I give a few examples, by way of illustrating the original
spoils system as it was applied in practice in the twelfth, thirteenth, and fourteenth centuries.

"Among the great officers of the Household which appear from the
pipe-roll to have been saleable are those of Dapifer, Marshal and Chancellor. The last mentioned officer, in A.D. 1130, owes £3006 13s. 4d.
for the great seal. The office of Treasurer was bought by Bishop
Nigel for his son, for £400. . . . In Norfolk, Benjamin pays
£4 5s. to be allowed to keep the pleas of the crown. . . . John
Marshall pays forty marks for a mastership in the King's Court.
. . . Richard Fitz Alured pays fifteen marks that he may sit with
Ralph Bassett on the King's pleas in Buckinghamshire. At the
same time the officers of the ancient courts are found purchasing *relief
from their responsibilities* . . . anxious, no doubt, to avoid
heavy fine . . . for neglect of duty."

These examples of that refinement of royal and official infamy, under which not only was the highest of human function

---

[1] For example: "In 1245, Henry III. ordered all shops in London to be
closed for fifteen days for the benefit of fairs proclaimed by him at Westminster. Henry the VI. having bought some alum for £4000, sold it for
£8000, granting in the sale an exclusive privilege of dealing in alum for a
term of years. Henry the VI. conferred upon a Tuscan merchant the privilege of importing a quantity of merchandise and prohibited its importation
by any one else until he had sold it off. America was only suffered to be
colonized under the permission of trading monopolists.—*Princeton Review*,
March, 1878.

—that of administering justice  thus openly sold for money, but by which also another price was taken in advance for impurity in the merciless and corrupt abuse of this purchased authority, lend a deeper significance to that celebrated clause of the great charter, extorted from King John, which declares that " no man shall be taken, or imprisoned, or outlawed, or exiled, or anywise destroyed : nor will we go upon him, nor send upon him, but by the lawful judgment of his peers or by the law of the land.  To none will we sell, to none will we deny or delay right or justice."  To this charter, some of the great principles of our constitutions are to be traced.

If in some appropriate form we had incorporated into them the principle of the forty-fifth article, which makes the King promise that " we will not make any justices, constables, sheriffs, or bailiffs, but of such as *know the law of the realm* and mean to truly observe it," is there any reason to doubt that primary justice in this country would have been far better administered ?  This clause of *Magna Carta* may be justly said to be the First Civil Service Rule—the first authoritative provision for securing due qualifications for an office—to be found in English history ; and I have not noticed that the constitution of any State of the Union has yet come up to its spirit.  The majority is hardly yet convinced that a justice needs to know the law provided he is only zealous for the party.  As a consequence there are thousands of justices in this country as ignorant of law as they are efficient in politics, and tens of thousands of the victims of their ignorance and their prejudices help to swell the volume of public discouragement and discontent by reason of our bad administration.  It cannot be matter of surprise that, in an age when the conception of such principles was possible only during the uprising of a high national sentiment, they were neglected and scorned as soon as those in rebellion had laid aside their arms.  The old abuses were renewed.  " So intimate is the connection of judicature with finance under the Norman kings, that we scarcely need the comments of the historian to guide to the conclusion that it was mainly for the sake of the profit that justice was administered at all. . . . The Treasurer, the Chancelor, the Justiciar, pays a sum of money for his office, or even renders an annual rent.  This practice runs on to the thirteenth century, when so many of the dignities became hereditary." "A great court and council was held at Nottingham, attended by . . . archbishops, bishops, and earls.  On the first day the King removed the Sheriffs of Lincolnshire and Yorkshire and put up the offices for sale.  Yorkshire fell to Archbishop Geoffrey, whose bid of an immediate payment of 3000 marks and 100 marks of increment was accepted in preference to the lower bid of the Chancellor, who proposed 1500 marks for Yorkshire, etc.  . . .  The sheriffs, as we learn from the rolls, were nearly all displaced."  " He (the King) brought together a great council at Pipewell, . . . where he gave away the vacant bishoprics, appointed a new ministry, *and raised a large sum of money by the sale of charters of confirmation.*"  "The Bishop of Durham had paid heavily for his honors ; he had bought the justiciarship and the earldom of Northumberland."  " Beneath a thin veil of names and fictions, the great ministerial officers, and the *royal interference by writ in private quarrels,* were alike matters of purchase."[1]

A statute[2] of this period so forcibly illustrates its spirit and is so ingenious a contrivance for giving impunity to all kinds of official corruption and tyranny, that I cannot forbear quoting from it.

" Whereas it is contained in the statute of the second year of our lord the King that none be so hardy to invent, say, or tell any false news, lies, or such other false things, of the prelates, Dukes, Earls, Barons, and other nobles and great men of the realm ; and also of the Chancellor, Clerk of the Privy Seal, Steward of the King's House, Justice of the one bench or of the other, and *other great officers of the realm ;* and he that doth shall be taken and imprisoned until he hath found him of whom the speech shall be moved."

The magistrates were the mere dependents of the higher officers.  Official records and doings were official secrets. No man could prove a charge from that quarter.  It was only needed to treat what was disagreeable as being " false," to

---

[1] See Stubbs' Const. History, vol. i., pp. 317-502, 496, 497, 384, 387, and 355.
[2] 2 Richard II., chap. 11.

make this law a terror to every man who thought to expose corruption. In condemning this device of tyranny, let us not forget how generally a rule prevails with us, within the public service, as demoralizing as this statute was without the service. So long as our subordinate officers can be dismissed without cause and without explanation, they are no more likely, than was a subject of Richard II., to expose official delinquency in high quarters. Year after year it may continue with no exposure from subordinates who are silenced by the fear of an arbitrary dismissal.

While considering the condition of civil administration at that interesting period when the English people, as the first instance in modern history, arose in their might to arrest its abuses, I wish to present some further facts which show the identity of such abuses in ages and under forms of government remotely separated. It is generally believed that such frauds as often come to light in our large cities in connection with the offices of coroners, sheriffs, justices, marshals, and clerks of courts, are original with us, and that they are the inevitable evils or drawbacks of universal suffrage and free institutions ; and this belief unquestionably discourages efforts for their prevention. Nothing can be more unwarranted than such opinions. A statute enacted more than six centuries ago,[1] having recited " that forasmuch as mean persons, and indiscreet, now of late are *commonly chosen* to the office of coroners, when it is requisite that honest persons should occupy such offices," proceeds to enact " that no coroner shall demand or take anything to do his office, upon pain of great forfeiture to the king." Another clause of the same law enacts " that no sheriff or other King's officer shall take any reward to do his office, . . . and if he do he shall be punished at the King's pleasure ;" and still another provides, in substance, that no clerk shall take anything but his fees for doing his duty, and if he does he shall pay twice as much as he has taken and also lose his place for a year : and still another forbids any " marshall, or cryer, or other officer of justice," taking money wrongfully, and declares " that there

---

[1] In 1275, 3 Edward I., chap. 10.

is a greater number of them than there ought to be, whereby
the people are sore aggrieved," and forbids such abuses in the
future, which are to be followed by a forfeiture of the office
and "grievous punishment at the King's pleasure."

In recognizing these familiar offences of our day, flourishing
under a royal and feudal government, it is worthy of notice
that the punishment denounced—especially the forfeiture of
office—is more drastic and effective in its nature than we have
generally provided. The twenty-ninth chapter of the same
law reaches another abuse not less familiar to us. It provides
that "if any pleader . . . or other do any manner of
deceit or collusion in the King's Court, or beguile the court or
the party, . . . he shall be imprisoned for a year and a
day : and if the trespass require greater punishment, it shall
be at the King's pleasure."

In 1344, a statute prohibits justices from taking gifts or
rewards : but a later statute [1] breathes a less stern morality,
for it makes this exception, "unless it be meat or drink, and
that of small value." [2]

The practice of extorting extra fees or arbitrary payments on
the part of officers of the treasury, is not an abuse of republican
origin, but was well developed under royalty before this continent was discovered. A statute of 1455 [3] recites that
" whereas officers in the King's Exchequer do take fees, . . "
and also do take gifts and rewards for the execution of their
offices . . . by extortion, . . . ." and then denounces
penalties. So also the vexatious wrongs practiced by baggage
searchers and other officers of customs are not original here,
but were well developed in the old country four centuries ago.
In a statute of about the same date as that last referred

---

[1] 12 Edward III.

[2] This easy kind of morality seems indigenous in despotic states. Speaking of Russian administration, a late author says : " The officials, quite puz-
zled by the severe punishments as to how to mask their corrupt cupidity, at
last invented a curious trick. They placed in their houses a great number
of religious pictures. Those who desired to win the ear of the judge, or of
any other official, suspended their presents as a sort of religious homage !
An ukase was thereupon published, that only seven or eight roubles' worth
could be suspended to the pictures.

[3] Henry VI., chap. 3.

to,[1] it is recited that " whereas divers water-bailiffs, searchers, comptrollers of the search, and others, their deputies and servants, within the ports of this realm, . . . do, by color of their office, wrongfully take, by constraint . . . of goods and merchandise, . . . and cause great charges and impositions, . . . and by such wrongful impositions, they do discourage said merchants and do great damage, . . . contrary to law and conscience . . ." ; and the act then goes on to provide a remedy. This law is well adapted to arrest the old abuses in the New York Custom House, which so many think are quite original in that office.

" As early as 1377 we find interference with the freedom of elections of members of Parliament by the executive officers made a ground of serious complaint by the people."[2] Even the great offence of false counts, certificates and returns of votes by inspectors of election and returning officers (generally deemed to be emphatically republican offences, if not incurable), were fully developed and ingeniously dealt with in England near two centuries before even a town meeting had been held on this continent. A law of Henry VI. contains an elaborate provision on that subject. It recites that " sheriffs for lucre" have not made due " elections of knights" (members of Parliament), and " no return of knights lawfully chosen," but " knights . . . have been returned which were never duly chosen ; and sometimes the sheriffs have not returned the writs which they had to make elections ; but the said writs have been embezzled ; and made no precept."

The congeries of frauds of omission and commission, referred to in this statute, would seem to indicate a royal original for all the devices of rascality, for which the politicians of Louisiana and Florida are thought to have shown unrivalled powers of invention.

" Under an absolute king, whose will is law, that which he chooses to sell passes for justice :" and there can be no doubt that the long practice of making merchandise of public authority had vitiated and benumbed the moral sense of the English nation on the subject, so that reform had become

[1] Henry VI., chap. 5.
[2] Green's History of the English People, p. 250.

tenfold more difficult ; just as the moral sense of this nation
has, from like causes, become blunted to the immorality of
levying assessments and bestowing office for mere partisan purposes.   It was not, it is well to repeat, mere offices and places
that were bought and sold—that great officers in Church and
State haughtily treated as their perquisites, which they might
hand over to the highest bidder or give to please a favorite or
conciliate an enemy—but every possible exercise of official
authority, by every grade of officials, from the lowest to the
highest, was in the market as merchandise, at the time when
Civil Service Reform may be said to have commenced in England.   It was not merely such universal and long-continued
precedents of venality that were to be encountered by any
reform, but there was also a false and pernicious public opinion,
developed through centuries, to the effect that such abuses were
inevitable ; because neither in England nor in any part of the
world were there any examples to the contrary.   In France,
for example, " the purchase of office was legalized.   A bureau
was opened for their sale. . . .   The kings of France,
in order to raise money, made the judicial offices in Parliament saleable." [1]   In every European country, in a certain
stage of its civilization, offices have been bought and sold.
And besides all this ground of discouragement, there was
the great fact that those who sanctioned and practised such
corruption, and who gained money, authority, and influence
thereby, were the ruling, the high-born, the educated classes
—the royal family and the nobles—the bishops and the priests—
the ministers and the generals—great lawyers who had become
judges—all persons in places of authority or social influence.

   Then, as now and ever, from its very nature, the cause of
administrative reform was the cause of the common people—
the cause of justice and equal rights among them, the cause of
personal merit against every one having special privileges and
perquisites—against the whole official or partisan body.   But the
great body of the people were utterly ignorant and were hardly
represented at all.   The public press, and other great modern
agencies for awakening and combining a public protest, did

---

[1] Young's Sketches of the French Bar.

not exist. Freedom of speech did not exist; the right of petition was not recognized. In such a time, it might well have been said that a reform of such abuses seemed impossible. To attack them was, indeed, hardly less than a rebellion; and the question raised by a reformer was a constitutional question of disturbing the balance of power in the state, by an elevation of the masses.

"The nobility, and the knights and members of knightly families, made up a warrior caste, who termed themselves gentle by birth, and who looked down upon the great mass of the lay community as beings of almost inferior nature. . . . The peasantry and the little allodialists were ground down with servitude and forced to till the soil as abject dependents of the barons." [1]

In those times the spoils system was neither an anachronism nor an importation, but a congenial growth in keeping with general despotism, injustice, and violence. To assail that system required not simply the little courage which suffices to dissent from one's party platform, or the small patriotism needed to forbear a nomination to a little office, but the forecast of a statesman in advance of his times, the courage of a patriot ready to defy a domineering class and a merciless king, or perhaps the resignation of a martyr ready to go to prison if not to the block. It is plain that to interfere with such a system was nothing less than an assault upon the power of the king. But in those times the king ruled, in popular estimation, by the favor of Heaven. His government was a divine institution.

This added vastly to the awe it inspired and the power it wielded. In the language of Mr. Lecky, "It placed the sovereign entirely apart from the category of mere human institutions;" and (I may add) it therefore made a civil service reformer a rebel against Divine Providence as well as a traitor against the king. He is with us only a visionary and an enemy of the party. This divine attribute, in those old times, was thought to extend to the physical person of the king, and to give him power over the ills of men—a power the exercise of which

---

[1] Creasy's History English Constitution, p. 82.

was for centuries used, with great political effect, in the cure of diseases; every instance of which was accepted as a fresh proof of the king's right to rule and of the smile of Heaven upon him. This perverse veneration—even surviving the cruelty of Mary and the treachery of Charles I. and James I.—was extended to the contemptible voluptuary who succeeded Cromwell. In a single year Charles II. touched for the king's evil 8500 times, and nearly 100,000 persons fell on their knees before him for that healing touch during his reign. Nor was it the humble and ignorant alone who were deluded; for in 1687 the King touched more than 700 sick in the centre of learned society at Oxford.

The delusion did not end with the seventeenth century. A solemn service for touching by the Queen was printed in the Common Prayer-book of the State Church during the reign of Queen Anne. Her Privy Council issued a proclamation stating where the Queen would perform the miracle. Dean Swift made an application to her in 1711 to cure a sick boy. In a single day, in 1712, two hundred persons were touched by her, and among them was the celebrated Samuel Johnston, then a scrofulous child. Even so late as 1838, a minister of the Shetland Islands asserts that no cure for scrofulous diseases was at that time there believed to be so efficacious as the royal touch. Nor could the democratic spirit of this land at once dissipate the madness. Mr. Lecky says that "a petition has been preserved in the records of the town of Portsmouth in New Hampshire, asking the assembly of that province in 1687 to grant assistance to one of the inhabitants who desired to make the journey to England in order to obtain the benefit of the royal touch." How brave and audacious must a reformer be to challenge any use of a prerogative in the hands of mortals thus favored by the powers above.

Returning again to the progress of the spoils system, we find two great popular uprisings against it during the arbitrary times we have been considering; the one in the fourteenth and the other in the fifteenth century; the first three hundred years before party government or even great parties existed in England. These uprisings were really the first distinct attempts to bring about civil service reform in England, though the rebellion under King John had in part the same end in view. And perhaps the violence and blood these rebellious reforms involved were the unavoidable means of gaining a hearing for civil abuses in those feudal ages.

It certainly cannot be said that, in the rebellion of 1377, in which Wat Tyler was the military leader, he had the spirit or acted the part of a civil service reformer. He only appeared when the popular protest had passed the limits of law and order. But it is as certain that, in that rebellion, the people of England, for the first time, made the abuses of their civil administration a great national issue and battle cry for reform, as it is that the same issue became national with us, for the first time, in the last Presidential election. Nor was Jack Cade any more such a reformer in his own person, in the rebellion of the next century, in which he was the military chieftain ; but the continuance of the spoils system, only a little curtailed, and still leading to outrageous corruption and oppression, was one of the greatest causes, if not the main cause, which drove the people a second time to revolt. It is worthy of notice that these two rebellions of our ancestors are the only instances of their taking up arms on their own account in the whole period from the Norman Conquest to Charles I.

There are facts connected with the earlier rebellion which have a practical bearing upon civil service reform, even in this enlightened age.

The open sale and prostitution of official power in manifold forms ; the granting of monopolies ; the extortion of money for the forbearance of injustice ; the exaction of illegal fees ; the invasion of private right by official favorites, male and female ; gross injustice in the courts ; oppressive taxes to maintain a great army of sinecurists and supernumeraries in offices and public places ; domineering and insulting conduct on the part of high officials—all these abuses, to which I have referred as existing at an earlier date, had continued to grow and poison and exasperate until they led to the outbreak early in the reign of Richard II., in 1377. The very vices and luxuries which such debasement of official power fostered, indirectly contributed to raising the condition of those most oppressed. This result was brought about by a process which in itself is one of the best illustrations that can be given of the degradation of all official and social influence. "The luxury of the time and the pomp of chivalry . . . drained the purses of knights and barons, and the sale of freedom to the serf . . afforded an easy and tempting mode of filling them. In this process Edward III. himself led the way. Commissioners were sent to the royal estates for the special purpose of manumissions."[1] The very lowest placeman at an office door, as well as the highest near the King, were equally venal and unscrupulous. Even the King, "with a jest took a bribe" for the exercise of the pardoning power.[2]

In the mean time the people had become bolder, as they had gained in liberty and in the knowledge of the cause of their grievances. It was the generation of Wyckliffe, and great ideas were beginning to stir the heart of England. In the domain of politics, as of religion, we find at this era the beginnings of those brave and true utterances which, in later generations, shook the Church and the State to their foundations. They are the first predecessors of the pamphlets of Milton and of Burke.

Foreign wars, made more disastrous by incompetent officers, had led to crushing taxation; and a poll tax brought a vivid sense of their cost to the people. If this obnoxious tax most directly aroused the masses, which Wat Tyler led, we yet find the real cause further back. "The poll tax interpreted to the individual far more intelligently than any political propaganda the *misdoings of the rulers.*"[3] To add to the public exasperation, the royal and lordly officials interfered with the freedom of elections in 1377; and this, Mr. Stubbs declares, "is the first occasion on which any definite signs are traceable of an attempt to influence an election for a political purpose." And in view of the bloody resistance to which it then contributed, as compared with the tame submission with which

[1] Green's History of the English People, p. 262.

[2] "There was no check (Stubbs' History, vol. ii., p. 434) on dishonesty and extortion among public servants, nor any determination to enforce the constitutional law; and some of the highest officers of the court, the closest friends and associates of the King, were among the chief offenders."

[3] Stubbs' History, vol. ii., p. 452.

we endure the same abuse, it is certainly a striking illustration of the demoralizing effect of long familiarity with vice.

The haughty statesmen of the day did not mistake the real cause of the threatened outbreak, and as they saw its angry spirit and vast proportions, they took measures to avert it. These measures failed. A Parliament was called (after the war), which entered upon the detailed work of reforming the administration; and it accomplished so much that it has always been known in history as the "Good Parliament." A hundred and forty petitions for the redress of grievances (a most unprecedented number in that age, when so few could write, and when even to petition involved the perils of imprisonment) were considered by that "Good Parliament." An examination of public accounts was demanded and granted. Some of the results read like a modern report about Washington or New York City. Latimer, the King's Chamberlain, was found "guilty of every sort of malversation." Richard Lyons, "the King's agent, had been a partner in some gigantic financial frauds." The great offenders were impeached and removed from office. Women as well as men were found guilty. Among those banished for corruption (and for a violation of an ordinance against women practising law) was Alice Perrers; but Alice got into her old place again years later. A council was elected by Parliament to act as a check on patronage. One of the petitions called for the reform in the conduct of justices, another of marshals, another of sheriffs, and another prays "that officers convicted of default or deceit may be permanently incapacitated from acting."

In the hope of allaying popular indignation, at this period, the aristocratic leaders in Parliament proposed a grand inquest of abuses, which was ordered, through a high commission.[1] It was the first great inquiry ever ordered in England into the abuses of public administration; and few in that country have been more sweeping and comprehensive. In this country none so thorough has ever been provided for. Every grade of office and every branch of administration and expenditure—high and low, civil and military, ecclesiastical and judicial, national and

---

[1] 12 Richard II., chap. 1.

3

municipal, domestic and foreign, including all forms of the exercise of official functions—were included. The concise enumeration of abuses to be investigated fills over four pages of this ancient statute. The act opens with a solemn recital of the pervading abuses of administration, saying " that whereas by the grievous complaints . . . it appears that the rents and revenues of the realm . . . by insufficient counsel and evil government of . . . great officers and other persons, be so wasted and destroyed, . . . and there is so great and outrageous oppressions, . . . and the laws are not executed, nor justice nor right done, to the people, . . . and great mischief and damage has happened." Parts of this recital are as flattering to the dear people as any modern platform made to catch votes in a canvass, and it was as basely disregarded by its authors. The work of the commission was entered upon and some abuses were exposed by it, but its great undertaking was never completed. The powerful nobles at its head, like the venal, partisan managers of our day, never intended to have their income, their authority, or their patronage much curtailed. The battle had gone in favor of the king's legions, and against the undisciplined people. In the language of the historian of the times, " What the politicians wanted was not so much reform of abuses as the possession of power." What they did was the equivalent in our day of a series of sonorous resolutions for economy and reform adopted by a national convention and trampled upon by the party that adopted them.

Here, therefore, in the first struggle for civil service reform, we find the unscrupulous politicians—the legitimate predecessors of those of our time—uniting with the great nobles under an arbitrary prince, and intriguing and working together to hold down the people under abuses in the civil administration so great that they were ready to fly to arms for their redress.

While the question whether the people would take up arms hung in fearful suspense, " the Parliament of 1377 resumed its work of reform and boldly assumed the control of the expenditure by means of a standing committee of two burgesses of London ; and that of 1378 demanded and obtained an account of the mode in which the subsidies had been spent." [1]   Official corruption has so weakened the executive department and so aroused the anger of the people, that Parliament having up to this time but little if any patronage is able to stand boldly forth for reform, with all the prestige of disinterestedness and popular indignation in its support. But it is worthy of notice that it so exerted its new authority from the outset as to secure substantial patronage at the expense of the Executive. Various new officers were for the first time appointed by its own vote. It exerted a controlling influence over other appointments. And we shall find as we proceed that, with the steady increase of the power in the legislature, there was also a continued usurpation of executive functions and a growing abuse of patronage by members of Parliament, until that body finally became more corrupt than even the Executive. As a consequence, Parliament at last became the great obstacle encountered by the people in that final contest for reform, which, in this generation, has established the Merit System in Great Britain. At every stage, corruption has prevailed, in either department, in the proportion that it has had control of patronage—or, in other words, the management of a spoils system of office.

The rebellion, I have said, had not been arrested. Partly because the reforms came too late, partly because they were believed to be deceptive, and largely because when popular indignation has been awakened it readily passes all bounds of reason, the people took up arms, by hundreds of thousands, demanding vengeance on official plunderers. It is not for me to describe the bloody scenes that followed, nor even to recount how a hundred thousand men from the country, headed by Wat Tyler, marched on London, when its common people opened its gates and Tyler and his followers did execution upon officers, whom they believed had grown rich on the spoils of office ; nor even to narrate how, all over the land, officials were stoned or slaughtered, licenses for extortion and grants of monopoly were seized and destroyed, or, in some quarters, how lawyers who had justified exactions and defended corruption were savagely put to death. While taking merciless

¹ Green's History of the English People, p. 265.

vengeance on the spoilsmen, high or low, who had ravaged the State, they not less mercilessly flung to the flames the men from their own ranks who were guilty of pillage. The soldiers proved too strong for the undisciplined people, and peace was soon restored. The spoils system, with its poison and its corrupting methods, was left essentially unchanged; though, for a considerable period, its greater abuses were arrested.

It would take me too far from the main subject were I to attempt to describe the many ways in which this terrific demonstration of the might and wrath of the common people contributed to the wholesome prestige of public opinion. It put some limits to the intolerable insolence and insatiable extortion of those in office. From that date, perhaps, the officials began to be in some small measure a *public* service, and hence in the same degree ceased to be a mere official tyranny. The direct gain of political influence, however, was rather on the part of the middle than of the lower class. What the latter gained was personal freedom and not political rights, which came later. From this date, there began in a small way to be a public opinion demanding that offices be bestowed with some regard for merit—an opinion which has grown stronger and stronger until the final victory it has achieved during this generation.

But there is one authentic expression of the reform spirit of this period so unique and remarkable that it must not be overlooked. I refer to the provisions of an act passed in 1388.[1]

Nothing uttered by Wyckliffe was more original, more in advance of the age, or evinced a deeper conception of the evils of the times and of the conditions of their improvement. It was no more to the taste of Richard II. or his court than was the Great Charter to that of King John, or the Habeas Corpus to that of Charles II., or the Declaration of Independence to that of George III.; but, like those memorable acts, it utters the high and just demands of an indignant people, when oppressive taxation and corrupt officials have aroused them to a great effort of patriotism and self-preservation. I give the language of the statute:

---

[1] 12 Richard II., chap. 2.

" *None shall obtain office by suit or for reward but upon desert.*

" Item : (1) It is accorded that the Chancellor, Treasurer, Keeper of the Privy Seal, Steward of the King's House, the King's Chamberlain, Clerk of the Rolls, the Justices of the one Bench and of the other, Barons of the Exchequer, and all others that shall be called to ordain, name, or make justices of the peace, sheriffs, escheators, customers, [1] comptrollers, *or any other officer* or minister of the King, shall be *firmly sworn.*

" (2) That they shall not ordain, name, or make justices of the peace, sheriffs, escheators, customers, comptrollers, nor other officers of the King, *for any gift or brokerage, favor or affection.* [2]

" 3) Nor that none that pursueth by himself or by others, privately or openly, to be in any manner of office, shall be put in the same office or any other.

" 4 But that they make all such officers and ministers of the best and most lawful men, and sufficient to their estimation and knowledge."

When we consider the spirit of the age, the fact that Parliament was in great measure the reflection of those who shared the profits of the despotic spoils system—that that system was the bulwark of authority in the hands of the titled and privileged classes, which were supreme in the government—I might say, when we consider that no State of this Union has (so far as I am aware, except in a single instance [3] within this decade) yet come even nearly up to the moral stand-

[1] That is, Custom House officers.

[2] Even the celebrated rule of Jefferson which our public men have generally accepted as the supreme standard of ideal duty, falls far short of the requirement of this statute of Richard II. in passing no censure either upon professional office seeking, or upon bestowing office for "gift, favor, or affection."

[3] In 1877, the Legislature of New York, for the purpose of arresting the gross extravagance and corruption that had long prevailed, under the partisan spoils system of managing its prisons, enacted the following section (Laws 1877, chap. 24), in a law regulating the future government of the prisons, in conformity with the amended State Constitution : § 3. "No appointment shall be made, in any of the prisons of this State, on grounds of political partisanship ; but honesty, capacity, and adaptation shall constitute the rule for appointments ; and any violation of this rule shall be sufficient cause for removal from office of the superintendent."

Already under the new system, discipline has become much more efficient, expenses have been materially reduced, and earnings largely increased.

ard of this statute, in dealing with public office—we may
well be astonished at its provisions; which doubtless are to be
accounted for only by considering how high public aspiration
will rise, when aroused by flagrant wrongs, and how great was
the dread of a repetition of the bloody scenes of the war then
just ended. It may be justly regarded as the second series of
civil service rules ever promulgated in England. It plainly
affirms the great and fundamental principles of all reform in
the public service—viz., that the appointing power is not a perquisite and must not be exercised as matter of favor; but is
a public trust, requiring those clothed with it to withstand all
the pretensions of birth, wealth, and social prestige, and to
make all appointments out of regard for personal merit and
the public welfare. Such a view (while of course exactly
in the spirit of our institutions) was so utterly repugnant
to the feudal tyranny of the fourteenth century, that it
requires no ordinary effort of the imagination to conceive
a force or fear strong enough to extort its recognition
from a despotic king and a parliament of armed knights and
haughty lords and bishops, whose lofty castles looked down
upon every part of the land where their dependents humbly
toiled. This unique statute must forever shine out conspicuously upon the dark horizon of a rude and ignorant age.
And may we not well believe that it will be the ultimate
judgment that the principles it affirms were as well worthy of
adoption into our system, and that they are as essential to our
well-being as a nation, as the Habeas Corpus or the trial by
jury: for these latter safeguards, perhaps, become less important as civilization advances; while the need of worth and capacity in office increases all the more with wealth and numbers
and the magnitude of public affairs?

As might well have been expected of a law so much in advance of the age, when the grave danger was passed, and the
old system had had time to regather its strength, this beneficent
statute and those who defended it were disregarded or defied.
In a milder and more secret form, the spoils system became
again supreme, and continued wars, both foreign and domestic,
aided its growth. Indeed, so bold did the spoilsmen become
that they undertook to vindicate their favorite system by deny-

ing that it had been the cause of the war; but Parliament formally resolved to the contrary.

"It laid before the King a scheme for the reform of his Household *and administration, the abuses of which they declared to have been the causes of the revolt,* and earnestly prayed for a general pardon for the severities committed in putting down the rebellion. . . . A commission for the reform of the Household, to begin with the person of the King himself, was elected."[1]

I have said that the uprising under Tyler failed to secure the political rights (though it advanced the personal freedom) of the lower class; but it did greatly strengthen the power of the middle classes for the future work of reform. It is a striking fact that the lords of the spoils system, while forced to such concessions to personal merit, did yet, in the true spirit of that system, still exert their power mercilessly to keep down the lower classes. The very Parliament by which that statute was enacted, for example, passed other acts, with the following significant titles:

"CHAP. 3. No servant shall depart from one hundred to another without a testimonial under the King's seal, on pain of being set in the stocks.

"CHAP. 4. The several penalties for taking more wages than are limited by statute.

"CHAP. 5. Whosoever serveth in husbandry until twelve years old shall so continue.

"CHAP. 11. The punishment of him who tells lies of the peers or great officers of the realm.

"CHAP. 13. No manner of artificer or laborer who hath not lands . . . shall keep any dog or ferret, . . . or net, for to take any deer, hare . . . or other *gentleman's* game, upon pain of one year's imprisonment."

Another act of 1389 is entitled that, "No shoemaker shall be a tanner, nor tanner a shoemaker."

Among the petitions of this period is one of great landed lords, praying that "no bondman or bondwoman shall place their children at school, as has been done, so as to advance their children."

[1] Stubbs' Constitutional History, vol. ii., p. 462.

What I have stated concerning the origin and methods of our inherited spoils system, in connection with this first great effort of the English people to arrest it, enables me to dismiss, with a few words, the subsequent rebellion against it to which I have alluded. It occurred in 1450. When it had passed its peaceful stages of petition, protests and parliamentary efforts to bring about a redress of abuses, and had culminated in a fearful uprising, especially of the middle classes, and when the populace was ready to join in the work of death, the soldier, Jack Cade, became its military leader. He, like Wat Tyler, led an armed multitude to London, and again corrupt ministers were made victims of the wrath of the people. The great popular demand was set forth in a formal and well considered " complaint," framed by the " Commons of Kent," where the people first flew to arms. Its scope and the whole aim of the revolt are clearly stated by the latest historian of the period in a single sentence.

" With the exception of the demand for the repeal of the statute of laborers, the programme of the Commons was now not social but political. The complaint calls for *administration and economical reform*, for a change of ministry, a more careful expenditure of revenues, . . . for *the restoration of the freedom of elections*, which had been broken in upon by the interference both of the Crown and the great landowners." [1]

I have already recited a statute of this date, which illustrates these election abuses ; and other laws passed about the same date give a clear idea of the frightful oppression and corruption which finally forced the people a second time to take up arms. An act of 1444 limits the term of sheriffs to a single year, for the significant reason that, so demoralizing was their official life, that a longer term tended " to the upholding of manslaughter, perjury, and great oppression of many of the King's liege people." Another act [2] contains this recital : " Considering the great perjury and oppression

[1] Green's History of the English People, p. 295.
[2] 2 Henry VI., chap. 9.

which be and have been in this realm by sheriffs, . . . clerks, coroners, stewards, bailiffs, keepers of prisons, and others officers," a recital which, in view of the fact that the government, in all its branches, was in the hands of the high-born classes, and that Parliament was a body of placemen, we may well believe, does but scanty justice to the shameful official degradation which this old spoils system had a second time produced. This second rebellion, like the first, arrested the grosser abuses ; but the sources and the methods of the old system itself were but little disturbed. They were not long in reproducing in milder form the same old evils in the administration.

Public opinion, however, acquired a greater power : officials were taught a wholesome lesson of caution and forbearance ; and all the lower grades of society were raised in the same degree that feudalism and despotism lost their strength and their terrors. But however mitigated, the spoils system itself survived. It was never really much broken in upon until the time of Cromwell. In fact, it was not possible to remove that system without removing much of the very framework of the old British constitution, or without repudiating the great theory of government upon which it reposed.

The insulted and pillaged merchants, artisans, and tenants of those times could see clearly enough that royal purveyors and revenue collectors, who bought their offices for a round sum of money—that sheriffs and bailiffs, who were the tools if not the stewards of the great lords of the country, pledged to make their own salary and fill their masters' treasury from the profits of their offices—that beadles and priors, who brought home to the family fireside the arbitrary power and exacting demands of the Church—were generally men without any sense of honor or justice to which they could appeal. But never having been accustomed to question the great power belonging to those officials, or much to consider ultimate causes in politics—they naturally thought that such a civil service law as I have cited, requiring that only men of "desert" should be appointed, and that professional office-seekers should be disqualified, would of its own virtue give adequate relief. They did not inquire what power there was to enforce such a law.

I find no evidence that the authors of the reform statute of Richard II. had any conception of the entire repugnance of its principles to the theory and organization of the government to which they had sworn allegiance. Much less did they foresee that such principles could be carried into practice only after centuries of conflict had changed the base of power in the State a struggle for authority and monopoly on one side, and liberty and justice on the other—to be marked by blood and martyrdom, by conflicts between Crown and Parliament, and between Parliament and the people—during all which liberty was to increase and education to be extended ; until, when the people should finally win the battle, they would stand, if nominally under the old monarchy of orders and privileges, yet in reality with something near the political equality of a republic, and with almost every right and protection which a republican freeman could expect.

We ought not to judge very severely the failures of the men of the fourteenth century. In our own times, we find many who fail to see that the parts of the spoils system which we have revived are in their very nature hostile to the whole spirit of liberty, justice, and equality in which our government is founded. They hardly take notice that the system is as destructive to public morality and economy as it is injurious to the great cause of education and to the salutary activity of political parties. Nor are the numbers still small among us who do not seem to comprehend much better than the subjects of Richard II., that no such statute can be made effective, except when re-enforced by a system of executive regulations providing proper tests of fitness, upon compliance with which persons of merit may secure the opportunity of appointment independent of mere official or partisan favoritism.

# CHAPTER III.

## INFLUENCE OF DESPOTISM ON ADMINISTRATION

An Aristocratic Monarchy hostile to the just claims of merit.—It tends to venality in bestowing office.—To require every little officer to defend the doings of the President, Senators and party leaders a Republican imitation of a feudal tyranny.—The old spoils system more courageous and consistent than the modern.—How the sale of offices prevented assessments and frequent removals.

Not the spirit of the government alone, but its very organization and modes of action, under the Plantagenets and Tudors, tended to produce a spoils system of favoritism, influence, nepotism, and venality, which frowned on personal merit and scorned the idea of official responsibility.

In an arbitrary monarchy, a primary necessity of its existence is absolute subordination and obedience to those in power ; and hence official authority must be so exerted as to preserve the monopoly and exalt the influence of the official class, to the end that they may overawe the common people. All authority comes from above—from the King. The ruling force is fear. Such a government, in its very theory and administration, says to the people that office should be obtained without regard to personal merit. The king, the source of all office, on that theory acquires his great place. The hereditary lords, who make laws and hold social and political precedence, gain and hold their offices irrespective of personal merit. They and the councils they form fill nearly every subordinate office in their discretion, and they are intended to do this not in a way that will promote merit or do justice, but in such way as will exalt the king, preserve their own rank, and secure obedience in all ranks below them. From giving an office at pleasure, on the condition of servility—from taking office by right of birth, however unworthy the heir—to selling it for money, is only a step. When once it is admitted that office is to be given, not to benefit the people, or reward merit among them, but to preserve a crown and nobility, to enforce gradation of rank, to put down aspirations for freedom, the spoils system becomes inevitable, or rather it is already in vigorous growth. If a rough royalist may be made a sheriff because he will coerce an election, or enforce the payment of an arbitrary tax in the interest of the Crown, then the office upon the same principle may be sold to him for such a purpose. If the office belongs to the king, duke or bishop to give to whom he will, in principle it belongs to him to sell to whom he will. If he may fix the terms on which he will give it, he may fix the terms on which he will sell it. To say that a man is entitled to an office simply because he is a man of worth and capacity and not otherwise, is in principle to say that he is entitled to be a knight, a baron, a duke, or a king for the same reason—obviously a principle as utterly repugnant to the theory of all arbitrary governments as it is essential to the prosperity of a republic. Therefore the spoils system was the natural outgrowth of despotism and aristocracy. It is in its very nature a royal and aristocratic and not a republican agency of government.

When Blackstone says that the king is the fountain of "justice, honor, office and privilege;" that "it is impossible that government can be maintained without a due subordination of rank;" that the king may make war and peace, that he may create corporations, that he "has the prerogative of conferring privileges upon private persons;" when he declares that for "the maintenance of his dignity and the exertion of his prerogative," the king has three councils to advise with—the Parliament, the law courts, and his "privy council," named at his pleasure, which last council, by way of eminence, is the principal; that "the person of the king is sacred even though the measures pursued in his reign be completely tyrannical and arbitrary"—we have presented before us in these outlines a form of government and a theory of executive power and responsibility in which the individual character and capacity of the officers and the welfare of the citizens are everywhere made subordinate to the interests of the class in power and the policy of the king and his great officers.

In the very nature of such a government, the number of officers, the salaries, the tenure of office must obviously be secondary to such essential conditions of its existence. When, therefore, our Declaration of Independence justly denounced George III. because " he made judges dependent on his will alone for the tenure of their offices and the amount and payment of their salaries," and because he created new offices and sent over officers to harass our people, we really assailed the theory of the government and complained of abuses which every generation of Englishmen before the expulsion of James II. had suffered, and against which they had struggled with small success. But, the strength and pernicious influence of this royal and aristocratic spoils system will be greatly underrated, if we do not bear in mind that the king became the head of the Church as well as of the State, and that the system extended to social order and consideration which it regulated, and to the Church which it dominated; pursuing a policy in the spheres of religion and society, quite as unjust and demoralizing as any that prevailed in politics.

It would perhaps require some apology for these few words in support of propositions so nearly self-evident, were it not that the difficulties in making any reform in our civil service, and the faith of the people in its practicability, are unfavorably affected by a loose theory, held by many persons, that such reforms are easier in a monarchy than under our form of government. They regard the spoils system as so original and congenial in our institutions that they incline to tolerate it as quite inevitable; when, in fact, our spoils system is only a faint reproduction, in an uncongenial age and government, of vicious methods, of which the coarse and more corrupt originals are to be found in the most despotic periods of British history. It is in fact that part of medieval despotism, inherited by us, which we have allowed to survive—even slavery.

The theory that a president may require that every petty executive officer shall hold his views of politics, and may compel him to exert himself to promote executive policy, is a feeble reproduction of the theory and practice of the worst of the Tudor and the Stuart princes, which were that everywhere the officer must be a believer in the divine right and perfection of the king, and an active advocate and champion of royal prerogative. The theory that a State Senator may selfishly use his patronage, and that all his appointees must assent to his faith and promise to use their official influence, to promote his prestige and his re-election, are but tame and puny imitations of that arrogant, old, feudal prerogative by reason of which every noble was the local ruler of his vicinage and all political action and all social life were obedient to his will, as a perpetual representative in a feudal Senate. The theory that a party may prostitute its authority and patronage in order to gain offices and levy assessments, and must do so to keep itself in power, is the cunning, cowardly, modern form of the old despotism, under which the king, the nobles, the knights, the squires, and the gentlemen—being the party forever dominant—perpetuated their supremacy by using official authority in every form of injustice for keeping the great body of the people in subjection. The only parts of our system, I am compelled to believe, which Henry VIII., or Elizabeth, or James II., or George III., would like, would be those theories of bestowing office under which personal merit may be overlooked in the pretended interest of keeping a party in power, and of causing executive policy or partisan opinions to be advocated by the carrier of every mail-bag and the keeper of every office-door. But more consistently they would also require that every priest and beadle of the Church, and every general and corporal of the army, as well as all the members of the legislature, should exhibit the same evidence of true faith and allegiance.

In fact, one of the marked distinctions between the original despotic-spoils system and the modern partisan-spoils system is this: that the old system was bold, consistent, and outspoken—not pretending to make selections for office out of regard for personal merit or economy, or the general welfare. It plainly asserted that those in power had a right and duty to keep themselves in power and preserve their monopoly in any way which their judgment should approve, and that the people were bound to submit ; while the modern system, at all times carrying the spirit of the original as far as it dares, falsely pretends to be guided by personal worth and the public interest.

If it shall be noticed that in the examples given in illustration of the original spoils system, it does not appear that the modern abuse of frequent removals and of levying assessments upon officers and placemen, or even the common forms of bribery, are very prominent, the explanation is easy. In the practice of the original system, the theory that the appointing power and all official authority are mere perquisites was carried to its legitimate results. Offices and places, royal prerogatives of every grade, and great and little official favors, were, as we have seen, openly sold, or were used as bribes and threats in whatever way found most available. In order that the market rate should be high, it was necessary that the purchaser should be assured that he could retain the commodity bought, and that it would not be made valueless by the further exercise of official authority in levying taxes. A nobleman or minister could sell an office or a monopoly for but a poor price, if any body of ministers and lords, or even the king, could thereafter tax that office or monopoly at pleasure, or remove the owner. In other words, the greater corruption of open sale and barter of offices in great measure excluded those peculiar and minor abuses of removals and assessments. So strongly, indeed, did this influence of general venality tend to permanence of tenure in the subordinate offices, and to cause them to be farmed out to non-resident agents, after the Turkish fashion, that non-resident officers were forbidden in 1402. And in 1519 [1] an act was passed with this title : " Customers,[2] controllers, searchers, etc., shall be removable at the pleasure of the king and shall be resident upon their office."

For similar reasons bribery of electors or members of Parliament—which, in later years, became one of the most serious abuses in Great Britain—was as yet but little known. Electors felt small interest in officers sure to be servilely obedient to the king and the nobles ; and members of Parliament were almost without patronage and wielded only a small portion of the legislative power which, in later centuries, growing to be almost supreme, made the vote of a member and even of an elector of value in the great market of politics.

---

[1] 1 Henry IV., chap. 13.    [2] Custom-House officers.

# CHAPTER IV.

## ADMINISTRATION UNDER THE TUDORS AND UNTIL CROMWELL.

Venality under Henry VII.—Boroughs created to control Parliament.—Its independence assailed.—Elections interfered with.—Dock-yard influence.—Spoils system extended to the Church and its effect.—Leads to royal assumptions of absolute power.—James' interference with the judges.—Great corruption under James.—Lord Coke and Lord Bacon.—Parliament grows bolder.—The Petition of Right.—Our party assessments repugnant to that memorable statute.

HAVING, I trust, sufficiently explained the origin and spirit of the spoils system, which we have so largely reproduced, it is unnecessary, and it would be tedious, to follow the details of its application, or even to note all the ways in which, from time to time, its worst features were removed. While there were various modifications—sometimes toward what was worse, and sometimes toward what was better—there was no essential change of the system after the opening of the fifteenth century until the time of Cromwell. In the reign of Henry VIII., the crown itself was treated as a mere personal perquisite of him who wore it, which he was authorized by statute to dispose of by last will and testament, and Henry did so dispose of it. The great and exciting religious questions and the frequent wars by which the politics of the period were embroiled and the higher thought of the nation was absorbed, were in every way unfavorable to good administration. I need not recall the political history of the reigns of Henry VIII., Edward VI., Mary, Elizabeth, or James I., as it is familiar knowledge that they cover a period in which men seem to have been almost willing to forego civil liberty and official morality, if they could have plenty of angry contentions and bloody scenes over church dogma and ecclesiastical forms. The leading minds were given the great subjects of church reformation. There can be little doubt that the long continuance of political corruption greatly debased official morality, and, as a natural consequence, private morality; and it is even a question whether, on the whole, both the morals of politics and methods of government did not degenerate during this period.

A few illustrations of the abiding spirit of the old system, which have an important bearing upon later changes, are all the notice I shall need to take of those times. So irresistible was the spoils system, and so little fearless public opinion was there under the first two Tudor princes (1485 to 1547), that almost the only resistance made to the government was directed against arbitrary taxes levied by the Crown. Speaking of the first of them (Henry VII.), Hallam says [1] that "even the King's clemency seems to have sprung from the sordid motive of selling pardons; and it has been shown that he made a profit of every office in his court, and received money for conferring bishoprics." Early in the next reign, we begin to find the strong manifestation of that pernicious appliance of the spoils system, through which, frequently, in the succeeding centuries, Parliament became little more than a body of servile placemen, named by the king and the great nobles, to endorse their policy and pay their henchmen and relatives in office. Referring to the reign of Henry VIII., Mr. Hallam says that "a considerable part of the Commons appears to have consisted of the King's Household officers."

In order to secure compliant members, as Parliament increased in importance, Edward VI. created twenty new boroughs, Mary fourteen, and Elizabeth as many as sixty-two; nor did the government "scruple a direct and avowed interference with elections." It was the habit of the Tudor kings to cause letters to be sent to the electors stating "our pleasure and commandment," as to who should be elected to Parliament. One of Mary's letters, written in 1554, "admonishes the electors to choose Catholics." Speaking of Elizabeth's reign, Mr. Hallam says: "The ministry took much pains with elections.
. . . The House accordingly was filled with placemen, civilians, and common lawyers grasping at preferment." Re-

---

[1] Constitutional History, vol. i., p. 27.

4

ferring to about the same date. Mr. Froude says : [1] "Either a circular was addressed to the sheriffs of counties or mayors of towns, simply naming the persons who were to be chosen, or the electors were instructed to accept their directions from some members of the privy council. In some instances the orders of the Crown were direct to the candidate himself." Here we find the original of our modern interference with the freedom of local elections by the national administration and the party managers. And when Mr. Froude says that, "in Portsmouth and Southampton the government influence was naturally paramount, through the dockyards and establishments maintained in them," I think we may naturally infer that the venal and corrupt use of dockyard sinecurists and custom-house-patronage coercion for carrying elections are not of republican origin, but are at least three and a quarter centuries old. The early leaders of the spoils system did not, however, stop with dictating as to who should go to parliaments ; but, with inflexible consistency, they endeavored to control, arbitrarily, the tongues as well as elections of their members. Blackstone tells us that " the glorious Queen Elizabeth made no scruple to direct her parliaments to abstain from discoursing of matters of state." Mr. Hallam says the Queen used to send messages to Parliament " to spend little time in motions and make no long speeches." With us it is only the tyranny of the party majority that suppresses debate on disagreeable subjects. "It became the common whisper that no one must speak against licenses lest the Queen and council should be angry." And at the close of the session, "the Lord Keeper severely reprimanded those audacious, arrogant, and presumptuous members who had called her Majesty's grants and prerogatives in question." The modern partisan managers only send a few thousands of assessment collections to the district of an independent member and defeat his re-election. We have not, to be sure, admitted that the practice of interfering with the freedom of elections, in aid of the party, as it is called, would justify a like interference with the freedom of debate ; but is it quite certain that, under our more partisan

---

[1] History, vol. v., p. 428.

application of the spoils system, the freedom of debate i not as much hampered, or that it does not require as much courage and as much imperil a re-election, to oppose the commands of the party, as it did to oppose those of Henry VIII. or of Elizabeth? The same system which accorded to noblemen a sort of monopoly of all offices not directly filled by the king or his ministers, also gave them formal patents for " the privilege of importing wine free of duty for the consumption of their households"—patents which we know have hardly been needed by the lords of our patronage system, to secure them a still more extensive exemption from the payment of duties.

During this period, as in the earlier periods to which I have referred, the spoils system was not kept within the sphere of politics, but was boldly extended to that of religion as well; and with results equally demoralizing. " In the country[1] the patron of a benefice no longer made distinction between a clergyman and a layman. . . . He presented his steward, his huntsman, or his gamekeeper. Clergy, even bishops—who called themelves Gospellers—would hold three or four or more livings, doing service in none ; or if, as a condescension, they appointed curates, they looked out for starving monks who would do the duty for the lowest pay —men who would take service indifferently under God or the devil, to keep life in their famished bodies. . . . The cathedrals and churches of London became the chosen scenes of riot and profanity. St. Paul's was the Stock Exchange of the day, where the merchants of the city met for business and the lounge where the young gallants gambled, fought and killed each other. They rode their horses through the aisles and stabled them among the monuments."

How naturally such a spoils system, prevailing through so many centuries, and forever saying to kings and nobles, " Your right it is to rule through officers and favorites selected at your caprice, without regard to merit, economy, or the general welfare," led on to the Star Chamber, to Charles I. and James II., to Laud and to Jeffreys—is too obvious for comment. Nothing but the influence of such a system, in spirit

[1] Froude's History, vol. v., p. 255-257.

asserting omnipotent and irresponsible power in the ruler, makes it conceivable that even James I. could ever have used those words of sublime audacity : " As it is atheism and blasphemy in a creature to dispute what the Deity may do, so it is presumption and sedition in a subject to dispute what a king may do in the height of his power." And I am persuaded that the feeling so general even to this day, that it is a less offence to use the appointing power for a corrupt or selfish purpose than it is to use the public money for the same purpose, has its source far back in those arbitrary centuries during which all example, all law, all teaching, impressed upon our ancestors the doctrine that the use of official authority was absolute and irresponsible in him who possessed it, even if that possession was not a divine favor too sacred and awful to be questioned by ordinary mortals. We may find the root of this pernicious distinction in the theory of King James himself, for even his doctrine of the divine right of kings did not mean that he might use the public money or the public stores at his pleasure or corruptly, but that he might so use his " prerogative royal "—the power to appoint and remove officers and placemen—and herein he agreed exactly with partisan managers of modern times. The King and Laud scrutinized the religious opinions of office-seekers as carefully as they did their political opinions ; and orthodoxy in the former, not less than in the latter, was an indispensable condition of royal favor.

It was as much a part of this old spoils system [1] that every officer should obey every direction of his superior, as it was that an appointment might be made or sold at pleasure ; and this they extended to military and judicial offices as well. The unflinching champions of that system at this period refused to see any distinction between claiming an arbitrary right to make a judge or a justice out of a compliant, incompetent favorite (with the intent that he should be obedient),

---

[1] There was another old method of strengthening the opinion and policy of the government, quite remarkable for its arbitrary forecast. " The rapid increase of London [says Mr. Hallam] " continued to disquiet the court. It was the stronghold of political and religious disaffection, hence the prohibitions of erecting new houses, which had begun under Elizabeth, were continually repeated."

and the right to command him if disobedient ; or between a
political test for office and a religious test for office. And
although we may all the more for this reason admire the
heroic sense of justice which caused Lord Coke to refuse to
give judgment as King James ordered, we can hardly deny
that the king's commands were very much, if not more than
the refusal of Coke, in harmony with the constitution of that
day and with the practice under it.[1]

When James prohibited the judges from " wounding his
prerogative under pretext of the interest of private persons,"
and Coke was first suspended and then dismissed from his
office because he answered, " that when the case should arise
he would do what should be fit for a judge to do," he was
naturally thought in official circles to be disobedient and
erratic—a view of the matter not so strange when we reflect
that he assrted a principle of official independence which, in
our generation even, has cost many a manly officer his place
when he attempted to protect " the interest of private persons" against the tyranny of partisan dictation. Sinecurists
and placemen swarmed in all the offices, and extravagance and
inefficiency prevailed everywhere in Church and State, in the
army and the navy. The peace expenditures of James I.
exceeded the war expenditures of Elizabeth. According to
Mr. Hallam, the terrific powers of the Star Chamber (a natural
growth of the spoils system) were resorted to by James I. as
much " to eke out a scanty revenue by penalties and forfeitures" as for any other purpose. Lord Bacon's official
corruption was punished, not so much because it was of a
kind uncommon as because it was that of the Lord Chancellor,
the keeper of the king's conscience, and the highest subject
of the realm. Mr. Hallam says that " shameless corruption
characterizes the reign of James beyond every other in our history." Mr. Green[2] says, " Payment of bribes to him (the
Duke of Buckingham), or marriage with his greedy relatives,
became the only road to political preferment." James not

---

[1] Under the Tudors "the Judges in the application and exposition of the
criminal law were servile tools of the sovereign."—Creasy on the English
Constitution.

[2] History English People, p. 480.

only had offices sold and shared the proceeds with his favorite ministers, but he sold his prerogative of making corporations and granting monopolies ; getting, for example, a large sum for a starch-making monopoly and £10,000 for a soap-making charter. Nor was this the worst, for, more merciless than any modern tyrant of patronage, he revoked this soap-charter and exacted a large sum for a new one ; and out of " political resentment " he even extorted large fines from those who did not come forward and receive knighthood at his hands.

These administrative abuses, and the extravagant claims of prerogative to which they led on, were, as all the world knows, in great part at least the causes which drove the people to arms (for the third time in self-defence) during the next reign. While thus all official life, both lay and clerical, was becoming more and more a festering source of corruption and a vast agency of tyranny, the control of which tended to those extravagant claims of prerogative made by Gardiner and Laud, and Charles and James, there was on the other hand an increase of wealth and intelligence and a growing courage among the common people, whom the poison of the spoils system least touched. Parliament became more active and aggressive. Its members secured more influence over appointments ; and with this tendency there came a greater desire for seats in that body. In such a state of public morality as then existed, bribery was an inevitable consequence. In the session of 1571, a fine had been imposed for bribery in a parliamentary election. This is the first instance on record of the punishment of that offence in England ; an offence which for a long time grew more frequent, and which in some form, for more than two centuries, continued to be one of the greatest scandals of English politics.

Popular intelligence had become too great, and the virtues of private life too robust, to longer tolerate supinely the huge vices bred in official circles. The spirit of resistance was aroused. The demand for reform first made itself greatly felt in the election of 1614, which brought such men as John Pym and John Eliot into Parliament. Puritanism, and the great law called the " Petition of Right," were the well-known expression of that reform spirit. And as we read the principal demand of that celebrated law, "that no man hereafter be compelled to make or yield any gift, loan, benevolence, or tax, or such like charge, without common consent by act of Parliament," and reflect upon the noble spirit by which it was extorted, it is well to remember that, although that high demand has long since been complied with in England, yet in this republican country (to which even Cromwell and Hampden sought to flee from the tyranny of Charles), tens of thousands of public officers and employees—national, state, and municipal—have long been compelled to annually make "gifts and benevolences," under the name of political assessments, at the peril of dismissal or with the hope of promotion—a threat and a bribe as great and as debasing as any that King Charles could have inflicted upon the meanest in his civil service.

The story is too familiar to warrant any repetition here, how the English people, when once aroused, carried on their contest against the spoils system of James I. and Charles I. But I cannot dismiss this period without a word of observation as to the debasing effect upon the public conscience of familiarity with flagrant public wrong. The readiness with which we supinely endure such exactions upon the members of our civil service and upon those who work for the public—such legalized pillage of the people's money (for that partisan tyranny which coerces the assessment also keeps up salaries and wages needlessly high in order that the assessment may be paid), at the same moment that we abhor and prohibit monopolies and the sale of offices—is certainly a remarkable instance of that effect. We seem to think it a wholly different wrong to sell an office or a franchise outright from that involved in handing it arbitrarily over to a servile dependent, on the condition that his master may exact from him an annual rent, to be fixed at his will, on the peril of ejection. The chances, I venture to think, are that he who holds by purchase will cherish the more wholesome and manly feeling of independence. That noble man, Sir Samuel Romilley, found a more honorable independence in a seat in Parliament he purchased than a partisan system would allow him to secure by an ordinary election. And perhaps John Hampden himself would not think Charles I. a greater tyrant, because he arbitrarily required a tax from all of his subjects alike for the purposes of the public treasury than he would consider that American President or Secretary to be who should, as arbitrarily, require a tax from those whom he has the power to dismiss, to be used, not in aid of the public treasury, but for the baser purposes of keeping himself and his friends in office, and his opponents out of office. But it is plain enough that such a President might be a far greater coward than the King; since real courage is required to practice extortion upon a whole nation, while any vulgar tyrant may enforce depredations upon a few thousand of his official subordinates. The justification made by James and Laud for levying the tax was in principle precisely that made by modern partisans in defence of party assessments, that it was necessary to uphold their principles and to keep their party in power.

# CHAPTER V.

## CROMWELL'S ADMINISTRATIVE SYSTEM.

He rejected the worst abuses of the old system, but relied on patronage.—
His situation similar to that of a party leader—A sort of partisan system
introduced.—He applied a joint test of religion and politics at the gates of
office.—Made important reforms.—The test applied to members of Parliament and army officers.—A better system hardly possible in his day.—
Marvel, Eliot, and Vane as reformers.

CROMWELL gave the first blow to the despotic spoils system
which was heavy enough to break in its framework. He was
no mere administrative reformer, but a mighty impersonation
of a new spirit in religion and politics, of better methods in
government and of grander conceptions of the duties and
responsibilities both of rulers and of citizens. It was principles
and ideas—a well-defined creed in religion, and large views in
politics—and not class interests or traditional favoritism, that
were to bear sway while he lived. There were neither party
platforms nor parties in the modern sense, but (excepting a
few gathered separately) there were two great, hostile bodies in
the state—the one standing together for the divine right of
kings, for rank, privilege, and the old spoils system generally,
and the other for Cromwell and the principles and spirit of the
great revolution of which he was the leader. Cromwell and
his fellow-officers recognized themselves as representing at least
that portion of the people who believed as they did ; and
hence they regarded themselves as responsible to them for
economy and efficiency in the administration. This placed
them much in the attitude of party leaders ; having imposed
upon them the obligation of justifying their use of official
authority to so many of the people as constitute the ruling
majority. This sort of responsibility, directly to at least a
great portion of the people, rather than to a privileged and

official class alone, marks the great advance of party over despotic government in the exercise of official power. Such a power may be used as corruptly by a party as by a despot (as I shall have occasion to point out), but not so despotically ; and hence a partisan use of such authority seems to be naturally an intermediate stage of progress between the arbitrary use of that power by a despot and its use by officers who, regarding their authority as a public trust, make appointments on the basis of personal merit.

It is plain that Cromwell must have men of capacity in the public service, or his rule would be short ; and neither his temper nor the spirit of the times tended to make him any more scrupulous about slaughtering the innocents and driving out those who did not accept his creed in the public service than he was of cutting down his enemies on the field of battle. It was a time of bloody antagonism and desperate measures. He had no leisure for perfecting methods of administration, and the violent sentiment of the times demanded retaliation and proscription.  He made some reforms of great importance, with a wise regard to the interest of the people ; and, in his own interest and that of his favorites and followers, he applied the partisan system with a vigor and a logical consistency from which its modern votaries would shrink. Himself a member of Parliament, he was, perhaps, the first to advocate the salutary doctrine that legislators ought not to hold executive office or interfere with its proper duties, but he fell from the great principles of his speech by remaining a member while he held the most influential executive office in the army.  He struck from the pay rolls many drones and sinecurists.  He dealt heavy blows upon court favoritism and extravagance generally.  He infused vigor into every part of the administration, and character and economy were more regarded in his appointments than ever before.  He gave members of Parliament a voice in the appointment of minis ters, and, for a time at least, he allowed them full legislative authority ; but he also dispersed one Parliament at the point of the sword, and he locked the members of another out of their hall until they promised to approve his policy.  He made a creed and a policy of his religion and his politics united ; and he enforced it in selecting the members of his regiment as well as the members of his civil service. He was too manly and statesmanlike to allow predatory levies or assessments by anybody upon his officials ; but he used intrigue and coercion, if he escaped venality, in the exercise of the appointing power. He caused rotten boroughs to be swept away, and members to be sent from unrepresented towns ; but he disfranchised Catholics and Royalists.

In his own way he gave the partisan system a most vigorous trial. For Cromwell not only gave office and titles, confiscated lands, and bribes of other sorts to his favorites and to those he wished to conciliate, but he added a religious to a political test for office. And to induce others to think as he did, he placed the creed of Congregationalism at the door of his conventions and parliaments, as we place the creed of our party at the doors of the post-offices and custom-houses. He not only nominated those who were to be voted for as members of a Parliament, but he also required them to get a certificate of orthodoxy from his council before they were allowed to pass the doors of the House. Being substantially in the position of a great party leader, he did not see any reason why executive and partisan coercion and tests of opinion might not be applied to legislative officers, and to those in the army, as well as to officials in the civil service proper. And can we deny the logical consistency of his reasoning ? Those of opposing faiths and factions were as proscriptive and as vigorously demanded that political spoils should be made the reward of victory as has ever been the case in the most violent partisan contests of our times. No partisan manager ever used patronage more skilfully or more boldly than Cromwell. And he evidently believed it would strengthen his hold upon power and perpetuate his dynasty. Of one of his Parliaments it is said that " It was calculated that of the members returned, one half were bound to the government by ties of profit or place." [1] The system does not seem to have been any more effective than in our day in securing model men for the customs service. For example, one of his statutes recites that " Carmen, por-

[1] Green's History of the English People, p. 576.

ters, watermen, and others employed on the quays, . . .
and also on the River Thames, are very ordinarily drunk, and
do also profane and blaspheme the holy name of God by curs-
ing and swearing." He punished such offenders, however,
with a vigor that we have never reached : for he gave his
customs officers the powers of justices of the peace, with
liberty to appoint deputies, each of whom, without special
warrant, might arrest any of these drunkards and blas-
phemers.

Neither Robert Walpole nor General Jackson could deny
that this first trial of the partisan system was in able hands.
But not even the mighty genius of Cromwell was able through
that system to secure for himself or his party any abiding
position or official gratitude. As he went on under it, his
power steadily declined. Upon his decease, his followers
melted away. Almost without a struggle, England resumed
allegiance to the heir to her throne, utterly base and unworthy
as he was. The greatest genius for government England ever
produced was not able, through the most skilful use of patronage, to leave gratitude enough behind him to save his
own bones from being dragged from the grave and exposed on
a gibbet to the jeers of the royalists. It is quite probable
that in the intolerant period in which he lived—when un-
popular opinions took men to the block—when men fought
about religious dogmas—when even slavery stood unchallenged
by the popular judgment—when the noblest man of his time
was executed for treason in violation of the pledge of a king
—any less mercenary and partisan system than his would
have failed of support ; just as in such times it would have
been impossible to have manned fleets or filled up armies, or
to have led either successfully, without the hope and the enjoyment of sacks, pillages, and spoils—which were so long
believed to be equally justiable and inevitable in warfare—and
from the terrible reality of which the designation of " spoils
system," in politics, has been derived.

It cannot therefore be said that Cromwell really broke up
the spoils system as a whole, but only in part : but his administration caused some salutary changes in public opinion upon
the subject, as well as in the modes of carrying on public

business. The number of those who thought and acted boldly upon political questions was permanently increased, and the old system lost much of its prestige, which it never regained. It was made easier for Parliament to become a great power at the expense of the Crown and the nobility. The Star Chamber, the Court of High Commission, and the arbitrary levy of taxes were at an end. In the minds of a great portion, and that the more intelligent portion, of the middle classes, the awe and majesty which had hedged about a king, and made a manly scrutiny of his doings almost impossible, was to be no more.

The great political contests in the times of Charles I. and of Cromwell had turned upon the fundamental principle of civil and religious liberty, and the time had not arrived when patriots and statesmen could in quiet sit down to the study of the problem of honest and economical administration. But an age that could produce Hampden and Pym, Eliot and Marvel, Milton and Vane, and could place them in Parliament or in high offices of state, gives reason to expect that the solid virtues and statesmanship nourished in the private life of the people will in due time make themselves felt in the execution of the laws. In the writings of Marvel, we find perhaps the first systematic attack upon administrative abuses recorded in English history ; sinecurists, placemen, and corrupt and subservient court favorites being so roughly handled by him that he was in danger of assassination. His acts were in the spirit of his words ; and at a time when he was so poor as to need to borrow a guinea, Charles II. tried in vain to bribe him with a £1000. He is said to have been the last member of Parliament who was paid for his services. But he served his constitutents with wonderful ability and fidelity, sending them a daily account of the proceedings of Parliament in letters which were thought worthy of publication even after the elapsing of a century. The abolition of all compensation to members was admirably calculated and was probably designed to keep out of Parliament poor men like Marvel, who were genuine representatives of a free and pure sentiment steadily growing among the people. Reformers were becoming troublesome in that age.

In a noble speech of Sir John Eliot, made in the House of
Commons in support of the " Petition of Right " in 1628, he
used this courageous and prophetic language : " For the next,
the ignorance and corruption of our ministers, where can you
miss of instances.   If you survey the court, if you survey the
country ; if the Church, if the city be examined ; if you
observe the bar, if the bench, if the ports, if the shipping, if
the land, if the seas—all these will give you variety of proofs ;
and that, in such measure and proportion as shows the *greatness of the disease to be such that, if there be not some speedy
appliance of remedy, our case is almost desperate.*"   And he
demanded that a great inquisition " should be speedily made
into these alarming abuses."   In that age a reformer had not (as
in England a century later, or now in this country) merely to
encounter small sarcasm or the coarse misrepresentation of
those whom he might scorn, but to withstand the despotic
power and the vindictive passions of those who could put his
liberty and life in peril, as Eliot well knew and soon experienced.   He must be such a man as Mr. Gladstone says he
found in Zachary Macaulcy, who " expected little comfort in
this world, and looked for his reward only beyond the grave."
The inquisition which Eliot demanded was not made ; and
his bold arraignment of the government caused this great
patriot and reformer, whom Hallam declares to be " the most
illustrious confessor in the cause of liberty whom the times produced," to be speedily thrown into the Tower by the King's
order, where his health giving way, after great suffering, he
died in 1632.   These facts are very familiar history ; but it
is not so generally noticed, I think, how greatly the administrative corruption and incompetency which, if not removed
by " speedy appliance of remedy," Eliot declared would
make the condition of the kingdom " desperate," had to do
with driving the people to arms and bringing Charles himself
to the block only seventeen years later.

It is, however, in the life and character of the noble Puritan statesman, Sir Henry Vane—whom Cromwell and Charles
both feared—and in the fact that he was long a member of
Parliament and in various other high offices, that we may find
the best evidence of the great strength which the liberal and

reforming spirit in that age had attained. He had the disinterestedness, the courage, and the constructive capacity essential to a great administrative reformer. He gave up to the government the fees of his office as Treasurer of the Navy, which amounted to £30,000 a year; and, as chairman of a committee, he reported a bill for parliamentary reform. But he was too far in advance of his age to achieve the important reforms he desired. It was on account of his great liberality in religion and politics that in early life he was opposed by Winthrop and was defeated as a candidate for governor in the Puritan colony of Massachusetts. As a leader of the Independents, he rendered great service in behalf of New England; and, befriending Roger Williams after he fled from official tyranny at Salem, it was the vast influence of Vane's character that procured that liberal charter for the Rhode Island colony, which was as much in advance of the general spirit of the New World as it was of that of the Old. The King feared his virtues. Parliament and the great leaders were too base to save him; and thirty years after the death of Eliot, Vane was beheaded. So great in those days was the peril of being a patriot and a reformer.

# CHAPTER VI.

Corruption gross and universal.—Bribery of members of Parliament becomes systematic.—Prostitution of the appointing power.—Parliament crowded with placemen.—Officials make great fortunes.—The King himself bribed.—Religious tests for office.—Administration as imbecile as it is venal.—Gerrymandering boroughs and packing Parliaments.—Removals, and revocation of licenses, on account of opinions.—The spoils system extended to the army.—Noble examples of courage and self-respect on the part of officers and candidates.—Favoritism and corruption unsuccessful.—The judiciary invaded by the spoils system.—How far that system contributed to the fall of James II.

It is not in the reign of an idler and a sensualist like Charles II., nor in that of a corrupt tyrant and bigot like James II., that we are to look for reform in public affairs. But these reigns are full of admonition; and they afford striking illustrations of the extent to which administrative abuses are independent of forms of government.

The surprise expressed by some historians that no conditions in favor of good administration were exacted on the restoration of Charles II. would perhaps be less if they had reflected that the privileged classes were opposed to such conditions, and that a vast army, in great part old officers and placemen, expected to become officials again, and to enjoy the spoils of the old system revived. Cromwell had established no method except the arbitrary exercise of his will and that of his officers for official selections. That method, in the hands of a monarch like Charles II., in an age of reaction against Puritanism as well as all morality and religion, was precisely what the most corrupt and desperate villains in politics, and all the dependents of the privileged classes, most desired. It included all the essential conditions of a saturnalia of official corruption, and therefore facilitated the loss of no small portion of what had been gained for good government by the revolution. Quite as unscrupulously as at any other period, public authority in the hands of the King, his favorites, and the privileged classes was now used in every grade of official life as a prerogative for gain, a bribery fund, and a terror; to the debasing demands of which every one seeking to enter the public service must prostrate himself, and every one in it must conform. No man of high capacity could act the part of a patriot or a reformer who had not the stalwart virtue that could withstand offers the most tempting and threats the most formidable. It was in this reign that the systematic buying of votes in Parliament began, and the abuse spread with great rapidity. We shall never realize how vast have been the reforms in Great Britain, without looking into the profound depths of the corruption and villainy which followed the Restoration.

On two points Charles was in earnest : (1) " he would not have a company of fellows¹ looking into his actions and examining his ministers and accounts ;" and (2) he would have titles and estates for his mistresses, and would use the appointing power freely to gratify his passions, please his court, reward his favorites, punish his enemies—caring as little as the most mercenary partisan demagogue of later days for the cost of the service or the rights, honor, or morals of the people.

" The public service was starved that courtiers might be pampered." . . . " The personal favorites of the sovereign, his ministers and the creatures of those ministers were gorged with public money." . . . " The regular salary was, however, the smallest part of the gains of an official man of that age. From the nobleman who held the white staff and the great seal down to the humblest tide waiter and gauger, what would now be called gross corruption was practiced without disguise and without reproach. Titles, places, commissions, pardons were daily sold in market overt by the great dignitaries of the realm ; and every clerk in every department imitated, to the best of his power, the evil example. Whitehall, when he dwelt there, was a focus of political intrigue and fashionable gayety."

¹ He meant by " fellows" members of Parliament, and it must be borne in mind that members of Parliament had not yet got so much patronage as to be involved in the corruption of the times.

5

" Whoever could make himself agreeable to the prince or could secure the good offices of the ministers, might hope to rise in the world without rendering any service to the government, without even being known by sight to any Minister of State.  This courtier got a frigate, and that a company ; the third the pardon of a rich offender; a fourth a lease of Crown land on easy terms."

" If the King notified his pleasure that a briefless favorite should be made a judge or that a libertine favorite should be made a peer, the gravest counsellors, after a little murmuring, submitted." [1]

" The immense gain of official men moved envy and indignation. Here a gentleman was paid to do nothing.  There many gentlemen were paid to do what would be better done by one."  . . .  " The house swarmed with placemen of all kinds—Lords of the Treasury, Lords of the Admiralty, Commissioners of Customs, Commissioners of Excise, Commissioners of Prizes, Tellers, Auditors, Receivers, Paymasters, Officers of the Mint, Officers of the Household, Colonels of Regiments, Captains of Men-of-war, Governors of Forts."

Parliament made no serious attempt to reform in this reign.

" There was great servility and no small amount of corruption among its members.  A minister of Charles II. declared that to pocket the bribes, members flocked around him like so many jackdaws for cheese." [2]

The King and the court actually became pensionaries of great corporations, and franchises and titles were bartered for money.  Childs, the Chairman of the India Company, bribed Charles II. with a present of 10,000 guineas from its funds, and James II. with the same amount.

" All who could help or hurt at court, ministers, mistresses, priests, were kept in good humor by presents of shawls and silks, bird's-nests and attar of roses, bulses of diamonds and bags of guineas.  . . . James ordered his seal to be set to a new charter." [3]

Imitating Cromwell, Parliament in this reign applied a theological as well as a political test to office.  The Test Act required, in addition to the oath of allegiance and supremacy,

[1] Macauley's History, vol. I., p. 303 and 359.
[2] Palgrave's Lectures on House of Commons, 1877.
[3] History, vol. vi., p. 249.

that every one in the civil and military employment of the State should make a declaration against transubstantiation and also partake of the sacrament according to the rites of the Church of England. This theory of strengthening a creed in religion may seem very absurd at first blush ; but are we certain that it cannot be defended upon every ground upon which parties have, in our times, justified a test of political faith for every petty office ? Not having practised the political art of propagating religion in that way, we call it oppression and have little faith in its success.

From Charles II. to James II. the short step is downward from one corrupt administration that was graceful and cautious to another that was brutal and reckless.

James II. cannot be said to have brought any new system into the public service ; but he combined together the worst elements of the despotic spoils system and the partisan spoils system, to both of which he added a taint of his own character. Far more arbitrary than Charles I., and quite as corrupt as Charles II., he imitated Cromwell, without his respect for merit, in the enforcement of a theological test in politics, and made a sort of political party out of Catholic sympathizers. He had no higher conception of the appointing power than to make it the instrument of his vengeance, his vanity, his lust, and his bigoted ambition. In the true spirit of the spoils system, of which he was the head, he became a pensionary of the King of France, pocketing the gold of that country as a condition of betraying his own.

Jeffreys, his favorite judge, ordered hanging and judicially levied blackmail as boldly as ever Barnard, under his view of the spoils system, granted illegal injunctions, or any of his associates plundered the public treasury. The Queen and the King's favorites collected commissions on fines and forfeitures imposed by the King as freely as ever the wife of a republican secretary made a levy upon army posts, or the partisan leaders in a republic ever levied percentages on salaries fixed by Congress.

" The naval administration moved the contempt of men acquainted with the dock-yards of France and Holland." . . . In the navy

done James seems to have made some reforms. "The military administration was worse. The courtiers took bribes from the colonels, the colonels cheated the soldiers ; the commissaries sent in long bills for what they had never furnished. Keepers of arsenals sold the stores and pocketed the price. From the time of the Restoration to the time of the Revolution, neglect and fraud had been almost constantly impairing the efficiency of every department of the government. Honors and public trusts, peerages, baronetcies, regiments, frigates, embassies, governments, commissionerships, leases of Crown lands, contracts for clothing, for provisions, for ammunition, pardons for murder, for robbery, for arson, were sold at Whitehall, scarcely less openly than asparagus at Covent Garden, or herrings at Billingsgate. Brokers had been incessantly plying for customers in the purlieus of the court ; and of these brokers the most successful had been, in the days of Charles, the harlots, and in the days of James, the priests. From the palace, which was the chief seat of this pestilence, the taint had diffused itself through every office and every rank in every office, and had everywhere produced feebleness and disorganization." [1]

It is worthy of notice in what small measure the contemporaries of these events comprehended how perilous administrative corruption is to a nation's peace and strength. At that time little importance was attached to the modes of appointing officers, the methods of doing the public business, or to character in public places. It is only since administration has been made a sort of science by English statesmen, that they have looked back and got a clear view of the fearful perils and costs in which official incapacity and dishonesty had involved the nation.

There is nothing new in the partisan (and generally supposed to be modern) theory of manipulating election districts, packing legislatures, or supporting the party right or wrong.

"Returning officers [says Macaulay] were appointed who would avail themselves of the slightest pretences to declare the King's friends duly elected. Every placeman, from the highest to the lowest, must be made to understand, if he wished to retain his office, that he must at this juncture support the Throne by his vote and interest. The

---

[1] History, vol. iv., p. 61 and 62.

high commission in the meanwhile would keep its eye upon the clergy. The boroughs, which had just been remodelled to serve one turn, might be modelled to serve another turn. By such means the King hoped to obtain a majority in the House of Commons."

Here is *Gerrymandering*, complete, from the brain of a royal bigot and despot, put in actual practice, three quarters of a century before Elbridge Gerry or this republic was born; and it is but another instance of old abuses which so many suppose to be original in a republic, and not a few palliate as inevitable in our politics, if, indeed, they are not held to be a very justifiable means of partisan success.

Under James II. also, the champions of the spoils and patronage system as vigorously denied the right of a member of Parliament, a judge, a magistrate, a bishop, or even a colonel, to hold political opinions different from those of his chief, as the advocates of that system now dispute the right of a gauger, a book-keeper, a collector, or a rural postmaster, to such liberty of opinion. King James wanted a parliament to suit himself; and, like Cromwell, seeing no reason why members of Parliament, as well as those holding office in the executive departments, should not be required to be of his way of thinking, he acted accordingly. The same author says: "King James also determined to revise the Commissions of Peace and Lieutenancy, and to keep in power and to retain in public employment only such gentlemen as should be disposed to support his policy." Here also Jackson has small claims to originality, and was greatly outdone in his own line of fame by James II. The King pursued a similar course in regard to municipal corporations; threatening the revocation of charters if the support of his policy was not pledged. In case of the attempted coercion of the Lieutenants, we find perhaps the first plain utterance—and, if not the first, certainly one of the most striking examples—of that manly, self-respecting feeling in the official life of England, which, contrary to the common belief, I fear that even the independent spirit of republican officials does not always surpass. For the historian adds that "half the Lieutenants of England peremptorily refused to stoop to the odious service which was required of them." . . . "They were immediately dismissed."

Similar attempts on magistrates and candidates for Parliament met with a resistance equally honorable and equally successful. " Arguments, promises, threats were tried in vain. . . The candidates and magistrates of four counties unanimously refused to fetter themselves by the pledge which the King demanded of them." In parts of the kingdom, where the King had great hopes, out of sixty only seven made so much as a qualified promise to support the royal policy. The candidates for Parliament in 1687 framed and signed a paper, and sent it to the King, which is so just and manly that legislators of the present day, from whom mercenary caucuses or the great chiefs of politics attempt to extort pledges, could hardly do better than to adopt it, if indeed they have the courage. These are the material parts : " As a member of the House of Commons, should I have the honor of a seat there, I shall think it my duty carefully to weigh such reasons as may be adduced in debate for and against a bill, . . . and then to vote according to my conscientious convictions." . . . " As an elector, I shall give my support to candidates whose notions of the duty of a representative agree with my own." Perhaps clerks in the departments, when coerced as to his vote by members of Congress, could not do better than refer their persecutors to this dignified language of their political ancestors, addressed to King James II. For the progress made in civil liberty since his reign is well illustrated in the fact that a large portion of the members of Parliament then sustained relations to the Crown quite as dependent as those our ordinary clerks now sustain to members of Congress. The elections went against the King and in favor of those who thus stood on principle and duty, but had no patronage. A motion having been made to inquire into the abuses in the elections, King James answered it in the same way that General Jackson answered those who opposed his election : " The members who had voted against the court were dismissed from the public service." Charles Fox quitted the pay office ; the Bishop of London ceased to be Dean of the Royal Chapel, and so on down the official list. In one particular the King proposed to carry the theory of the spoils system and the doctrine of passive obedience to those in authority further, perhaps, than any of its advocates have proposed to carry it in our days, however much they may have in secret practice followed King James' precedent. He insisted that none but those who approved his policy should have a license for selling wine, beer, or coffee ; not seeing any good reason, I suppose, why the faithful constable or magistrate, who might be called on to deal with an offending coffee-stand or beer-cellar, should, any more than the voter (who had got the favor of a license he had broken) be placed under a pledge to support those who gave him his privileges.

"Every battered old cavalier (says Macaulay) who, in return for blood and lands lost in the royal cause, had obtained some small place under the Keeper of the Wardrobe or the Master of the Harriers, was called up to choose between the King and the Church. The Commissioners of Customs and Excise were ordered to attend his Majesty at the Treasury. There he demanded from them a promise to support his policy, and directed them to require a similar promise from all their subordinates. One custom-house officer notified his submission to the royal will in a way which excited both merriment and compassion. 'I have,' he said, 'fourteen reasons for obeying his Majesty's command : a wife and thirteen young children.' "

That system was all the more terrible in the King's hands, because it was carried to its logical results of allowing him to remove, and he did remove, judges and justices at will, as he did all other officers. "The packed judges of the Court of King's Bench gave, as a matter of course, judgment in favor of the Crown."[1] Wielding this all-pervading power, he used it everywhere, as an unscrupulous party majority might use it, and his strong hand was felt in every local election. "Its effect was to place in the hands of the Crown the nomination of a large portion of the members of the House of Commons, and also to give its adherents the power of domineering in all the daily detail of local municipal politics. The court put in force every artifice and used injustice and violence of the gravest kind throughout England to manage the elections. . . . An eminently servile House of Commons was the result."[2]

[1] Creasy on the English Const., p. 308.
[2] Creasy on the English Const., pp. 308 and 310.

I hardly need say that all this use of patronage and spoils, of threats and solicitation, alike failed to increase the power of King James. The feeling of independence and the sense of public duty, the patriotism and the manhood, among the people from whom we sprung, were, under an arbitrary monarch near two centuries ago, too great and fearless to submit to such abuses. They saw that one of two results must soon happen—either that all the justice and liberty enjoyed by Englishmen must be lost in an intolerable despotism, or that the prostitution of official authority must be arrested. The world knows how England decided that issue—what angry cries hurried Jeffreys to the Tower—how a nation, indignant, drove its King from its soil and called a foreign prince to the throne. James, his tyranny and his civil service system fell together, never more to be tolerated in England.

It may be difficult to decide in what measure the direct causes of these great events had their origin in any positive usurpation on the part of Charles II. and James II., or in what measure they may be traced back to the extravagance and corruption, the annoyance, humiliation, and oppression, the royal necessities and presumption, the pride of birth and the tyranny of official station. These were the natural outgrowth of that false and vicious system of public administration which, while repudiating all moral standards and all official responsibility, had for centuries flouted and scorned high character and capacity in the common life of the nation. That system treated the bestowal of the highest offices, and the management of what is grandest in the executive affairs of a nation, as royal and aristocratic perquisites and monopolies to be dispensed as a favor or bargained for money and influence. But without attempting any estimate on the subject, no one can fail now to see, as Marvel, Eliot and Vane and other great statesmen had foreseen, that it was necessary that this system should be arrested, or liberty, intelligence, and public virtue, in England, would be dwarfed forever.

# CHAPTER VII.

## THE NEW SYSTEM OF ADMINISTRATION UNDER WILLIAM III.

Low character and capacity of those he found in office.—The Bill of
Rights.—Executive officers excluded from Parliament.—Tenure of judges
to be during good behavior.—Third series of Civil Service Rules.—Experiment of opposing leaders for executive advisers and its failure.—Factions
lead politics.—Origin of British Cabinet.—Party government originated in
1693.—Its significance.—Partisan system of office developed.—Its meaning.
—Power of Parliament increased.—The British Cabinet compared with that
of the United States.—Power of appointment and removal and conditions
of administration similar in the two countries.—William as a reformer.—
Bribery increases with the increased authority of Parliament.—Relation of
party government to the partisan system of appointments.

THE vicious methods of selecting officers, and the corruptions which had existed in administration, during the last two
reigns, naturally debased the character of those in official life.
When William, Prince of Orange, came to the throne in
1688, the official life of England was at the lowest stage of
degradation it had ever reached. With rare exception, all
those in office and all those connected with the court or politics were seething sources of corruption. The very fact of a
man being a public officer or a politician brought a suspicion
upon his integrity and his manhood.

The same causes which had kept men of purity and capacity
from official places had also filled them to overflowing with
venal minions of the court, decayed stewards of lords and
bishops, and the servile henchmen of the privileged classes
generally. Self-respecting manhood had no chances, and sinecurists drained the public treasury. William could never be
certain that any of those he found in office would be either faithful or competent in an emergency. "The standard of honor
and virtue among our public men was, during his reign, at the

very lowest point.    His predecessors had bequeathed to him a
court foul with all the vices of the Restoration, a court swarming with sycophants, who were ready, on the first turn of
fortune, to abandon him, as they had abandoned his uncle.
Here and there, lost in the ignoble crowd, was to be found a
man of true integrity and public spirit." [1]

It is at this time, and at such profound depths of official
degradation, that we may begin to trace the motions of those
purer currents that led slowly on to great improvements.
From the beginning, the movement for reform was republican
in its spirit—a struggle in which the privileged classes contended for their old monopoly, and the unprivileged classes for
equal chances to enter the service of their country.

" The politicians of the Upper House were deeply tainted with the
treachery and duplicity common to most English statesmen between
the Restoration and the American Revolution.    Most of the bills for
preventing corrupt influence in the Commons  .  .  .   were crushed
by the influence of ministers in the House of Lords.    The country
was long seriously burdened, and some of the professions were system-
atically degraded, in order to furnish lucrative posts for the younger
members of the aristocratic families ; and the representative character
of the Lower House was so utterly prevented by the multiplication of
nomination boroughs, in the hands of the peers, that a storm of indignation was at last raised, which shook the very pillars of the constitution." [2]

In his own person, the King brought a purer moral tone as
well as habits of business to his high station.    The English
people had gained wisdom since they called Charles II. to the
throne without guaranties for good administration.    They
therefore, at the accession of William, imposed some conditions upon the crown ; but the low state of morals in political circles allowed these conditions to be far less stringent
than the public safety required.    Still some of them have a
vital bearing upon our system.    They clearly show the increased power of the higher sentiments.    It was a part of the

---

Macaulay's History, vol. iv., p. 60.
[2] Lecky's England in the Nineteenth Century, vol. i., pp. 198 and 199.

great results of this revolution to limit the power of the Crown and to increase that of Parliament and of the higher public opinion. In order to prevent the King and the army of civil officers from everywhere controlling elections, as they had formerly done, the Bill of Rights of 1688 declared that "elections of members of Parliament ought to be free." In the same spirit it was provided, in the Act of Settlement of the next year, "that no person who has an office and place of profit under the King, or receives a pension from the Crown, shall be capable of serving as a member of the House of Commons:" [1] and also, "that judges' commissions shall be made *quamdiu se bene gesserint*, and their salaries ascertained and established; but upon the address of both Houses of Parliament it may be lawful to remove them." And I may anticipate a little by adding that in the first year of the reign of George III. (1760) [2] it was enacted that the judges should continue to hold their offices notwithstanding the demise of the King, and that they should continue to enjoy their salaries during their terms, which shall be "during good behavior."

Taken together, these provisions may be designated as another (a third) series of "Civil Service Rules." They broadly break into the old spoils system in various ways, but more especially by raising the judiciary above executive interference. The former rules (I have referred to) related mainly to qualifications for appointment; here, however, for the first time, we find independence secured in the proper discharge of duty while in office. These precedents (so far as they relate to the judiciary) we have followed; for they are the well-known originals of our constitutional provisions that judges "shall hold their offices during good behavior," and shall not have their compensation diminished during their continuance in office. But the difference in the two countries has been that, while in England the same tenure has been gradually extended to nearly the whole civil service, we have, more

---

[1] Such a law would of course have excluded members of the Cabinet from membership of either House of Parliament, and thus have disastrously changed the whole balance of the executive system of Great Britain.

[2] Statutes George III., chap. 23.

especially in later years, confined it to judges alone.[1]  This
provision of the Act of Settlement, however, was too much
for the disinterestedness of the members of the then existing
Parliament, but was not beyond that which they were willing
to demand of their successors ; and so they speedily changed
the provision to the effect that it should only apply to members elected after 1705 ; but even that provision was modified.
In the mean time, however, an act passed in 1694, for a new
revenue board for stamp duties, provided that its members
should not have seats in Parliament ; and this, Mr. Hallam
says, is the first exclusion from membership of that body on
account of employment.   A law of 1699 extended the exclusion to various other excise officers.   It will be perceived that
these are material limitations of the opportunities of official
tyranny under the old spoils system ; and it is a good illustration of the survival of parts of that system that we now often
see our State legislatures protecting themselves against executive officers, as the British Parliament did near two centuries
ago, by excluding them from membership.

But we have never yet, in our federal legislation at least,
acted upon the salutary precedent of the Bill of Rights, by
preventing such officers interfering with the freedom of elections.   We have, on the contrary, so tamely surrendered ourselves to official dictation, that a late mild attempt of the President to vindicate such freedom at elections was denounced by
partisan leaders as an interference with the just liberty of
officials   as if the exertion of official authority over elections,
rather than freedom on the part of the private citizen in taking part in them, was the right to be protected.

During the first five years of William's reign his position
was peculiar.   Strictly speaking, there were no parties, but
factions ; and yet the power of the King was not despotic.
Despotism was at an end, but neither parliamentary nor party

---

[1] We have not, in the States, as is well known, generally maintained that
tenure even for judges, but have elected them for short terms.  The tendency now is toward a longer tenure ; New York, for example, has lately
changed her judicial tenure from eight to fourteen years.  Our federal statutes go the full length of the Bill of Rights in excluding executive officers
from the legislature.

government had begun.[1] The condition was that of rival noblemen and unscrupulous factions among the higher classes contending for the favor of the King and the control of patronage. Parliament had become stronger and more ambitious than ever before, but it had then secured but little patronage. The King, seeking to harmonize contending factions, took opposing elements into his council. Being a sovereign of commanding ability and great experience in administration, he seems to have thought that he could bend rival factions to his policy ; or at least that he could make a strong administration by pursuing a middle course. He gave the experiment a thorough trial during five years. So far as royal authority had, under the Stuarts, not been absolute, it had been shared by the *Privy Council*, a large body, of which the kings had really consulted only a small number, and those of course royal favorites. William seems to have become convinced, after five years' experience, that neither any large body, nor any body though not large, which contained antagonistic elements, could successfully exercise executive power.

" It would cause infinite delay and embarrassment in governing the kingdom." " Want of harmony caused want of vigor."[2] " Some of the most serious difficulties of his situation were caused by the conduct of the ministers on whom he was forced to rely. There was indeed no want of ability among his chief councillors, but one half of their ability was employed in counteracting the other half. . . . "The two Secretaries of State were constantly laboring to draw their masters in diametrically opposite directions."[3]

Such a state of things could not be long endured. Unity of policy was found to be as essential as unity of action. In short, the King's experiment of reconciliation and harmony had failed utterly. A remedy for the difficulty was proposed by Sunderland and approved by William, in 1693 : which was this : that a small number, since called the " Cabinet," or the

[1] Hallam says that political factions were so violent in the early part of William's reign, that they were " regardless of all the decencies of political lying."
[2] Creasy on the English Constitution, p. 332.
[3] Macaulay's History, vol. iv., pp. 63-70 ; and vol. vii., pp. 246-256.

"Cabinet Council," should be selected from the party in majority in Parliament, under whose advice the King should carry on the government, leaving to the ancient Privy Council only a small portion of its original authority. The Cabinet soon discontinued the practice it first adopted of consulting the Privy Council at all. The members of the Cabinet were called "Cabinet Ministers." Yet this "Cabinet," which keeps no records, yet controls the highest affairs of a vast empire, which is the original upon which our Cabinet is modelled and the embodiment of what all the world has come to designate as parliamentary government, is not, nor are its members, named in any law or known to the English Constitution.[1]

This important change in the method of exercising executive authority marks—or perhaps, I might say, was in itself—the *origin of political parties* in the modern sense, and of *party government* in England, and, indeed, in the world. This change, so pregnant of vast consequences in every way, enormously increased the power of Parliament over the civil service : since from its majority the members of the Cabinet were to be taken, and upon their failure to receive the support of that majority they were, according to the new theory, to resign. It tended greatly to secure harmony and vigor in the administration, which at all times (apparently at least) represented the majority of the nation. It hardly need be added that it also developed two great parties, each of which struggled for that majority which would give the victor the control not only of all legislation, but of all administration. There being no separate States to share the power and dignity of government, the central party majority was really made (in a more absolute sense than has ever been the fact in this country) supreme throughout the domain of politics. Such vast power, as well as all patronage (which Parliament could grasp), and the direction of every officer (save the judges), the enactment of all laws and the interpretation of the constitution itself, constituted the grand objects for which party warfare was

---

[1] By making the Lord Chancellor a member of the Cabinet, and not giving to the Vice-Chancellors a tenure during good behavior, the English equity system was left far more dependent than is our own upon political favor.

thereafter to be waged. This great change was what naturally and speedily led to the development in England of the partisan system of appointment to office. Under this system the sharing of the opinions of the party in power and the unhesitating support of the policy of its administration, are conditions paramount to personal merit, of receiving or retaining each and every office, however humble ; and the proscriptive use of patronage in that sense is one of the great agencies relied on for party strength. In a strict sense, this system was new in English politics, though Cromwell and some of the kings had ruled in its spirit. Never elsewhere has that system offered so splendid and so tempting a prize to party victory. And never elsewhere had the government of a country held its power by a tenure so precarious ; for on no day could a prime minister be sure that to-morrow he and his cabinet would not fall.[1]

I have thought it important to recall those events, because at this date commences the long trial, in Great Britain, of the efficiency of a partisan system of administration of the same kind, in general theory and practice, as that known by the same designation in our politics. It went into effect (as far as the situation would allow) in 1693, and was continued, though somewhat modified in detail, without fundamental change, for one hundred and sixty years, or until 1853, when the first elements of the *Merit System* were formally introduced. While there have been dissimilar conditions in the two countries, effecting to some extent the bearing of the experience of the one upon the other, I think it will appear that there is hardly a phase of administration in the United States upon which that of Great Britain, under the partisan system, will not be found to throw a valuable light. For some years after 1693, the power of the great nobles and families unquestionably caused the administration to be as much aristocratic as partisan ; but there was a steady growth of parliamentary influence, and hence of the influence of the great parties, at the expense of the Crown and privileged classes. As the power of Parliament and

---

[1] There have been in fact, I believe, three cabinets in the same month in England, though the average duration of each has been about three and a half years.

of popular opinion increased, the House of Commons more and more encroached upon the old prerogatives of the executive, and, in similar measure, of course upon its patronage. Members seeking patronage naturally conditioned their support of aspirants for seats in the Cabinet upon pledges of such patronage ; and here we have the origin of members of the legislature dictating local appointments. Much in the same ratio that members of Parliament grasped patronage, parliamentary elections became corrupt and the votes of members became venal. As a consequence, bribery of voters and of members so increased that we shall soon find the greater corruption in the administration standing, for the first time in English history, in connection with Parliament rather than with the executive.

Before proceeding to the practical effects of the partisan system, it will be useful to consider how close is the similarity in the two countries between the methods of exercising executive authority. Between an hereditary king and nobility on one side, and an elective president and senators on the other, the difference of course is vast ; but practically authority over administration in Great Britain is now neither with the Crown nor the Lords, but, as here, is with the Cabinet and the heads of departments. I have said that our Cabinet is modelled upon this original Cabinet of 1693. The imitation is one of both substance and form. We borrowed the English name. Like the Cabinet of England, our own keeps no records. Ours, like hers, is unknown to the constitution and the laws. The authority of either is nowhere defined nor is the action of either anywhere legally subject to review. In each country alike, the Cabinet, in a large way, has the care of its great affairs in peace and war ; the one with a king, the other with a president, in whose name everything is done ; and in the president is united nearly all the powers of the king, with perhaps all those of the prime minister. The modal difference is this : that in England the king names a prime minister from the party majority of members elected by the people to Parliament, and the member so named selects the other members of the Cabinet from the same party majority, subject to the assent of the king, which he is almost certain to give ; while, with us, the president (himself elected by the party majority) selects the members of his Cabinet from that same majority, subject to the assent of the Senate, which it is almost certain to give. The one grand difference in the two governments, touching the civil service, is the power of the United States Senate in the matter of confirmation, to which no executive authority possessed by Parliament corresponds ; but, as a sort of offset, the president freely uses the veto power, which for more than a century no British sovereign has used, and which may therefore be regarded as obsolete.[1]

Both methods alike bring into the control of the administration men who stand for the principles and policy of the party majority of the nation, and it is their duty to interpret those principles and to carry that policy into action. With us the same policy may be pursued for four years, unless arrested by supply bills, even though the party majority has changed. But, in England, a change of the popular majority will be at once followed by a change of the Cabinet, unless Parliament is prorogued, and a new election ordered. In England the permanence of the Crown and the House of Lords, and in the United States the fixed term of the President and the conservative influence of the Senate, put some check upon the sudden and dangerous oscillations in policy which the too rapid changes in the popular majority might otherwise produce. The constitutions of both countries give the appointing power, and by implication the power of promotion, removal, and control of subordinates, to the executive (which in Great Britain, for nearly all administrative purposes, means to the Cabinet and departments), but in neither constitution has it been defined how that power should be exercised, nor are there any adequate safeguards against its use for selfish or partisan ends. Whether it be a trust for the public benefit or an official perquisite, each constitution leaves to inference. Hence it may be said, with equal truth of both governments, that in principle those who administer them may give

[1] There is this further difference in practice, that in Great Britain the sovereign does not preside at or attend Cabinet meetings, while with us the President always presides. Originally the practice was the same in Great Britain, but is said to have been discontinued because George I. could not speak the English language.

" to the party in power those places where harmony and vigor
of administration require its policy to be represented," and
that both alike " permit all others to be filled by persons
selected with sole reference to the efficiency of the public
service and the right of all citizens to share in the honor
of rendering faithful service to their country." Neither government, more than the other, seems to require that all subordinate officials should be active politicians or hold the same
political opinions as the high officers who control its policy.
The divisions into departments—State and Foreign Affairs,
the Treasury, War, Naval Affairs, Public Justice, the Post
Office Department, with subdivisions into bureaus and offices
having various grades of official and clerical duty—are, with
formal difference, in the main the same in the two countries,
except that this great difference grows out of the very nature
of the two governments — viz., that ours most encourages
supreme regard for personal merit and accords the least importance to wealth, birth, and official and social prestige.
With these elements of similarity in mind, we may consider
the great trial of the partisan system and its results in Great
Britain.

A few more words will suffice as to the reign of William.

The greatest statesman of his age and the ablest man that
had sat on the English throne in modern times, he was the
first of her kings who had any sense of the vital importance
of good administration ; an importance all the greater in the
fearful stress of arms and of civil discontent in which so much
of his reign was involved. Finding so few officials worthy of
confidence, he became a practical reformer himself ; taking
time, in the midst of the most exacting duties, to make investigations into the departments ; for example, going in person
day after day to the Navy Department and to the Treasury,
and overhauling records and accounts which disclosed the most
flagrant incompetency, neglect, and corruption. He removed
many sinecurists, enforced economy in various ways, and
brought able men into the public service. He was his own
Secretary for Foreign Affairs, and reformed that branch of
the service. He vetoed several bills, and (except in a single
instance) he was the last English sovereign who has thought it

prudent to use that high authority. He did not allow members of Parliament to acquire much control over patronage, but he used it in the hope of strengthening the Whig party. Still in his reign there began to be a strong indication of patronage falling into the hands of members. His influence was in favor of retaining efficient officers as long as they were honest, and this much strengthened the example of the permanent tenure of judges. But he resorted to pensions, sinecures, and venal patronage to influence Parliament. Though in advance of his age, he did not wholly keep clear of its corruptions. His high example, however, in favoring some reforms and in giving reformers exemption from the courtly annoyance and the lordly scorn and sarcasm, to say nothing of the injustice and persecution, they had before encountered, so emboldened the reform spirit that even Parliament itself was driven by public opinion, for the first time since Cromwell's death, into making a real investigation into the abuses of the public service. Mr. Macaulay says, " The House fully determined to make a real reform, and in truth nothing could have averted such a reform except the folly and violence of the reformers." The common fault of underrating the power of those organized about abuses of long standing, and of believing the attempt should be made to remove all evils by one drastic operation, was fatal for the time. The House even had the rashness and folly to vote that no person employed in the civil service (save the Speaker, judges and ambassadors) should receive more than five hundred pounds a year. All the higher officials combined for self-defence, and the cause of reform was arrested by causes that may be traced back to the incompetency and impetuosity of its own friends.

While the partisan system in its early stages tended greatly to increase the influence of members of Parliament and of public opinion, and hence in many ways was productive of good, it early showed its inability to much raise the moral standard of official life. Even before the close of William's reign it greatly increased the practice of bribery. " Burnet assures us that, at the election of 1701, when William was still on the throne, a most scandalous practice was brought in of buying votes, with so little decency that the electors engaged themselves by subscription to choose a blank person before they were trusted with the name of the candidate." . . . In a pamphlet (published by Defoe) in 1701, he tells us that there was a regular set of stock-jobbers in the city who made a business to buy and sell seats in Parliament, that the market price was 1000 guineas, and that Parliament was in a fair way of coming under the management of a few individuals." [1]

The stronger and most corrupt interest in these elections was the new influence over appointments which members of Parliament had unfortunately acquired with their enlarged legislative authority.

In considering the effects of party government, and the partisan system for appointments and removals, now on trial, it is important to have clear views of their relations to each other. It by no means follows that party government must enforce a partisan system in carrying on the administration. Patriotic motives may prevail and personal worth may be prized higher than party zeal. It is unquestionably essential to such government that a few of the higher executive officers at the head of affairs, who are to carry into effect the policy, both domestic and foreign, of the dominant party, should share the opinions of that party and have faith in its policy. Such higher officers guide all executive affairs, give instructions to all below them, and enforce official obedience everywhere. [2] The political opinions of the vast body of subordinate officials, including the whole clerical force, in a properly regulated civil service, are not material to the success of such policy ; nor would such subordinates be active politicians if not com-

---

[1] Lecky's English History in the Eighteenth Century, vol. i., p. 397.

[2] In British administration there are from thirty-four to fifty of these higher officers, who are regarded as political, and who go out when their party suffers defeat. They include, of course, all the members of the Cabinet, and certain of the heads of departments. Various of the departments —the Treasury, Admiralty, War, Customs, Inland Revenue, for example— have Boards at their head, a part of the members of which (except of the two latter) are regarded as political. But there are permanent members of these Boards who are specially charged with the care of the administrative work. Foreign ministers are not generally displaced by a new administration, but may be, if important questions of policy are involved ; though transfers are more frequent than removals.

pelled to be in order to prevent their own removal. It is quite open to a party in power, therefore, either to enforce a proscriptive, partisan system in the civil service, or to select those to fill the subordinate places with paramount reference to personal merit, and to leave them undisturbed so long as their duties are well performed. Whether party government will insist on having a partisan civil service will, of course, depend on the relative strength of its moral and patriotic elements as compared with its corrupt and proscriptive elements. In Great Britain the latter elements were for a long time controlling, and they can hardly be said to have been subordinated by the other until 1853, when, as I have said, the *Merit System*, in a qualified form, was introduced, without any change in the essential features of party government.

# CHAPTER VIII.

## PARTY GOVERNMENT FROM ANNE TO GEORGE III.

Attempted union of opposing elements in her Cabinet.—Advantages of party government.—Parliament takes power from the Crown.—Uses patronage corruptly.—Officers in postal services prohibited from interfering with elections.—Gross injustice in contested election cases.—Turning out officers to make places a high Tory device.—Increase of bribery.—Office-holders excluded from Parliament.—The partisan system degrades official life and becomes a spoils system.—Religious tests for office and their consequence.—Partisan censorship of the press.—Sales of boroughs.—Parliament grows more corrupt.—Robert Walpole, his theory, and gross corruption of his rule.—Public despair.—Duke of Newcastle.—Growth of higher public opinion outside official life.—John Wesley.—William Pitt.—Drunkenness and gambling, crime and violence, have increased.—Fearful condition of prisons.

COMING to the throne in 1702, Queen Anne brought to it no personal qualities likely to affect the administration, except purity of character and decided Tory sympathies. Looking at the party conflict from the Tory side, as William had from the Whig side, she also sought peace and a good execution of the laws through an administration of which the leaders of both parties were members. "Her ideal was a government in which neither Whig nor Tories possessed a complete ascendency." [1] Until near the end of her reign she persevered with such a Cabinet; but, like King William's experiment of the same kind, it was essentially a failure, and she finally yielded to the advice of the stronger party. This part of the policy of the two sovereigns has, I believe, never been tried by any of their successors. Referring to the contemplated adoption of the same policy in the next reign, Mr. Hallam [2] says: "But the mischief of a disunited, hybrid ministry had been

---

[1] 1 Lecky, p. 46.        [2] Constitutional History, vol. ii., p. 759.

sufficiently manifest in the two last reigns ; nor could George, a stranger to his people and their constitution, have undertaken without ruin that most difficult task of balancing parties and persons, to which the great mind of William had proved unequal." When this theory of balancing party influence in the Cabinet was at an end, party government had its first great opportunity.

Party government as such (that is, as distinct from a partisan and corrupt system of administration) was an immense advance in political justice and civilization. In spirit, it declared the majority of the people, instead of the King, the privileged classes and court favorites, to be the ruling power. It affirmed that great political principles, and not royal and aristocratic pleasure and interests, were the true standards of public duty. It widened the circle of those who enjoyed the monopoly of office, transferring it from the King, the nobles, and their favorites, to the King, the dominant party (or at least the managers of that party), and their favorites. It thus tended strongly to a larger liberty and equality, at the same time that it stimulated public thought and gave to personal worth and capacity larger opportunity of influence. It tended also to inspire a higher conception of the dignity and power of government, as having all its action conformable to great political principles ; and it aroused a loftier feeling of self-respect in the citizen, since through his party he could make his influence felt, and was himself recognized as a part of the nation. Party government, in its larger spirit, had also this salutary effect upon the administration—that it tended to make it harmonious, public and national. In earlier times each minister, head of department or great office was independently appointed, governed, and removed by the King ; each acted as an independent chieftain within his own autocratic sphere of duty ; and the administration therein was as diverse as it was secret, capricious, and arbitrary. The subordinate officers or agents were mere hirelings of the heads of departments. When party government was established, the Cabinet became in theory one body standing for a policy, and administering the national affairs as a whole. It is also one of the good results of the partisan system itself (as compared with the despotic system), to be set off against its manifest evils, that it introduced third persons—the dominant party and its leaders—whom it recognized as having a right to be heard in the disposal of office. In earlier times the giver and receiver were the only parties to the contract. The introduction of this third party tended to greater publicity, since in a measure it opened the secrets of patronage and of the spoils system to public criticism. If it only conceded a right to share office to those of the dominant party, and not to the people at large, it was at least a great and essential step toward recognizing the just claims of merit.

The appointing power and the control of administration passed as largely from the Crown to Parliament, in the reign of Queen Anne, as it did in this country from the President to Congress in the twenty years following the close of General Jackson's second term. It was something like a revolution, which threatened the counterpoise of legislative and executive power, under each government. The newly acquired appointing power was more and more, under Queen Anne, used by the dominant party for corrupt and merely partisan purposes; foreboding a reproduction of the spoils system in another form.

Party government was thus put to a severe test in its very outset. It became more and more clear, as its trial went on, that there was no virtue in it adequate for the reform of the great abuses which it had inherited; and, on the other hand, the new order of things soon developed serious evils of its own. Parliament having ceased to be subservient to the Crown, turned around and made its appointees subservient to itself. Indeed, it soon became itself tyrannical.

It was early perceived that the only hope of reform was in a coercive influence, from a higher public opinion, to be developed outside official circles. The time was favorable for the formation of that opinion; as never before had there been such eminent men who gave their talents to political literature; for example, Swift, Bolingbroke, Atterbury, and Prior on the side of the Tories; Addison, Steele, and Defoe on the side of the Whigs. The *Tatler*, the *Spectator*, the *Guardian*, and the *Englishman*, and many less celebrated journals, show the tendency toward popular discussion. To a better public opinion thus aroused, we may attribute legislation (during some years later) that helped to arrest those new evils. The independent, reforming sentiment to which these times gave an ineffective utterance acquired a vast power when proclaimed by Burke and Chatham in the next generation. A law enacted early in the reign of Queen Anne [1] is an example of the demand of this public opinion. Referring to the various postoffice officials, it declares that if any of them "shall by word, message, or writing, or in any manner whatsoever, endeavor to persuade any elector to give or dissuade any elector from giving his vote for the choice of any person . . . to serve in Parliament," he shall be liable to a fine of $500, and on conviction "shall become disabled and incapable of ever bearing or executing any office" under the Crown. That law is still in force, and is printed in the standing instructions before the eyes of every postmaster in the United Kingdom. To its salutary influence we may doubtless attribute the exemption from partisanship and in no small measure the unrivalled efficiency of the British postal service; while the absence of such a law in our service has allowed so many of our postmasters to be politicians and their offices to be electioneering agencies.

The proof that patronage newly acquired by members of Parliament, and used in a partisan spirit, was rather a source of corruption than of purification, is decisive. The appetite for patronage was as insatiable as it was demoralizing on the part of members of Parliament. Hallam [2] says of this period: "No check was put on the number or quality of placemen in the lower House. *New offices were continually created and at unreasonable salaries.* Those who desired to see a regard to virtue and liberty in the Parliament of England could not be insensible to the enormous mischief of their influence;" nor, I fear, can we be insensible to the fact that, to this day, similar causes continue to produce similar effects in our own legislatures.

Mr. Lecky [3] says that the old corruption, within Parliament, "increased rather than diminished after the revolution." In 1694, for example, Sir John Trevor, the Speaker

---

[1] 9 Anne, ch. 10, § 44.  [2] Const. History, vol. ii., p. 733.
[3] England in Eighteenth Century, vol. i., p. 396.

a cousin and warm friend of the infamous Jeffreys), was convicted of receiving a bribe of 1000 guineas from the City of London for his services in carrying a bill through the House of Commons.[1]

Mr. Hallam[2] shows how early there was a dishonest use of power in contested election cases ; "there was the grossest partiality . . . and contrary determinations for the sole purpose of serving rival factions," by reason of which a statute[3] was passed by the House to check its own corruption, which renders the last determination of the House of Commons conclusive as to the right involved. The modern proscriptive policy of turning out all the lower officers to make room for friendly partisans was adopted by the very generation that originated party government. That policy began with the high born Tories. Bolingbroke, their great leader, says Hallam, exposes "their intention to fill the employments of the Kingdom, down to the meanest, with Tories ;" at the same time declaring the Tory belief to be that such a use of patronage and the great property of the Tories would keep them in power during the whole of the reign of Queen Anne. But greatly to the surprise of the Tory leader, what happened was that the Whigs, though without control of patronage, actually got control of the administration before the end of her reign.

Bribery became so bold that, after outside public opinion had forced Parliament to enact laws against it (between 1703 and 1708), they seem to have been disregarded even by those who enacted them. Mr. Lecky[4] (citing Defoe) says :

" Never was treating, bribery, buying of voices . . . so open and barefaced. . . . In 1716 we find bitter complaints in Parliament of the rapidly-increasing expenses of election, . . . and a great number of persons have no other livelihood than being employed in bribing corporations."

---

[1] As Speaker, Sir John was forced to the ignominious duty of putting the vote in the House that adjudged his own infamy ; but he did it with a sublime effrontery perhaps without example in a legislative body, until William M. Tweed rose in the Senate of his State to vindicate the purity of partisan rule in the city of New York. Trevor's corruption and expulsion did not prevent him continuing to hold the office of Master of the Rolls for twenty-two years thereafter !

[2] 2 George II., chap. 2.

[3] Vol. ii., p. 640.

[4] Vol. i., pp. 397 and 398.

In a short passage, Mr. Lecky,[1] places in very clear light not only the fact that the new partisan system was powerless to elevate the public service, but the further fact that the party majority, in Parliament, had no disposition to reform the gross abuses in that body :

"The question in home politics, however, which created most interest in the nation, was of a different kind, and it was one which for very obvious reasons Parliament desired as much as possible to avoid. It was the extreme corruption of Parliament itself, its subserviency to the influence of the executive, and the danger of its becoming in time rather the oppressor than the representative of the people. *This danger had been steadily growing since the Revolution*, and it had reached such a point that there were many who imagined that they had certainly gained little by exchanging an arbitrary King for a corrupt and often tyrannical Parliament."

Though members of Parliament exercised without scruple their new patronage,[2] they had spirit enough to enact laws for limiting the influence of the executive in their own body. By one act[3] all persons holding pensions from the Crown were rendered incapable of sitting in the House ; and by another[4] this prohibition was extended to those who held them for a term of years ; but a bill of the House requiring an oath by each member that he was not pensioned, was defeated in the House of Lords ; a further fact showing that the greater corruption was in the old ruling class.

But the inherent incapacity of party government to raise the moral tone of official life, except as coerced by an independent public sentiment, is shown in the steady growth of corrupt favoritism, until its most profound depths were reached under the administrations of Walpole, Pelham, and Newcastle, during the reigns of George I. and George II. Nor shall we find that justice and liberty, except as protected by that senti-

---

[1] England in Eighteenth Century, vol. i., p. 470.
[2] "Patronage," in British politics, seems to include not merely the legal right to appoint, but controlling influence in respect to an appointment. When a member of Parliament could influence an appointment effectively, he was said to have the patronage of that appointment.
[3] 6 Anne, chap. 7.  [4] 1 George I., chap. 56.

ment, were much more cared for by an arbitrary party majority than they had been by an arbitrary King and nobility.[1]

Following the worst examples of the reigns of James and
Charles, the party majority, led by men of no religious principles, enforced a religious test in Queen Anne's reign, not
only for all officers under the national government, but for
officers in corporations; and this (in the language of Mr.
Lecky, and also, I may add, in the language of modern partisans) " on the ground that it was necessary for the *party* interests."    These tests required the reception of the eucharist,
according to the rites of the Church of England; and so shame-
lessly was one of the most solemn sacraments of Christianity
trailed in the mire of official corruption, and so repugnant was
the spectacle to the better sentiment outside of partisan politics, that " it became the general custom for the minister, before
celebrating the communion, to desire the *loyal* communicants
to separate themselves from those who were come there purely
for the sake of devotion.[2]

In the ninth year of the reign of William III., a law was
enacted for political effect which required that any Catholic
priest who should perform a marriage between a Catholic and
a Protestant should be hung; there were other laws in the
same spirit; and in 1729, in the reign of George II., a Fran-
ciscan friar died in Hurst Castle, in the seventy-fourth year of
his age, and the thirtieth of his imprisonment, under one of
these savage laws.    When, in 1701, the party majority had,
in pursuit of its factious policy, delayed the public supplies
(just as we have seen them delayed in our time), and a respectful and constitutional petition from the people was presented,

---

[1] Party government, in these earliest years of its trial, adopted one pernicious practice which we have seen despotic partisans continue in this generation.    " The mode adopted by the Commons of tacking, as it was called,
the provisions for this purpose to a money bill, so as to render it impossible
for the Lords even to modify them without depriving the King of his supply,
tended to subvert the constitution and annihilate the rights of a coequal
House of Parliament."—Hallam's Constitutional History, vol. ii., p. 703.

[2] In one of the states of Germany this proscriptive practice is said to have
been, in its application to licenses, carried so far that the courtesans were
required to partake of the Communion as a qualification for opening a
bawdy house.

justly reflecting on such conduct, the House voted the petition-
ers seditious, had them arrested, and held them in prison for
two months.

Members of Parliament claimed that the proceedings of
their own body (in the same spirit that arbitrary kings had
claimed that the causes and records of their appointments and
removals) were a part of their own secrets, as to which it was
an impertinence for the people to seek any information. If
the right of nominating to office was an official perquisite, with
which the people had nothing to do, why was not knowledge
of the doings of the Commons also an official privilege? It is
well known that it was only after a long and dangerous struggle
(during which Parliament sent many a reporter to prison), ter-
minating in the reign of George III., that the right of printing
debates in Parliament was won by the English people.

It was not until 1836—four years after the passage of the
great reform bill—that the votes in Parliament were published
by its own authority. The party majority also carried on a
censorship of the public press, on the theory that its control
was as rightful and as essential as was the partisan use of the
appointing power, in order to maintain the dominant party in
position and to keep down its adversaries. And, on this
theory, Steele and others were expelled, Defoe was prosecuted,
and Tutchin and several besides were whipped by the hang-
man, by order of the House of Commons ; and several writers
were compelled to apologize on their knees at the bar of the
House—all for the offence of having written in opposition to
the party majority of the hour. Nor was any check put to
this tyranny until Parliament was prorogued by reason of a
crisis produced by its order in committing to Newgate four
officers of the Court of King's Bench engaged in carrying out
judgments of that court for maintaining the rights and liberties
of the people.

The injustice and corruption in the matter of contested elections, which Hallam mentions as existing in the reign of William, grew to be far worse under the two first Georges. Mr.
Lecky [1] says : " They threatened to subvert the whole theory

_____
[1] Vol. i., pp. 477 to 479.

of representation :  .  .  .  the evil had already become apparent in the latter days of William, but some regard for appearance seems then to have been observed ;  .  .  .  soon, however, all shame was cast aside.  In the Tory Parliament, in 1702, the controverted elections, in the words of Burnett, were adjudged in favor of the Tories with such barefaced partiality that it showed that the party was resolved on everything that might serve their ends.  When the Whigs triumphed in 1705, they exhibited the same spirit.  In the Parliament which met in 1728 there were nearly seventy election petitions to be tried, and Lord Harvey has left an account of how the House discharged its functions.  ' I believe,' he says, 'the manifest injustice and glaring violation of all truth in the decisions of this Parliament surpass even the most flagrant and infamous instances of injustice of any of their predecessors.  .  .  .  People grew ashamed of pretending to talk of right and wrong, and laughed at that for which they ought to have blushed, and declared that in elections they never considered the cause, but the men, nor even voted according to justice and right, but from solicitation and favor.' "

This reference to " solicitation and favor " as a rule for a decision that ought to have been impartial and non-partisan, shows how readily the corrupt standard of bestowing office by favor perverts all political action ; that rule being in this case carried even into the sphere of judicial procedure.  The celebrated Speaker Onslow says the rule " that the right is in the friend, and not in the cause, is almost avowed, and he is laughed at by the leaders of parties who scruples upon it ; and yet we should not bear this a month in any other judicature of the Kingdom."  Here we see that an independent tenure, so lately conferred, had already developed a higher standard of duty in the courts.

The utter demoralization, on the part of those engaged in political functions, which these facts disclose, and the tone of despair and desperation (not unknown in our time) with which all honorable standards of political conduct were referred to, is also strikingly illustrated in Mr. Macaulay's essay on Lord Chatham, where he says :

" These men wished to transfer the disposal of employments and the command of the army from the Crown to the Parliament, and this on the very ground that the Parliament had long been a grossly corrupt body. The security against malpractice was to be that the members, instead of having a portion of the public plunder doled out to them by a minister, were to help themselves."

There have been several bills presented in our Congress within the last ten years which have proposed the equally revolutionary measures of substantially giving to members of Congress all the patronage which they have not already appropriated. And some of their advocates, for want of a better reason, have justified themselves in the same way as the men referred to by Macaulay. The baneful results of the new spoils system, in the control of the dominant party, were not, however, more conspicuous within Parliament than they were in the election of its members.

Mr. Lecky, quoting the writers of these times, says :

" Boroughs are rated at the Royal Exchange like stocks and tallies : the price of a vote is as well known as of an acre of land, and it is no secret who are the moneyed men, and consequently the best customers."

The Lord Chancellor (Macclesfield) during Walpole's administration was impeached for official corruption in selling masterships in his own court. Robert Walpole, an able man, but utterly unscrupulous, who had himself been in the Tower for official corruption, naturally became the great impersonation of the partisan spoils system of this age. For the larger part of the time from 1708 to 1742 he was Prime Minister or in the Cabinet. It was as much a part of his theory and that of his coadjutors that it is necessary for a party, in order to keep itself in power, to break open the letters of its opponents in the post-office, as it is of partisan leaders to-day that they must fill all offices with their minions : and therefore he freely ransacked his opponents' letters for their secrets, and even literary authors, like Pope, were victims of his pillage. According to Mr. Macaulay, he established a regular practice of giving places on condition that a part of the salary or perquisites should be paid over to some third person, and this prac-

tice seems to have continued long after his day.   This is the
nearest approach in British administration to our abuse of
levying party assessments, and is really the same in principle
and its equivalent in mischief.[1]

"He governed," says Mr. Lecky,[2] "by means of an assembly, which was saturated with corruption, and he fully
acquiesced in its conditions and resisted every attempt to improve it.   He appears to have cordially accepted the maxim
that government must be carried on by corruption or by force,
and he deliberately made the former the basis of his rule.   He
bribed George II. by obtaining for him a civil list exceeding by
more than £100,000 a year that of his father.   He bribed the
Queen by securing for her a jointure of £100,000 a year. . . .
He employed the vast patronage of the Crown, uniformly and
steadily, with the single view of securing his political position,
and there can be no doubt that a large proportion of the immense expenditure of the secret service money, during his
administration, was devoted to the direct purchase of members
of Parliament.   The government, . . . by the votes of
its numerous excise or revenue officers, by direct purchase, or
by bestowing places or peerages on the proprietors, exercised
an absolute authority over many seats ; and its means of influencing the assembled Parliament were so great that it is
difficult to understand how, in the corrupt moral atmosphere
that was prevalent, it was possible to resist it.   Great sums of
secret service money were usually expended in direct bribery,
and places and pensions were multiplied to such an extent that
it is on record that, out of 550 members, there were in the first
Parliament of George I. no less than 271, and in the first
Parliament of George II. no less than 257, holding offices,
pensions, or sinecures."   "Almost every man of weight in
the House of Commons," says Mr. Macaulay in his essay on
Walpole, "was officially connected with the government."
Macaulay says that in 1742 the Solicitor and Secretary of the
Treasury received £1,147,211 of secret service money, and

---

[1] I have before explained the reasons why the identical abuse seems never
to have prevailed in England, and it is, perhaps, the only one in our service
without a complete and generally a more extreme English precedent.

[2] Vol. i., pp. 395, 471, and 472.

avoided giving any account of it, Walpole's agent evading the answering of questions as to the use of the money, on the ground that his answers would tend to criminate himself.

Walpole and his party were true to the spirit of the spoils system to the last. In the course of his ministry he had bestowed upon his sons permanent offices, chiefly sinecures, amounting in all to about £15,000 a year, and had obtained the title of Baron for his eldest son, and the Orders of the Bath and of the Garter for himself. He also procured for himself the title of the Earl of Orford and a pension of £4000 a year, and for his illegitimate daughter the rank and precedence of an earl's daughter. In view of such vast agencies of power and influence, concentrated in the hands of an able leader of a ruling party, having an overwhelming majority in Parliament and in all official circles, it would seem almost impossible that a minister like Walpole could ever be overthrown. But such was not a true view of the situation; and, while his unrivalled sagacity was wholly unimpaired and the devotion of his party was without abatement, he was hurled from office in 1742 by the irresistible power of public opinion. He did not make a fortune in public life. But he had no faith that there could be any disinterestedness in public affairs, and he distrusted all appeal to patriotism or duty. His only reliance was self-interest and adroit management. His shrewdness and good judgment in estimating the strength of all the more selfish forces of politics were proverbial and were probably never surpassed by any party leader. But, like most of the partisans of later days who have acted on his system, he was by nature incapable of measuring the force, or even of appreciating the spirit, of that more unselfish, patriotic public opinion outside official and partisan circles, born and cherished in the common life of every enlightened people; and which, when mere party managers least expect it, may come mightily forth, sweeping all their plans and favorites before its irresistible advance. Walpole and his confederates did not comprehend that, during the period in which their corrupt use of official authority had been degrading the moral tone of official life, and of all men and women [1] within the in-

---

[1] In this early stage of the spoils system, bright intriguing women acted

7

fluence of politics, there had been developing in the virtuous houses of England a high-toned and patriotic demand for purer methods in politics, which the elder Pitt was soon to lead to victory and glory. Nor did Walpole any more comprehend that, in this same period, a stern and fervent spirit of religious revival was growing strong and active, by reason of the apathy and formalism of the State Church, which, under the lead of Wesley and Whitefield, was soon to shake the whole ecclesiastical system at the same time it would elevate the moral tone of the nation. Walpole, therefore, with the fatuity of a blind man rather than with the sagacity of a statesman, tried to suppress William Pitt (the future Lord Chatham) by depriving him of his commission in the army. He met those who protested against abuses, and who complained of his contempt for moral duty, " in a strain of coarse and cynical banter.   .   .   .   and sneeringly called them patriots,' saints, Spartans, and boys." But the sentiment he had scorned, and the power he could not comprehend, were what laid him low.

" Above all," says Mr. Lecky, " there was the public opinion of England, which was doubly scandalized by the extent to which parliamentary corruption had arisen, and by the cynicism with which it was avowed, and on this point, though on this alone, Walpole never respected it. Like many men of low morals and of coarse and prosaic natures, he was altogether incapable of appreciating, as an element of political calculation, the force which moral sentiment exercises upon mankind ; and this incapacity was one of the great causes of his fall."

Had the saturnalia of corruption, of which he was the chief, occurred a century or two earlier, there might have been an

a vicious part. The Duchess of Kendall, the Countess of Platen, the Duchess of Yarmouth, and Mrs. Howard made and unmade officials, and were generally quite as successful in partisan politics as Mrs. Jencks, or any female office-broker of our day. Even the mother of Lord Chatham tried the virtue of a bribe of a thousand guineas to procure a position for her brother.

" A patriot, sir. Why, patriots spring up like mushrooms. I could raise fifty of them within four-and-twenty hours. I have raised many of them in one night."—Walpole's Speech in reply to Sandys.

opportunity for another Wat Tyler or Jack Cade; for "the cry of the people for his blood was fierce and general, and politicians of most parties had pledged themselves to impeach him."[1] But the English people were now seeking reform by peaceable methods.

Yet at this crisis again we find that the public understanding of the real causes of corrupt administration was no deeper than this: they were believed to have been brought about by a corrupt minister, or they were the result of combinations of bad men in official places. It was not yet generally perceived that there could be no permanent relief until the partisan spoils system itself was uprooted, and a different system put in its place. Indeed, the time had not arrived when public investigations had disclosed to the people the secrets of administration. Hence the same historian tells us that "to the mass of the nation the fall of Walpole was the signal for the wildest rejoicing. It was believed that the reign of corruption had at last ended; . . . that all pensioners would be excluded from Parliament; that the number of placemen would be strictly limited,"[2] just as in our day the people have so generally believed that corruption is to end with the fall of each official villain, which that system has produced as regularly as any seed produces its kind. The partisan spoils system itself was hardly challenged, and it survived Walpole unchanged in its modes of action, and only modified in practice.

It would not shed much additional light on the subject to enter into any detail concerning the ministry of Pelham or of the Duke of Newcastle, which carry us down to 1760, when George III. came to the throne. But in the mean time William Pitt, representing the purer and more non-partisan sentiment, had become, just at the end of the reign of George II., one of his ministers. His influence, in a general way, raised the moral tone of the administration, but he was compelled to leave the disposition of patronage almost wholly to the Duke of Newcastle. And under Newcastle, as under Pelham for the most part, Parliament was managed, officers and places were disposed of, sinecure salaries were paid, honors and titles were granted, on the basis of favoritism, bar-

---

[1] Lecky, vol. 1., p. 431.                    [2] Ibid., p. 428.

gains, and influence, to strengthen the ruling party and fill the pockets and gratify the ambition of its favorites.

How the system had been gradually extended, so as to establish a general tyranny and arrest the advance of every person who did not accept the creed of the dominant party and conform to the discipline of its leaders, is well illustrated in the case of the great commentator, Sir William Blackstone. He was recommended by Mr. Murray (afterwards Lord Mansfield) to the Duke of Newcastle for the Professorship of Civil Law at Oxford. The Duke said to him :

"'Sir, I can rely upon your friend Mr. Murray as to your giving law lectures in a style beneficial to the students ; and I dare say I may safely rely on you, whenever anything in the political hemisphere is agitated in the university, that you will exert yourself in our behalf.' 'Your grace may be assured that I will discharge my duty in giving the law lectures to the best of my poor ability,' was the response. 'Ay,' replied his grace, 'and your duty in the other branch, too ?' Blackstone coolly bowed : and a few days after Dr. Jenner was appointed professor."[1]

At the conclusion of the reign of George II. party government had been on trial for more than sixty years ; and, at least after the death of William in 1702, it had not been greatly influenced by the Crown. Ministers especially under the two Georges had with little interruption controlled all officers and patronage, and had exercised every kind of authority at will. If, during nearly the whole period, the dominant party had been dragged down by the spoils system, the union with corruption was voluntary, and the party in power was at all times free to select its officers with supreme reference to personal merit.

It undoubtedly cannot be justly said that all abuses that existed are to be attributed to the spoils system itself ; since some of them may have been the inevitable consequences of the moral tone of the age. The decisive question on that point is whether party government, in union with the system adopted, kept the public service on the moral plane of public opinion, or whether the service fell below that plane. And

[1] Memoir of Sir William Blackstone.

it is clear that the latter was the case, and that corruption flowed over from every office and place in politics into the great plane of private life. The causes of Walpole's fall, the exultation of non-partisan people upon it, the spirit that Pitt brought into office, the fact that when he came into public life poor he refused the old perquisites of the paymaster's office, also prove this fact. " For the corruption about him he had nothing but disdain ; . . . his real strength was not in Parliament, but in the people at large. His significant title of the Great Commoner marks a political revolution." " During his struggle with Newcastle, the greater towns backed him with gifts of their freedom and addresses of confidence." [1]

" History owes to him this attestation, that at a time when everything short of direct embezzlement of the public money was considered as quite fair in public men, he showed the most scrupulous disinterestedness ; that at a time when it seemed generally taken for granted that government could be upheld only by the basest and most immoral acts, he appealed to the better and nobler parts of human nature." [2]

And he not only did this, in the same noble spirit that he justified the heroic patriotism of our fathers, but, overawing not only dukes and bishops, but all the confederated hosts of partisans and corruptionists, he advanced higher than any man but Cromwell had done the character and martial glory of his country, at the same time that, in the name of honor, duty, and justice, he acquired a respect, affection, and power, wherever the English language was spoken, such as no other English statesman has ever commanded. And now— when only infamy covers the memory of Walpole, Pelham, Newcastle, Bolingbroke, and the whole corrupt and partisan generation, who sneered at public virtue and religion, and scoffed at the possibility of honest ways in government—the name of Chatham is a part of the glory of his country, and every American recalls it with pride and gratitude.

Mr. Lecky [3] quotes contemporary authority, which speaks

---

[1] Green's History, p. 718.   [2] Macaulay's Essay on Lord Chatham, p. 11.
[3] History, vol. i., p. 509.

of "the administration of justice as generally pure" (from which the partisan spoils system, as we have seen, had been for some years excluded), but beyond that he points out "the ever widening circle of corruption which *had now spread from the Parliament to the constituencies,* and tainted all the approaches of political life."

After referring to the fact that, at an earlier period in the century, worthy scholars had been aided by government, he says [1] that "in the reign of the first two Georges all this changed. The government, if it helped any authors, helped only those who would employ their talents in the lowest forms of party libel."

In respect to religion the tendency of the partisan system was equally downward, until it was arrested by the accession of Pitt to the Cabinet in 1757. "There has seldom been a time in which the religious tone was lower than in the age of the first two Georges. [2] On the death of the Queen (Anne), church patronage, like all other patronage, degenerated into a mere matter of party or personal interest. It was distributed, for the most part, among members or adherents of the great families, subject to the condition that the candidates were moderate in their views and were *not inclined to any description of reform.*"

In 1745, "good judges spoke with great despondency of the decline of public spirit, as if the energy of the people had been fatally impaired." [3]

It is, then, abundantly clear that party government, when upholding the partisan system of appointment, had failed as signally as any despotic or aristocratic administration ever tolerated in England had failed, to raise or even prevent the degradation of the moral tone of politics. But the important question remains, What was the effect upon the actual execution of the laws? The answer is very clear. The minor officials and the standard of duty were such as the system would naturally produce. They were degraded. Owing to the

---

[1] History, vol. i., p. 505.

[2] It is said that not more than five members of the House of Commons were at this period regular attendants upon any place of worship.

[3] Lecky's History, vol. i., pp. 505, 506.

party in power courting the support of the liquor interest, and to the subserviency of venal officials to that interest, intoxication and drunken brawls fearfully increased in the time from Anne to George III. "In 1749 more than 4000 persons were convicted of selling spirituous liquors without a license, and the number of private ginshops within the bills of mortality was estimated at more than 17,000. At the same time, crime and immorality of every description *were rapidly increasing.* The City of London urgently petitioned for new measures of restriction. . . . In 1750 and 1751 more than 11,000,000 of gallons of spirits were annually consumed, and the increase of population, especially in London, appears to have been perceptibly checked. . . . There is not only no safety of living in the town but scarcely any in the country now, robbery and murder are grown so frequent. . . . The watchmen and constables, utterly inefficient, are as a rule to be found more frequently in the beer shops than in the streets, and were often themselves a serious danger to the community. . . . One is forced to travel, wrote Horace Walpole, even at noon, as if one were going to battle. . . . The weakness of the law was also shown in the great number of serious riots which took place in every part of the Kingdom. . . . Outrages connected with smuggling were in many parts of the Kingdom singularly daring and ferocious, and they were often countenanced by a large amount of popular sympathy."

This was the generation of the famous burglar, John Shepherd, of the famous thief, Jonathan Wild, and of the famous highwayman, Dick Turpin — all of whom were hung in the period between 1724 and 1739. Fielding says of the justices at this time that they were "never indifferent in a cause, but when they could get nothing on either side." Smollett, speaking of 1740, declares that thieves and robbers were now become "more desperate and savage than they had ever appeared since mankind was civilized." An address to the King from the Mayor and Aldermen of London, in 1744, complains that "persons armed with bludgeons and pistols . . . now infest the streets and places . . . at such times as were heretofore deemed hours of safety."[1]

[1] Lecky's History, vol. i., pp. 518–590.

The prisons were loosely and inhumanly managed.    The
wardenship of the Fleet Prison, bought for £5000 in the time
of Lord Clarendon, was publicly sold for the same sum in 1728.
In 1730 the judge and several members of the Bar lost their
lives from jail fever caught while trying prisoners in London ;
and in 1750 the disease raged to such an extent in Newgate
Prison that the Lord Mayor of London, an alderman and many
of inferior rank were its victims while an assize was being
held.    In 1759, Dr. Johnson computed the number of imprisoned debtors at not less than 20,000, and asserted that one in
four died every year from the treatment they underwent.
Often the criminals staggered to the gallows, and some of the
most noted were exhibited for money by the turnkeys before
their execution.    Dr. Dodd, a clergyman convicted of forgery,
was exhibited for two hours for a shilling a head.  All the
high officials, even Addison, took shares in public lotteries,
which were not suppressed in England until 1823.

Demoralization extended even to the stage (as it did in New
York City in the time of Barnard and Tweed), and " the English
stage," says Mr. Lecky, " was far inferior to that of France
in decorum, modesty, and morality."    Miss Pelham, daughter
of the Prime Minister under George I., was one of the most
notorious gamblers of her time, and in the palmy days of the
partisan spoils system under Walpole gambling in England
reached its climax.    An illustration of the higher moral sentiment, outside the sources of corruption, may be found in the
fact that, at this period, there were many active societies " for
the reformation of manners" (or rather morals) ; and their
members became a sort of voluntary police.    In 1735 their
aggregate prosecutions in London and Westminster alone had
reached the enormous number of 99,380.

No one at all acquainted with the influence of the liquor interest over official appointments under our spoils system—no
one who knows the extent to which gambling and lottery
ticket selling are encouraged and protected by the associations
and the corrupting influences which grow out of a venal and
partisan bestowal of office—no one, especially, who has witnessed prison life degradation in some parts of New York, or
in any prison given over to corrupt partisan control, whether

in village or country—in this generation— will fail to see the
significance of the facts I have cited, as illustrations of the character and effects of early partisan administration in England.
I have thought it all the more desirable to bring out pretty
fully the character and methods of such administration in its
early stages, especially because they bring us close upon the
time of our Revolution ; and altogether they show the system
inherited by George III., who used all its vicious resources
(against the influence of Chatham, Rockingham, and Burke,
and all the true friends of administrative reform) to reduce our
fathers to political slavery.  In view of such abuses, it seems all
the more strange that so few safeguards were provided against
them in our constitution and early Federal laws ; an omission
only to be accounted for, I venture to think, by the fact that
in this country they were hardly known at our Revolution, and
that, even in England, they had in but small measure become
a part of general information.

# CHAPTER IX.

Its condition and public opinion in 1760.—His theory of governing.—Tries to break up party government and to govern through "The King's friends."—Meddlesome and arbitrary.—Lord Bute.—Favoritism and venality.—Bribery.—The King urges on war against America.—Corrupt lotteries to pay its expenses.—King interferes with Parliament.—Guilty of bribery.—Religious tests.—Great obstacles in way of reform.—Spoils system in the State, Church and the Army.—Borough abuses in England, in Scotland, in Ireland.—Municipal corruption and intolerance.—Power of impressment used politically.—Dominant party opens letters and employs spies.—Debates state secrets.—Liberty of the press not allowed.—General warrants issued by ministers.—Spoils system extended to America.—First reform administration.

Such was the condition of administration and the temper of the public mind in 1760 when George III. came to the throne.

Corruption, extravagance, inefficiency everywhere in the domain of politics, except where the influence of William Pitt and his followers was felt. A high-toned, rapidly growing public opinion abroad among the people—the strength of Pitt and Burke in politics, and of Wesley and Whitefield in religion indignant at the pervading abuses, crying aloud for reform, but ill instructed as to their deeper causes, and without experience in the ways of their removal. Party government, having been on trial for sixty-seven years, was in full vigor. As an agency for expressing the opinions and interests of a nation, for embodying them in national policy, and for carrying that policy into effect, there was no great protest against it ; and it may be added there has not been any such protest to the present time. The party method of governing, which originated under William III., stands, in its essential features, unchanged and unchallenged by the British nation to this hour.

The sentiment which was to separate that method, first, from the partisan spoils system of appointment, and, next, from the partisan system itself, was, when George III. came to the throne, only a great unorganized mass of public opinion, not knowing either its own power or how to attack the corruption which it was its high mission to overthrow. That traditionary loyalty which was universal, and that servile spirit of obedience which was general, forgetting the past, hopefully and blindly trusted the future to the pleasure of a fresh young king—even at the moment that he adopted the spoils system, as being altogether as much a part of his heritage as the crown itself ; just as at our elections we have trusted that reform was certain as successive presidents have made a fresh application of the same old spoils system.

Great changes took place in public administration during the sixty years George III. was on the throne. For about twenty years after his accession he had, for the most part, his own way. At the close of that period the reform spirit had become too bold and strong for the King. An ascending plane of administration was then entered upon, which has ever since been held. During the first period, he pushed the spoils system generally to extremes of tyranny and corruption almost as great as it had ever reached ; and, in some particulars, he was the worst administrative tyrant (except James II.) ever on the English throne. Narrow, proud, obstinate, and relentless, yet highly patriotic and sincere, he was a sort of Andrew Jackson, crowned. He was unfaithful to party government itself : not that, like William and Anne, he tried to amalgamate parties or to rule by compromise councils ; for his aim was to build up a party of his own, called " The King's Friends," based on patronage and prerogative, and to subordinate everything in the government to his own arbitrary will. And, for a time, he had apparently great success. But, in fact, this specious success contributed to that bold sentiment among the people, demanding liberty and reform, which, within twenty years, gave the death-blow to the worst parts of the spoils system itself, arrested the arbitrary power of the Crown, reinstated party government in its true position, and so humiliated the King that he ordered his royal yacht to be made ready for his retirement to Hanover.

There never has been in times of peace a more desperate struggle between official coercion and mercenary influence on the one side, and a few noble men, standing for public honor and duty, and leading the higher sentiments of a nation, on the other, than the earlier period of this reign presented. It is especially interesting as showing how a king may apply a spoils system to break down the very parties which had matured it for their own selfish purposes.

" The King desired to undertake, personally, the chief administration of public affairs, to direct the policy of his ministers, and himself to distribute the patronage of the Crown. He was ambitious not only to reign but to govern. . . . It was the King's object, not merely to supplant one party and establish another in its place, but to create a new party, faithful to himself, regarding his personal wishes, carrying out his policy, and dependent on his will. This party was soon distinguished as ' The King's Men ' or ' The King's Friends.' " [1]

" Day by day George himself scrutinized the voting list of the two houses, and distributed rewards and punishments as members voted according to his will or not. Promotion in the civil service, preferment in the church, or rank in the army was reserved for the ' King's friends.' Pensions and court places were used to influence debates. Bribery was employed on a scale never known before. Under Bute's ministry, an office was opened at the Treasury for the bribery of members, and twenty-five thousand pounds are said to have been spent in a single day.

. . . " Not only did he direct the minister in all important matters of foreign and domestic policy, but he instructed him as to the management of debates in Parliament, suggested what motions should be made or opposed and how measures should be carried. He reserved for himself all the patronage, he arranged the whole cast of the administration, settled the relative plan and pretensions of Ministers of State, law officers, and members of the household, nominated and promoted the English and Scotch judges, appointed and translated bishops and deans, and dispensed other preferments in the Church. He disposed of military governments, regiments, and commissions,

[1] May's Constitutional History of England, vol. i., pp. 23, 24, and 60.

and himself ordered the marching of troops. He gave and refused titles, honors, and pensions. All this immense patronage was steadily used for the creation and maintenance of a party in both Houses of Parliament attached to the King himself, and its weight was seen in the dependence to which the new ministry was reduced."[1]

Macaulay, in his essay upon Lord Chatham, after stating that all ranks from the highest to the lowest were to be taught that the King would be obeyed, and that lords-lieutenants of several counties were dismissed, adds (in language as applicable in spirit to this generation and in this country as to the royal despot whom our fathers fought) :

" But as nothing was too high for the revenge of the court, so also was nothing too low. A prosecution, such as had never been known before and has never been known since, raged in every public department. Great numbers of humble and laborious clerks were deprived of their bread, not because they had taken an active part against the ministry, but merely because they owed their situations to the recommendation of some nobleman or gentleman who was against the peace. The proscription extended to tide-waiters, to gaugers, to door-keepers. One poor man, to whom a pension had been given for his gallantry in a fight with smugglers, was deprived of it because he had been befriended by the Duke of Grafton. An aged widow, who, on account of her husband's services in the navy, had many years before been made housekeeper in a public office, was dismissed from her situation because it was imagined that he was distantly connected by marriage with the Cavendish family. The public clamor, as may well be supposed, grew daily louder and louder."

The corrupt intrigues and the fierce contentions about collectorships and postmasterships, and all places in the customs and the excise service, were not carried on by bodies corresponding to our primary organizations, for the mass of the people were not allowed to vote ; nor did members of the two houses of Parliament bestow so much of their time and thought, as have our Senators and Representatives, in planning and scheming in connection with such offices ; for members of Parliament had not then secured that complete control over pat-

[1] Green's History of the English People, pp. 732 and 737.

ronage which they were able to usurp during the next generation ; but these struggles were carried on between borough-
mongers and the agents of great officers and nobles, or between
ministers, bishops, royal favorites, and the nobility in person.  There is nothing new, however, in our constant and
unseemly contentions about petty offices and small local patronage except the station in life and the official designation of
those who most engage in them.

Everywhere the freedom of elections was invaded and the
whole power of the Crown and of the ministry was used to in-
timidate, bribe, or cajole the voters.

" In a letter to Lord North, in 1772, the King says : 'I expect
every nerve to be strained to carry the bill.  .  .  .  I have a right
to expect a hearty support from every man in my service, *and I shall
remember defaulters.*'  And in a letter a few days after he says :
'I wish a list could be prepared of those that went away and of those
that deserted to the minority (on the division in the committee).
*That would be a rule for my conduct in the drawing-room to-morrow.*'"

Here we see that it was not merely royal and official power,
but social opportunity and ostracism as well, that were to be
coercively used.  It is not easy to say whether James II. or
President Jackson would have most admired this theory of
George III., but both of them would have felt at home with
him.  It is certain that President Jackson has by no means
such claims to originality as are generally conceded to him.

Such a policy naturally called for an unscrupulous man like
Lord Bute [1] to lead in its execution.  He was a facile agent in
using money, offices, sinecures, increased salaries and pensions,
titles and every form of intimidation, flattery and bribery in
support of the government.  The following letter illustrates
the relation between ministers and their supporters in Parliament in those times :

---

[1] He rested under a charge of betraying his country for money in a treaty,
and of illicit intercourse with the widow of the Prince of Wales.  His ideas
of literature and of office were quite in keeping, for he expended $50,000 of
his dishonest fortune in a great work on botany, but had the plates destroyed when twelve copies were struck off, in order that the work might
be exclusive.

Nov. 26, 1763.

*Honored Sir :* I am very much obliged to you for that freedom of converse you this morning indulged me in, which I prize more than the lucrative advantage I then received. To show the sincerity of my words pardon, sir, the perhaps over-niceness of my disposition , I return, enclosed, the bill for £300 you favored me with, as good manners would not permit my refusal of it when tendered by you.

Your most obliged and obedient servant,

SAYE & SELE.

But all these venal influences, so long effective in British administration, and all the power of the Crown united with them, were now unable to keep Lord Bute in power for more than ten months. He had not preserved the proper secrecy, and the honest public opinion of a nation—of which the letters of Junius and the unprecedented boldness of the public press were an utterance—began at this time to be more than ever before a power in the State. Mr. May[1] says, " The government was soon at issue with the press. Lord Bute was the first to illustrate its power. Overwhelmed by a storm of obloquy and ridicule, he bowed down before it and fled. . . . Vainly did his own hired writers endeavor to shelter him. Vainly did the King uphold his favorite." This was the first great triumph of the higher sentiment at this period. And it powerfully contributed to the civil service reform policy which, as we shall see, was a few years later inaugurated.

But the King and his favorites adhered to the spoils system as long as possible. Vast sums of money were raised for the public use by lotteries as well as by loans. Officials made large sums dishonestly, in 1763, out of these loans. In 1767, there were huge stock-jobbing transactions, in which as many as sixty members of Parliament, including the Chancellor of the Exchequer himself, were involved. In 1769, it appeared that 20,000 lottery tickets, on the raising of a public loan, had been disposed of to members of Parliament, which sold at a premium of £2 each. A motion in that virtuous body, in the same year, to prohibit members receiving more than twenty tickets each (and backed by charges that as many as fifty mem-

[1] Constitutional History, vol. ii., p. 110.

bers had subscribed for as many as five hundred tickets each) was voted down. But what may perhaps enable us to more fully appreciate the influence and resources of the spoils system at that time is the fact that, in 1781, Lord North, in order to raise £12,000,000 with which to carry on the war against this country, resorted to a sale of lottery tickets, and so disposed of a great part to members[1] of Parliament as to make them corruptly interested in the success of the loan. Lord Rockingham declared the loan was made " for the purpose of corrupting Parliament to support a wicked, impolitic, and ruinous war." The King persisted in the more corrupt parts of the spoils system, even after an indignant public opinion had begun to overawe his minions. As late as March, 1781, he used this language in a letter to Lord North : " Mr. Robinson sent me the list of the speakers last evening, and of the very good majority. I have this morning sent him £6000 to be placed to the same purpose as the sum transmitted on the 21st of August." The King was as lavish of titles of nobility as he was of money ; and Mr. May says there were three hundred and eighty-eight conferred during his reign.

But the facts now presented by no means convey an adequate conception of the strength, the oppression, or the manifold resources of the British spoils system of a century ago, and therefore fall far short of presenting the hostile influences which later reforms have had to overcome. Some further illustrations will be useful. They will show how much more difficult reform was in England than it would be with us.

1. The King, having all executive power, and the House of Lords, with half the legislative power, united with a vast preponderating social and moneyed influence, have their foundation in a political theory and custom utterly hostile to the just claims of personal merit and common right before the law. Indeed they represent in large measure only birthright, favoritisms, property, and privilege -- or, in a word, feudalism. Every nobleman (and I might add every bishop) had a strong personal interest — to say nothing of the safety of his class—in maintaining the old system under which, for

---

[1] Seven members subscribed £70,000 each, others £50,000, and one £100,000.

centuries, the sons, the decayed stewards, and the favorites of his ancestors had monopolized the offices and places, both in Church and State. Whoever advocated a reform that based selections for the public service on personal worth was compelled to challenge the privileges of the nobility.

2. The administrative system, in an old country, carries with it the immense influence of usage, which is indeed a vital part of the English constitution itself. It was a part of that ancient usage—in fact, it was and is now a part of the system of government itself—to bestow titles, orders, and decorations—always conferring social rank and often political power—as a mere matter of favor ; and with the common understanding that they imposed an obligation of grateful allegiance and friendly service ; a practice, in spirit and influence, utterly hostile to the paramount claims of personal merit and common right, to which all true civil service reform must respond.

3. The partisan system, in the time of George III., was as paramount in the State Church as in politics. According to its methods, bishops, deans, and vicars secured their places.

" The piety of a churchman brought him no preferment, unless his political orthodoxy was well attested. All who aspired to be prebendaries, deans, and bishops sought Tory patrons and professed the Tory creed." [1]

Advowsons,[2] presentations to livings, and clerkships in the Church were as unscrupulously conferred by favor as were the meanest civil offices, and they were as openly advertised and sold as calves and cabbages. The Sacrament of that Church was a legal test at the gates of nearly every office, national, municipal, and corporate.

" The incapacity of dissenters extended not only to government employments but to the direction of the Bank of England, the East India Company, and other chartered companies. The City of London had perverted the corporation act into an instrument of extortion by electing dissenters to the office of sheriff, and exacting fines when

[1] 2 May's History, 48.
[2] And they are openly sold at this day, as I shall more fully point out.

8

they refused to qualify." That is by taking the Sacrament after the manner of the Church of England.) No less than £15,000 had thus been levied.

The creed of that Church was practically a condition of entrance to the great universities and professions. Its bishops had seats in the House of Lords ; and throughout the nation its monopoly of official station, its vast wealth and social prestige, its friends everywhere controlling the local magistracy, and in manifold ways influencing the private life of the people, made it a vast power opposed to reform in the civil service. Its sympathies were therefore strongly with the King and the nobility ; and the King and his ministers had no more scruples about using Church patronage [2] than about using political patronage.

4. That system also extended to the army and navy. I shall have occasion to point out that the English regular army remained under a sort of spoils system — commissions being openly bought and sold as well as secured by influence and favor  long after we had made provision, at the national cost, for high personal qualifications for office in our regular army. By orders of the King, worthy military officers like General Conway and Colonel Barré (who sympathized with this country) were, on account of votes in Parliament, deprived of their commands. Political proscription extended to all grades of office in the army.

Having fortunately (yet with far less consistency than the original English system) taken our army offices out of partisan politics, but leaving our civil officials embroiled in them, we look with surprise at the old English practice ; while, on the other hand, modern Englishmen, who, (until within this decade saw offices in their army bought and sold,) finding their civil offices now conferred upon merit, look upon our favoritism and partisanship in civil administration with astonishment and disgust. Mr. May quotes Mr. Grenville, while

[1] 2 May, pp. 315–324.
[2] The king, after keeping the Bishopric of Osnaburgh open for near three years, contrary to the custom which allows but six months, bestowed it upon his son, a new-born child, before it was christened. The revenue was about £25,000 a year.—Walpole's Memoirs of George III., vol. i., p. 320.

minister to George III., to the effect that " he never would admit the distinction between civil and military appointments." The King maintained that position until Mr. Pitt became minister, when he was forced, by public opinion, to forbear enforcing political proscription against army officers : and the practice has never since prevailed.[1]

5. The elections and the methods of appointment in the boroughs, (from which members of Parliament were sent,) were even more corrupt and exclusive than any other part of the administration. The outrageous monopoly of the franchise, in a few hands, defeating the fair expression of the better public sentiment at the elections, made the franchise venal beyond all example in history. Parliament was practically controlled by a few great families. Out of a population of about 8,000,000 there were scarcely 160,000 legal voters. I can give space for only slight illustration of borough politics. In the boroughs of Buckingham and Bewdley the right of election was confined to thirteen persons ; at Bath to thirty-five ; at Salisbury to fifty-six ; at Gatton to seven ; at Tavistock to ten ; at St. Michael to seven. It would seem that ninety members of Parliament were returned by forty-six places, with less than fifty electors each ; thirty-seven members by nineteen places, having less than one hundred electors each ; while Leeds, Birmingham, and Manchester had no representation whatsoever. Eleven members owed their places to the Duke of Norfolk, nine to Lord Lonsdale, eleven to Lord Darlington ; several lords had six members each ; and members were actually holding their seats in the Commons under claim of *hereditary* right.

" Boroughs had been publicly advertised for sale in the newspapers ; and there was a set of attorneys who rode the country and negotiated seats in the most indecent manner."[2]

The borough of Sudbury " publicly advertised itself for

---

[1] Our laws of 1862 and 1866 (12 stat. p. 596 and 14 stat. p. 92) afford a curious commentary upon official tenure in the army and navy. The first gave free scope for the practice of the very abuses of which Geo. III. was guilty, and the second brought us back to the rule which that king was compelled to submit to.

[2] Walpole's Memoirs, George III., vol. i., p. 157.

-ale." In the borough of New Shoreham, the majority of electors, calling itself the "Christian Club," under the guise of charity, were in the habit of selling the borough to the highest bidder and dividing the spoils among its members. The prices generally paid are not given, but Mr. May says there are instances of a person spending £70,000 in contesting a borough. The practice of buying and selling boroughs gave a new word to the language and a new calling in life—"borough-mongers" "borough-mongering." Boroughs were not only sold, but they were rented for annual sums when the member was unable to buy. Some of the noblest men of the times, like Sir Samuel Romilly, were compelled to buy a borough as the only means of getting into Parliament with any independence.

In 1762, an act was passed imposing, for the first time, pecuniary penalties on the offense of bribery. But it was far from being adequate for its purpose. The mayor and ten of the aldermen of Oxford were imprisoned in 1768 for receiving bribes for the borough vote. But Mr. May says that " while in Newgate they completed a bargain which they had already commenced, and sold the representation of this city to the Duke of Marlborough, . . . and the town clerk carried off the books of the corporation which contained the evidence of the bargain : and the business was laughed at and forgotten."

The state of things in the boroughs and local districts of Scotland, was no better. There property, revenues, franchises, and patronage were vested in small self-elected bodies. The public property and revenues were corruptly alienated and despoiled sold to nobles and other favored persons at inadequate prices. Incompetent men and even boys were appointed to offices of trust. At Forfar an idiot for twenty years filled the place of town clerk. " Lucrative offices were sold by the councils. Judicature was exercised without fitness or responsibility." [1]

In Ireland, if possible, it was worse. While the corrupt proscription of the dominant party and the Sacrament of the State Church were in the name of the majority supreme in

---

[1] 2 May's History, 470, 471.

the politics of England, in Ireland a despotism not less corrupt
and far more galling was enforced in the interest of a small
minority of the population. A sectarian creed excluded from
the franchise five sixths of the Irish people. In her Parliament
not a single representative of this vast Catholic majority was
allowed a seat. Peerages were given almost exclusively to
large borough-owners, and it would seem that fifty-three peers
controlled the election of one hundred and twenty-three members of the Commons.[1]

"Two thirds of the House of Commons, on whom the government
generally relied, were attached to its interests, by offices, pensions, or
promises of preferments. . . . Places and pensions, the price of
Parliamentary services, were publicly bought and sold in the market.
Every judge, every magistrate, every officer—civil, military, and corporate—was a Churchman. No Catholic could practice law or serve
on a jury. . . . Protestant Nonconformists, scarcely inferior in
numbers to Churchmen, fared no better than Catholics, . . . being excluded from every civil office, from the army and from corporations."[2]

The King was himself a participant in borough corruption.
In one of his letters to Lord North, in 1779, he says : "If the
Duke of Northumberland requires some gold bills for the
election, it would be wrong not to satisfy him." Besides this
kind of corruption at the polls, there were other forms of election abuses with which we are familiar. The use of the minor
government officers, clerks, and placemen as a band of political regulars, bound to support their superiors, right or wrong,
was in full operation. Speaking of such officers and servants, Mr. May[3] uses language which this generation of Americans can understand : "It was quite understood to be part of
their duty to vote for any candidate who hoisted the colors of
the minister of the day. Wherever they were most needed by
the government their number was the greatest. The smaller
boroughs were secured by purchase or overwhelming local interests ; but the cities and ports had some pretension to independence. Here, however, *troops of petty officers of customs*

[1] 2 Lecky, 247.                    [2] 2 May's History, pp. 479–482.
[3] 1 History, 277, 278.

.... ... driven to the polls, and, supported by venal freemen, overpowered the independent electors."

It hardly need be added that the dominant party of that day was as exacting in local appointments as it has ever been in our own times. Referring to city appointments, Mr. May says: "None but jealous adherents of the government could hope for the least share of the patronage of the Crown."[1] And with still another phase of municipal abuses then prevalent we are equally familiar, except that we are a little shy about the political use of religion, or what passes for it.

"Generally of one political party, the borough electors excluded men of different opinions, whether in politics or religion. . . . Neglecting their proper functions—the superintendence of the police, the management of the jails, the paving and lighting of the streets, and the supply of water—they thought only of the personal interests attached to office. They grasped all patronage, lay and ecclesiastical, for their relatives, friends and political partisans, and wasted the corporation funds in greasy feasts and vulgar ribaldry. Many were absolutely insolvent. Charities were despoiled. . . . Jobbery and corruption in every form were practised. . . . Even the administration of justice was tainted by suspicion of political partiality. Borough magistrates were at once incompetent and exclusively of one party. . . . But the worst abuse of these corrupt bodies was that which too long *secured them impunity. They were the strongholds of parliamentary interests and corruption.*"[2]

6. But the spoils system of that age had yet other powers of seduction and terror unknown in our day. The same arbitrary authority which, in order to strengthen the government or the party, might give places or make removals anywhere in the army, the navy, the Church, and the civil administration at its pleasure, might also, in the plenitude of its authority, impress soldiers for the regiments and sailors for the ships—"nay, we even find soldiers employed to assist the press gangs; villages invested by a regular force; sentries standing with fixed bayonets; and churches surrounded during divine service, to seize

---

[1] History, vol. ii., p. 48.        [2] 2 May's History, 464–466.

seamen for the fleets." [1]  And this formidable power was effectively used to influence elections and overawe the spirit of independence and reform.

It was a part of the same system that government could no more get along without paid spies everywhere than it could get along without servile henchmen at every government desk.  " Throughout that period," says Mr. May, " society was everywhere infested with espionage."  In 1764, " we see spies following Wilkes, dogging his steps like shadows, and reporting every movement of himself and his friends to the Secretaries of State."

In the same spirit, the high officials of George III. claimed the right, for the protection of the party in power, to break open and read the letters of their opponents, while in the mails or public offices ; and they did so without shame or hesitation. They thought no administration safe without the exercise of this power.  And perhaps no abuse of public authority did so much to arrest independent utterance and embarrass that organization and co-operation essential to crush so fearful a tyranny.  Mr. Pitt complains that even his correspondence with his family was constantly ransacked in the post office.  Nothing written by a political opponent of the government was safe from the pillage of the post office official and government spies. And while the Parliamentary majority claimed such powers, it refused to allow its own proceedings to be reported.  It prosecuted or imprisoned those who attempted to furnish the people with adequate reports.

7.  The partisan tyrants of these times also sought to make the public press, then threatening to become a dangerous enemy of the spoils system, either its servant or its victim.  The law of libel of that day—under which any servile justice of the peace (holding office by appointment made by a member of the Cabinet) could arrest any person charged on oath with a seditious libel, and according to which juries were not judges of the fact of libel—greatly favored such results.

Besides all this, Secretaries of State—as the law was interpreted—might issue general warrants to search for authors, printers, and publishers and their papers throughout the Kingdom. This power, unscrupulously exercised, was sufficient to overawe any ordinary reformer, and it caused the imprisonment and financial ruin of not a few. Even John Wilkes had his house ransacked, and was brought a prisoner before the ministers on such a warrant. Years later, so fearless a writer as William Cobbett was driven from England to this country by the mere fear of its exercise.

It needs no argument to prove how naturally the spirit of such a system, and the exercise at will of a power so vast and irresponsible, developed in the King and his ministers an exaggerated idea of prerogative and official authority. It completely blinded them to the state of public opinion, at the same time that it gave them the means of carrying forward whatever arbitrary undertaking they might decide to enter upon. "What a king and ministry habitually do, soon comes to be regarded as involving their rights and their honor."

If in the application of such a system all merit and all justice among the people might be disregarded ; if municipal corporations might be converted into partisan entrenchments : if money coming from taxation and from the endowments of charity at home could be used in the interest of the party and the ministry  upon what theory could little colonial settlements along the borders of the ocean and the forests of a remote continent expect any higher consideration for their property or their rights ?  Indeed, the very extravagance and the insatiable demand for offices and places which such a system developed only made those colonies the more certain to become its victims. They could be outraged and pillaged without offending any Parliamentary voter, except such rare men as Burke and Chatham, who felt indignant when in any quarter of the world a British subject was wronged.

In this view the familiar fact that George III. personally insisted on taxing, coercing, and fighting the American colonies, (when he might have known that the higher, if not the larger, public opinion of England condemned that policy,) is no evidence of malice in the King or his ministers, but only shows the consequences to which the spoils system of administration, with its false standard of official "right and honor," had carried them.

" The King continued, personally, to direct the measures of the ministers, more particularly in the disputes with the American colonies, which, in his opinion, involved the rights and honors of his crown. . . . The persecution of Wilkes, the straining of Parliamentary privilege, and *the coercion of America* were the disastrous fruits of the court policy." [1] " The colonies offered a wide field of employment for the friends, connections, and political partisans of the home government. The offices in England available for securing Parliamentary support fell short of the demand, and appointments were accordingly multiplied abroad. . . . *Infants in the cradle* were endowed with colonial appointments to be executed *through life* by convenient deputies." [2]

Mr. May quotes a letter of a British general, written in 1758, which says : " As for civil officers appointed for America, most of the places in the gift of the Crown have been filled with broken-down members of Parliament, of bad if any principles ; *valets de chambre*, electioneering scoundrels, and even livery servants. In one word, America has been for many years made the *hospital of England.*" Measures of oppression against the colonies were so ingeniously contrived as to take away their liberties at the same time that they made more places to be filled under this voracious spoils system : for example, in 1774 [3] the Elective Council of Massachussetts was made appointable by the Crown, and the selection of judges, magistrates, and sheriffs was also added to the royal patronage.

It is a not less interesting fact to us that, if this country was the place of the most unprovoked and unscrupulous application of the spoils system, it also affords about the last illustration of its extreme enforcement. [4] The failure of the King's policy against us dealt the King, his party, and the spoils system a blow from which they never fully recovered.

Lord North's administration fell in 1782, four months after

[1] 1 May's History, pp. 48, 49.     [2] 2 May, 529.
[3] 14 George III., chap. 45.
[4] From Horace Walpole's Memoirs it appears to have required about $6,700,000 in 1788 to satisfy promises made under that system to American traitors, mildly called Royalists.

the fall of Yorktown. It was succeeded by that of Lord Rockingham, the *first ministry distinctly pledged to administrative reform*, or faithful to its duties, which England had ever seen. The leading friends of reform were the leading friends of America : Rockingham, who had declared the war " wicked, impolitic, and ruinous ;" Burke and Chatham, whose noble defence of our cause all the world knows ; Conway, Barré, and others less distinguished.

If the horrors of the French Revolution, late in the reign of George III., arrested for a time the cause of reform, we shall, with that exception, find that it made a steady advance after our independence was recognized. Such, then, was the theory of the appointing power—the system of administration the moral tone of party politics—in England during the generation of Washington, Madison, Hamilton, and all the founders of our system, and even within the lifetime of persons now living. It seems not improbable that but for the corrupt and proscriptive system of administration which prevailed, our Revolutionary War might have been a far less protracted and costly struggle.

Our fathers framed a system repugnant to that of England in some of the principles of equality and justice upon which it rests, yet substantially identical in the arrangements, methods, and official character required for good administration. Birthright, privileges, class distinctions, religion, Church Establishments, property, and every element of feudalism they discarded, as foundations of government or qualifications for official service. By the strongest of all conceivable implications, they declared competency for office to be character and capacity. Yet, in face of such an experience in the mother country, they directly said, or provided for, almost nothing on a subject so vital, beyond declaring that the President should be a native ; that judges should have a fixed tenure and salary (provisions copied from English statutes) ; and that Senators and Representatives in Congress should be of a certain age. The States generally fell short of even such meagre provisions. The nation and the States alike left the great and dangerous power of removal to the merest implication. This is not to be mentioned against them as a reproach ; for their thoughts were absorbed in the vital questions of personal liberty and national independence. The subject of good public administration, as one of the vital and permanent conditions of national peace, morality, and prosperity, was only a mooted question even among the older nations which had centuries of misrule before their eyes. Indeed, it could hardly be said to be before their eyes, for the procedure and the corruption in the great offices, like the debates in Parliament, had been treated as party or official secrets. There was but little in print, and perhaps nothing on this side of the Atlantic, from which they could be learned. It cost the greatest efforts and long litigation to bring to light abuses in the departments and the municipalities, and the veil of secrecy is not yet torn from some parts of the administration of the City of London.[1]

The subject of administration had hardly been considered at all on this side of the ocean. And in sparsely settled colonies, without great cities or great fortunes, or any experience in large public affairs, it is not strange that no provision should be made for the character, capacity, or discipline of that great army of officers, and those vast and complex affairs which were only to exist in a future generation. Need we doubt that adequate safeguards would have been provided in the constitution, had its framers foreseen the abuses of the last forty years?

[1] At this time (Jan. 16, 1879) a proceeding is being taken before the courts, in the City of New York, in order to get at the facts of habitual extortion and other corruption in the municipal offices, which are charged, and generally believed, to be, in character, quite analogous to those prevailing in English cities a century ago.

# CHAPTER X.

On the accession of George III., Parliament had, for the first time, assumed control over the personal expenditures (the "civil list") of the Crown ; but that servile body allowed the law to remain a dead letter. In less than nine years the king had exceeded the allowance by more than £500,000. The climax of the last phase of the spoils system in English politics was reached under Lord Bute ;[1] and with his fall the era of practical reform opened. The public opinion demanding it had become bold and threatening. The theory of making a party of mere office-holders and favorites was at an end, and that of ruling through party leaders was restored.

In 1765, the king was forced to accept, as Prime Minister, the Marquis of Rockingham, the leader of the opposition, whom he had just dismissed from his lieutenancy, and, as a

---

[1] The Union with Ireland, effected in 1799, was, in a pecuniary sense, one of the most corrupt of all the official transactions of that generation. Government bought out the borough interests, openly treating patronage as property. The patrons of boroughs received £7500 for each seat. The total compensation for boroughs amounted to £1,260,000. It appears that the original estimates of expenses were as follows : Boroughs, £756,000 ; county interests, £224,000 ; barristers, £200,000 ; purchases of seats, £75,000 ; Dublin, £200,000. Besides all which, there were peerages conferred, places multiplied, and pensions increased. Lord Cornwallis, the Lord Lieutenant, most bitterly complained of the "dirty business," and "longed to kick those whom his public duty obliged him to court."

Secretary of State, General Conway, whom he had just deprived of his regiment. It was a condition, made by this administration, that military officers should not be disturbed for political reasons. It also compelled the king to disclaim the old practice[1] of influencing members of Parliament by bribes, patronage or prerogative. These were two great victories, poorly as the king kept his promise. The king[2] was intensely hostile to the independent reforming spirit of his new cabinet; and, aided by divisions among the Whigs, was before long able to overthrow it. For ten more years, there was little apparent progress, but a public opinion was growing, more enlightened, more exacting and more audacious than had ever been known. For the first time, the character and the practical methods of the administration became a great issue before the people. The public was angry over abuses.

The first of the letters of Junius appeared in January, 1769, and that to the king, the boldest and most defiant ever written by a subject, before the end of the year. So audacious did the popular protest against the royal spoils system become, that Mr. Nast, in our day, has not dealt more boldly with high officials. One caricature sold upon the streets represented a high official wheeling the king on a barrow with his crown, with the legend " what a man buys he may sell ;" and, in another, the king was exhibited on his knees, with his mouth open, into which Warren Hastings was pitching diamonds. In the law courts, Wilkes recovered £4000 against the Secretary of State, who had caused his house to be ransacked under a general search warrant. It would require far too much space to trace, historically, the many reform measures by which abuses existing in the early part of this reign have been removed or reduced. A brief outline must therefore suffice. The days for sneering at reform and for scorning the higher sentiment of the nation pretty much expired with Walpole and his generation. But the details of public abuses had not

[1] The celebrated Lord Mansfield defended the king.
[2] The king treated reformers as rebels against the laws, just as modern partisan tyrants treat them as rebels against the party; and, in a proclamation, he warned the people " against rebellious insurrection" to resist *or reform* the laws.

even yet, become much known to the people. They had no definite theories about the best way of reforming the exercise of the appointing power. They knew that fearful abuses existed, and they had three distinct convictions on the subject : that the corruption and favoritism in the administration were serious matters : that their rulers ought to give their attention to them : and that they might be reformed. The greatest and most practical statesmen of the age held the same views. From that day to this, administrative measures in England have been recognized as among the most vital questions in her affairs : and the reputation of nearly every eminent statesman since the time of Lord North has largely rested upon his efforts in connection with administrative reform. Administration has been converted into a sort of science, which all the leading statesmen have studied. The bold and brilliant speeches and writings of Mr. Burke called attention to the details of official abuses. The struggle for reform was opened in Parliament by Lord Chatham in 1766, the same year in which he spoke against the Stamp act, and openly " rejoiced that America had resisted." Seeing the angry mood of the nation, he declared that " before the end of the century, Parliament will reform itself from within, or be reformed, *with a vengeance*, from without."

The press, by reason of Parliament, being too corrupt to represent the higher sentiment, had suddenly become a political power ; and, repeating the thoughts of the great statesmen, and giving voice to the popular indignation, it awed both the Parliament and the king. In 1780, " numerous public meetings were held, associations formed, and petitions presented, in favor of economical reforms, complaining of the undue influence of the Crown, and of the patronage and corruption by which it was maintained."[1] It was this aroused feeling among the people which encouraged Mr. Burke[2] to bring forward his celebrated reform bill, the

---

[1] 1 May's History, p. 54.

[2] Lord Talbot, about the same time, had tried to carry through a bill for reducing the officers, sinecurists and various expenses in the king's household : but Mr. Burke said he failed, " because the king's turnspit was a member of Parliament."

next year, which was supported in a speech by the younger Pitt. It provided both for a reduction of officers and a diminution of expenses in many ways.

"I bent the whole force of my mind (Mr. Burke says) to the reduction of that corrupt influence which is, in itself, the perennial spring of all prodigality and of all disorder ; which loads us with . . . debt, takes vigor from our army, wisdom from our council . . . and authority and credit from the more venerable parts of our constitution."

Mr. Pitt (the younger) brought forward a reform bill of his own, in 1783, and twice pressed it upon Parliament. When coming to office himself in the same year, he was (in his own person) true to his principles : for though so poor that he had an income of only £300 a year, he declined the sinecure perquisites, amounting to £3000 a year, which the old spoils system tendered him.[1]

About the same time the Duke of Richmond also brought in a reform bill, and the people began, for the first time at this period, to petition on a large scale for the removal of abuses ; earnestly calling for " parliamentary and economical reform." One of these petitions from Yorkshire was signed by eight thousand freeholders, and one from Westminster by five thousand electors. It required some boldness, under the law of libel of those days, to sign an outspoken petition.

Instead of fearing to promote any reform, lest the party majority should be offended (as has so generally and so unfortunately been the case with our party managers),[2] the great party leaders of that day (1780) formed a society " to instruct the people in their political rights and to forward the cause of

[1] But William Pitt, as Prime Minister, made a partisan, though, strictly speaking, not a corrupt, use of titles, decorations and patronage, to an extent that has not been equalled by any of his successors.

[2] English writers of the most liberal views, and who are ready to do justice to our public virtues, cannot forbear noticing this habitual cowering to the party majority. Speaking of English public opinion, in this decade, Mr. May says (2 History, p. 215): " Opinion—free in the press, free in every form of public discussion—has become not less free in society. *It is never coerced into silence or conformity, as in America,* by the *tyrannous* force of a majority."

parliamentary reform." Among its early members were the Duke of Richmond, Mr. Fox, Mr. Pitt, and Mr. Sheridan.

"Political societies and clubs took part in the creation of public opinion, and . . . proved that Parliament would soon have to reckon with the sentiments of the people at large."[1]

But it was the fall of Lord North in 1782, and the coming in of the Marquis of Rockingham, a second time, as Prime Minister (under whom Burke held office), which dealt the heaviest blow the spoils system had ever received : a blow from which it has never recovered. "It must be added, to the lasting honor of Lord Rockingham, that his administration was the first which during a long course of years had the courage and the virtue to refrain from bribing members of Parliament. . . . None of his friends had asked or obtained any pension or any sinecure, either in possession or in reversion."[2] It was then that the proud king felt so humiliated, that he ordered his yacht ready with a view of leaving the country. Parliament was overawed by the stern tone of public opinion. Mr. May thinks that bribery of its members, with money, "did not long survive the ministry of Lord North," and Mr. Green says it then ceased altogether. The new administration declared, as part of its policy, "*independence to America*, abolition of offices, the exclusion of contractors from Parliament, and the disfranchisement of revenue officers ;" and this policy was carried out. "Many useless offices were abolished, restraints were imposed on the issue of secret-service money, the pension list was diminished, and guarantees were provided for a more effectual supervision of the royal expenditures."[3] And thus was our independence a twin birth with administrative reform in the mother country.

The effect of such measures and of such a public sentiment upon Parliament had been great. In the time of George II., there had been two hundred and fifty-seven placemen in that body, exclusive of army and navy officers, but at this time they had fallen to less than ninety. That venal but tyrannical body which, as late as 1771, had issued a proc-

[1] Green's History, p. 738.
[2] Macaulay's "Essay on Lord Chatham," pp. 172 and 178.
[3] May's History, vol. i., pp. 61 and 199.

lamation forbidding the publication of its debates—had brought printers to its bar, on their knees—had sent the Lord Mayor of London to the Tower—was now compliant in the presence of that indignant sentiment of the nation which fiercely demanded publicity and reform. "The public expenses were reduced and commission after commission was appointed to introduce economy into every department of the public service . . . Credit was restored. The smuggling trade was greatly reduced."[1]

The demand for reform continued to spread more and more widely among the people. And, had it not been for the reaction caused by the excesses of the French Revolution, results attained only in this decade might, perhaps, have been reached a half a century ago. As early as 1795, political meetings were held at which 150,000 persons are said to have been present, and at which universal suffrage and parliamentary reform were demanded. In 1797, a reform of the borough system was urged in Parliament by Lord Gray, but it was not carried until 1832, when he was Prime Minister.

The corporation and test acts—making the Sacrament of the Church of England a qualification[2] for office—lingered on the statute books until 1828, and Lord Eldon opposed the repeal to the last. Because the partisan tyranny of our day has only had the courage to deprive those in the public service of reasonable liberty of speech, we must not forget that, in these earlier times, the same tyranny was extended both to the public press and to the assemblies of the people. It was the theory—and for a long period the fact—that there was little more liberty to criticise the acts of government on the part of those beyond the public service, than on the part of those within it. It was against what remained of this official oppression, that the fierce and trenchant invective of Junius, the boldness and adroitness of Wilkes, the patriotic eloquence of Erskine, and the majestic justice of Camden were so effective. They seriously crippled an overshadowing despotism; which, however, was not wholly removed until the present century.

---

[1] Green's History, pp. 756 and 757.
[2] " To make the symbols of atoning grace,
      An office key and pick-lock to a place."

9

For, when neither courts nor juries would longer sustain
it, and high officials dared not act under restrictive statutes still in force (which they were too partisan to have repealed), the old spirit, just as hostile to popular intelligence as
to popular action, found utterance in the form of taxation.
And it was not until 1853 and 1855 that the advertisement
duty and the newspaper stamp were taken away. The duty
on paper did not fall until six years later.

It was not until 1829 that belief in the Catholic creed
ceased to disqualify a man, generally, for office. In that year,
Sir Robert Peel carried a reform bill, which removed that
test, opening Parliament and all political and judicial offices,
national and municipal, to the Catholics, except that of Re-
gent, Lord Chancellor, and Lord Lieutenant of Ireland. But
that precious piece of property, the patronage of the State
Church, was sacredly reserved. Here again the venerable
Lord Eldon led the opposition, but he was compelled in that
year to see Catholic peers take seats which had been vacant for
generations. The Jews were now the only persons, unable by
reason of their opinions, to hold office, civil, military or corporate. An effort to emancipate them failed in 1830. In 1845
they were allowed to hold corporate offices; and finally, in
1860, a roundabout way was provided for Jews to come into
the House of Commons. Only in so late times did England
remove the official test of opinion and grant such limited measure of justice and liberty; while we proclaimed them, without
limitation, at our national birth. Yet it is one of the anomalies of national development that, in this decade, opinions are,
practically, a pervading test for subordinate office with us,
while in England not opinion, but personal merit alone, is that
test. Never have efforts been made on a scale so large,
in forms so varied, or with a perseverance so great, to keep
administrations in power by patronage, to enforce opinions by
official influence, or to strengthen creeds by a monopoly of
office. In these records, we see their futility and their fate.

For what but these have been the results? Administrations
struck down by the popular verdict against the very favoritism and corruption on which they leaned; Ireland, to-day,
more overwhelmingly Catholic than ever; the Jews more

than ever numerous, respected and prosperous; Dissenters grown to be more than half of the people of England ; the old official system detested and abandoned, and the memory of its champions held in execration ; the government of England itself, under the forms of a monarchy, closely approximated to a republic, toward which it is slowly drifting.

# CHAPTER XI

## THE IMPROVED CONDITION AFTER THE FALL OF LORD NORTH.

The Partisan system in last part of reign of George III.—Members of Parliament secure patronage.—The higher public opinion asserts itself.—Various reforms.—Clerks no longer mere department employés.—Freedom of elections protected.—Those in the public service disfranchised.—Office brokerage prohibited.—Legislation against it stringent and comprehensive.—Drastic bribery laws.—British legislation compared with American.—Severe laws against official abuses in India.—Superannuation allowances and their effect.

WE have seen that the fall of Lord North and the independence of America mark the period when the power of the higher public opinion began to be felt in the departments and feared by the executive and by Parliament. With some interruption by George III., party government prevailed during the residue of his reign. Pecuniary corruption and aristocratic supremacy were steadily decreasing, and patronage was dispensed with a more and more strict regard to partisan interests. The mental derangement of the king and the growing political activity and enlightenment of the times facilitated the transfer of power and patronage from the executive; and Parliament was able to appropriate what the executive lost. " Members of Parliament eagerly sought the patronage of the Crown." [1] The party leaders in that body promised patronage to their friends in the House, as well as out, in return for support. And when these leaders were called into the cabinet, (as one party or the other became dominant), they performed their part of the bargain, and the elections in boroughs and municipalities felt the consequences. In that age, the basis of a call to the cabinet was party influence in Parliament and in the boroughs, and such influence was generally measured by the num-

---

[1] 1 May's History, p. 18.

ber of pensions and titles promised to fellow members and constituents. It is plain that this practical working of party government tended to make the administration intensely partisan and to concentrate all patronage in the hands of members of Parliament. That tendency continued almost unchecked during the residue of this reign. The people, generally, did not at that time see that the great contest in which, after a struggle for centuries, they had destroyed monopoly and tyranny in the civil service on the part of the king and his ministers, was about to be succeeded by a contest, hardly less formidable, with the same monopoly, which was then being usurped by members of Parliament. In the public eye, Parliament, rather than the executive, was the popular body and stood for liberty and justice ; and therefore its silent and steady usurpation was less noticed. We shall find that this new parliamentary monopoly of the appointing power gained strength for about half a century, when it had become an oppressive and demoralizing tyranny, against which the higher public opinion then began to make open war. It is in this period between 1800 and 1853 that the administrative situation in Great Britain was, in its general features, most analogous to what our own has been during the last fifty years, except that there a steady improvement was taking place. There the plane of advance was slowly rising (but not so rapidly as public intelligence and virtue), while with us it was slowly falling. To make the nearest accordance, the order of time must be reversed in one country. Among the greater obstacles to reform in both countries was a monopoly of patronage in the hands of members of the legislature. In Great Britain, as with us, the contest was really between the people, standing for freedom and equality, as to sharing public service and emoluments, on the one side, and the members of the legislature with some high officials, claiming and enjoying a monopoly of both, on the other side ; while the executive, sometimes favoring one side and sometimes the other, failed to gain much popular support, because so rarely rising to a standard above that of the monopolists of whose encroachments it justly complained. I can give but a brief outline of the reforms made in this period.

1. It would seem that, in the first half of the reign of George III., or perhaps earlier, a practice had grown up in certain of the larger offices, without the aid of any act of Parliament, of providing, (mainly by collections from the salaries of those in the public service,) a fund out of which those who might be disabled in the discharge of duty, or who might retire after long service, should receive an allowance for their support. This voluntary action appears to have been the basis of that pervading system of superannuation allowances in the English service, to which I shall more fully refer.

2. *Subordinates in departments elevated in rank.* Until 1810,[1] those employed in any department appear to have been little more than private clerks or employés of the head of that department. They were not, in law, recognized as public officials at all. They were paid out of a fund made up of the fees collected in the department or office ; and the balance of the fund, like the appointing power itself, was treated as a part of the perquisites of the minister or head of the office. It was a part of the old spoils system which had prevailed, under which offices and places in the civil service were official property to be sold. This statute seems to indicate that the balance of the fund above expenses is to be paid into the public treasury, and it requires that any deficiency of the fund to pay salaries should be made up from the treasury, thus making those employed in the departments public servants. It regulated pensions and allowances and required annual statements of those employed and of their compensation to be laid before Parliament. This statute, with an act of 1816,[2] and some later amendments, made all those engaged in the established service public officials with fixed salaries. Their dignity and self-respect were thereby much increased, and the tyranny and profit of high officers were in the same degree diminished.

3. *Official interference with freedom of elections.* The corruption and partisan activity in the civil service, (caused by the whole body of inferior officers, except officers in the postal service, whom we have seen a statute of Anne had prohibited tak-

---

[1] Statute of 50 George III., chap. 117.    [2] 56 George III., ch. 46.

ing any part in elections, being in confederacy with members of Parliament and other high officials, by whom they were in great measure appointed), and the coercion of elections which was a natural consequence, were too great to be longer endured. All milder remedies having failed, the disenfranchisement of these in minor offices seemed to be the only effective remedy. An act passed in 1782 [1] is entitled " An act for better securing the freedom of elections, . . . by disabling certain officers from giving their votes," etc. It provides that " no commissioner, collector, supervisor, gauger, or other officer or person, whatsoever, concerned or employed in the charging, collecting, levying, or managing the duties of excise, . . . or concerned or employed in the charging, collecting, levying, or managing the customs, . . . or any of the duties on stamped . . . parchment and paper, . . . or of the duties on salt, . . . windows or houses, nor any postmaster, postmaster-general, or his deputy or deputies, nor any person employed under him or them, . . . shall vote for members of Parliament. . . ." The number of persons thus disfranchised, and the great check put upon official dictation, at elections, may be inferred from the fact that one of the four schedules of duties attached to a customs revenue law, of 1809, defining the articles to be taxed,[2] fills one hundred and twenty-five closely printed pages of the act, making the bewildering number of more than two thousand separate classes of customs duties to be collected. All officers required for such a vast service are of course in addition to those in the inland revenue and post office service, which were also disfranchised. Such was the result in England, before the adoption of our constitution, of the indignation of her people aroused by the same abuse against which we now more and more protest, under the name of interference with local elections, by custom-house and other officials. And thus members of Parliament, having neither the disinterestedness nor the patriotism required to refrain from making use of the unworthy subordinates, whose appointment they had procured, for the purpose of coercing their own election, and not being able to withstand

---

[1] 22 George III., chap. 41.        [2] 49 George III., chap. 93.

a non-partisan public opinion which demanded the removal of
that abuse, instead of attempting to justify it, as has too often
been the case in our day, boldly disfranchised the whole body
of subordinates in the executive department.    They greatly
limit the abuse on the side of the minor officials, while cun-
ningly preserving their usurped patronage and retaining the
full measure of the evil on their own side.    Whether the remedy was the best practicable or not, it shows a stern determination to have an end of a great public evil ; and the act is further worthy of notice as being, perhaps, the first (since the celebrated statute of Richard II.) which aims directly at raising
the character of the civil service.    And I may add that both
the great parties in England found it necessary to maintain this
restriction until July, 1868, when the salutary effects of introducing *the merit system* (that is, examinations and competitions) made it safe to restore the franchise to all those officers.[2]
In that year it was restored : and public officers, clerks, and
employés in Great Britain can now, as freely as any other persons, vote at all elections.    Having come into the public service on their own merits, and holding their places by no tenure
of servility to any high official or domineering party leader,
they, like other citizens, vote or decline to vote, with entire
freedom, of which no one complains.

4. *Sale and brokerage of offices.*    But even when deprived
of the right of voting, those in the public service might intrigue and bargain for promotions and for increase of salaries.
Those not in the public service might promise votes and electioneering work for appointments in the gift of members of
Parliament.    An act of 1809[1] is entitled " An act for the
further prevention of the sale and brokerage of offices."
It re-enacts the prohibitions of the law of Edward VI.
(already referred to), and such prohibitions are extended
to nearly all officers.    How thoroughly it deals with the
subject may be inferred from the following provisions : Any
one is made guilty of a misdemeanor who shall give or assist
to give any money or thing of value, . . . or prom-

---

49 George III., chap. 126, and chap. 218, § 3.
[2] 31 and 32 Vict., chap. 73, and see 37 and 38 Vict., chap. 22.

ise to give any, . . . "for any office, commission, place, or employment," or . . . "for any appointment or nomination or resignation thereof, or for the consent or consents or voice or voices of any person or persons to any such appointment, nomination, or resignation. . . ." And the same punishment is incurred by "any person who shall receive, have, or take any money, reward, directly or indirectly, for any promise, . . . assurance ; or *by any way, means or device, contract . . . for any interest, solicitation, petition, request, recommendation, negotiation,* . . . under pretence of . . . or in or about or anywise *touching, concerning, or relating* to any *nomination, appointment, deputation, or resignation* of any such office, commission, place, or employment." The keeping of any office, place, or agency for procuring or selling offices, employments, or places, " or for *negotiating* in any manner whatever *any business relating to vacancies,* or *in or to* the sale or purchase of any *appointments, nominations, or deputation to, resignation, transfer or exchange of any offices,* places, or employments, in or under any public department," . . . is also made a misdemeanor. The purchase and sale of commissions in the army upon the conditions and at regular rates fixed by authority are excepted. It hardly need be mentioned that such a searching law is equally remarkable as illustrating the grave and varied abuses to which a bad system inevitably leads, and as declaring the stern, practical demand of the English people that these abuses shall come to an end. How much further this act goes than any of the laws we have, in making criminal not only barter and trade concerning salaries and officers, but all negotiations relating to vacancies, exchanges, nominations, resignations, removals, and transfers—in short, every form of corrupt use of the power of appointment and confirmation, and every pernicious kind of solicitation and bargaining— hardly need be pointed out.

But it should be particularly noticed that, it is not merely the giving, promising, or accepting of money or a *valuable* consideration, which is made penal, but the " making or taking of any promise or agreement whatever" of a corrupt nature as a consideration : and that not for office or place merely, but

for any " appointment, nomination, resignation, voice, or consent to any *appointment, nomination, or resignation*, or for
any " negotiation concerning an office or appointment ;" and
" every such person, and also every person who shall wilfully
and knowingly aid such person, shall be deemed guilty of a
misdemeanor." It would seem that such a statute would reach
every form of corrupt bargaining and promising, in connection
with nominations and confirmations, whether or not any money
or thing of value was promised ; and therefore presents a significant instance of the more exacting demands of English legislation aimed at securing official fidelity.

Indeed, on several of the important points covered by this
law, I believe our laws are silent. And it is, to say the least,
very doubtful whether our courts would feel authorized to follow the English decisions. Perhaps this statute is comprehensive enough to make penal the habitual bartering and trading which takes place in regard to nominations, appointments,
and elections between public officers, party managers, and patronage brokers in our municipalities, and sometimes in our legislatures, if not in higher quarters. It places the exacting demands of the times in which it was enacted in curious contrast
with the loose morality which had before prevailed ; for it declares that, if any one has an office, which he took " on an
agreement to pay a charge or part of the profits to a former
holder," *he is still left liable to make such payments ;* and it
further recites that ' whereas . . . it has always been
customary in the appointment of the masters and six clerks
and . . . the examiners of the Court of Chancery of
Ireland *to allow the having or receiving of money or other valuable consideration for such appointments ;*" and though it
is a practice fit to be discontinued, etc., " yet it is reasonable
that the persons . . . who now hold the said offices
*should be permitted to dispose of them in the same manner ;*"
and it permits them so to do. If we wonder at such indul-
gence, we cannot wonder less at the rapid rise in public sentiment, as shown in the general provisions of the law.

5. *Bribery.* An act of 1809 [1] shows how the English Gov-

---

[1] 49 George III., chap. 118.

ernment struck at the partisan spoils system through her laws against bribery. It is declared to be " An act to secure independence in Parliament and prevent the attaining of seats by corrupt practices," and is a part of the laws against bribery. One of its recitals is worthy of special notice. The Bill of Rights had declared that " the election of members of Parliament ought to be free." Now this act, after reciting that money . . . and "*offices, places,* and *employment are promised and given to secure elections,*" declares that not only are such gifts but " *such promises are contrary to the freedom of elections.*"

It was a great step in the reform of the civil service to lay down the rule of law that a promise of an office, place, or employment, or of official influence in securing either under the government, in consideration of votes and work for candidates, was as real and dangerous an invasion of the freedom of elections and as fit a cause of punishment as to promise money or anything of direct pecuniary value for doing the same thing. But this statute carries the principle even further in the same direction. For, after declaring in the first section that it is a penal offence to " promise any sum of money, gift, or thing of value" as a consideration for procuring or endeavoring to procure the return of any person to Parliament, it declares in the next section that if " any person shall by himself or other person give or procure to be given, *or promise to give or procure to be given, any office, place, or employment, to any person or persons whatsoever,* upon any express contract or agreement that such person . . . shall by himself, or by any other person or persons, . . . their solicitation, request, or command, procure or endeavor to procure the return of any person to Parliament," . . . the candidate *knowing and consenting to such* agreement, is " declared to be disabled and *incapacitated to serve in Parliament;*" and the person promised the said office, place, or employment is declared incapable of holding the same, and is made liable to pay a fine of £500. And in addition, "any person holding any office under the Crown *who shall give any office, place, or employment* under a contract for procuring or endeavoring to procure the return of a person to Parliament," is made liable by the same section to a fine of £1000. The bearing of this provision upon such habitual arrangements as are made in connection with our elections, for giving offices and places as a consideration for votes, resignations, and influence, must be apparent. Is there any way of avoiding the admission that in this statute, English political legislation had thus early reached a level ours has not yet attained? If I am not laboring under some misapprehension, the passage of such a law by Congress would not only produce a great sensation in the lower circles of our politics, but would be a great and salutary reform in our official life. And have we any right to be surprised at the higher moral tone and greater efficiency now claimed for the British civil service, when, for more than half a century, it has been guarded and protected by such salutary statutes?

A law of 1827 [1] is in the same spirit. That is also a law to prevent corrupt practices in elections, and for diminishing election expenses. It provides that "If any person shall, either during any election of members of Parliament or within six calendar months before or fourteen days after . . . be employed as counsel, agent, or attorney, . . . or in any other capacity for the purposes of such election, and shall . . . accept from any such candidate, *or from any person whatsoever*, for, in consideration of, or with reference to such employment, any sum of money, retaining fee, *office, place, or employment, or any promise or security* for any such money, . . . *office, place, or employment,* . . . such person shall be deemed incapable of voting at such election." These laws were consolidated and extended by a law of 1854 [2] which declares that "every person who shall directly or indirectly . . . give or procure, or agree to give or procure, . . . *or endeavor to procure any office, place, or employment* to or for any voter, *or to or for any person in behalf of any voter*, or to or for any other person, . . . in order *to induce him to vote or refrain from voting*," . . . is guilty of bribery. "Every person who shall, in consequence of any such promises, . . . endeavor to procure any such . . . return or vote, . . .

---

[1] 7 and 8 George IV., chap. 37        [2] 17 and 18 Vict., chap. 102.

is also guilty of bribery." It is further provided that every voter who shall, before or during the election, . . . agree or contract for any money, etc., "*or any office, place, or employment for himself or any other person for voting, agreeing to vote, or refraining from voting at any election*," is also guilty of bribery. This act also places salutary restrictions of various kinds upon election abuses too numerous to be detailed here. They show that far more consideration has been given to the subject in all its bearings than it has ever commanded in this country. Some of the prohibitions were doubtless made more necessary for the reason that the ballot was not in use ; but most of them are hardly less efficacious since it has been introduced. The more important of them relate to making merchandise of the appointing power independently of elections. Among other important precautions of the act are those providing for a public " auditor of election expenses," before whom all such expenses must be publicly stated and proved, and without whose approval of them they are neither binding, nor is it lawful for the candidate to pay them. I think there can be no doubt but these provisions as to expenses have been most salutary in England, and could be adopted here with good effect in checking the secret and corrupt use of money and other bribes to effect elections.

There are strong reasons for thinking that these British statutes have contributed largely to the formation of that salutary public opinion in Great Britain—sure to attract the attention of a candid foreigner—which now condemns the use of authority over the public service for promoting the interests of ambition and partisanship, almost as strongly as it does the direct use of public money for the same purpose. That opinion and these statutes plainly regard the honest exercise of the power of appointment, promotion, removal, and employment in the public service as being a duty as absolute as that of accounting for the taxes or guarding the treasury.

It is worthy of serious reflection that our Federal statutes, on the subject of bribery, though sometimes framed in language which suggests a knowledge of the English precedents, have stopped short of prohibiting the corrupt use or the promise of the use of influence or official authority to procure offices, places, or employments in the public service as a consideration for votes or support. And, so far as I have been able to learn, our State statutes on these subjects go little further than the Federal statutes or are silent.

The United States Revised Statutes, § 5449, relating to bribing judges ; § 5450 and § 5500, relating to bribing members of Congress ; § 5501, relating to other officers generally, are meagre and narrow compared with the British statutes ; only prohibiting the use of "money or any promise, contract, etc., for payment of money, or for the delivery or conveyance of anything of value." Were these words "delivery or conveyance" put in connection with "thing of value," to make it certain that the statute should extend to nothing but a bribe in material property of some kind ?

And such important provisions as those contained in § 1781 to § 1784, inclusive, seem to be framed in the same restrictive spirit ; almost suggesting that, while it is a grave offence to receive a sum of money for prostituting a public function, it is no offence at all to promise or give an office or a promotion for doing the same thing. Indeed, the British crime of "office brokerage"—that is, the making of merchandise of the use of official authority and influence, in the guise of promising offices and places—the criminality of which has long been a salutary force for civil service reform in Great Britain—appears to be unknown in our Federal legislation. I know of no fact more significant of the demoralizing effects of the partisan spoils system in our politics than these defects in our laws : unless it be that public opinion, which so generally fails to perceive that a public officer has no more right to use the authority than he has the money, with which the people have entrusted him, to advance private or partisan interests at their expense.

A thoughtful writer has declared it to be important "that the national institutions should place all things that are connected with themselves before the mind of the citizen, in the light in which it is for his good that he should regard them."[1] Is there not reason to fear that these false teachings of the laws —laws which in their very phraseology reflect the domineering

[1] Mill on Representation, p. 173.

supremacy of the partisan theory of politics—are in a large measure responsible for the idea so generally accepted, that there is no right to inquire into the abuse of official discretion, provided it falls short of actual peculation—that its use, in the selfish interests of a party, is almost if not quite commendable, if not a sheer necessity? The simple facts are that we now tolerate the corrupt use — the virtual bargain and sale—of power and influence connected with office, precisely as I have shown that the English so long tolerated the bargaining and sale of the offices themselves.

The extent of the differences I have pointed out, between the English and American statutes, as to using public functions and offices for selfish and partisan purposes, is emphasized by the decisions of our courts. Though popular elections of judges for short terms have brought our judiciary (in most of the States) sadly under the influence of party politics, the judges have still tried to go beyond the language of our statutes in arresting official corruption; and their reliance has been the English statutes and decisions. Thus, where one public officer paid money to another for a resignation in his favor, the courts of Rhode Island could find no law of the State or of Congress forbidding the abuse, but held the transaction illegal under English precedents.[1] The same in substance was the fact when the United States Supreme Court declared void a promise to pay a percentage to one who lobbied a claim through Congress.[2] So when, in New York, one of two candidates for an inspectorship agreed to withdraw, to support the other and to share fees, the agreement was held void, not because the meagre New York bribery law or any American law was against it, but because English statutes and precedents were against it.[3] It was decided by Lord Thurlow that a suit on an agreement to pay for recommending one to an office should be enjoined.[4]

6. *India Civil Service.* The world knows the fearful abuses that once pervaded it. A law of 1784[5] affords a further illus-

[1] Eddy v. Capron, 4 Rhode Island Rep., 394.
[2] Trist v. Child, 21 Wallace, chap. 450.
[3] Gray v. Hook, 4 Comstock R., 449.
[4] Harrington v. Chatel, 1 Bro. cases, 124 ; Greame v. Wroughton, 1 Eng. L. and E. Rep.                              [5] 24 George III., chap. 25.

tration of the painstaking manner in which English statesmen at this period attempted to bring purity and vigor into that branch of administration. No law upon our statute book will bear any comparison with this for the thoroughness of its dealing with the principal elements essential to a good civil service remote from central supervision. I have no space for details. Promotions by favor and patronage, having resulted in disgraceful corruption, inefficiency, and injustice, a trial was ordered of a system of promotion mainly based on seniority, and to prevent abuses, it is declared that the India authorities shall keep and transmit a report to the directors which shall contain "a full and perfect entry to be made upon their minutes, specifying all the circumstances of the case, and their reasons and inducements at large," whenever in making promotions, they shall depart from the general rules laid down in the law.

And I may say that similar rules had prevailed in some of the home offices of England, in regard to promotions, and that such records have been the efficient means of taking promotions to a considerable extent out of party politics and personal favoritism. But seniority had its own evils. Another section of this law is perhaps more stringent and comprehensive than any we now have against public officers receiving payments or bribes ; and the same remark may be extended to the following provision from the 50th section : "The making or entering into, by any officer, of any corrupt contract for the giving up or obtaining or in any manner touching or concerning the trust and duty of any office or employment under the said company in the East Indies, . . . shall be deemed and taken to be a misdemeanor."

But the 55th section of this act is the most remarkable, and is certainly a very unique and probably effective remedy. Its re-enactment by Congress would give a shock to our territorial officials, and it would be so well adapted to the cases of some of our Indian agents that I give the material part of it in a

---

[1] § 55. And for the better preventing or more easily punishing the misconduct of the servants in the . . . affairs of . . . India, be it further enacted, That every person now being, or who shall hereafter be, in the service . . . in India, shall, within the space of two calendar

note.¹ Not only is the complete inventory in that section required to be made under oath, but, *at any time within three years*, it may be shown to be false by *any one ;* and in that case, or in case of any misrepresentation in it, or in the public examinations under oath concerning its contents, to which the maker may be subjected, he is not only made guilty of perjury, *but he also forfeits his entire fortune*. By such laws, the English people illustrated their resolve to have brought to an end that robbery and corruption in India with which the eloquence of Burke has made the world familiar. It was by such laws, giving authority and permanency to the higher moods of the people, that great encouragement and strength were imparted, three-quarters of a century ago, to that reforming spirit, in which were laid the deep foundations of those methods in the civil service which have so much raised its standard in the present generation over that of the past. Without citing such laws, I have feared I shall be thought guilty of exaggeration when I come to state how high that standard now is.

7. *Superannuation allowances.* The next class of the legislation of this period, to which I shall refer, aims at making

months after his returning to Great Britain, deliver in upon oath, before the Lord Chief Baron of his Majesty's Court of Exchequer in England, or any two of the other barons of the said court for the time being respectively (which oath the said Lord Chief Baron, and other barons, are hereby respectively authorized to administer), duplicates of an exact particular or inventory of all and singular the lands, tenements, hereditaments, goods, chattels, debts, moneys, securities for money, and other real and personal estate and property whatsoever, as well in Europe as in Asia, or elsewhere, which such person was seized or possessed of or entitled unto, at the time of his arrival in Great Britain, in his own right, or which any person or persons was or were seized or possessed of in trust for him, or to or for his use or benefit, at the time of his said arrival in Great Britain, or at any time after ; specifying what part thereof was not acquired, or purchased by property acquired, in consequence of his residence in the East Indies ; and if any of the real or personal estate or property of any such person shall have been conveyed, alienated, transferred, or otherwise disposed of, after his said arrival in Great Britain, then such person shall also, in and by said particular or inventory, set forth an accurate description and specification of all such parts of his said real or personal estate and property as shall have been so conveyed, transferred, or disposed of, and how and in what manner, and to whom, and at what time, and for what price consideration, the same shall have been so conveyed, alienated, transferred, or disposed of respectively.

10

the public service more attractive through provisions for disability and declining years ; whereby also it was believed that, at least equal capacity and more fidelity might be obtained, at a smaller expense to the public treasury. A law of 1809 [1] provides for superannuation allowances to persons in the excise service. It clearly defines the policy on which it proceeds in this preamble : "Whereas no provision is made by law for persons employed in the revenue of excise *to the great discouragement of such officers and other persons, and to the manifest injury of the revenue,"* and it then authorizes certain payments out of the public revenue to those disabled by age or infirmity after ten years' service ; the allowance being proportional to salary. Allowances are also to be made to those who shall meet with accidents in the discharge of official duty. A law of 1810 [2] shows a fact already suggested, that the voluntary contributions of those in certain branches of the service had provided a sort of retiring allowance from a fund in the nature of an insurance fund. This law provides, for the first time, that statements shall be annually laid before Parliament of all persons in the public service, giving their salaries, pensions, and allowances, and of all increase and diminution of either : the act being the equivalent and precedent of our statements annually laid before Congress. The act also established a system of superannuation allowances. The next year, [3] the old system was abolished in the customs service, and the payment of the allowances, so far as the old fund was inadequate, was regularly charged upon the public treasury. The new system having been found to contribute to efficiency as well as economy, after long trial, has never been very materially changed, though modified from time to time. The final revision of these laws was made in 1859. [4] Under this act, it is the rule that, if there has been no more than ten years' service, there can be no allowance. The retiring allowance, after ten years and before eleven years of service, is at the rate of ten-sixtieths of the current salary being paid at that time. At eleven years of service, the allowance is at the rate of eleven-sixtieths of the salary, and so on, increasing at the rate of one-sixtieth for every

---

[1] 49 George III., chap. 96.  
[2] 50 George III., chap. 117.  
[3] 51 George III., chap. 55.  
[4] 22 Vict., chap. 26.

year of service, after ten years, until forty years of service, after which there is no increase. It is also a part of this method for securing faithful and efficient officers that most of the salaries are regularly graded, so that there are regular additions, dependent upon length and efficiency of service. There are also carefully guarded provisions for the granting of discretionary allowances up to a fixed limit, in cases of exceptional merit, severe bodily injury, disability in the service, *abolition of offices*, and also in cases of special service of great value to the public ; the same being, in principle, analogous to pensions in military life. On the other hand, a deduction may be made from such allowances against any person when " his defaults or demerits in relation to the public service . . . appear to justify such diminution." The act further provides that thereafter no person (save a few especially excepted) shall be deemed to be in the civil service, in such a sense as to entitle him to any superannuation or retiring allowance, " unless he has been admitted to the civil service with a certificate from the *Civil Service Commissioners :*" or, in other words, he must have got into the service, not by favor or influence, but through a public examination and open competition with his fellows who sought the same place.

I have departed from chronological order, for the purpose of bringing together all I have to say upon this important subject. It seems to be demonstrated, by the experience of England during three-quarters of a century, under such a method (which we have adopted, by applying it in a very limited way to the judges of the Supreme Court, and in spirit in our army and navy pension system),[1] that the provision it makes for old age and misfortunes, besides promoting a better feeling in the service towards the State, and making effective discipline easier, actually enables the State to purchase the services of its officers at a less cost to the public treasury. The allowances for special merit and the deductions for bad conduct are based on records kept in the departments, and they are considered to have a salutary influence, (analogous to promotions, prize money, and brevet rank in the naval and military service,) in stimulating honorable exertions in the public interest.

[1] It has lately been applied to the police force of New York City.

# CHAPTER XII.

The better public opinion a growing power in politics.—Condition of the public service from 1820 to 1830.—Partisan system supreme, but pecuniary corruption has nearly ceased in appointments.—Bribery of members of Parliament at an end, but not of electors.—Few removals for political reasons.—Members of Parliament cling to patronage.—Inefficiency and supernumeraries in the service.—Members foist incompetent favorites upon the public Treasury.—Theory of promotion.—The Treasury and its authority.—The existing abuses explained.—Great Reform Bill of 1832. —Failed to break up the partisan system.—The "Patronage Secretary" of the Treasury and his functions.

GEORGE IV. came to the throne in 1820. In the laws to which I have referred, it abundantly appears that the higher public opinion had already achieved considerable victories over official tyranny and all the corrupt elements of politics. Of that tyranny Mr. May says : " Henceforward we shall find its supremacy gradually declining and yielding to the advancing power and intelligence of the people. . . . From this time public opinion became a power which ministers were unable to subdue, and to which statesmen of all parties learned more and more to defer. . . . From the accession of George IV. it gathered strength until it was able, as we shall see, to dominate over ministers and Parliaments."[1] The establishment of the Society for the Diffusion of Useful Knowledge in 1826, and of the Society for the Promotion of Christian Knowledge soon after, mark the spirit of the period. Since that time, the utmost latitude of criticism and invective has been permitted. Prosecutions for libel, like the censorship of the press, fell out of the system of government. The time of George IV. (1820 to 1830) has a peculiar interest, because,

[1] History, vol. ii., pp. 201-213.

during that period, the element of "spoils" (in its true defini-
tion) in the partisan system of appointment almost wholly disappeared from English administration, while, by a strange contrast, the way was, at that time, opened for the spoils and proscriptive elements to come more readily into our politics. For
the act of 1820, limiting the term of numerous officers to four
years, tended to make the election of the President decisive of
their tenure, and hence to involve all those officials in that
contest, as in a struggle for life. The administrative system of
the two centuries then passed each other, one on an ascending
and the other on a descending plane. It will be useful to note
the character of British administration at that period.

1. Bribery of members of Parliament was past ; though
bribery of electors continued a very serious evil until after the
great Reform Bill of 1832 ; and it was considerable until the
introduction of the ballot in 1871, since which the situation in
that regard has been, I think, much the same as our own.

2. Party government becoming more absolute as the power
of the Crown and nobility declined, a proscriptive application
of the partisan system, everywhere setting up political opinions
as a test, prevailed in making all appointments and promotions.

3. Patronage--that is, the right of selections for official
places below heads of departments—was substantially in the
hands of members of Parliament ; and it was freely used for
the purpose of gaining influence for themselves and making
places for their favorites.

4. Grave abuses, inevitable from a partisan system in the
control of members of legislature, existed. It caused a vicious
activity and rewarded demoralizing intrigues in Parliamentary
and even in municipal elections. The election involved the
awarding of patronage ; and hence other issues than those of
principle and the merits of the candidate were often controlling.

The practice was also fatal to economy and disastrous to the
character and efficiency of the public service. Legislation was
often controlled by patronage, and the departments were crowded with incompetents and supernumeraries.

5. It had, by the force of public opinion, without any law
on the subject, come to be the rule, almost universally acted

upon, that those in the civil service below cabinet ministers and a few political assistants (less than fifty in all, besides foreign ministers and certain consuls) should not be removed except for causes other than political opinions. To the number thus liable to be removed for political reasons, postmasters must be added : though they were not removed with the frequency of such removals in our service. There was no practice of removing one subordinate merely to make place for another. These facts are of some importance as bearing upon the extent of the implied power of removal declared by the Senate, in 1789, to belong to our Executive : the question being whether in principle it is a power of removal for cause, or upon caprice merely.

6. As those in the subordinate civil service were no longer allowed to vote, they were little inclined to activity in party politics. Not being liable to arbitrary removal, they were not forced to fight at every election in self-defence.

7. No abuse corresponding to what we call " political assessments" existed : and I have pointed out the reasons why it never existed in the English service. It was, in more corrupt times, merged in the greater evil of selling offices, the purchaser insisting on getting a title free of annual taxation. Besides, for a long time after members of Parliament had become the dominant power in politics, all those in the service below heads of bureaus, being regarded as the servants of high officers, were paid from fees, the balance of which belonged to the head of the office. This system did not allow party assessments. Perhaps the great officers contributed to election expenses from the balance of the fee fund.

8. No examinations of any sort stood between the appointing power on the one side, and the favorites urged upon it by members of Parliament and party leaders on the other side. As a rule, those exercising that power were forced to accept whoever was most strongly backed.

9. There was not at this time, nor has there been since, any legislative authority in England, participating in executive functions, which is the equivalent of the power of confirmation in our Senate. Still, in other ways, the party majority in the legislature was made perhaps almost as influential as with us.

The members of the Cabinet were members of the Parliamentary majority. What was called The Treasury had (subject to the influence of members of Parliament) something like a control over the greater number of the appointments and promotions. There was a permanent Secretary of the Treasury ; and in addition there were the following (political) officers who went out with each administration—viz., the first Lord of the Treasury (generally the Prime Minister), the Chancellor of the Exchequer, and several junior lords, which together constitute " *The Treasury*."

Such, in substance, appears to have been the condition of the English civil service in the period from 1820 to 1830 ; the relative power of the Crown, the Cabinet, The Treasury, and the members of Parliament over appointments and promotions being very inadequately defined, and by far the greater evil being patronage in the control of members of Parliament. The system of administration, in short, was at this date the partisan system, in its most characteristic and extreme form, but without the spoils element in the mercenary or more corrupt sense.

The evidence illustrating the abuses of patronage in the hands of members of Parliament, to which I might refer, is so great in variety and volume that I have no space to do justice to it. It is to be found throughout the many thousands of pages of evidence and reports which have been printed, as the results of the numerous investigations into the working of the civil service. I submit a few illustrations. Mr. Lowe, Chancellor of the Exchequer under Mr. Gladstone, said, on his examination before a committee in 1873 (referring to the partisan system after the introduction of the merit system) : that " Under the former system, I suppose there was never such a thing known as a man being appointed to a clerkship in a public office because he was supposed to be fit for the place." [1] Mr. Baxter, the Financial Secretary of the Treasury, describes that system in his examination :—" Question 4672. Is much pressure brought upon the Treasury with respect to public establishments outside ? Answer. The most unpleasant part, as I find it, of the duty of the Financial Secretary of the

[1] Report Parliamentary Committee, 1873, p. 231.

Treasury is to resist the constant pressure brought day by day, and almost hour by hour, *by members of Parliament in order to increase expenditure by increasing the pay of the classes, and granting larger compensations to individuals or to classes ;* . . . and that pressure, which is little known to the public, as I said before, is the most unpleasant part of my duties, and it occupies a very great deal of time which probably might be better spent. Question 4682. You spoke of the constant parliamentary pressure. . . . Do you allude to proceedings in Parliament as well as private communications, or only to the latter? Answer. I did. . . . But of course my answers might be extended to those motions in the House which are resisted without effect by the government, and *which entail great expenditure upon the country.*"[1] In another report, the head of a large office makes this statement :

"I have made out a return of 55 persons . . . who were nominated by the Treasury between 1836 and 1854. . . . Several of them were incompetent from their ages. . . . I found some perfectly unqualified. . . . I also found persons there of very bad character : one person in that list had been imprisoned by the sentence of the court as a fraudulent debtor. . . . Then with regard to health, there was one man whom I was forced to keep in a room by himself, as he was in such a state of health that he could not associate with the other clerks. . . . There was a case in our offices (Board of Audit), in which a gentleman was appointed who really could neither read nor write, he was almost an idiot, and there was the greatest possible difficulty in getting him out of the office."[2]

The report of the committee last referred to declares that, "where the spirit of patronage rules, the appointments are given, to a great extent, as a *reward for political services, without the least reference to the ability, knowledge, or fitness of the persons appointed.*"[3]

In 1855 a large volume[4] was printed by the British Govern-

[1] Parliamentary Report of 1873, p. 248.
[2] Parliamentary Report on Civil Service, 1830, p. 176 and p. x.
[3] Report on Civil Service, 1860 p. 287.
[4] That volume will be hereafter cited as Civil Service Papers.

ment, made up of valuable papers, containing the opinions of
many persons of great experience in administration upon its
previous condition, and setting forth the causes of existing
abuses. The following extracts are from that volume : [1]

" I have known many instances of individuals boldly stating they
were not put into the service by their patrons to work. . . . The . . .
majority of the members of the Colonial Department in my time
possessed only in a low degree, and some of them in a degree almost
incredible, either the talents or the habits of men of business, or the
industry, the zeal, or the knowledge required for the effective performance of their appropriate functions. . . . The existing defect of the
civil service is, in my opinion, its want of that high moral tone
which is so essential in conducting the common affairs of life. . . .
The most feeble sons in families which have been so fortunate as to
obtain an appointment, yes, and others too, either mentally or physically incapacitated, enter the service. The more able and ambitious
sons seek the open professions. . . . The fault of the present system
lies principally in the fact that almost every branch of the Permanent
Civil Service is connected more or less with politics through the heads
of the respective departments . . . and that the selection of officers
generally proceeds on political grounds, and for political purposes. . .
The needless and very inconvenient increase of the numbers borne on
the clerical list—the frequent transfer of many of their appropriate
duties to ill-educated and ill-paid supernumeraries—and the not infre-
quent occurrence of mistakes and oversights are so serious as occasionally to imperil interests of high national importance. . . . Every
person who has had experience in conducting a large office will admit,
that if all were really efficient . . . it could be probably executed
by *two-thirds of the number of clerks at present employed.* Let any one
who has had experience, reflect on the operation of patronage on
Elections, Parliament, and the Government. Over each it exercises an
evil influence. In the Elections, it interferes with the honest exercise of
the franchise ; in Parliament it encourages subservience to the administration ; it impedes the free action of a Government desirous of pursuing
an honest or an economical course, and it occasions the employment
of persons without regard to their peculiar fitness. It is a more pernicious system than the mere giving of money to Electors or members of Parliament to secure their votes. It is bribery in its worst
form. . . Notwithstanding the constant interference of the House

[1] Pages 52, 53, 54, 73, 80, 81, 74-236, 302, 271, 272.

of Commons in matters relating to the civil service, the reform of the civil service remains just where it was. Their single panacea for all the evils they supposed to exist in it is, was, and ever will be, retrenchment, the abolition and consolidation of offices, and the diminution of salaries. The mode of making the service efficient seems never to have entered their minds ; and the real reform of the civil service is still left for the civil service itself to accomplish.''

The point made by the last writer was that members of Parliament, wishing to preserve their patronage and to use it in their own interest—to reward their favorites and supporters— would never consent to any tests of character and capacity that would limit their own arbitrary authority by keeping out the unworthy. This was the greatest obstacle in the later stages of reform in Great Britain. The disinterestedness required for a surrender of that patronage was too great for Parliamentary patriotism. No candid person, I think, can read these statements of the condition of the British civil service in the last generation without being impressed with its great similarity to that of our own in this generation. And that the causes which produced both were substantially the same perhaps hardly admits of a doubt. Great as had been the reforms already achieved, it is not strange that when public attention became concentrated upon this new phase of abuses, the demand for their removal was expressed with great vigor. Neither parties nor members of Parliament, however, at that time, showed any inclination to surrender their patronage. The statesmen of that day may have thought that a reform of the Parliamentary representation itself would be the best means of mitigating if not of removing such abuses. However the fact may have been, they bent themselves upon that reform. How long and stormy the struggle that secured a great victory for liberal government in the reform law of 1832, is well known. I have already referred to the monstrous injustice and corruption at which it was aimed. Lord John Russell took the lead in the struggle in which it was carried. It was the greatest and most desperate civil contest in modern history. On one side of the issue hung the rights of the people to be better represented and protected, and on the other the waning supremacy of the aristocracy and the cor-

rupt borough system.   All England was for several years in a
ferment of agitation.   It required the most formidable dis-
play of the police and military to keep the peace, and even
that failed.   Monster meetings, fired with anger and indignation, were held in all the great cities.   One at Birmingham,
in 1831, was attended by 150,000 people, and it voted " to
refuse to pay taxes as Hampden had refused to pay ship
money," if reform was not granted ; and it petitioned Parliament to withhold supplies.   Great bodies of people paraded
the streets of the larger cities in an angry mood, and assaulted
distinguished noblemen.   During two days, the city of Bristol
was in the hands of a riotous mob.   Custom houses, excise
offices, and bishops' palaces were carried by storm.   The ex-
tinction of the peerage was threatened, and the throne itself
was in danger.   In 1831, the second reading of the bill was
carried in the Commons by a majority of one, in a vote of
608, the largest number that ever voted in Parliament.
Another year of fearful agitation followed.   There were monster meeting assuming attitudes of intimidation, and filling the
air with threats of violence.   It was not until the danger of a
general collision between the government and the people was
imminent, and the perils of the nation could be read in smok-
ing harvests and burning castles and mansions, that the bill was
passed.   The close monopolies at elections were set aside, and
a £10 household franchise was established.   Fifty-six boroughs,
having less than 2000 inhabitants, and returning one hundred
and eleven members, were swept away.   The disfranchisement
extended to one hundred and forty-three members.   Twenty-
two large towns and districts were allowed two members each,
and twenty more one each.   These changes secured a fairer representation of the better public opinion, and greatly limited
but by no means prevented bribery.[1]   A large body of intelligent and worthy persons of small means were, for the first
time, enabled to vote.   Royalty and aristocracy lost a great
deal of power which that class of voters gained.   The cause

---

[1] Soon after, the laws against bribery were made more effective by allowing general proof of bribery to precede the proof of agency of the members'
supposed bribing agent ; and still later by a law authorizing the personal
examination of sitting members and candidates. (4 and 5 Vict., chap. 57 ;
14 and 15 Vict., chap. 99.)

of good administration was thus strongly reinforced. But it soon appeared that even this vast extension of suffrage had left the cause of reform too weak to take nominations from members of Parliament, or to install merit in the place of favoritism at the gates of the public service. The partisan system was too strongly entrenched, and its managers too skilful, to be captured in that way. They resisted to the utmost. With more votes to win and more vigorous political criticism to withstand, the partisan managers of the reformed Parliament only saw the greater need of using every fragment of patronage to perpetuate their monopoly. Though the higher leaderships and better public sentiment which prevailed, after 1832, were able (in 1833) to abolish slavery in the British Colonies; to terminate the monopoly in the East India trade; to reform the poor laws and the tithe laws; to provide an admirable municipal system in the two years next following; to inaugurate popular education in 1834, and greatly extend it in 1839; to overthrow the corn laws monopoly in 1846 after a contest only less desperate than that which carried the Reform Bill; and to improve the administration in many ways which I need not mention in detail—yet moral forces equal to such high achievements were altogether too weak to take a young man of merit and put him into the public service without the formal consent of some member of Parliament, or of the official heads of the party in power; a consent which was almost sure to turn upon personal or partisan reasons.

It was not till long after 1832 that the inherent mischief of the partisan system became manifest to the great body of thinking people. When that result was attained, the final struggle with patronage in the hands of members of Parliament began on a larger scale. It seems to have been, even then, foreseen by the best informed that it could not be removed by any partisan agency. They began to see the need of some method by which fitness for the public service could be tested otherwise than by the fiat of a member of Parliament or the vote of the Cabinet or the Treasury. What that method should be was one of the great problems of the future. No government had then solved it. That there must be tests of fitness independent of any political action, or

mere official influence, became more and more plain to thinking men.

The leaders of the great parties soon began to see that a
public opinion in favor of such tests was being rapidly developed, which seriously threatened their power, unless the
party system itself could be made more acceptable to the
people. Parliament (after a fashion with which we are
familiar) held long debates and ordered frequent investigations
into the details of the public service, but always passing by the
great evil for which its members were responsible. They
could see and were ready to attack any abuse except their own
prostitution of patronage. Talk of economy was as long,
loud, and frequent as it has been in our Congress. The party
in power commended itself to the people from time to time by
exposing the extravagance of its opponents, by having the
salaries of officers cut down, by lopping off a few of the
many supernumeraries, by removing some of the many complications. And above all, there was an abundance of fine
promises made. But no member gave up his patronage—no
way was opened by which a person of merit could get into an
office or a place except by the favor of the party or the condescension of a member. The partisan blockade of every port
of entry to the public service, which made it tenfold easier for
a decayed butler or an incompetent cousin of a member or a
minister, than for the promising son of a poor widow, to
pass the barrier, was, after the Reform Bill as before, rigidly
maintained. Fealty to the party and work in its ranks—subserviency to members and to ministers—and electioneering on
their behalf—these were the virtues before which the ways to
office and the doors of the Treasury were opened. Year by
year, the public discontent with the whole system increased.
Certain parts of it had already been found so degrading and
intolerable that an ingenious mitigation had been contrived.
In Walpole's time, a Parliamentary bribery agent had been
employed, with plenary authority to make contracts with
members and to comply with their terms in the distribution
of the corruption fund. After this analogy, there had been
provided, for the present exigency, a broken general in patronage called "The Patronage Secretary of the Treasury,"

whose duty it was to stand between members and partisan managers appealing for places for their favorites, on the one side, and the heads of offices who needed to have these places filled with competent persons, on the other side. This Secretary measured the force of threats and took the weight of influence ; he computed the political value of a member's support and deducted from it the official appraisement of patronage before awarded to him. It is said that actual accounts, Dr. and Cr. were kept with members by this Patronage Secretary. Degrading as such an arrangement was, it was far better than to have members of Parliament going from department to department and from office to office, now suggesting favors and then assaults in Parliament—here using threats and there persuasion  in aid of his purpose of foisting a dependent or an electioneering agent upon the public treasury. This comptroller-general of patronage continued in full sway until competitive examinations, upon the introduction of the merit system, had made an end of patronage. He still feebly survives, but only as the withered skeleton of the great political potentate which he once was—in whose presence members took off their hats and their dependents fell to their knees.

# CHAPTER XIII.

THE demand for administrative reform has now become concentrated against the great monopoly of designating all persons for the civil service, which is held potentially by members of Parliament. How to break up that monopoly and to open the public service to merit without influence, has become a great question. The people do not challenge party government itself, but thoughtful men are concerned at its prostitution. They concede that the party majority should elect all legislators and enact all laws ; that it should make up the Cabinet and select all those higher officers who shall stand for and carry into effect the policy, both foreign and domestic, which the majority of the people have approved at the polls. But the rest—the sixty thousand or more subordinates who are bound to obey the instructions of those superiors—and whose politics, to say the least, are not so important as their capacity and their character—these they insist should be selected with reference to personal merit and not partisan convictions. What should be the test and how applied ? This, after the Reform Bill, became a much mooted question.

I have said that, since the time of Mr. Pitt, the fame of nearly every leading English statesman has in large measure rested upon his reform policy. We now find new illustrations of this fact. That of Lord John Russell stands on the Reform

Bill of 1832.  Sir Robert Peel was, perhaps, the most practical statesman England had produced, and as little as any
flattered by the seductions which an aristocracy can offer ; for
he refused a peerage and the highest Order of distinction the
Queen could tender him.   In 1816, he brought about a great
reform by the passage of the Irish Constabulary Act ; in 1822,
he carried a measure for reforming the criminal laws ; and a few
years later he caused the Metropolitan Police law for London to
be enacted, with its stringent provisions for excluding politics.

" To check the introduction of patronage into the Metropolitan
Police force, Sir Robert Peel provided that no one should be admitted as qualified for the office of inspector or superintendent who had
not been trained by actual service in *each* subordinate rank." [1]

To these measures of administrative reform, he brought the
whole force of his character.   It is after these models that the
police system of New York city, and all the best police laws
we have, are framed.   These police laws were the first laws (since
the act of Richard II.) that, in principle, made personal qualification in an officer paramount to political opinions or the favor
of some great lord or politician.   Despite the pressure of members of Parliament, who demanded every scrap of patronage,
those administering the government had, at an earlier date,
been forced by sheer necessity to resort to other than political
methods for securing adequate ability.   Lord Liverpool set the
example in 1820, and his example was followed by Mr. Canning.
" Before that time, all the higher appointments in the customs
service, the collectors and comptrollers of the outposts, were
filled by members (of Parliament) from the posts,   .   .   .
and from certain boroughs which regularly returned government members.   .   .   .   There was a commission of inquiry
into the customs service which reported in that year and made
a strong presentation of the abuses that existed.   .   .   .
Upon the recommendation of this commission, Lord Liverpool
sacrificed all that patronage, and laid down the principle that
all superior officers in the customs should be supplied by promotion from the inferior ranks. . . . Lord Grey, in 1830 . . .
gave up all exercise of patronage, in matters relating to pro-

[1] Civil Service Papers, p. 149.

motion, and it has so continued ever since." [1]  To comprehend
the statesmanship and disinterestedness and the moral tone in
party leaders required for such a change, we must imagine an
American Secretary of the Treasury as abandoning all idea of advancing partisan interests by selecting political managers for the
collectorships or the other high places in the customs service, and
as filling its offices (with the consent of those leaders) by the
promotion of the most worthy subordinates in that service.   If
the relief from lamentable controversy and demoralizing intrigue, which such a change would produce, are indescribable,
we can at least in that way get a better idea of the reform thus
made in England nearly sixty years ago.

During the Melbourne administration, between 1834 and
1841, a demand for examinations, as a condition for admission
to the service, came from two very different quarters.  One
was the higher officials, who declared that they could not do the
public work with such poor servants as the partisan system
supplied. [2]  The other was the more independent, thoughtful
portion of the people, who held it to be as unjust as it was demoralizing for members of Parliament and other officers to
monopolize the privilege of saying who might enter the public
service.   Lord Melbourne then yielded so far as to allow *pass*
examinations to be instituted in some of the larger offices ; and
he was inclined to favor *competitive* examinations, but it was
thought to be too great an innovation to attempt at once.
These examinations—several of them being competitive—introduced by public officers in self-defence many years previous
to 1853, had before that time produced striking results.   In
the Poor Law Commission, for example, they had brought
about a reform that arrested public attention.   Under the
Committee on Education, they had caused the selection of

---

[1] Report on Civil Service, etc., 1860, p. 69.

[2] "It used to be by no means uncommon to have a fine, fashionably
dressed young man introduced as the junior clerk.  On trial he turns out fit
for nothing.  The head of the department knows from old experience that
a representation of this fact to higher quarters would merely draw down ill
will upon himself. . . .  Besides there is the imbecile, who is below
work. . . .  The public offices have been a resource for many an idle,
dissipated youth, with whom other occupations have been tried in vain."
(Civil Service Papers, p. 181.)

11

teachers so much superior " that higher salaries were bidden for them for private service, . . . and they were taken away to a seriously inconvenient extent." In the General Board for Public Works, both superior servants and greater economy had been the result of examinations in so marked a degree that " the local authorities of twenty-five cities and towns . . . have practically abandoned the principle of patronage by requesting the General Board to name an engineer for . . . taking responsible superintendence. In all sixty-nine towns have . . . abandoned the principle of appointment by patronage. . . . The result has been improved local administration, *local party agitation has been checked,* . . . fewer persons are put on the lists to carry appointments or contracts, and the attendance of persons of higher qualifications on the local boards : and business has been better transacted." [1] If I had space for the facts, it could be shown that the reform in municipal administration in Great Britain has hardly been less than in its national affairs ; and that the same methods of improving the character of the official force and of advancing economy have been found equally applicable in both.

Such were the first distinct encroachments made by the Executive upon the partisan system by a partial introduction of the merit system through examinations. These examinations were steadily extended from office to office down to the radical change made in 1853. It is worthy of notice that these examinations—the theory of placing personal merit above politics in selections for office—originated not in Parliament—not by that body showing any willingness to surrender patronage which it had usurped—but in the executive department, where the evils were most felt and the responsibility for good administration rested. The aim and tendency of the examinations were not to aggrandize the Executive, but rather to limit its discretion, by opening the public service in some measure to the whole people. We shall find that, in all stages of the later reforms, the Executive has held this position, and that the people, and not the Crown, have gained influence and

---

[1] Civil Service Papers, pp. 142–150.

opportunity. Parliament did not aid, but was compelled by the people to acquiesce, in this reform.

The higher public opinion had been making rapid progress, and it now overawed Parliament and gave direction to State policy. The leading statesmen were too clear-sighted not to see that the time had come when a great party, which should attempt to confront such an opinion, and to rule through patronage, must go to the wall. A strictly partisan system of administration was no longer practicable. Both parties seem to have reached this condition about the same time. Melbourne, Peel, Russell, Aberdeen, Palmerston, and Derby, the leaders of both parties—who certainly were neither theorists nor *doctrinaires*—and whose administrations together cover the whole period from 1834 to 1868—acted upon this view of the situation. They clearly considered the partisan system as doomed, from the moment it should be found practicable to substitute a better system, and that any party was also doomed that should refuse to make a practical test of examinations as a basis for a better system. This was not because there was little party spirit; on the contrary, party spirit was as vigorous and exacting as it ever has been in this country. For example, Sir Robert Peel (between 1836 and 1841) refused to form a ministry because Queen Victoria would not dismiss certain ladies of her household who had Whig connections. This state of public opinion naturally prevented the question of civil-service reform ever being made a direct issue between the great parties in England; but caused it, as naturally, to be made for a long time an issue in each party between its more unselfish, patriotic elements on one side, and its more partisan and corrupt elements on the other side. "The question of reforming the administration did not so much divide the two parties as it did each party within itself, according to the moral level of its members."[2] Each party claimed—as we have seen opposing parties claim, and with no more sincerity—to be

---

[1] In 1821, such men as Lord Castlereagh, Mr. Huskisson, and Lord Palmerston ridiculed Mr. Joseph Hume for firmly supporting reform : but thirty years later Mr. Hume was still in Parliament, and was regarded " with unfeigned and cordial respect by leading members of all sorts of politics." (Miss Martineau's Biographical Sketches, p. 305.)

[2] Civil Service Report, 1860.

the special friend of reform, and appealed to the people for
support on that basis. There can be nothing original in this
country in that line of policy. The state of public opinion in
England at that time, upon the subject of admissions to the
public service, was similar to what is with us now, though
somewhat more advanced. Neither party dared defy the reform sentiment, and both, while courting it, were too ready to
depart from its principles. From the time that the beneficial
results of examinations had become known to the people, it
was seen to be impossible ever to suppress them, unless upon
the substitution of examinations of a better kind. Before
1853, at which time they had been in practice for about twenty
years, they had done much to improve the public service,
though they were very defective, and had been applied in only
part of the offices.

These examinations attracted attention in this country, and
they led to the enactment of the law of 1853,[1] which divided
our clerks in the Treasury, War, Navy, Interior, and Post
Office departments into four classes, and provided that " no
clerk shall be appointed . . . until after he has been examined and found qualified by a board to consist of three examiners." In 1855,[2] similar provisions were extended to the
State Department.[3]

The great difference in the action of the two countries, at
that time so nearly in harmony, has been that we fell away
from the policy on which the laws of 1853 and 1855 are based,
while England has continued to advance steadily in the same
direction, and thereby has more and more elevated her civil
service. But the continuing encroachment upon the partisan
system which such examinations threatened were not to be
allowed without a struggle. It was clearly seen that they
were democratic in tendency, and that they challenged, not
merely the partisan monopoly of the members of the House, but
the vested interests and the prestige of the aristocracy as well.

---

[1] Ch. 97, § 3.                        [2] Laws 1855, chap. 175, § 4.

[3] In some sort of fashion, pass examinations have been since made under
these laws, except during the time the civil service rules were enforced
pursuant to the statute of 3d March, 1871 (now Revised Statutes, § 1753),
under which President Grant, through the Civil Service Commission, provided for uniform competitive examinations.

Pointing out the tendency of the new method, one writer says it will increase " until at last the aristocracy will be altogether dissociated from the permanent civil service of the country." . . . Another says, " The encouragement given to education would no doubt be great, . . . but it will be all in favor of the lower classes of society and not of the higher." Another says, . . . " The principal objection which I have heard . . . is, that appointments now conferred on young men of aristocratic connexion will fall into the hands of persons in a much lower grade in society." [1]

The strength of a custom of a hundred and fifty years, in a conservative old country like England, in favor of any system, thus united with the interests of the privileged classes in its preservation, were indeed a formidable power. Those who stood for patronage and those who stood for class distinctions naturally joined hands to break down these examinations, and to change the public judgment which sustained them. Their sarcasms, their ridicule, and their cunning policy (of which I shall give examples), as they stand recorded, leave little chance for doing or saying anything original by those who oppose reform in this country. The friends of reform met those attacks not only by argument, but by demanding open competitive examinations, common for all the departments and free to all the people, and the *merit system* [2] of appointments and promotions. They also insisted that it was an injustice, a usurpation, and a source of manifold evils for members of Parliament and other high officers to hold a monopoly of patronage, so that none could go into the public service without their consent. Before proceeding further, it will be

[1] Civil Service Papers, pp. 44 and 289.

[2] By the *merit system* I mean that theory of government (and the proper method of examinations and promotions through which it is applied, and the proper regulations for attaining economy and efficiency) which treats personal qualifications, rather than the political opinions or the partisan services of applicants for office, as the true and paramount basis for appointments; which regards office, including the appointing power, as a public trust and not as an official perquisite or a partisan agency for propagating political opinions or keeping a party in power. From the despotic system, under the Norman kings, through various spoils systems under arbitrary kings—through a sort of partisan system under Cromwell—through fearful corruption under James and Charles—through a sort of aristocratic spoils

useful to give some particulars concerning these examinations, as they will not only render more clear what is to follow, but have a direct bearing upon difficulties in our civil service.

*Kinds of examinations.* There are three distinct kinds of examinations : the pass examination, the limited competitive examination, and the open competitive examination. The two last are in England usually designated as "limited competition" and "open competition." These examinations are very different in principle, and in their adequacy to bring about the best results. I shall not now enter upon the question of their utility. It was never any part of the theory upon which either is based, that it should extend to judges, to any legislative, or other officer elected by the people, or to any member of the Cabinet, or to foreign ministers (as such), or to any high officer of the executive department (in England there being not exceeding fifty excluded officers, besides those elected) who can properly be regarded as the representative of the principles or policy of the party in power. Officers who are properly regarded as political must, of course, be selected in reference to their political opinions and ideas of policy, and it is they who are clothed with authority, to compel the subordinate members of the civil service (from collectors and postmasters to doorkeepers, to whom the examinations apply) to obey all proper instructions. They thus carry out the great policy, foreign and domestic, which the popular majority has approved. Obedience to them and to the laws is the duty of all their subordinates. It is because these subordinates have no more legal right or ability to carry into practice their political opinions, than they have to carry out their personal theories (contrary to the instructions of their superiors), that such opinions should not control in their selection.

Examination may be made through examiners named and acting separately in each department office ; or there may be one

system under William and Anne—through a partisan spoils system under George I. and II. and a part of the reign of George III.—through the partisan system in its best estate in later years—we have traced the unsteady but generally ascending progress of British administration ; and, in 1870, we shall find it to have reached a level at which office is treated as a trust and personal merit is the recognized criterion for selection for office. That was the inauguration of the merit system.

examining board for all departments. Uniformity of requirement for admission to the service could hardly be brought about by independent examiners. The mutual jealousy of departments and examiners, and disparity in practice, would be sure to be damaging to such a method. It is otherwise inherently weak. No examiner would represent the power or policy of the Executive, but only that of a particular secretary or the head of a bureau. And further ; each examiner, so separately appointed, being exposed to the whole pressure of all those who wish to force unworthy persons upon the service, and not being directly supported by the Executive, has no such power of resistance as is possessed by a central board of examiners, directly appointed by the Executive, which acts uniformly in his name in every department and office.[1]

It hardly need be added that partisans and patronage-holders favored these isolated examinations and learned how to make their influence most effective with detached examiners. It was natural too for secretaries to favor great party leaders by making their special examinations vary to suit them. It has been found, after great experience in England, that it was highly important that all examinations of whatever kind should be conducted by one central examining board backed by the whole power of the government. Nor is any other method one of common justice to all those in the public service.

1. *The pass examination* is one under which each person allowed to present himself is separately examined as to whether he comes up to some prescribed standards. He is put in comparison with nobody. No one need be or is usually present with him except the examiner, and very likely the patron by whom he has been presented. In the case of a nominee of a member of Parliament who wishes to get in with inadequate qualification, it is easy to see that it would not be one of the members only, but many having similar interests, who would join to push him past the examiner. If the nominee was the favorite of a minister, a bishop, or a great nobleman, or a partisan clique, and not utterly a knave or a dunce, the

---

[1] " I agree with you in thinking that the examination cannot be conducted in an efficient manner throughout the service if it is left to each department to examine the candidates. " (Civil Service Papers, p. 132.)

pressure would be still more nearly irresistible. If the qualifications presented came nearly up to the prescribed standard,
it is easy to see how solicitation and threats would cause their
acceptance by an isolated examiner, perhaps in peril of his
place. The standard once thus depressed, the next effort
would be to go in at a still lower level ; and hence a tendency
to constant depression. Still, with all its inherent tendency
to feebleness, even this method of examination raised the civil
service of England. Mr. Mill said that, at their worst, pass
examinations only kept dunces out, but as many dunces were
presented, even that effect was no small blessing. It was impossible to preserve the standard. " It became so much a
matter of form that we used to have an examination paper
which was generally known about the office. When a young
man came into the office, he had to pass the examination by a
superior clerk, who perhaps was the friend of his father or
his uncle. There was a feeling that it was not right to reject.
It was a leaping-bar-test, and if the clerk did not come up to the
bar, it was somewhat lowered." [1]  " These unknown men of
talent witness daily their inferiors advancing before them, who
may have been put into the service through interest, and who
probably passed what is termed an examination, but such as a
charity boy would smile at." [2]  Another defect of pass examinations was that they allowed the party managers and the
holders of patronage to designate all the persons to be examined ; so that it was no check upon the parliamentary and
partisan monopoly of nomination, but only a limitation upon
the incapacity which they could foist upon the public service.
It gave the people, outside official favoritism, no opportunities.
It is plain, therefore, that the most inefficient and objectionable
of all methods of examinations, and hence those most acceptable to spoilsmen, are pass examinations, conducted by separate
examiners, named by and acting for each department or office
separately. And only such examinations were made in this
country before 1872, and, with very limited exceptions, only
such were made in England before 1854. They showed the
same defects with us that they did in Great Britain.

[1] Report Civil Service, etc., 1860, p. 221.
[2] Civil Service Papers, p. 53.

2. *Limited competitive examinations* are those in which a certain number of selected persons are examined in competition with each other, with a view to give appointments only to those who show the highest qualifications. The selections for examinations were of course made by those having patronage or controlling influence. This kind of examination was therefore entirely consistent with the claim made by members of Parliament to designate those outside of whom the executive department should not go in making its appointments. It was also no less compatible with the partisan theory that none but those who adopt the party creed shall go into the public service. It allows the partisan toll gate to stand, where all who enter must accept the creed and swear allegiance. But going through that gate does not bring one into the service, but only into competition with all the others who have passed it. Nevertheless, it was found to be a great improvement upon mere *pass* examinations : for, unless the competition was, by reason of the vicious and exclusive mode of selections for it, confined (as, in fact, it occasionally was) to a dead level of dunces and imbeciles, superannuated coachmen, valets, and stewards, sickly sons and shiftless cousins, the competition would infallibly throw down the good-for-nothings, and give the appointments to those who were most competent.

3. *Open competitive examinations* are founded on broad principles of justice, liberty, and equality. The meaning attached to their being "open" is, that every citizen is permitted upon the same conditions to join in the competition, and that the right of no one to be examined is dependent either on any official or any party. Each is to come publicly and fairly to the examination with the others who present themselves ; and those who show the highest measure of the qualifications which the government requires in its service, as laid down in fixed regulations, will win the chances of going into that service. All that fall below a fixed standard are excluded by their incompetency thus demonstrated. In their very nature, competitive examinations affirm these principles : (1) That every citizen—whether high-born or low-born, whether with great influence or wealth or without any influence or wealth—stands on an equality before the laws and in the right to enjoy an

open and manly contest with his fellows for the honor of entering the service of his country ; (2) That the government needs
in its service, and seeks most to honor and reward, those who
represent capacity and worth, and not those who represent
partisan or official influence, political opinions, or intrigue ;
(3) That the right and propriety of members of Parliament or
any other high officers taking to themselves the monopoly and
the profit of opening and shutting, at their pleasure, the gates
of the public service—to all those who do not accept their politics and pay court and swear fealty to them—is utterly denied
and intended to be made impossible in practice ; and (4) That
the affairs of the nation being the greatest of all human affairs,
and its interest to have the people educated and of good character being a paramount interest, therefore a just test of relative character, attainments, and capacity is enforced in the
common cause of good morals, good government, and general
education.  It is clear that open, competitive examinations
must be everywhere destructive of a monopoly of the right of
saying who may be examined.  The poorest and humblest
may apply without the consent of any officer or any politician.
No member of Parliament, or other official, when they apply,
could look over his constituents and say, " This relative of
mine, these old worn-out servants of mine, those who elec-
tioneered for me at the last election, those who will promise
to work for me at the next election or for my schemes of
profit—and those alone—may be examined.  You are not
among them."  The introduction of open competition is the
death sentence of the last phase of official feudalism.

All members of Parliament, who cared more for patronage
than for good government, were as hostile to open competition
as that is fatal to their patronage.  It was of course opposed
by corrupt party managers.  It is one of the salutary conditions of open competition that it has that publicity under
which fraud or favoritism is hardly possible.  Every one who
competes is interested in the marks and in the character of
every other who competes.  He looks to see that others are
not marked more liberally than himself.  He makes inquiries
whether his fellow-competitors are persons of good character.
The competitions arrest public interest and curiosity, and are

reported in the public press. The young man or woman, with a vulnerable reputation, must be very bold indeed, who would dare offer himself or herself in such a contest. Any one below may strike a person of frail repute from the list above, and thus advance his own chances by exposing the bad character of his competitors. The value of the places to be won are in the nature of prices to the worthy for their worth, and they are hardly less prices offered for the exposure of the bad character of any scoundrel who may have the impudence to join in the competition. Such competition tends continually to raise its own standard ; for in every contest the best are preferred, no matter how high it rises. The victor wins by a test which commands his own self-respect as it does the respect of his competitors, of the community which watches the contest, and of the government which gives the prize to merit.

" The simple nomination system gives to the candidate expectations on which he relies, . . . so that if he is neglected on the *pass* examination, he is discredited and disappointed. The disappointment is shared by his friends and his patron, and leads to dissatisfaction with the examining authorities and with the system generally ; whilst under the system of open competition, each candidate is well aware that he has only a chance of success, and that if he fails the failure may be ascribed to the merits of others and not to defects on his own part." [1]

The method of reaching the public service through open competition would seem to be republican in spirit, because based on common justice and absolute equality before the laws. The child of a chimney sweep or the orphan from a ragged school, if worthy, may, under this method—in the most aristocratic nation of the world—without the consent of any officer or politician whatever—go and win a place in the service of his country over the favorite of a cabinet or the son of a duke. The examination papers of each, with their marks and gradings of relative merit in the competition, are preserved ; and years hence, as well as at the moment, the justice of the decision can be verified. The same Civil Service Commission applies the same rules of competition and the same tests of

[1] Report on Civil Service, 1870. p. 300.

merit in every department and in the several localities where examinations are held. Thus the government, everywhere the same in its system, and everywhere through a process untouched by any suspicions that influence and favoritism have prevailed, gains the most worthy and the most capable of those who wish to enter its service. I have not intended in this outline to state everything that is material to be known about open competition; but only to set forth its principle and so much of the method as is essential to an understanding of the final struggle in which it won the victory over Parliamentary patronage and official favoritism. If I have implied an opinion of its merits, before presenting the evidence, I can only say now that such evidence will not be wanting.

*Probation.* But it should be added that it has been at all times a part of the competitive system that those who won in competition should serve at least six months on moderate pay, under probation, during which their ability and fidelity in business affairs could be tested before they receive any actual appointment. Probation had also been, in form, applied under pass and limited examinations, though when influence pushed a man into and through the examination, it generally pushed him beyond probation as well. But it was easy to apply the probative test effectually against the competitor who came alone and had no influence to back him. The fact that it will be applied generally keeps away those young men who know, or whose friends know, they have no practical qualities for business.

# CHAPTER XIV.

The principles involved.—Arguments for and against Parliamentary patronage.—Is a partisan system essential to party government?—The evils that
result from nominations in the hands of members of Parliament.

THE decisive part of the contest between patronage and
open competition was between 1845 and 1855, though the
victors did not take possession of the whole field until
1870. No two systems could be more antagonistic in principle than one based on open competition and one based on
patronage, favoritism, and spoils. The difference was one
which involved the nature of office, the duties of public servants, the theory of party government, the authority and functions of Parliament, the common rights of the people to hold
office, and the relative claims of character and capacity as
compared with those of partisanship and subservience upon
the respect and honors of a great nation. Are offices public
trusts for the common good, or are they partisan outposts for
the special benefit of those who can capture them? Were
officers in the subordinate service to be first of all electioneering agents and obedient representatives of high officials, or
were they to be the common servants and guardians of the
community? Should parties seek their strength in sound
principles and a wise policy, carried into effect in a pure, vig
orous, and economical administration, or should they seek it in
the adroit use of patronage and the skilful manipulation of
elections? Ought members of Parliament to confine themselves to a courageous and thorough scrutiny of the acts of the
Executive, and to preserve that independence of patronage
which would enable them to do so, or was it better that they
should grasp and use all the patronage possible, each being in

the line of his duty alike, while searching through the offices
for as much as he can gather, and while using it to suit his
official caprice or to discharge his election pledges? Did or
did not an election to Parliament, as matter of law or of principle, confer the right to a fractional part of all the appointments in Great Britain, as personal perquisite, or partisan
spoils? Were her people for ever to allow all chances of entering the public service to depend upon the will of a member
of Parliament and a few high officials, or, in the name of common justice and equality, should it be demanded that free and
open access to office should be opened to the most worthy?
Should education and character be encouraged by conferring
office upon merit, or should partisan tyranny and political intrigue be encouraged by bestowing it as the reward of influence and servility? These were the issues involved in the
struggle. There was nothing in the form or the history of
the government to make such a struggle less severe than it
would be with us; but quite the contrary. Members of Parliament loved executive power and knew how to use specious
arguments to defend its usurpation. There was no purer era
of public administration in the country, before that authority
was usurped, to which reference could be made as a reason for
its surrender. If it must be conceded that the power of selection, in the hands of members, was a clear usurpation of executive authority, it could not be denied that it was acquired
at the time when Parliament began to stand more bravely for
liberty and common rights.

During the one hundred and fifty years in which that patronage had increased, and party government in England had
acquired its solid frame, it could not be denied that liberty,
education and political power had vastly increased among the,
people. In no country is usage so formidable or so generally
accepted as evidence of right as in England. By far the
greater part of the aristocratic influence of the country was
against an innovation so democratic in spirit and so hostile to that
regard for wealth and conservativism which are the strength
of an aristocracy. All available arguments were used for and
against Parliamentary patronage, and a slight outline of them
may be useful :

1. To the argument that England had prospered under favoritism, it was replied that she had also prospered while sharing the slave trade, neglecting to educate her people, and denying them the right to vote ; but that since she had emancipated her slaves, widened her suffrage, and founded a better system of education, she had prospered all the more. As the body of her people had become more intelligent, and class divisions and aristocratic privileges had decayed. the protest against official patronage and favoritism had gained strength.

2. To the argument that the old-fashioned patronage system was necessary to the stability and good effects of parties, it was replied that they had never been more vital, vigorous, or honest than in that period during which examinations had been encroaching upon patronage. On an average, under the partisan spoils system, a party had not been able to keep an administration in power more than three and one half years ; and in 1834-5. it failed to keep Sir Robert Peel in power even one year. For every person or faction that was conciliated by an appointment, there were many offended who had sought the same appointment. It was very likely that changes of administration would be less frequent if there were no appointments whatever to be made. If appointments, on the other hand, were increased a hundredfold, was it not clear that party struggles would be more bitter and politics far more corrupt ? Patronage and spoils were as disastrous to the moral tone and discipline of a party as the right of sack and pillage had been to armies and fleets. The theory that a party can be kept together only by the hope and reality of spoils, is in fact but the survivorship, in a milder form, of the once universal theory that an army could only be raised and kept in efficiency by the prospects of pillage. "When the measures were first proposed for the abolition of patronage, . . . the old political officers treated it with the like incredulity that the old Mahratta chieftains treated the notion of European armies in India being moved or maintained in the field without regular plunder." [1] This theory is wholly false alike. in war and peace, in politics and in military service. The more largely a party relies upon patronage and spoils, and the less

[1] Civil Service Papers, p. 144.

it appeals to the public, on the basis of principle and good administration, the more certain that party is to suffer defeat. The simple fact that year by year the popular protest against favoritism and the demand for open competition had increased, despite all the efforts of party leaders to arrest it, was conclusive of the intrinsic weakness and failure of the partisan system. As the result of his broad survey of British politics, Mr. Hallam declares, " There is no real cause to apprehend that a virtuous and enlightened government would find difficulty in resting upon the reputation justly due to it."[1]

3. It was asserted that members of Parliament lived among the people, knew the local needs of the public service, and many persons well qualified to supply them. Members, like other officers, were patriotic, and were to be trusted to look to the general welfare. To a certain extent, this argument was admitted to be well founded. The best evidence, however, of the controlling aim of members in holding on to patronage, was the use they had made of it and the effects of their action upon the administration. That use was being year by year more and more emphatically condemned by the people. It was notorious that dependents and electioneering agents of members abounded in the public service. Salaries and supernumeraries were not reduced, merely because such legislation would be damaging to the favorites of members. Persons not connected with the executive department were not good judges of its needs, or of those most fit to serve it. Members of Parliament were so dependent upon votes at elections as to be in the worst possible situation for forming an impartial judgment. If it was worthy, competent persons that members knew in their localities, and whom they wished to get into the public service, why do such persons fear the test of open competition? However disinterested the motives of many members, the system of patronage subjected them to dangerous temptations, and was far too seductive for the patriotism of not a few. They knew best and thought best of those who worked most for them in their political contests. They could not, without the greatest self-denial, refuse to promise nominations to their henchmen. The scandalous suggestion at-

[1] Const. Hist., vol. ii., p. 782.

tached to the very name of patronage, and the avowed purpose of so many of the noblest men in Parliament to be rid of
its exacting and humiliating demands, left no room for doubt
on these points. It is as indefensible in principle for members
to select executive officers as it would be for the Executive to
select subjects upon which Parliament should legislate, or
names for the committees it should appoint. What would be
said if the Executive should claim a right to nominate the officers of either House of Parliament ?

The duty of a member of Parliament is, in its very nature,
such as to require him to have a constant and supreme regard
to the effects of the old laws, and to the need of new laws, in
their relation to the common welfare of the people. And this
duty is inconsistent with his use of an appointing power (without executive responsibility) through which he becomes interested in keeping certain persons in office, in bringing other
persons into office.[1] Under the present state of things, bills
are supported or opposed in reference to their probable effect
upon the patronage of members.[2]

It is inconsistent with that independence, dignity, and disinterestedness which the people require in a legislator, as well
as a bad use of valuable time and talents, for a member of
Parliament to act as an office or patronage broker, and to go
about from department to department and office to office,
begging or bullying, to-day this, and to-morrow that officer,
in order to make a place for perhaps a needy dependent, or
perhaps an unscrupulous and unrewarded supporter at an
election.

" Considering the pressure that is put on the treasury by
men having powerful Parliamentary interest, and that which
is put on the heads of departments, both by Parliamentary interest and by the claims of private friendship (and the object

---

[1] As to the vicious effects of Parliamentary patronage, see chap. xii.

[2] How interest in office may influence the conduct of a legislator and may
cause even a great and pure man to make, perhaps unconsciously, a damaging record against himself, is shown in the letters of Macaulay while a
member of Parliament. " There were points in the bill of which I did not
approve, and I only refrained from stating these points because *an office of
my own was at stake.*" (Life and Letters of Macaulay, by Trevelyan, vol.
i., p. 165.)

12

of the persons possessing this influence is generally to palm off on the public service such of their sons or nephews as are fit for nothing else), it is impossible to estimate too highly the importance of a preliminary examination, conducted by an independent and competent Board of Examiners." [1]

The fact that a member has such a power tempts him to promise places for votes, subjects him to suspicions, and brings upon him solicitations in a thousand ways as pernicious as they are troublesome. They degrade the morals of official life, at the same time that they dissuade the best men from standing for Parliament. Members of Parliament were worn out with the annoyance patronage gave them. [2] The possession of patronage by members introduces a corrupt element, and especially the damaging belief that there must be corruption, in elections, because the ability of a member to control places under the government causes the more active and unscrupulous managers of local politics to give their support to the candidate who will promise most places and is likely to work most persistently to obtain them. Thereby the chances of the most partisan and unscrupulous candidate are increased, and the better sort are disgusted and discouraged.

5. Patronage in members also tends to bring the public service into disrepute, and to convert public officers into active politicians. For no officer can have great self-respect, or much respect for his fellows, when he gets his office, and they theirs, through official favor, if not through demoralizing subserviency; nor are the public likely to have a better opinion of the public service than its members have of themselves. A mistaken duty of gratitude is held to require that one who is receiving a salary obtained for him by a member of Parliament should serve that member whenever the opportunity presents. Thus a great portion of the public service is brought into subserviency to members of Parliament.

6. And looking beyond any particulars that can be specified, it is plainly discreditable to a great and free country, and unbecoming the exalted position of those who make its laws

[1] Civil Service Papers, p. 132.

[2] " As I know from experience that it would relieve members of Parliament and official men from a most disagreeable portion of their labors." (Civil Service Papers, p. 231.)

and interpret its constitution, that they should desire to possess an authority to barter and bargain in nominations, or should be willing to use their official influence to enforce a partisan test upon the conscience and manhood of the nation. A member of Parliament should scorn a system which thus inevitably degrades his high office, subjects him to suspicion, and demoralizes the politics of his country. The final decision on these issues was early foreshadowed. For some years before 1853, it seems to have been tacitly conceded by the leaders of both parties that Parliamentary patronage, if not the whole partisan system, must be very soon abandoned. The great question was, What should be put in its place? It was not regarded as a mere question of administrative details or as having its greater interest in its probable effects upon a general election, but as a vital issue of principle and national policy, of which the influence would be felt to the very foundation of government and of social order. The eminent men consulted by the administration—whether hostile or friendly to a competitive system—equally recognized its grave importance, and its sure encouragement of education and of liberty. " Why add yet another to the many recent sacrifices of the royal prerogative? . . . I . . . call your attention to the almost incalculable magnitude of the political changes which the proposed abdication of all the patronage of the Crown in the public offices must invoke. . . . The proposal to select candidates for the civil service of government by a competitive examination appears to me to be one of those great public improvements, the adoption of which would form an era in history. . . . It still seems to me that the ultimate result of open competition will be a *democratic civil service*, side by side with an aristocratic legislature. Open competition must necessarily be in favor of the more numerous class. The natural ability of that more numerous class—*i.e.*, of the lower or less rich class—is not inferior to those of the higher or richer class." [1]

Such were the divergent views expressed. Neither party dared defend the old system any longer, or maintain that nothing better was possible. Lords Derby and Aberdeen, the min-

[1] Civil Service Papers, pp. 79, 80, 92, and 288.

isters and party leaders of the period, were not theorists, but
practical statesmen of great experience. Both appear to have
reached the conclusion that a reform must be undertaken. It
fell to Lord Aberdeen's administration to begin it. But before considering the measures for introducing open competition
into the civil service at home, it will be useful to refer to what
was done, in the same direction and about the same time, to
improve the administration of British India.

# CHAPTER XV.

Patronage a failure there.—Pass examinations and a college course found inadequate.—The public service in a threatening condition.—Open competition provided for in 1853.—Report of Mr. Macaulay and Lord Ashburton.—Nature of the competition.

ATTENTION has already been called to several statutes of the reign of George III., which showed that, thus early, careful study had been made into the conditions of good administration for India, and that official corruption was even then more stringently dealt with than it has yet been in analogous cases in this country. It would be easy, but it can hardly be useful, to refer to later statutes, framed in the same spirit, under which several experiments were made, in the hope of increasing the purity and vigor of the civil service of India. It is enough to say that patronage, in the hands of the Board of Directors having control of its administration, was found to be as intolerable as such patronage was at home in the hands of members of Parliament. For this reason, it had been provided, long before 1853, that those designed for the civil service of India should not only be subjected to a pass examination, but should, before entering the service, be subjected to a course of special instruction at Haileybury College, a sort of civil West Point. This college was abolished in 1854, but equivalent instruction was elsewhere provided for. The directors had the patronage of nomination for such instruction, much as our members of Congress have (or rather take) the patronage of nomination for our military school. If it seems strange that a severe course of study, for two years in such a college, was not sufficient to weed out the incompetents which patronage forced into it, we must bear in mind that the same influence which sent them there was used to keep them there, and that it has required a high standard of proficiency and the sternness of military discipline, which force out a very great portion of those who enter, to prevent incompetent favorites from graduating at West Point.    The ablest administrators England could supply had been sent to India for the purpose of raising its civil administration to a condition compatible with the public safety.    Every promising method, consistent with such patronage, or short of a radical change of system, had been tried.    The evils which the India administration disclosed grew not so much out of mere partisan zeal and recklessness as out of the general demoralization sure to result from every system which allows an appointing power, without executive responsibility, as a mere appendage to a public office, or permits that power to be exercised with no enforced regard to the worth and capacity of those nominated.    Both the Derby and the Aberdeen administrations, in 1852 and 1853, took notice that the civil service was in a condition of peril to British India ; and, without distinction of party, it was agreed that radical reforms must be promptly made.    There was corruption, there was inefficiency, there was disgraceful ignorance, there was a humiliating failure in the government to command the respect of the more intelligent portion of the people of India, and there was a still more alarming failure to overawe the unruly classes.    It was as bad in the army as in the civil offices.   " In the years 1851 to 1854, both inclusive, 437 gentlemen were examined for direct commissions in the Indian army ; of this number 132 failed in English, and 234 in arithmetic.    The return requires no comment."[1]    There was, in short, a hotbed of abuses prolific of those influences which caused the fearful outbreak of 1857.    It was too late, when reform was decided upon, to prevent the outbreak, but not too late to save British supremacy in India.

A change of system was entered upon in 1853.    The 36th and 37th clauses of the India act of that year provided " that all powers, rights, and privileges of the court of directors of the said India Company to nominate or appoint persons to be

---

[1] Civil Service Papers, pp. 376, 377.

admitted as students . . . shall cease ; and that, subject to such regulations as might be made, *any person, being a natural born subject of her Majesty*, who might be desirous of presenting himself, should be admitted to be examined as a candidate." [1]

Thus, it will be seen, Indian patronage received its death-blow, and the same blow opened the door of study for the civil service of India to every British citizen ; allowing him to come and prove himself, if he could, to be the better man to serve his country, without having to ask the consent of any director, minister, member of Parliament, caucus, or party manager whatever. It was the clearing of the way for the introduction of the merit system, pure and simple, into civil administration in the home government. It was the first example of the kind—the first time that a nation had declared in its statutes that its officers should not have either a patronage, a privilege, a profit, or a monopoly, in the authority of saying, irrespective of merit,[2] which of its citizens shall be allowed to present his claims for a place in its service. It was the intent of the statute that open competition should take the place made vacant by the death of patronage. Mr. Macaulay, as is well known, had held office in India ; and he and Lord Ashburton were the leading men on the committee which the administration selected to draw up the regulations to which the statute referred. Their report was made in 1854, and provided for open competition, in which the best qualified would win the right of admission to the proper college, where two years of special study would complete their preparation for entering the civil service of India. The report was approved, and thereupon the merit system, based on open competition, was for the first time put into actual practice on a large scale. It was a bold and radical experiment full of peril ; and it may be said to have been, like our government, founded almost upon theory alone, since it was the first of its kind ever adopted by a nation. The rules for the competition provided for extended to such subjects as were deemed important to be understood by those engaged in the Indian ser-

[1] Report on India Civil Service, London, 1876, p. 13.
[2] Except the law of Richard II.

vice. In order to determine the relative standing of each competitor, he was to be marked in each subject, and the average of his aggregate marks, in all the subjects, would determine how he stood as compared with the others in the competition. There is no doubt that aristocratic influence was used to set up a standard most favorable to the classes from which that influence came ; but the authors declare in their report that they have adopted a standard which is not calculated to favor any class, school, or other institution of learning. When we consider the vast population and revenue of India, and how vitally the honor and credit of Great Britain are involved in her fate, we can more readily comprehend the magnitude of this experiment and the gravity of the abuses that must have forced a proud and practical nation to enter upon it. For to it were committed, not the hopes of a party merely, but the safety of an empire. At the proper time, the results of this unique experiment will be presented.

# CHAPTER XVI.

In 1853, the British Government had reached a final decision
that the partisan system of appointments could not be longer
tolerated. Substantial control of nominations by members
of Parliament, however guarded by restrictions and improved
by mere pass examinations, had continued to be demoralizing
in its effect upon elections, vicious in its influence upon legislation, and fatal to economy and efficiency in the departments.
The higher public opinion demanded the extension of those
better modes of examination for admission to the public service, which, in their limited use, had been so manifestly beneficial. Those responsible for good administration had a deep
sense of the need of relief from that pervading solicitation and
intrigue which everywhere stood in the way of the fit discharge of their official duties. It is plain, from what has
already been said, that the abuses from which relief was to be
sought were by no means of that gross and alarming kind which
had existed in earlier times. The laws and the policy, to which
I have referred, had greatly advanced the work of reform.
But public opinion, in the same spirit, had made not less advance ; and it now insisted on a standard of efficiency and
purity in official life which only the most advanced reformers had, half a century before, thought to be practicable in public affairs. Both the importance which govern-

ment accorded to administrative methods and the sound principles embodied in the statutes, I have cited had, doubtless, contributed to elevate the public standard of official duty. A brief outline will enable us to compare that standard and the character of administration in Great Britain in 1853 with our own at this time.

1. Neither political assessments nor any other form of extortion, by the higher officers from the lower, or by partisan leaders from any grade of officials or government employés, existed.

2. Officers were not removed for the purpose of making places for others ; and, so long as official duty was properly performed, no one was proscribed by reason of his political opinions.

3. In the great departments of customs and internal revenue (and in a large way, as a general rule, in other departments also), the higher places were filled by promotions from the lower ; and therefore such contests as we have over these higher places were unknown.

4. As a general rule, to which the exceptions were rare, those in office held their places during efficiency and good behavior (always excepting the members of the Cabinet and the few high political officers to which I have before referred), and therefore nothing analogous to the fear of removal and the vicious, partisan activity of officials in connection with elections (which that fear produces under our system) was known in Great Britain.

5. The law of Queen Anne (already cited), which prohibits post office officials trying to influence elections, and the laws of George III., which prevented them and nearly all others in the civil service from voting, were still in force, and they effectually protected the freedom of elections from invasion by executive officers. But they were not adequate to prevent members of Parliament and other high officers from giving places to those who had worked for them in the canvass. The grosser forms of bargaining, however, these laws had suppressed.

6. Members of Parliament monopolized patronage, but they must recommend their favorites through the *Patronage Sec-*

*retary* of the Treasury ; and to that officer the heads of departments and offices must apply for clerks. " The names are sent by the Secretary of the Treasury, who, in selecting them, is mainly influenced by political considerations. They are persons of whom he can scarcely ever have any personal knowledge, and who are recommended to him by the political supporters of the government." [1] The Secretary parcelled out places and salaries with as much exactness as a prize master ever apportioned the proceeds of a capture. Secret bargaining and intrigue was greatly limited by this open way of making merchandise of public functions. The reduction of favoritism and nepotism to a system was also a most salutary check upon the old habits of members of Parliament going whining and palavering, or bullying and blustering (according to their temper, or that of the official whose ante-room they besieged), from department to department, and from office to office, seeking places for their favorites.

7. There were pass examinations quite as effective (to say the least) as any we have applied, between nominations and admissions ; and, very generally, a six-months probation followed before an actual appointment was made. In addition, competitive examinations were being enforced (in mere self-protection) by the heads of some of the offices ; and, altogether, these safeguards were no inconsiderable check upon the selfishness and wantonness of official favoritism.

8. What might be called a spoils system (in the more corrupt sense of the term) had ceased to exist. Personal corruption in office had, for a considerable period, been of very rare occurrence. The public service, as a whole, was regarded as needlessly costly and inefficient ; but public opinion did not distrust official honesty, however much it might suspect politica partiality and prejudice. In public, as in private life, there were of course criminals, but on moral grounds the public service, as a whole, was respectable.

9. A strictly partisan system of appointments (and to some extent of promotions) prevailed. The right of nomination was treated as an official perquisite. Political opinions were recognized as paramount qualifications for office. Govern-

---

[1] Letter Sir George Cornwall Lewes, July 20th, 1854, Civil Service Papers, p. 108.

ment stood before the people as a grand agency (or, in the
language of our politics, as " a machine") that might be used
to keep in the offices those who at any time held them, and to
perpetuate the rule of the dominant party. The system
afforded the means of rewarding those intriguers and manipulators who supply the corrupt elements of elections, and beset
and seduce every officer having patronage. The gates of the
public service, being opened by influence rather than by
merit, those within naturally held a low place in public esteem,
and generally deserved nothing more. In all the elections,
which were as vigorously contested as they are in our politics,
the corrupting elements of patronage and partisan coercion
were present and exhaled an atmosphere of suspicion over
every issue of principle and of character. If the facts that
there were no removals and but few promotions, except for
cause, made this vicious element far weaker than in our politics, it was yet an ever-active source of debasement and distrust. In short, the bestowal of office was made upon the
theory of official and partisan favoritism, rather than upon
that of duty, justice, or the public interests, as the supreme
ends of government. So long as that theory prevailed, government and those who served it could never hold their just
place in the honor and respect of the people.

10. Stated in general terms, the great and primary source
of the evils in the British civil service, in 1853, was executive
patronage in the hands of members of Parliament, and the
obstruction it naturally caused in the way of bringing in and
promoting merit and of carrying on the administration
economically and efficiently. Questions upon the enactment
of laws were continually complicated by questions of Parliamentary patronage. Members were indisposed to cut down
salaries, or reduce numbers, or abolish offices, or repeal laws,
when their own favorites might be those prejudiced by the
change. The men it was for their interest to foist upon the
service were not unfrequently persons very unfit to discharge
its duties.[1] There were many more persons whom members
wished to oblige than there were vacant places in the Treasury.

Such were the evils which the British Government set

[1] See ante, p. 147 to 149.

about removing in 1853. How they compare with those in our service is too obvious for remark. In one particular—that of patronage in the hands of members of the legislature—the analogy is very close, though in consequence of our short terms for so many officers and of our making promotions and removals for political reasons, that evil in our service is vastly greater. Should it be suggested that, if our service were in the condition of that of Great Britain in 1853, there would be slight fault found with it, the fact would be only further evidence of an exacting public opinion there, which is due to the greater attention which statesmen have for a long time given to the subject of good administration.

Ingenious attempts had been made, especially since 1832, to remove the evils of the partisan system, and to make it satisfactory to the higher public opinion. In several ways, the abuses of the system had been curtailed. The more it was restricted, the purer and more vigorous party government had become. The results of all experience pointed to yet more salutary effects, as sure to result from an utter severance of party government itself from a mere partisan system of appointments. The last twenty years had been, beyond any in English history, distinguished by liberal measures ; and the time was fortunate in enlightened statesmen—Grey, Aberdeen, Peel, Russell, Cobden, Granville, Derby, Palmerston, Bright, Gladstone among them—whose names recall the great triumphs of justice, liberty, education, humanity, and national vigor with which they will stand forever associated. Fortunately, these men had no faith in a partisan system, nor was there one of them, whichever side he took in politics, who was willing to apologize for that system, or failed to see that it was hostile alike to the true life of a party and to the highest interests of a nation. It was at this period that those enlightened health laws were enacted, and that vigorous sanitary administration began, which have been an inestimable blessing to the British people—and especially to the poor—and which are also the basis of our best laws and regulations for the protection of the public health.

The administration, with Lord Aberdeen at its head, promptly decided to undertake a radical and systematic reform.

There was no little doubt as to the best plan to pursue. It was at first proposed to begin by offering a bill in Parliament, it being thought that nothing short of joint action by the legislative and the executive would either be at once effective, or binding upon succeeding administrations. But unanswerable objections arose. It was least promising of success. Members of Parliament were much more likely to acquiesce in reforms proposed by the executive than to initiate them by statute. They were not well informed as to existing methods or real needs in the executive department, and could never devise a good system, even if such an undertaking did not too directly concern both their future patronage and their favorites in office.

It would be shirking responsibility, and would raise suspicions of want of faith, for the executive not to take the initiative in a reform within its own sphere of duty. None so well as those in the executive department knew the abuses or the true remedy. Upon none did the duty so clearly rest to remove them. Nowhere else was there so much existing authority unused for that purpose. With what consistency could the executive call upon Parliament to reform administration, so long as executive authority remained unexercised, which, if not wholly adequate, was yet sufficient to accomplish much in that direction? Any lack of courage—any want of faith in the higher sentiments of the people—any attempt to shift responsibility, any resort to the tactics of its opponents, on the part of the Executive, it was perceived, must be fatal to such a reform.

" It has been too much the habit of the House of Commons to interfere in matters for which not they but the executive are responsible. It is the duty of the executive to provide for the efficient and harmonious working of the civil service, and they cannot transfer that duty to any other body far less competent to the task than themselves, without infringing a great and important constitutional principle, already too often infringed, to the great detriment of the public service." [1]

A new method must be very cautiously, if not gradually,

[1] Civil Service Papers, pp. 271, 272.

introduced, and it would be fatal to give a new and experimental system the rigidity of law at the outset. A statute may safely declare a principle of action, but not the details of that action. There must be tentative measures gradually adopted by the executive to the public needs.

" I may as well say that there was a considerable amount of vacillation and of tentative action, proceedings being afterwards recalled and alterations made in the conduct of the Treasury, according as we got fresh light and information ; . . . there were different rules in almost every department . . . we took a step in that year which we saw fit to retract the next year."[1]

Why should the administration be encumbered by regulations, theoretically devised, which might soon be found impracticable, but which could only be changed by the joint act of the executive and the legislature ? Whether regard be had to the usurpation of executive power by members of Parliament, or to the plain duty of the executive, independent of that encroachment, it was felt to be too clear for dispute that the most natural and the most effective opening of a reform policy would be for the executive to set an example of the discharge of official duty, in the spirit of the reform proposed, and to follow it up by the fearless exercise of all executive authority in that direction. Such an example would, in the public mind, silence all suspicion of lack of courage or lack of sincerity ; and, in Parliament, it would make the executive invulnerable, at the same time that it would turn public criticism upon members and other officers who should continue to justify abuses in order that they might enjoy patronage. Consistency, disinterestedness, fidelity to the principles on which the reform was to be based, at whatever cost, were felt to be indispensable to its success. Strong opposition was to be expected, but it must be boldly met on the basis of the reform policy alone.

But there were other reasons not less decisive. The greater effort was to make it certain, first, that the executive should be at liberty to select the best persons, as the constitution contemplated ; and, next, that its authority should be faith-

[1] Evidence of the Chancellor of the Exchequer, Report of Parliamentary Commission, 1873, p. 227.

fully exercised. The main reform sought is in the use of the executive power of appointment. If Parliament would surrender its usurpations and not again interfere, all that was needed was that the executive should perform a plain duty within its constitutional power. The authority of selecting officers covers the whole subject of their character, qualifications, age, promotions and removals; and that of executing the laws embraces all matters pertaining to the regulation and discipline of public servants. If left free to do so, and supplied with the necessary funds, the executive could bring about such reform. Why then should the executive begin the work of reform in its own department with a request that Parliament should further transcend its sphere? "I am firmly persuaded that if governments were more courageous in effecting reforms tending to the benefit of the community, we should hear fewer complaints of the difficulties arising out of the conflict of party interests." "After a few quiverings in the balance, the scale would sink down on the side of those whose wisdom and energy were steadily toward the promotion of the common weal." [1] Why assume that members of Parliament are as well acquainted with business in the departments as the experienced officers at their head? Why might not the executive as properly take part in making the business rules of the House of Commons as the House interfere with the business rules of the departments? It could not of course be denied that Parliament had a large and undefined legislative authority, that in many ways reached within the departments; and it unquestionably extended to salaries and to all matters involving expenditures. But, at most, Parliament should be only called upon to approve regulations for the government of executive officers, and that approval was implied in voting an appropriation. The course that members of Parliament would pursue was predicted with remarkable foresight, and the prediction has been almost as applicable to what we have seen in this country, as to what took place in the British Parliament; though, when once the members of that body had committed themselves to the reform before the nation, they did not arrest it by withholding money to pay its cost.

[1] Civil Service Papers, pp. 21, 22.

"I think the members of the House of Commons would in general support this scheme. Many of them would gladly be relieved from the importunities to which they are now exposed. Many more would advocate the new arrangement from a sincere conviction of its advantages. Of those who were inclined to oppose it, some would dissemble their aversion, through unwillingness to come forward at all as the champions of a system which they knew to be corrupt ; and other would be unable to offer more than a feeble resistance, being obliged to rest their arguments upon grounds different from those on which their views were really founded. They would raise objections on small points of detail, or would assert in a sweeping way that the plan was complicated, expensive, impracticable, and so forth." [1]

Such views prevailed, and the original plan was changed. It was decided that, in the outset, no application should be made to Parliament. The reform should be undertaken by the English Executive (that is, the Queen, and ministers, or administration) for the time being. The first step decided upon was an inquiry into the exact condition of the public service. Sir Stafford Northcote (the present Chancellor of the Exchequer) and Sir Charles Trevelyan were appointed in 1853 to make such inquiry and a report. They submitted their report in November of the same year.

I have no space to do justice to this able document, but a few sentences will indicate its spirit and some of the abuses of patronage for which it proposed a remedy.

"Admission into the civil service is indeed eagerly sought after, but it is for the unambitious and the indolent or incapable that it is chiefly desired. Those whose abilities do not warrant the expectation that they will succeed in the open professions, where they must encounter the competition of their cotemporaries, and those whose indolence of temperament or physical infirmities unfit them for active exertions, are placed in the civil service. . . . Parents and friends of sickly youths endeavor to attain for them employment in the service of the government. . . . The character of the individuals influences the mass, and it is thus that we often hear complaints of official delays, official evasions of difficulty, and official indisposition to improvement."

[1] Civil Service Papers, pp. 21, 22.

13

A system of competitive examinations is recommended which will test personal fitness for the public service.

"In the examinations which we have recommended, we consider that the *right of competing should be open to all persons of a given age*," subject to satisfactory proof of good health and good moral character.

These examinations "cannot be conducted in an effective and consistent manner throughout the service while it is left to each department to determine the nature of the examination and to examine the candidates."

The report was accompanied with a scheme for carrying the examinations into effect, from which I quote the following passages, as seeming to show that, from the very outset, the reform was neither royal nor aristocratic, but was advocated in the interest of common justice and population education : "Such a measure will exercise the happiest influence in *the education of the lower classes* throughout England, acting by the surest of all motives—the desire a man has of bettering himself in life. . . . They will have attained their situations in an independent manner through their own merits. The sense of this conduct cannot but induce self-respect and diffuse a wholesome respect among the lower no less than the higher classes of official men. . . . The effect of it in giving a stimulus to the education of the *lower classes can hardly be overestimated*."[1] Such was the spirit of the report. This was the theory of the *merit system*, then first approved by an English administration for the home government. I hardly need repeat that the examinations referred to as existing were (with small exception) mere *pass* examinations, and that the new examinations proposed were open, competitive examinations, being such as I have before explained. The examinations were to be general, so as to reach those qualifications which every person in the public service ought to possess, and also special to the extent requisite in the various parts and grades of the service, to ascertain the peculiar qualifications there needed.

A central board of examiners, with common duties, in all the departments and offices, is recommended as essential to

[1] Civil Service Papers, Appendix, pp. 4–31.

uniformity and independence in enforcing the rules of admission and probation. Such a body, for conducting them, would, we may readily see, impart the greatest vigor, uniformity, and justice to open competition. The proposal that merit should be the basis of promotion was of course quite hostile to the spirit of royalty and conservatism. It is worthy of notice that the report does not advise that any officers should be dismissed because they came in under the old system and were imbued with its spirit. If they should not act in good faith under the new system, they could be dismissed for cause. English statesmen have always regarded the government itself, and not its subordinates, as responsible for low qualifications and excessive numbers in the public service; and poor clerks have never, as with us, been suddenly and ruthlessly dismissed into the streets without notice or other employment. The report proceeds upon the theory that a complete removal of all abuses at once is impossible. But if merit, and not favoritism, should hereafter secure places in the public service, its whole spirit would be, at once, changed and its reasonable independence of politics would be in a short period established. Promotion from the places to the higher would inspire and reward honorable ambition, and in a few years the whole service would become as distinguished for administrative capacity as it had been for incapacity and servility. We shall see to what extent these hopes have been realized.

But the great feature of the report, which made it really a proposal for the introduction of a new system, was its advocacy of open competition. Except the experiment just put on trial in India, no nation had adopted that system. It was as theoretical as it was radical. While it seemed sound in principle, and had worked well in a small way, when it had been tried in isolated places in England and France, no one could be certain what might be its general consequences. Caution, candor, and a fair field were needed for its trial. It was of course particularly exposed to ridicule and misrepresentation.

It soon appeared that such a trial was too much to expect. Speculators in patronage, partisan leaders, high officers having some fragments of the appointing power, and, especially, all the scheming members of Parliament who had appropriated the bulk of that power, at once took alarm and combined for common attack and self-defence. They saw that their usurpation was threatened, not so much by the executive regaining what they had pillaged as by the people having the public service so freely opened to them that the most meritorious could enter it without their consent—without any other passport than superior merit. Such freedom and justice would be fatal to all official monopoly and all Parliamentary dictation. If the cabman's son John and the farmer's boy Peter, and the orphan at the head of his class in the public schools, could boldly go before the Civil Service Commission, in open competition, and prove themselves to be better qualified to enter the public service than the bishops's blockhead boy, the squire's or the earl's favorite, the member's electioneering clerk or decayed butler, or the party manager's most serviceable henchman, then, indeed, it would be pretty plain that a new system had come in and that patronage and favoritism must go out. This was too much for official and average Parliamentary patriotism, too much for conservative old England —too dangerous for any country without a precedent to bring about all at once. A chorus of ridicule, indignation, lamentation, and wrath arose from all the official and partisan places of politics. The government saw that a further struggle was at hand. It appeared more clear than ever that Parliament was not a very hopeful place in which to trust the tender years of such a reform. Its true friends were the intelligent classes outside official life.

In England, as with us, the most active opponents of the reform were those who had promised places and those who hoped soon to gain them through official favoritism and partisan coercion. The appeal, therefore, it was seen, must be made to the people themselves. They—that is, such of them as are neither in office nor seeking it – were the true and almost the only disinterested friends of the new system. With this view, the executive caused the report to be spread broadcast among the people, and also requested the written opinions of a large number of persons of worth and distinction both in and out of office. The report was sent to Parliament, but no action upon it was requested. The situation will be recognized as resembling our own when, under General Grant's administration, a similar report was prepared ; but the final executive action in the two countries was widely different.

The responses made in 1854 are printed in an interesting volume, to which I have already referred as " Civil Service Papers." The hostility manifested in Parliamentary and partisan circles soon appeared to be very formidable. But there were not wanting able, disinterested members who were ready to support the reform with patriotic zeal. At the other end of the scale of membership, there were partisan intriguers and noisy demagogues horrified at such an attack upon Parliamentary perquisites which had been enjoyed for more than a hundred years, and without which, they declared, no party could live, if indeed the constitution could survive. They were as ready to defend their monopoly as they were to defend their dog kennels, their inherited acres, or their seats at the horse races. Between these extremes were many goodish members, some of whom would faintly support reform in order to get rid of the annoyance and the dirty work imposed by patronage, and others of whom had just faith and principle enough to vote on what they might think would be the winning side. The result of an early appeal to Parliament would therefore be very doubtful, to say the least ; nor was the first response of the people (perhaps to be made before they had fully comprehended the issue) by any means certain. When we consider that an English administration has no other tenure than the support of a majority in Parliament, so that an adverse majority, for a single day, might compel the resignation of a ministry, we can appreciate that such an appeal to the people required faith and courage of a high order.[1] Those high qualifications were not wanting in the ministry in power. The government, faithful to its pledges and its sense of duty, resolved to persist in the reform at all hazards. The only

---

[1] " Those early supporters of it might be *counted upon the fingers*, and if the matter had been put to the vote in London society or the clubs, or even in Parliament itself by *secret* voting, it would have been rejected by an overwhelming majority."—Letter, Sir Charles Trevelyan to the Author. See Appendix.

alternatives were success or repudiation and disgrace. It decided to notify its purpose to Parliament, but not to ask any assistance at that time. Accordingly, the Queen's Speech, on the opening of Parliament, in 1854, contained the following language :

"The establishment required for the conduct of the civil service, and the arrangements bearing upon its conditions, have recently been under review : and I shall direct a plan to be laid before you which will have for its object to improve the system of admission, and thereby to increase the efficiency of the service." [1]

No such plan, however, was laid before Parliament at the time first contemplated. That body showed itself too selfish, unpatriotic, and hostile. But before considering the next step taken by the administration, I ought to notice the response made to the report by those of whom the government requested opinions.

[1] See Report on Civil Service Appointments, 1860, p. v.

# CHAPTER XVII.

## HOW THE NEW SYSTEM WAS RECEIVED.

Politicians and many officers oppose.—Non-partisans generally approve.—
Great disparity of views.—It is Chinese.—It is sound and salutary.—It is
Utopian.—It is wise and just.—It shoots above human virtue.—It responds
to public morality and intelligence.—It is ridiculous.—It is statesmanlike.
—It is the dream of *doctrinaires*.—It has the marks of practical statesmanship.—The present service is the best the world ever saw.—The present service is disgracefully incompetent and costly.—The new system
endangers the aristocracy.—The spoils system defended.—Ridicule.—The
new plan a bureaucracy.—It is the opposite of a bureaucracy.

THE volume of replies to which I have referred [1] discusses
the report of 1853 from every point of view. The prejudices
of aged officers wedded to routine, the natural hostility and
jealousy of partisan managers, the indignation and anger of a
certain class of members of Parliament,[2] the zeal of great reformers like John Stuart Mill, the honorable ambition of
young men wishing to rise by merit and scorning the degrading ways of subserviency, the alarm of old croakers and pessi-
mists, and the sober thought of good citizens in many callings
—each and all found expression. There was no small difference of opinion as to what would come of an experiment so
novel and so radical. The journals and reviews of England
resounded with the fierce debate. I might fill pages with interesting illustrations. Sarcasm, ridicule, denunciation, gloomy
prognostications of evil, high faith in the better sentiments, the

---

[1] Civil Service Papers published in 1855.

[2] The public press did not spare the selfish and partisan members of
Parliament. "Had not a long course of elective corruption blinded the
constituencies to its true import, and given members an instinctive antipathy
to any method for curtailing the means of corruption, such a measure
would have been hailed with applause."—*Times*, August 11, 1854, Civil
Service Papers, p. 250.

cunning sophisms of demagogues, and the calm reasoning of statesmen, were heard by turns. Those whose patronage and whose mercenary prospects of rising were threatened were especially exasperated, and insisted that their rights were being invaded. No bellicose woman at Billingsgate ever defended her herring-stand with greater fierceness, or greater apparent faith in the righteousness of her cause, than some of the monopolists of patronage brought to the support of their claim that justice, good policy, and the stability of the English constitution itself required that they should each keep a toll-gate to the public service ever open to favor and shut to merit. So complete was the discussion that subsequent originality has not been possible; and those who now employ stale sarcasm and ridicule, better uttered at that time, must be pardoned. Some denounced it as a Chinese system, because the Chinese were said to have originated examinations; not remembering that the same reasoning would deprive Englishmen of gunpowder, the compass, and the art of printing. Some sneered at the new system as " a perfect novelty, never hitherto enforced in any commonwealth except that of Utopia;"[1] not of course bearing in mind that free speech, which they so much enjoyed, was also original in that renowned commonwealth. One high officer, a Right Honorable, a Knight Commander of the Order of the Bath, and a Secretary of a great department, commends his objections by using the familiar argument (sound enough when fairly applied) that rulers must not attempt what is not practicable in their day and generation. He says : " The law-giver may keep ahead of public opinion, but he cannot shoot out of sight of the moral standard of his age and country. The world we live in is not, I think, half moralized enough for the acceptance of a scheme of such stern morality as this." He was reminded that public officers are very liable to mistake official opinion for the public opinion, and hence often shoot far below the moral tone of the people. He showed before he got through that it was fears about prerogative and not about morality that really troubled him. " Why add another," he

---

[1] Civil Service Papers, p. 77.

exclaims, " to the many recent sacrifices of the royal prerogative !" [1]

Just as with us, there were those who thought the old system a piece of perfection. " I reply that I do not consider that system capable of improvement, but think it *better than any other that has been suggested*, or that I am able to suggest." [2]

Even distinguished officers (a Right Honorable Secretary of State and the Secretary of the National Council for Education) had the hardihood to defend the worst features of the old partisan spoils system itself, in language that would have brought a blush of shame even to the face of the author of the declaration that " to the victor belongs the spoils."

" The principal ministers of the Crown (he said) are themselves so ill remunerated, that those high trusts are practically confined to persons born to ample fortunes.    . . .    But the range of choice will become still more narrow,    . . .    if the *remuneration* of these great offices be further reduced, by depriving the holders of them of all their most *valuable* patronage.    . . .    Considering the long . . .    habituation of the people to political contests, in which the share of office, not merely for its emoluments, but also for the sake of influencing administration, *reckons among the legitimate prizes of war*,    . . .    and that rank and wealth    . . .    hold the keys of many things,    . . .    I should hesitate long before I advised such a revolution of the civil service." [3]

The argument, so familiar with us, that the corruption we have is an inevitable evil that comes " with the best civil service the world has ever seen," is by no means original here, but is a stale falsehood born of English fatalism and conceit.[4] " Jobbing is a part, though an ugly part, of the *price which a free people pay for their constitutional liberty*. So long as there are Parliamentary constituents, they will ask favors of members of Parliament, and members of Parliament of ministers.    . ." [5]

---

[1] Civil Service Papers, pp. 78, 79.          [2] Ibid., p. 393.
[3] Ibid., pp. 104 and 105.                    [4] Ibid., p. 253.
[5] Ibid.

Polite sarcasm was ingeniously applied by high officials in language of which this is a specimen :

" I should be extremely happy if any scheme occurred to me by which pure, simple, unadulterated merit, without the slightest mixture of other ingredients, could be made the sole criterion of advancement. If such a discovery should ever be made, it would probably be founded upon some new view of human nature, and would certainly not be confined in its operation to the civil service, but would extend its benign influence over all services, trades and professions." [1]

Some arguments are noticeable as not having been yet reproduced in our discussions ; for example, in one, it is urged that if patronage is taken from members of Parliament, they will utterly neglect the civil service, whereby it will go to decay ; and, in another, that the real sufferers by existing abuses are, not the public service or the people, but " the members of Parliament and heads of departments, . . . who need sheltering from the irresistible attacks of their constituents and supporters, with which they often unwillingly and from necessity comply." [2]

The specious and familiar, old argument—the argument that no part of an abuse should be remedied unless the whole can be removed at once—that no thief should be punished unless all gamblers are sent to prison at the same time—was put with much adroitness, with a view of arousing the fears and hostility of the Established Church and of the owners of its patronage. Why should patronage and favoritism, in bestowing offices, be stopped (the writer asks), unless the sale of livings (that is, the sale of the right to be a minister in the State Church) shall also be forbidden ? " If the government will absolutely proclaim the abstract principle that nepotism is not to be endured, what will they say of nepotism in the Church ? There it is not an accident, but a system. It is an abuse, not furtively perpetuated, but ostentatiously avowed." [3]

By some the new system was opposed on the ground that the standard of examinations would be fixed so high that none

[1] Civil Service Papers, p. 394.
[2] Ibid., p. 357.   Civil Service Report, 1860, p. 224.
[3] Civil Service Papers, p. 78.

but learned pedants and college-bred aristocrats could gain admission ; and, by others, it was opposed for exactly the opposite, that it would be fixed so low that gentlemen would be overslaughed by a band of conceited, impracticable schoolmasters and book-worms, together with crowds of bright, vulgar fellows from the lower classes : so that the high flavor of honor and gentility, if not the moral tone of the service, would be lost. "Another objection to your system of competing examinations is to be found in the stimulus that would be given by it to over-education. There can be little doubt that great numbers of youths who are now content to seek to earn their subsistence in the lower ranks . . . would be attracted by the more captivating prospect of these government offices." [1] In reply, Mr. Mill and others commended the new system because it gave the poor and the humble an equal chance upon their merits, and they declared that if the sons of the rich and the high-born could not, on that basis, hold their own, the quicker they were driven from the public service the better. There were also attacks upon the new system on the ground that it would so largely draw young persons of ability and attainments into the public service, that private business, the pulpit, and the bar would suffer for want of them. To which it was replied that no affairs were so great and important as those of the nation, and that they demanded the service of the best of her children, in which their example and their influence would be most beneficent in all the ranges of private life. At the worst, it would be easy to lower the standard, if the nation should ever be found to be too ably and worthily served. It was claimed by some that the new system would tend to a bureaucracy, and thus become dangerous to liberty. The reply was that no system was so repugnant and fatal to a bureaucracy as that proposed. It opened the public service to every one upon equal terms, and those who came in entered it under the least possible commitment or obligations that would compromise their independence. The essential conditions of a bureaucracy, in a public service, were, first, that those in office should command the gate of that service, thus selecting those who should enter it ; and second,

[1] Civil Service Papers, pp. 133 and 134.

that the higher officers should domineer over the lower. These were the very conditions of the old system which the new was intended and was especially adapted to remove. How could a bureaucracy arise under a system where all the old officers in the service united could not prevent a young man of worth from coming in, and under which they must promote him for merit, and could turn him out only for cause, to be publicly stated?

The old argument, that parties could not prosper without at least as much patronage as they then enjoyed, was renewed. But, as it had been made by the party managers and overruled by the English people, at every stage of the progress of reform, and parties had continued to prosper all the more, it did not seem to have so much weight in England as it has with us: for the present generation of Americans has seen partisan patronage and coercion steadily increase, whereas the present generation of Englishmen has seen them as steadily fall away.

Another objection, which has been also urged with us, was that a general examining board would be too expensive, and that its duties would be found impracticable in their discharge. To which it was replied that experience would be the best answer: though there had been enough already to make it probable that the objections were without weight; that the intrigues, the consumption of the time of officers by rival applicants for office, the interruptions of public business by members of Parliament soliciting places, and the excessive numbers and salaries foisted upon the treasury, which were the inevitable results of the old system, were ten times more costly than any examining board could be. Still another objection, lately made familiar to us, was that the examining board would itself succeed to the patronage which its old possessors would lose, and thereby a sort of *Patronage Star Chamber* would be created: in answer to which it was explained that the board would not have the least authority over or participation in appointments, its duty being confined to making up a record from data, always open to inspection and review, and upon the face of which any unfairness would at all times be patent.

But the attack upon the new system most confidently urged was this: that, while an examination might test mere memory, brightness and quickness of parts, it could not test moral character, soundness of discretion, executive ability, or capacity to command. This was the consideration which caused not a few good citizens to hesitate, and which partisans urged with much force and effect. It could be urged in much fewer words than it could be answered, and it looked plausible at the first statement. No nation had then tried examinations on a large scale. Still, there had been considerable miscellaneous experience in England, and some in France, and that was fully set forth. The argument from experience, to which I shall call attention, is now, at the end of nearly a quarter of a century of actual trial, so full and decisive that it will hardly be useful to refer to what then existed or to dwell upon theory or probability. It was pointed out that a public competition is almost sure to expose and exclude bad characters. Examinations were not to be merely literary, but were to cover the practical duties of officers. They were not claimed to be infallible ; but it was believed that a public competition, between attainments and capacity, for such duties was far preferable to a private competition of influence, solicitation, favor, and coercion, which generally prevailed under the old system. Besides, the six-month probation would further test executive ability.

The reform was distinctly presented to the people as one in the interest of popular education, and of the common, equal rights of the people of every class and condition to share in the public service : and it was as distinctly opposed, because it was regarded as hostile to privilege and favorable to republican or democratic ideas. "A public opinion favorable to the elementary schools would spring up in the humbler classes of society, from this public recognition and sanction of it, as the means of qualifying men for responsible stations in life. . . . In the first place, we may expect to see it operate widely and deeply in the education of the country. Parents, even down to those of the lowest class, will be more solicitous than they are to secure the benefits of instruction for their children, when they see its direct bearing upon their prospects of advancement in life."[1]

---

[1] Civil Service Papers, pp. 24, 41, and 42.

To this language of its friends its enemies replied in this strain :

"I am free to confess that I can see no reason why the Crown should be deprived of the grace and influence which belongs to the nominations. . . . One obvious effect of the competition which is proposed by you would be to fill the offices with the picked, clever, young men of the lower ranks of society, to whom such offices would be a great object of ambition, which they would not in general be to men of the higher ranks." [1]

And yet, it would not be just to say that the aristocracy were all on one side and the common people (as they are called) all on the other.     To the credit of English statesmen of the most aristocratic birth and associations, it should be said that several of them have set examples of the surrender of patronage and of the support of measures clearly in the interest of common justice and humble life, which it would be an honor to high officers in a republic to imitate.  Lord Derby, Lord Russell, and Lord Palmerston, for example, supported the reform, as prime ministers, at the head of their respective parties, though assured by their subordinates (and I think by their own experience compelled to believe) that the inevitable consequence would be an advance of the influence and education of the people at large, by reason of which the privileged classes would suffer a loss of power in public affairs.  The line between those who supported and those who opposed the reform was not a party line, nor was it the boundary between the privileged and the unprivileged classes ; but it was a strata in the moral tone of all parties and all ranks, below which were the men whose faith was in management and the selfish forces of politics, and, above which, were those who trusted the higher sentiments and the nobler impulses of the people.  On the one side was all that survived in sympathy with Walpole and Newcastle, on the other, all that had grown in the spirit of Chatham and of Burke.

[1] Civil Service Papers, pp. 123 and 330.

# CHAPTER XVIII.

## THE FIRST ORDER FOR A CIVIL SERVICE COMMISSION AND COMPETITIVE EXAMINATIONS, MAY, 1855.

Lord Palmerston decides to go to Parliament only for an appropriation.—Executive order appointing a Civil Service Commission.—Applicants for office to be examined by the commission.—Only limited competition at first introduced.—Part of their patronage retained by members of Parliament.—No removals made.—Moderate changes thought most prudent.—Vote of Commons in 1855 adverse to new system.—The administration stands firm, and relies on the people.

ABOUT the time that English public opinion had pronounced its first judgment upon the official report, and before any final action had been taken upon it, the Aberdeen administration went out. The cause—the disastrous management of the Crimean war—was independent of the new system, except in so far as the lack of official capacity, both in the military and civil administration, for which the old system was responsible, contributed to that result. Lord Palmerston came into power early in 1855, than whom, this most practical of nations never produced a more hard-headed, practical statesman, nor one who had a poorer opinion of mere theorists, sentimentalists, and *doctrinaires*. Upon his administration fell the duty of deciding the fate of the new system advocated in the report.

Fortunately, he was no more inclined to shirk a plain duty than he was to follow an empty theory. He had had long experience in administration, and knew intimately the hopeless incompetency of the partisan system. He too held that the executive should discharge its own duty before going to Parliament. He had faith in his party, and believed it would gain more by removing grave abuses than by any partisan use of patronage. It was beyond question, however, that a majority of those most active in either party, and probably a majority of members of Parliament, were opposed to the reform. But he knew its strength with the people. Making no direct appeal to Parliament, and trusting to the higher public opinion, Lord Palmerston's administration advised that an order should be made by the Queen in Council for carrying the reform into effect ; and such an order was made on the 21st of May, 1855.

It recites that " it is expedient to make provision for testing, according to fixed rules, the qualifications of the young men who may from time to time be proposed to be appointed to the junior situations," . . . in the civil service. There were no women in the service at that time, and no provision was made for them. It also appoints three General Commissioners, with power to select assistants, under whom the examinations for all the departments are provided to be made. It directs that an estimate for their remuneration be laid before Parliament ; for it was believed that even members of Parliament would not refuse to allow a trial of the experiment, hostile as the majority was believed to be. The order requires that all young men proposed to be appointed to junior situations shall, before they shall be admitted to probation, be examined under the commissioners and receive a certificate of qualification from them ; but there is a carefully guarded exception allowing persons of mature age to be admitted to certain places where special qualifications may be required. Appointments are not to be made until after a six months' probation, which probation must have given satisfactory evidence of fitness. There are also proper directions for determining age, good character, and freedom from disqualifying physical defects.

Thus far the order was as broad as the report ; but the need of going to Parliament for an appropriation, the doubts of so many thoughtful men over so radical a novelty, the fierce opposition in official and partisan circles, and the angry mood of the public mind over the Crimean war, seem to have caused the administration to think it most prudent to modify the recommendation of the report upon the three following points, until some experience should be acquired : (1) the rules were to be accommodated in each department to the views of its head ; (2) the power of nominating and appointing, as then existing (but subject to examinations), was not to be taken away by the rules ; (3) the examinations were not expressly required to be competitive ; but it seems to have been understood they would be competitive, and in fact competitive examinations were held by the Board of Commissioners from the beginning of its duties.

This first order, therefore, did not really provide for uniform rules throughout the departments, but we shall find it hurried on and really produced that result. It did not in terms take away Parliamentary and official patronage, but, by submitting its favorites to competitive examination, under one central board, it gave patronage its death-blow. It was really limited and not open competition that was at first introduced, and mainly a competition, perhaps, between those of the same party. It was much as if all the nominations made by members of Congress for West Point, or for civil offices, were subjected to competition, and only a fit number of those marked highest, regardless of residence, were allowed to enter or have places. No one, I presume, will doubt that such a competition would greatly raise the average capacity and character of the students and clerks. The English service was therefore not really opened to the people, or made free to merit, but the old monopoly of office-holders and members of Parliament was made more odious by being made more conspicuous. As competition and the other tests would head off favorite dunces and rascals, the holders of patronage at once began to regard their perquisites as of much less importance. It was therefore a substantial triumph for the new system, which was very soon put in practice. If members of Parliament still nominally sat in authority at the gates of the public service, it was only to make their selfishness more conspicuous, by showing themselves ready to contend for the shadow of a monopoly, after its substance had been lost,—to maintain the forms of usurpation, after the fruits had been wrested from their hands.

Before proceeding to the effects of the new system, it will be useful to consider for a moment its theory and scope. The aim of the practical statesmen who promoted it was to take the whole body of the civil service of Great Britain out of

14

official favoritism and partisan control, and to raise official life to a higher plane. They knew there were many officers in the service, for a long time trained under the old system, who were opposed to the new, and who would not fail to disparage and obstruct it. But they left every such case to be treated upon its own merits, irrespective of the changes adopted. No removals were made, by reason of the introduction of the new system. The members of Lord Palmerston's cabinet and the unofficial friends of reform foresaw that the change they proposed would be only slowly brought about by the new method they established. Their long experience had convinced them that all expectations of suddenly changing the character and tone of the sixty or more thousand persons who make up the civil service of Great Britain—a character and tone which were the growth of generations—are utterly chimerical. They felt that even the attempt, to accomplish at one sweep the full reform that was desired, would recoil upon them with disastrous effect. Their reliance was upon the introduction of superior elements into the service—and almost wholly into its lower grade—from which promotions would be made on the basis of merit ; and thus, in a few years, higher character and a better spirit would permeate and in no long time would control the entire service. Neither the ministry nor the English people fell into the error of regarding that reform as trifling which, though not at once very much affecting the higher offices, really controlled the doors of patronage and favoritism, and determined who, a few years hence, would fill nearly every high office except that of cabinet ministers. They seem to have comprehended that the adoption, even in a limited sphere, of a principle by which partisan tyranny was condemned, was in itself no inconsiderable victory, which would not fail to lead on to far greater triumphs in the same direction. I have found nothing in the progress of this reform which has seemed to me a better evidence of a sound public opinion on the subject than this popular judgment. Wise methods steadily and faithfully applied, which educate public opinion at the same time that they close the fountains of mischief, and not sweeping, revolutionary proceedings, which assume that the moral tone of a nation's politics can be

changed by an assault or an exhortation, were, in the opinion
of the British public, the essential conditions of all administrative reform.

The evidence is decisive that the reform would have been
defeated had the original plan of going to Parliament in the
first instance been adhered to.   For, after it had been strengthened by all the power of the administration, it failed of a
majority when first brought before that body.   Members saw
that it was in principle fatal to patronage.   The order in Council of May, 1855, came before Parliament in July of that year,
and it was approved by only 125 votes to 140 which condemned
it.   It will be noticed that a very large majority of members did
not vote.   How many of those who dodged the issue really
detested the mean work which patronage imposed upon them,
yet wanted the courage to vote, I have no means of knowing.
The administration neither informed Parliament beforehand
that it would surrender to an adverse vote, nor abandoned its
duty or its pledges when that vote was announced.   The
struggle had been recognized as one in which the people, contending for common rights and pure government, were on one
side, and selfish officials, endeavoring to maintain a corrupt
monopoly of patronage, and all the partisan manipulators were
on the other side.   The ministers had set an example of submitting their patronage to the test of competition, and that example members of Parliament had refused to follow.   It was for
the people to decide between them.   To the people therefore
the appeal was made, whether they would approve the selfishness and the monopoly of their representatives or the patriotism and disinterestedness of the administration.

# CHAPTER XIX.

## THE FIRST FIVE YEARS UNDER THE NEW SYSTEM.

The system gains strength.—Subjects as to which examinations were made. —Many incompetent persons applied.—Examinations extended to Ireland and Scotland.—Competition shown to be practicable and popular.—Better men secured than by pass examinations.—The Commons, in 1856, change their vote, and approve the commission and open competition.—In 1857, the House, by vote, calls for an extension of competition.—It is steadily extended from office to office.—Examinations favorable to practical capacity and to the public schools.—In 1859, Parliament refuses the benefit of the superannuation allowances to those not examined before the Civil Service Commission.

THE members of the *Civil Service Commission* promptly entered upon the discharge of their duties. The administration was faithful to the spirit of the order in Council, and exhibited the self-denial and firmness which were essential to success in the great work. The commissioners' first report was made, March 4th, 1856, covering only a period of about nine months. Though not expressly required by the order, a great portion of the examinations were competitive from the outset. The first examination was held in June, 1855. Thirteen competitive examinations are mentioned in the first report. This able document—broadly circulated—very much strengthened that favoring public opinion which the frequent discussions of the action of the commission in the public press had tended to develop. The principal subjects of examination were writing, arithmetic, geography, composition, history, and book-keeping ; but some of the examinations included one or more languages : to which were added such practical subjects as the clerk most needed to understand in entering a particular office. A just system of marking and grading was adopted, according to which the relative standing of those examined, as between themselves, was so made up that both the

degree of excellence in each subject and the relative practical
importance of that subject, were embraced as factors. Those
who stood the highest in qualifications got the appointments.
It has struck me that the standard for admission was at first
fixed needlessly high, probably on some grounds of expediency
having reference to English opinion at that time ; and it is
very certain that it would exclude not a few of those who
enter our service. But it gave high capacity and character to
English official life ; and nothing is easier than to lower the
standard to any extent desirable. Indeed, it has been somewhat lowered in later years. In the outset the old aristocratic
element was powerful, and it could not be wholly disregarded.

The commission seems to have discharged its duties with
ability and firmness. The rules were extended to only a portion of the offices at the beginning. But in the few months
covered by the first report, 1078 persons were examined, of
whom almost one third—that is, 309—were regarded as not
competent. The 309 would seem to have been the class of
blockheads and incompetents — of partisan henchmen and
superannuated butlers—of which the report of 1853 had given
an account as swarming in the service. Of course, not a few
members of Parliament had such favorites thrown back upon
their hands and were angry. But the people were glad to see
them spurned from the public service, and praised the commission. Great pressure was brought upon the board, by members and high officers, to allow favorite dunces to pass, but in
vain. An important incident tested the character of the
board the first year. Lord Palmerston, the Prime Minister,
had the mortification of being informed that one of his own
nominees had failed in the examination. He sent to the
board for the papers, which would show why his favorite had
been rejected ; and he was probably never more astonished than
when told they could not be sent from the office, but were
open to his inspection there, as they were to the inspection of
all other persons. He graciously yielded to his own system,
and allowed the papers to remain and his nominee to go about
other business. This event was a sort of proclamation that
personal fitness would avail more for getting into the public
service than all the power of a Prime Minister. This first

report declared that the duties of the board were in their
nature judicial, and that a recognition of its independence
was essential to justice. And I may add that, from that
day to this, the Civil Service Commission, created in 1855,
has gone on in the discharge of its ever increasing duties,
with a justice that has hardly been challenged, and with a
good faith that has never been questioned. The order contemplated that examinations should be extended from office
to office, and even beyond London, as experience and convenience might suggest. The first report shows examinations
held in Ireland and in Scotland ; and that Lord Clarendon, the
Secretary of State for Foreign Affairs, had required that, both
his clerks and all persons entering the diplomatic service as
attaches or consuls, should be examined by the commission.
Perhaps the most striking illustration of the extent to which
these examinations, from the beginning, arrested incompetency, is found in the fact that, at a single examination, held
in November, 1855, for clerkships in the Council for Education, and confined to " *subjects deemed of indispensable necessity.*" 21 of the 31 candidates examined were rejected as disqualified.

If the people did not, in those first examinations, find all
their sons at liberty, without official endorsement, to compete
for a place in the public service, they did, for the first time,
see such of them as members and ministers might choose to
favor, compelled to submit to manly competitions between
themselves, in which those of the best character and the highest
capacity won the prizes. They did, from the first, see the nation thus openly declare its preference for young men of merit
rather than for beggars for places and sycophants in politics ;
they did see education honored and its victory, in honorable
competition, send official favorites and fawners to the wall.
This was a great advance in the right direction ; and neither
the people nor the monopolists failed to see that the success of
this limited form of contest would inevitably bring in free,
open, competition at no distant day.

The first experience of competitive examinations dissipated
the old objections that it would be found impracticable to conduct them, and that they would fail to arrest bright rascals.

In such an open contest, it was found that the public and the competitors alike took notice of the character and history as well as of the capacity of those competing. Young men of tarnished reputations dared not present themselves for a public ordeal of that kind, in which every one engaged searched the record of those who contended against him.

Even ridicule was soon turned against those who had laughed and sneered at examinations. The ten who had won the prizes, in the case last referred to, were cheered by the people and praised by the press, while the twenty-one incompetents were ridiculed, and with them the patronage system they represented : for it thus appeared that the system would, but for the examinations, have foisted two imbeciles upon the service for each competent person it produced. It was declared that if competition was made free to all, far better men would offer themselves, who would be greatly superior to the favorites recommended by members of Parliament. These favorites, like some of our students recommended to West Point, were not seldom found to be poor material for public officers : and their competition was compared to a Derby horse-race at which none but " sprained and sickly colts, ringboned, old racers, and heavy, wheezy coach-horses should be allowed to run." The reformers had their time to laugh when highly-recommended noodles walked out crestfallen from the examinations. The effects upon the public mind of these examinations, and of the discussions they called forth, were at once considerable. It was seen that patronage and favoritism were the losers by competition, and that what they lost was gained by good character and capacity. Still, pass examinations, by the commissioners, were not wholly discontinued ; but they were far more efficient than pass examinations by mere department boards. Members of Parliament soon appreciated the change which had thus come over public opinion, and comprehended that their old monopoly was no longer defensible. On the 24th of April, 1856, Parliament resolved, by a vote of 108 to 87 (from which it would appear that dodgers were still very numerous), that " the House has observed, with great satisfaction, the zeal and prudence with which the Commission has proceeded in applying a remedy to evils of a serious character, the previous ex-

istence of which *has now been placed beyond dispute ;*[1] and
also the degree of progress that has been made, with the sanction of various departments of the State, toward the establishment of a system of competition among the candidates for admission to the civil service,  .  .  .  and makes known to
her Majesty that, if she shall think fit further to *extend* them
and to make trial in the service of the method of *open* competition as a condition of entrance, this House will cheerfully
provide for any charges which the adoption of that system
may entail."

This certainly was a great victory for the new system ; and
it was won by the executive and the people.  A right of nomination had become of little value as a perquisite, the moment
that even limited competition was placed between the favorites
and the offices.  Recommendation no longer gave an office,
but only a chance to compete for one.  The great majority
that failed to vote, however, shows that not all the defeated
monopolists were willing to meet their fate in a patriotic and
manly spirit.  Still, the British Parliament, as a whole, must
be given the credit of having promptly accepted the public
judgment, and of having tendered the executive its promise
to sustain a trial of open competition, which, if successful,
would take from each member—from all officials of the empire
—from party managers—every particle of that coveted patronage which had belonged to them and their predecessors for a
hundred and fifty years.  This is the highest elevation of self-
denial and patriotic statesmanship that legislative action on
the subject, in any country, has ever reached.  And it can
never flatter our pride to compare this record with that of our
Congress, when, without a debate or a division, it refused to
vote a dollar to carry on a similar reform to which an American
Executive and a great party were equally committed.  Thus,
within three years from the time *the merit system* was pre-

---

[1] The evidence which had " placed such evils beyond dispute " was the
exposure and rejection, on the examinations, of incompetent nominees which
before had been pushed into the service.  The public had begun to take
notice of abuses which before had escaped censure, and members of Parliament could no longer deny an evil they had before considered it infidelity
to the party and scandalous to even suggest.

sented, in an official report, which was, at first, received by
hostile parties and an indignant Parliament, it had won both
the people and the legislature.

I must pass rapidly over the next four years, in which the
reform rapidly gained strength ; so rapidly indeed that, in
1857, the House resolved, *unanimously*, " that the experience
gained since the issuing of the order in Council of May 21st,
1855, is in favor of the adoption of the principle of competition as a condition of entrance to the civil service, and that the
application of that principle ought to be extended, in conformity with the resolution of the House agreed to on the 24th of
April, 1856."

The facts were that members of Parliament and officials generally experienced a great relief in being even partially protected from solicitation. Troublesome office-seekers could be
sent to competition, where the poorer sort were sure to be laid
out. When legislation and party action began to turn on
principle and not on patronage, official duty was found to be
as much less wearisome as it was more honorable. The
moment favoritism ceased to be powerful, it became contemptible. Each year, to this time, the Civil Service Commission has
laid its methods and proceedings fully before the public in an
annual report. The second report showed that competition
had been steadily extended, and with results equally satisfactory. The number of noodles and ignoramuses sent by members for examination were less than the first year ; but some
appeared who declared Germany to be on the Caspian Sea, the
Isle of Wight to be a part of Scotland, who had never heard
anything about the Alps, Mount Sinai, Athens, the Red Sea,
or the St. Lawrence ; nor could some of them tell where tea,
tobacco, or cotton came from. Such examples of ignorance of
course more and more turned the laugh upon the opponents of
the new system. From the report of 1857, it appears that 509
persons had been examined as letter-carriers before 1856 ; a
method which Postmaster James of New York city has lately
found greatly conducive to the rare efficiency of his administration. During the year, 34 competitive examinations were held.
Of all those examined over 38 per cent were rejected, and 1906
certificates of competency were granted. The third report

shows that the Directors of the East India Company had applied to the commission to examine the clerks for the home service of that company, and I shall soon have occasion to show how the system had been extended to its foreign service. The corporation of London, in the same year, took measures in the same direction. Examinations were about the same time instituted in Malta and were provided for in Canada. This report shows that 5682 persons in all had been examined. The ratio of rejections had fallen to about 28 per cent, apparently for the reason that dunces had come to understand that it was of no use to compete. The post office authorities, which had always been most hostile to the new system, this year notified their assent to competition. In this report, the general bearings and results of the competitions, which had turned in part upon literary attainments and in part upon practical capacity, are fully discussed ; and it is shown that attainments and business ability are so closely allied in young men, that on the basis of *76 competitions, it appears that out of 115 candidates the result would have been different as to nine only, had the examinations been limited to subjects wholly practical.* The stimulating and salutary effects of these public competitions— of the spirit that brought them into existence—speedily made themselves felt in places beyond the public service, proper ; and early produced striking results. For example, there is a central society—a sort of semi-official body—known as the Society of Arts, which has contributed largely to the improvement of scientific and artistic education. As early as 1856, I find this society conducting competitive [1] examinations, in " a large number of institutions of different kinds, . . . people's colleges, evening schools, and all sorts of bodies." From its centre in London, the examinations of the Society, in 1858, had extended to 36 places, and in 1859 to 63 places, in England, Ireland, and Scotland, everywhere superseding favoritism and solicitation, and giving new vigor to that growth of

[1] As illustrating the liberal spirit in which British noblemen have dealt with patronage (to which I have already referred), I may mention that Lord Granville declined the patronage of these appointments belonging to his office, and gave them to competition " to make them available for the purpose of encouraging education." Report of 1860 on Civil Service Appointments, p. 286. May we hope that Republican officers will do as much ?

education of every kind which has been so remarkable in
Great Britain during the last twenty years.[1]

The report for 1858 further illustrates the fact that the examinations gave results far more favorable to the common
people (to use an English phrase) and to the public schools than
to the aristocracy or to higher scholarship, and that the want
of practical knowledge, and not the want of mere book learning, determined the rejections ; though of course whatever
stimulated learning in its lower planes strengthened it in all its
higher grades.   For example, certificates were granted to 958
of the persons nominated ; and in 292 cases they were refused.   Now, of these 292 rejections, 286 were made by reason of incapacity in such elementary subjects as arithmetic and
spelling, and *only six* for incompetency in higher attainments.
A careful inquiry into the education and the occupation of
the parents of 391 of those who passed by competition, showed
that but 12 were sons of lawyers, that but 27 were sons of gentlemen, and that but 22 were sons of ministers of the Established
Church ; while 29 were sons of public officers, 14 were sons of
private clerks, and 174 were sons of tradesmen, artificers,
farmers, and manufacturers.   Of the 391, only eight *were
college graduates*, while 335 were educated in the different
grades of British schools.   Here we have the predictions, made
by the friends of the new system, that it would promote
school education, fully verified.   Such facts show us why this
reform has commended itself so much more to the great body
of the worthy English people, not high in the social scale, than
it has to the aristocracy, and why it has so greatly advanced
popular education.   In 1859, the new system came again before Parliament, in connection with a revision of the superannuation acts ; and so firmly had it and *the Civil Service Commission* been established in public favor, that it was enacted
(22 Victoria, ch. 26) that (with some slight exceptions) " no
person appointed after its date shall, for its purposes, be considered as serving in the permanent civil service of the State
unless admitted with a certificate from the Civil Service Commissioners ;" and, without being in that service, no one could
share in the superannuation allowances.              •

_____
[1] Report of 1860 on Civil Service Appointments, p. 283.

# CHAPTER XX.

AT this date, the new system had been on trial only five
years. It should be borne in mind that the greater part of
those competitions had been limited—that is, confined to persons selected by members of Parliament and other officers.
Though Parliament had, as we have seen, expressed its readiness to make appropriations for the trial of *open* competition,
the government had, with that caution which has marked the
whole progress of administrative reform, preferred to have
fuller evidence of the effects of what they had already done.
Some had complained that the standard of admission was too
high, some that it was too low. Conservatives had expressed
fears that the new system endangered the constitution ; and
partisans had got angry over the loss of patronage and spoils.
In 1860, therefore, a Parliamentary committee of fifteen was
appointed " to inquire into the present mode of nominating
and examining candidates for *junior* appointments in the civil
service, with a view of ascertaining whether greater facility
may not be afforded for the admission of properly qualified
persons."

It is worth noticing, as an illustration of the high importance
which the English Parliament and nation have long attached
to the character of those who enter even its *junior* civil service,
that this inquiry was not treated as matter of clerical detail,

nor intrusted to inferior members, but was placed in charge of some of the foremost statesmen of both parties ; and the thorough investigation made is beyond comparison with any similar inquiry ever conducted by our Congress.   The six first names on the committee are the following :

Sir Stafford Northcote (now Chancellor of the Exchequer).

John Bright, } both in Mr. Gladstone's Cabinet.  ⎰
Robert Lowe, }                                    ⎱

Monckton Milnes.

Lord Stanley (now Lord Derby).

Mr. Roebuck.

Lord Stanley was made chairman.   The interest felt in the subject is shown by the facts that he did not fail to preside at a single one of the numerous meetings, and that, though five was a quorum, there was not a meeting at which less than eight were present.   I call attention to such details, not as being important in themselves, but to contrast them with the neglect and indifference, with which, in this country, a subject vital to its safety has generally been treated by legislators.   It would require far more space than I can give to do justice to the elaborate report of this committee, presented in July, 1860.   More than 4500 comprehensive questions are answered. There are exhaustive explanations in the appendix on special points.   Those in every grade of the service, from heads of departments to messengers and copyists, were fully examined.

The action of Parliament that led to the inquiry, as well as the opening proceedings of the committee, showed that there was no thought of taking any back steps, but only of perfecting and extending the new system, and of removing collateral abuses that interfered with its good effects.   The committee give the whole number officially employed in the civil service of Great Britain in 1860 (not however including those serving in the colonies or in India, as I understand

it), as............................................. 58,504

To those are to be added artisans and laborers....... 29,613

Persons not wholly employed, women, etc.......... 14,941

In all..............................................103,058 [1]

---

[1] I think this includes none of the postmasters, but there is an indefiniteness of language on the subject.   Report, 1860, p. viii., and 247 and 362.

There were, of those designated as heads of departments, in all 190. Of these 190 only from *thirty-four* to fifty are classed as " political " - that is, as being the officers (exclusive of some of the foreign ministers) who go out and come in with an administration. *Beyond those, a change of administration in England does not change its civil service.*[1]

The committee say that, since the creation of the Civil Service Commission, and, before the end of 1859, there had been 10,860 nominations to which the order of 1854 applied ; of which 2479 had been rejected ; and that " it is worthy of notice that of these latter *all except 106 were rejected as deficient in arithmetic or spelling, a fact which your committee thinks ought to be borne in mind when complaints are made of the needlessly high educational requirements imposed on candidates for the civil service.* . . . The examiners emphatically deny that candidates have ever been rejected, as is frequently rumored, for failing to answer questions of a recondite or difficult character. . . . It does not appear that an examination paper has ever come *unfairly* into the hands of a candidate or his tutor. . . ."

It would seem from this report that about 500 new admissions are annually made into the 58,504 which make up the regular official civil service ; but these 500 vacancies are exclusive of those in the post office service. That department remained longer under political influence than any other. Yet even its average yearly appointments, for five years previous to 1859, was 111 clerks, 14 mail guards, and 535 sorters, letter carriers, and laborers. But in regard to the lower grade of postmasters, it would seem that there was still a considerable response to political influence in making appointments, but there were no removals without cause. The average appointments for

---

[1] Report, 1860, pp. 347 and 362.

It may be stated as explaining the large number of 190 heads of departments, that several offices are called departments that would not be so called with us. The inland and customs revenue, for example, is each under a separate department, each being in charge of several commissioners or heads, all in a limited way subordinate to the Treasury. So there are several Lords or Heads of the Admiralty and of the Treasury. But of these heads, I repeat, only about 34 to 50 are political, or go out with a change of administration.

five years of postmasters, sub-postmasters, and letter receivers had been 1264 annually.

The report brings out, in a striking way, the well-known fact that heads of bureaus and officers who have served under the patronage-favorite system are generally opposed to selection or promotion according to merit. They are also opposed to competition, for it not only takes away their arbitrary authority, but it may bring in or promote men brighter than themselves. Such officers had generally deprecated if not openly opposed reform; but the report shows that a majority of them had outgrown their prejudices. By some of these officers, opposition was unquestionably made for disinterested reasons. Mr. Helps and Mr. Trollope were distinguished for their hostility to the new system, and they stand almost alone among men of distinction who have conscientiously opposed it. The opposition of Mr. Trollope was so conspicuous that it is referred to in the report; and, as his peculiar views have been frequently quoted in this country, I give a question and answer from his examination before the committe, which will show the evil the new system was in his view bringing upon the country:

"Are you of the opinion that there is a *serious evil* to be apprehended in getting men who are, *too good* for their situation? I think so." [1]

---

[1] Mr. Trollope's view seems to have been that it was possible to get men who were above their business, an evil perhaps; but he did not say that this would be an effect of the new system, if found to exist at all, which could be easily prevented by lowering the examination. His fears, however, have not been realized. The views of Mr. Arthur Helps have also been often quoted in this country. Mr. Helps was the secretary of the Queen's privy council (one of the most aristocratic of the institutions that survive from early times), and Mr. Helps and such members of Parliament as Mr. Neate—the representative, of State Church doctrines and aristocratic philosophy, for the University of Oxford — condemn, competitive examinations "as bringing a lower class of society into the civil service." Mr. Helps, in his "Thoughts on Government," page 6, says, "I rather partake of the opinion of George III. (not altogether an unprejudiced observer) that the British Constitution is the best that has yet been devised by man." At page 82, we are told, "The conferring of honors is a most important function of government;" and at page 84 we

Having disposed of the objections, the report, in the language next quoted, states the ends sought by the wide range of the investigation the committee had made :

1. " To provide, by a proper system of examination, for the supply of the public service with a thoroughly efficient class of men."

2. " *To encourage industry and foster merit* by teaching all public servants *to look forward to promotion according to their deserts*, and to expect the highest prizes in the service if they can qualify themselves for them."

3. " To mitigate the evils which result from the fragmentary character of the service, and to introduce into it some elements of unity, by placing the first appointments upon a uniform footing, opening the way to the promotion of public officers to staff appointments in other departments than their own, and introducing into the lower ranks a body of men (the supplementary clerks) whose services may be made available at any time *in any office whatever*."

Such was the undertaking which, in 1860, the eminent, practical statesmen of both the great parties seemed to have thought to be more worthy of their attention than the manipulation of elections or the parcelling of patronage—plain as it is that only about a generation had passed since their predecessors were accustomed to give to these latter subjects the paramount importance with which we are so painfully familiar. And, I cannot forbear the remark that, so far as I recollect, such subjects have not yet commanded the attention of our leading statesmen, and that until they do there is great reason to fear that the abuses' of our civil administration will continue to be a subject of grave solicitude. I must pass over all the evidence relating to salaries, promotions, hours

---

are informed that the wisdom of a maxim of Napoleon, that " Religion and honors were the two things by which mankind may be governed," is so clear that it " will not be disputed by those who have had converse with their fellow-men." The value placed upon the eccentric judgment of this worthy and accomplished author may be inferred from the fact that the statesmen of the Privy Council, of which he was secretary, introduced competition for the selection of its clerks, in 1857, and that this method is still enforced in that office.

of service, classification, grading, discipline, superannuation, seniority, removals for cause, health, proper age for entering and leaving the service ; not because they are not full of interest and instruction, but because we shall never deal wisely with such matters, if even attention can be gained for them, until we have applied some salutary first principles to our service. In the present state of public opinion, they would only encumber the higher interests of the subject. I will therefore close my references to the report, with the leading conclusions of the committee.

1. Though the pass examinations, conducted by the Civil Service Commission, are far more effective than pass examinations, as before conducted in separate offices, they are yet greatly inferior to *limited* competition.

2. Limited competition would be much improved if more persons competed, and more should therefore be nominated for each competition. If they are to continue, there must also be preliminary examinations of those nominated by members to compete, so that there shall not, in the future, be competitions between mere dunces, blockheads, and ignoramuses.

3. The committee (whose report is unanimous) are convinced that open competition—free alike to every British subject, and an end, utterly, of the monopoly of patronage, now reduced to mere selections for examination—are what the public interest and the better public opinion demand, and that these results must very soon be reached. In not advising open competition at once, as the only entrance to the public service, they are influenced by prudential reasons. They fear a recoil of public opinion, if too great changes are made hastily. In the interest of open competition itself, they advise a cautious advance towards its complete introduction.

4. While such further experience is being acquired, the committee recommend that *pass* examinations be wholly superseded, that no place in the public service be filled save through a competition of five or at least three nominated persons, except that open competitions, wherever it be practicable, should be introduced after the plan of those which had lately been shown to be satisfactory in the East Indian service. The

15

salutary system of probation, according to which no one was to be appointed until after a trial of six months, was, I hardly need say, retained. Such were the conclusions reached in 1860. If it was a bold experiment to introduce the new system, it was certainly applied with prudence and watched with care.

# CHAPTER XXI.

## DEVELOPMENT OF THE NEW SYSTEM FROM 1860 TO 1870.

Government acts on report of 1860.—Examinations to weed out those unfit to compete.—Competition extended to various offices.—Two out of five nominated shown to be unfit even to compete.—Competition for the service of India.—Those educated in the public schools win in competition.—Have been 66,519 persons examined.—The new system becomes rapidly popular with the people.—Every one claimed to have an equal right to compete.—The official monopoly of nomination must be broken up.

IF the Parliamentary report of 1860 did not advance the *merit system* so rapidly as its more radical friends desired, it seems to have convinced its enemies that there was small chance of arresting it. It had taken a strong hold of the public mind. Its opponents were shown to be, with few exceptions, officers, partisans, and aristocrats, with the addition of a few excellent persons with peculiar views. Lord Palmerston's administration approved the report of the committee of 1860, and ordered its recommendations to be carried into effect. I must pass rapidly over the period of ten years of steady growth in the reform sentiment—of waning patronage and victorious competition—which brought in the great changes of 1870; making only slightest references to the annual reports of the Civil Service Commission, by which the public mind was being educated.

The report of 1861 shows that *The Treasury*, the great centre of patronage, promptly acted upon the suggestion of the Parliamentary committee of 1860—viz., that those nominated for competition should first undergo a preliminary *test* examination, in order to avoid the scandal of a competition between inferior persons alone. The need of such precaution was expressly shown by the facts that, during 1860, there were 66 nominated candidates examined for the admiralty service, out of which only 24 were competent, and that on a competition for clerks in the customs service, at Hull, not a competent person was found among the nominated champions sent there to compete.

The report says that "the desire is natural to provide for faithful and long tried servants, which has often led to the appointment of persons advanced in life" —in plainer phrase, it is natural for members of Parliament and other officers having the right of nomination to make the public service a hospital for the superannuated. Such facts more and more aroused the people to a sense of the imposition which members of Parliament and other high officials had long practiced upon the public service, under the pretense of selecting good officers from among their acquaintances. This same report shows that, hostile as the post-office department had been to the new system, even Mr. Trollope was ready for a competition for letter-carriers, based mainly on physical qualifications, which was also favored by the Postmaster-General, the Duke of Argyle. Competition is also shown to have been applied with success to apprentices in the dockyards and for the position of naval engineers, and also to the selection of young men to be sent to China and Japan to master the languages of those countries. The report for 1862 shows that competitions for engineer, dockyard and admiralty factory boys were successful, and that open competition was being extended elsewhere. The report for 1865 shows that of 364 persons nominated for competition, and subjected to a preliminary examination before being allowed to compete, 160, or in a ratio greater than two out of every five, were rejected as unworthy even to compete. No one can fail to see how natural it is that a system which arrests so many incompetent, official favorites should have bitter enemies, especially in official circles. This report also explains the successful progress of competition for the civil service of India, to which I shall soon call attention, showing that the natives of that country were winning official places in the contests.

It is shown, by the report for 1866, that 196 out of 411, and in 1867 that 244 out of 540, officially nominated for competition, were thrown out by the preliminary examination, as too stupid or ignorant to have a chance on a competitive trial, to say nothing of those who were superannuated. Those thus rejected doubtless corresponded to the troublesome fellows whom our members of Congress are said to sometimes send with an approving letter to a secretary, which letter is met by another declaring them to be blockheads or nuisances. There had, however, been some improvement in the class nominated : for, in 1859, out of 1107 nominated to fill 258 situations, only 397 were found qualified, and 710 were utterly rejected as incompetents.[1] It is also shown that of the whole number of marks gained in competition, in 1866, " eighty-two per cent were due to subjects included in the ordinary *curriculum* (studies) of a *public school ;*" and as further showing in what small ratio merely literary (or not directly practical) knowledge excludes those rejected, I may add that the report for 1867 shows that of 818 rejections in that year (from the 3038 examined) 805 were made by reason of deficiency in knowledge of " subjects connected with the practical work of the office," or of ignorance in the matters of " reading, spelling, arithmetic, and handwriting," and that only 13 were rejected by reason of a want of higher knowledge !

From the report for 1868, it appears that the whole number nominated for examination under the commission, during the thirteen years of its existence, had been (unless a few may have been twice nominated) 59,658. Some of them seem not to have had the courage to appear, for only 46,528 had been actually examined. Of these 9461 had been rejected ; of whom 480 were rejected for being physically disqualified, and 616 by reason of unsatisfactory character.[2]

This report also shows that competition had been extended to the public service at Ceylon and Mauritius, to the Irish constabulary force, to dockyard artificers, and to the public inspectors of schools throughout Great Britain.

The report for 1869 shows that the whole number of candidates for examinations whose names appeared on the books in

[1] Report on Civil Service, 1860.

[2] But (as I understand) the two last classes of rejections are independent of those who were rejected for the same causes for want of proper certificates before any examination took place.

the office of the commission—that office having become the
great centre of information relating to official life—had reached
66,519.   In addition to those who had failed to appear, 10,558
had been rejected as disqualified for various causes ; and, included in this number, were 2283 who had been preliminarily
rejected, as not even fit to be allowed to go into competitions.   These figures mark the extent of the prostitution of
Parliamentary nominations.   If by reason of so numerous rejections, many enemies of the new system were made among
officials, party leaders and their dependents, yet, on the
other hand, its keeping of incompetency out of the public service, and the honor it conferred on education and good character, had gained for it fiftyfold more friends among the
people at large.   The report for 1869 shows that during the
fourteen years of examinations under the Commission, 8169
persons had been rejected as deficient in mental ability and
literary attainments.   How few of these failures were due to
anything but stupidity or disgraceful ignorance may be inferred
from this extract : " If the subjects of examination be divided
into two classes, one including reading, spelling, handwriting,
arithmetic, and (in the case of each department), the subjects
connected with the practical work of that office ; the other
comprising those which are prescribed as tests of general intelligence and cultivation ; the number of rejections caused
by failures in the latter class of subjects has been only 271, as
against 7899 cases of failure in the former class."   In face of
such facts, it was, of course, impossible longer to pretend that
ornamental attainments won the day or that essential and practical knowledge were not decisive.   The old Parliamentary
monopoly of nominations had become not only untenable, but
ridiculous.   The change in public opinion, since 1850, had
been as great as that which had taken place, in this country on
the slave question, between 1840 and 1860.   The popular support of the merit system had become so overwhelming—indeed
so nearly universal—that opposition by any one cast something
like suspicion upon his motives.   The thought even of making it a party or Parliamentary issue had ceased to exist.   The
cause of civil service reform had become identified with that
of common justice, popular education, and official integrity ;

all of which it had greatly strengthened.    The people of England had finally decided that it was a public disgrace and a gross injustice to allow a monopoly of selections for appointment in the public service, on the part of members of Parliament or any other officials, to longer continue.    They demanded, as the right of every citizen, that he should be at liberty, without any official interference or consent, to present himself, in conformity to just regulations, for examination by the Civil Service Commission, for a place in the public service.    " I think that all persons have, *primâ facie*, an *equal right* to be candidates, if they are fit ; and if you do not concede that right and make it accessible, you do injustice, first, to the public service, and then to her Majesty's subjects generally who are excluded." [1]    Here is a principle of democratic equality and common justice maintained in a monarchy, but yet unrecognized in this republic.    We shall next see how this principle was reduced to practice in 1870.

[1] Report on Civil Service, 1860, p. 286.

# CHAPTER XXII.

## THE ORDER FOR OPEN COMPETITION IN 1870.

Right of nomination lost its value.—Officers not willing to defend their monopoly of nominations.—Order for open competition.—Its provisions.—
Probation retained.—Exceptions to open competition.—Nature of the opposition made.—General principle of the new method provided for.

THE demand for the suppression of the official monopoly of
patronage had become too strong for the administration to
withstand, had it been so disposed. Even the more partisan
members of Parliament had ceased to care much for a right to
nominate : because the inevitable result had been that a great
portion of those whom they most wished should secure places
were thrown out in disgrace by the preliminary examination,
and not a few of the residue had been distanced in the competition. To enable their *protégés* to succeed, they must
nominate the most worthy young men, but that necessity deprived their perquisite of most of its value in their eyes ; since
it would neither aid an election nor make a place for an old
servant. None but the most brazen-faced and unscrupulous
were willing to appear longer as sponsors of the prostitution
of the executive power they had ' usurped, now that the people
comprehended that it was prized by its possessors in the exact
ratio that it was costly and demoralizing to the public service.
A monopoly which had prevailed for more than a hundred and
fifty years was almost without a claimant or a defender.

On the 4th of July, 1870, the administration, through an
executive order in Council, and without any action by Parliament, gave effect to the wishes of the people by abolishing
official patronage and favoritism (and limited competition as
an incident), and substituting open competition in their place.[1]

---

[1] " Our object was to introduce competition. I think that everything we
did, so far as I know, was rigidly subordinated to that."—Testimony of the
Chancellor of the Exchequer, Report of Committee, 1873, p. 226.

The order declares " that the qualifications of all such persons as may be proposed to be appointed, either permanently or temporarily, *to any situation or employment*, in any department in the civil service, shall, before they are employed, be tested by or under the directions of said *Commissioners ;* and no person shall be employed in any department of the civil service until he shall have been reported by the said Commissioners to be qualified to be admitted on *probation* to such situation or employment."

" All appointments which it may be necessary to make after the 31st of August next (1870), . . . shall be made by reasons of *competitive* examinations according to regulations, . . . *open to all persons* (of requisite age, health, character, and other qualifications prescribed in the said regulations), who may be desirous of attending the same." '

These provisions do not extend to mere day laborers or to wholly unskilled labor, but they do extend to skilled laborers in continuous public employment. And there are exceptions of three classes of official persons (very few in all), whom I shall more particularly describe. The order then provides that the Civil Service Commissioners, the Commissioners of the Treasury, and the chiefs of the departments shall frame proper rules or regulations for putting open competition into practice. The regulations or rules provided methods of ascertaining the age, character, and physical health as well as the attainments and practical capacity for the public business of those who offer themselves for competition. The appointments were to be given to those shown by the competition to have the highest qualifications for the service ; and it will be noticed that it is not mere ornamental or literary attainments which are to be made the subject of the examinations, "*but knowledge and ability to enter on the discharge of his official duties.*" And to secure a still higher guaranty of practical, executive capacity, the long-tried rule of probation was retained and made more stringent. No actual appointment was to be made except at the end of a six-months' trial of official

---

' Subject to the payment of small fees which were intended to cover the expenses of the examinations, but they have been made so light as to pay only about one third of such expense.

work, during which time "a formal record of the particulars
of the result of such probation" (of course covering deport-
ment as well as capacity) was to be kept, "and the chief of
the department" (as used here nearly the equivalent of a chief
of bureau with us) must sign and declare satisfactory this
record, and send it to the Civil Service Commission for preservation.

So far from such provisions being an inadequate test of
practical capacity, as some mistaken people have supposed,
they have been found to be highly effective. They have been
objected to as being much too severe, since young men might
lose their places by reason of an unsatisfactory probation.
The answer was that applicants, or their friends, must, at
their own peril, form a correct judgment of their ability for
practical work.[1]

Before considering the practical effects of the great changes
which this order introduced, we may well reflect a moment

---

[1] A few words of explanation may make the exceptions to competition
more intelligible. There are three classes of them. The first embraces the
34 to 50 political officers who go out with an administration, and to which I
have before made reference.

There are some provisions as to the second class in this order of 1870 ;
and the clauses of the Superannuation act before referred to are to nearly
the same effect. The two provisions together cover cases (always very few
in number) where persons of maturer years may be needed in the public service, who shall possess professional or peculiar attainments of a high order
not acquired in the usual course of public instruction or of experience in
the service. In such cases, the Lords of the Treasury, together with the
head of department where such an appointment is needed, may make a
selection, and thereupon there is to be a special examination and certificate
of qualification by the Civil Service Commissioners, upon which, the same
being satisfactory, the appointment may be made, but not before.

The third class of exceptions from open competition covers promotions.
They are, in the main, based on merit, either tested by limited competition
among those within the departments, or otherwise tested, as I shall have
occasion to explain. In some offices meritorious seniority is given weight.

It will be seen, therefore, that the entire exceptions to open competition,
as the rule for admissions under the order of 1870, can hardly exceed one
per cent of the whole number in the public service. The lower grades of
post-offices, however, are not included in that order.

But in order to guard against any unforeseen embarrassments from a
change so sweeping, provision was made for taking particular officers out
of competition as public exigency might require.

upon its nature and the convictions which enforced its adoption. We should take notice that the order not merely arrested all interference by the members of the legislature with executive appointments, but it also involved, and in substance proclaimed, a surrender, by the members of the Cabinet and by every other high officer (with the small exceptions just pointed out), of all opportunity to make any selfish or partisan use of the appointing power. Recognizing the inherent duty of always using that power so as to secure the persons best qualified to serve the people, the order declared that the open competition provided for was the most reliable means of ascertaining such persons ; and that, upon their being ascertained, the duty of appointment was imperative. The usurped authority thus reclaimed from the members of the legislature was not an increase of executive power in any arbitrary sense, or even in any sense whatever ; for the freedom of open competition was at the same time extended to the whole body of the British people ; and hence it was not the Executive, but the people themselves—common justice, general liberty, personal character and capacity—which had really won the victory and made the gain. If the executive had, in one sense, a larger discretion than before, it was only a discretion to discharge a public duty, by recognizing and rewarding merit, as tested by fair public standards which all right-minded men approved. It was no discretion to grant favors or to encroach on liberty. The order was, in short, a grand triumph of patriotism, character, education, and capacity over selfishness, official favoritism, partisan intrigue, and whatever else had been corrupt, immoral, or unjust in the action of parties or the bestowal of office. It marked the highest elevation of justice and official self-denial that governmental action, in any country, had ever reached ; for though examinations and competitions had been used in a qualified form in France, Germany, Sweden, and several other European countries, they were not wholly without official dictation nor were they free to all citizens alike. Open competition, thus established in Great Britain, said, in substance, to every British subject : The administration confers no favors by appointments, the great parties are not allowed to coerce you, the high officers are forbidden to use the appointing power capriciously ; and, subject to the just regulations prescribed, each of you is at liberty to compete for, and, if you are the most worthy, you will win a place in the public service of your country, there to remain as long as you serve her honorably and efficiently and her interests require you. The able and experienced statesmen who, after the partisan system had been tried for more than five generations, thus brought in the *merit system* in its completest form, with no protest from either party, must, I think, be regarded as condemning, more emphatically by their action than they could by any language, the entire theory of securing power for parties, stability for administrations, or economy, purity, or safety for nations, by a partisan use of the appointing power. They did not condemn party government in its true form, or when acting by just methods : but only its prostitution to the purposes of a partisan system of appointments. Thus, the British people—with whom party government originated, and by whom it has been given the most absolute sway—have, after a long and earnest discussion of the subject—such as has taken place in no other nation—demanded and applauded that great change —and, by their acts, have expressed their profound conviction that all that is salutary in political parties will survive the loss of all that is corrupt or venal, and their determination that, thereafter, those in power shall seek support, not through intrigue and manipulation, or through influence secured by the prostitution of the appointing power, but upon their record of good administration. In approving this order, they practically said to the Crown, to the administration, and to the great parties : Hereafter, as before, the party majorities may carry all elections, name all members of the Cabinet, make all laws, and guide all national action, whether domestic or foreign. In those high spheres, the principles of parties, the worth and ability of their leaders, the wisdom of their policy must gain public favor or fail in the attempt. With such prizes to win, elections can never lose their wholesome interest, nor citizens be indifferent to their results. The examinations will cause the most worthy to be selected as subordinates to carry into effect the instruction of their superiors.

But we neither wish, nor will we allow, any action by parties, or anything to be done by postmasters, collectors, or other subordinate officers, or any processes of electing members of Parliament, which depend upon making merchandise of the appointing power or upon treating public places as perquisites or spoils. After the *partisan system* in its long trial under its favorite forms had failed, we allowed party managers and public officials to decide, during the period from 1855 to 1870, who should be examined for admission to the public service. The records show that inferior and unworthy persons were generally nominated. Members of Parliament did not nominate the most worthy among their acquaintances, but they used their monopoly in a selfish and partisan spirit. We now therefore suppress the monopoly. We order the trial whether parties cannot make their issues upon sound principles and good works ; whether better men will not apply for admission to the public service, now that official and partisan tyranny has been dislodged at its gates ; whether the moral tone of politics will not rise, now that patronage and favoritism have been expelled from the departments.

# CHAPTER XXIII.

## FIRST EXPERIENCE OF OPEN COMPETITION.

Competitions extended to the military schools.—Competition in India.—An aristocratic division into classes.—Numbers competing.—Extended to various offices, civil, military, and naval.—Better men secured by open competition.—Obstructions by officers.

THE report of the Civil Service Commission for 1870 shows that the whole number of those who had been before the commission during the period of limited competition had been 71,971 ; a number considerably greater than the whole body of those in the British Civil Service, who are properly designated as officers or clerks.[1]  It also shows that examinations for admissions to the Military College at Sandhurst, for the Military Academy at Woolwich, and for direct commissions in the army, were thereafter to be conducted under the Civil Service Commission ; and that one *open* competition had just been held for such admission.  It is an interesting fact that, though we instituted examinations for admissions to our naval and military schools before such examinations were introduced in England, the English Government, encouraged by the success of their tests of merit for civil appointment, has rapidly made her selection of cadets for the army and navy far more independent than ours, both of official favoritism and of partisan dictation.  I need not enter into the details concerning the new rules, the general principles of which I have already explained.  I may say, however, that they not only provide for examinations in elementary subjects (essential for all or nearly all candidates to understand), but for examinations extending to that special information and skill necessary in particular officers or kinds of service : or, in other words, they range, in their prac-

---

[1] Exclusive of postmasters.

tical bearing, from reading, writing, and the elementary rules of arithmetic, to knowledge of materials and skill and attainments adequate for applying the patent, customs, and inland revenue laws, so that fraud may be detected and the money due to the government may be more efficiently collected. I might quote pages, if it was worth while, in answer to the popular and superficial criticism so often made, to the effect that examinations and probation cannot test the attainments or capacity needed for the real work of the offices. But if the fact that the most practical nation in the world—the nation having the most complex and difficult civil administration that has ever existed—has, as the result of varied and long continued trial, demonstrated to its satisfaction that such theoretical criticism is unfounded, shall not be regarded as decisive, surely a more extended discussion of the subject would be useless.

In the report for 1872, the first results of open competition on a grand scale are set forth at length.[1] So democratic or republican an innovation as that of opening the whole civil service to the free competition of all classes, very naturally, not a little alarmed the more aristocratic officials; and they were strong enough in 1870 to enforce a division of the new clerks into two classes, known as Class I. and Class II., the attainments and work of the former to be of a higher order. If this division was not in the liberal spirit of the order of 1870, it was quite in the spirit of the division of the legal profession into barristers and attorneys, and of the legislature into Lords and Commons. We shall find that this aristocratic distinction has been disapproved and substantially abolished by that same just and liberal sentiment which demanded open competition, though not before it had produced both jealousies and expensive complications. The belief was so general that open competition would introduce a better class of

---

[1] This report, very inexpressive in form, with the examination papers and correspondence appended (covering both the domestic and Indian service), fills more than 800 large pages; and the annual reports that follow are not much less voluminous; the whole action of the Civil Service Commission being set forth at length, in order to give the utmost publicity to proceedings peculiarly liable to be prejudiced by charges of unfairness, if any part of them should be involved in mystery or confusion.

public servants, and thereby enable a reduction to be made of the number, and hence of expense in the service, that preparation for that result was made in the outset ; and it was fully realized. The report for 1872 shows that since open competition, under the order of 1870, had commenced, 2684 persons had competed for 355 places (exclusive of those in the Post Office Department), and those 355 places had been assigned to the most meritorious. Besides these competitions, there was open competition for selecting boys to fill the junior clerkships in the Post Office Department, for newspaper sorters and for telegraph messengers ; 1995 such situations having been filled between July, 1870, and June, 1872, by the most worthy as indicated by competition between 10,065 persons. Postmaster James, of the New York City Post Office, now keeps his "sorters" up to their rare condition of efficiency by the same kind of examinations. Nor do these include all ; for there were also the competitors for the admiralty and military service, and for the Irish constabulary, raising the total candidates to 14,123. And even this immense number is exclusive of the examinations for the entire public service of British India. In these competitions, we have the means of making the first practical comparison, on a large scale, between those who presented themselves for examination, directly and freely from the people, and those who had been sent in by the nomination-monopolists ; and the language of the report on this vital point is as follows : "But it is more important to observe that the standard of proficiency exhibited by the successful competitors, and even by many of the unsuccessful, has been very satisfactory, and *far in advance of that which we found it possible to enforce under the previous system of nomination.* Nor can we refrain from expressing a confident hope that, while an important branch of the service will thus gain by the appointment of officers of superior intelligence, a further and wider benefit will result to the public generally from the stimulus which these large competitions for valuable privileges must impart *to elementary education in each of the numerous districts in which they are held.*" They were held from time to time in various parts of England, Ireland, and Scotland ; and weekly in London.

Instructive examples are next given of the successful use of open competition for the selection of persons required to possess technical, scientific, and even mechanical proficiency, but I cannot spare space for them.[1]  The report further shows that such competition had been applied for the selection of clerks in the House of Lords ; and also by Earl Granville, the Secretary of Foreign Affairs, for the selection of *student interpreters* in the consular service.[2]

The eighteenth report of the commission brings the new system down to January 1st, 1874.  It shows that under various pretences causing delay in applying open competition, and through the facilities afforded by the complication of offices in an old country and the natural desire of officials to retain unlimited authority,[3] a considerable number of places had still been filled through nominations and limited competition.  Yet open competition had rapidly advanced.  It had been for the first time extended to appointments to cavalry and infantry regiments, and to applicants for places in the commissary department of the army.  Besides those examined for the military service, and for service in British India, it appears that 23,261 had come before the commission since the order of 1870.

[1] See Report 1872. pp. X. and XI.

[2] It would seem that great influence had been used to take certain places out of competition under the order ; and a moderate number had, for apparently good reasons, been excepted.

[3] My theory is, that all persons in authority are the natural enemies of competition, and that if they have an opportunity of evading it, they will use it.—Investigation, 1874, vol. i., p. 125, Evidence of Mr. Lowe.

16

# CHAPTER XXIV.

A thorough investigation ordered.—Economy the object.—Patronage being at an end, members are ready to reduce numbers and salaries.—Spirit and scope of the inquiry.—Sinecures brought to light.—How open competition tends to economy. Officers allowed to vote.—No official fraud or corruption found.—Open competition approved.

THE investigation of 1873 is mainly instructive for reasons peculiar to itself. The committee consisted of seventeen members of the House of Commons; and its membership shows that the importance of the subject had not fallen in the estimation of that body. Sir Stafford Northcote, the present Chancellor of the Exchequer, was chairman; Mr. Childers (of Mr. Gladstone's cabinet), Mr. Smith (now of Mr. Disraeli's cabinet), Mr. McLaren (a brother-in-law of John Bright), and Mr. Vernon Harcourt were upon the committee. The report, in three volumes, was, if possible, even more thorough and searching than those already referred to. I should think it safe to say that, if all the investigations made by us since the formation of our government, with a view to economy in our civil administration, were united into one, such united reports would fail to bring together so complete and important a mass of facts and explanations. The third volume of the report alone would fill nearly a thousand pages of our documentary size; and it contains answers to more than five thousand questions, besides many subordinate reports and special statements. Every class of officials and employés, from the Lord Chancellor and the head of the Treasury down to messengers and post boys, were examined, and nothing was allowed to screen scandalous secrets. The special—I may say the only—object of this investigation was to " inquire whether any and what reductions can be effected in the expenditures for the civil service." The prior investigations had been directed to the best means of selecting and promoting officers, to the discipline, duties, and methods best adapted to secure honest and efficient administration. This had for its object retrenchment and economy, in harmony with the new system. Nothing is more significant, in connection with this inquiry, than the facts that it could be ordered with such breadth and carried forward with such completeness and severity. When members could see that retrenchment might abolish places they wished to fill, send back to them their poor dependents, or cut down the salaries of the partisan henchmen to whom they owed a debt of gratitude—to say nothing of the scandals of which such results might provoke a disclosure—how could they be expected to have courage for economy? But limited competition, from 1855 to 1870, having excluded most of the unworthy, and open competition, since 1870, having closed the doors of patronage and favoritism, members of Parliament had no longer the same interest to resist retrenchment. The investigation of 1873 was, therefore, a natural outcome of the new system of selections. I cannot take the space required to do justice to this great inquest of economy; and I fear we are not likely to appreciate its value until we shall have taken patronage away from our officials and freely opened our public service to the personal worth of the nation. Some general explanations must suffice. The inquiry was not confined to questions about the lowest salaries that would secure clerks and the fewest clerks that could be made to do the work at the period of the reports. It extended to the whole subject of organization, official authority, subordination, discipline, hours of labor, mechanical appliances, holy days, health and sickness, ventilation of offices, pride in the service, honesty efficiency in making collections, satisfaction in performing public duty, promotions, increase of pay with length of service, retiring allowances, proper age for coming into and going out of the public service—in all the aspects in which these matters bear upon economy and efficiency of administration in its long range. I say, in its long range: for while a purpose of promoting direct economy is everywhere apparent, it is not less apparent that it was regarded as one of the surest means of inducing young men of worth to enter and remain in the service, at a low salary, that they should feel that their compensation and tenure were not utterly precarious, and that their official relations would not be needlessly degrading or disagreeable. The authors of the report evidently believe that if the surroundings of a man, in the minor civil service, are not inconsistent with a manly self-respect, and if he is not liable, every hour, to be dismissed upon the spite of an official or the greedy claim of a party manager, he is not only more likely to be honest and efficient, but certain to be willing to accept a lower salary. The purpose of making the public service honorable and manly, and hence attractive and economical, everywhere finds expression. I am strongly impressed with the fact, so often shown in these reports, that, in this aristocratic, old country, those in the public service are treated with more consideration and justice than are those in our public service. Their freedom of opinion is as much greater as their tenure of office is more secure. Under the partisan system, they had been disfranchised by the statutes of George III., as the only means of securing freedom of elections ; but the merit system had made it practicable to remove that disability, and since 1868 [*] they had been as free to vote as any other citizen ; and, having a tenure during good conduct and capacity, they were no longer driven into election contests to make sure of their own places. And here I will repeat a fact, emphasized in the inquiry of 1873 that where excessive numbers have been employed, it is treated as the fault of the government or of its higher officers, for which the nation is responsible ; and the supernumeraries are not arbitrarily dismissed, but are given the first vacancies for which they are qualified. Our practice in that regard would be looked upon as cruel in England. Even when an office is abolished, some provision as a general rule is made for him who filled it. And I hardly need add that, as a natural consequence, British officials, in the lower grade—such as doorkeepers and boatmen—not less than the highest, cherish, as I am compelled to believe, much kinder

---

Act 31 and 32 Vict. ch. 73, as amended, in 1874, by 37 and 38 Vict. ch. 22.

and more respectful feelings than are found among our officials towards their superiors and towards the public service generally. Nor can I doubt that such provisions, by awakening gratitude and a sense of duty, advance economy and fidelity alike. But I have departed too much from my general plan, which is to reserve the practical results of the new system for the last topic. Before dismissing this inquiry of 1873, I will refer to a few illustrative facts which this new courage for retrenchment brought to light. They show what sums members of Parliament had been willing to vote, if only their favorites were retained in the public service. There was an old office designated as " Patentee of Bankrupts," which had many years ago ceased to have more than the merest nominal existence ; yet the persons holding or pensioned for it, and doing nothing whatever, appear to have received altogether nearly $2,500,000, and there was being expended, on account of it, the sum of $60,000 a year of the public money.

Clerks of assize were shown to be drawing salaries at the rate of $2500 annually, and yet not serving the public more than twenty-five days in the year. There were cases brought to light of the same person holding several offices, and very suspicious examples of nepotism and extravagance on the part of high officials. The Treasury had been compelled, during the last year, to rebuke the Master of the Rolls by letter for giving clerkships to his son and his nephew, and it was done in strong and plain terms. Even the Lord Chancellor had to make an explanation in writing ; his secretary having been receiving a salary of $6000 a year, and the clerk of the secretary a salary of $2000 a year ! The committee were also very free in their raillery and scrutiny in regard to purse bearers, porters of the great seal, court-keepers, ceremonial ushers and other needless or overpaid officials, which the vicious patronage system had allowed to survive from the royal times of old. The overhauling of patronage, in the hands of judges of the higher courts, was as severe as it was needful. It was shown that certain *registrars*, being part of the old patronage of the Chief Justices of the King's Bench and Common Pleas, had no duties whatever, the whole work being done by deputy registrars ; yet it would appear that the registrars for the county of Middlesex alone had been collecting fees at the rate of from $10,000 to $15,000 a year. But the bankrupt court was the great headquarters of sinecurists. The annual cost of the court was shown to be $710,000; of which $280,000 was being paid for the services of officers no longer performing any duty whatever!

I can spare no more space for such examples. But the following, from the evidence of the permanent Secretary of the Treasury, is worthy of quotation: " Under competition, you have no patronage, and there is therefore no motive to increase establishments beyond the strength which is required for the work which they have to do; on the contrary, there is a very strong motive in the departments themselves to keep the establishment down, so as to have the credit of economical estimates."[1] Of which I may add this practical illustration from the same report—viz., that, in 1853 (before competition was introduced), the customs service cost $5,250,000, in 1868 it cost only $4,950,000, and in 1872 only $4,600,000. There is one more important consideration connected with this report to which I must refer. The thorough and fearless scrutiny of the committee extended over several months and into every office, without respect of station, high or low—a scrutiny that brought the head of the Treasury and the Lord Chancellor to their bar, not less than the humblest clerks and doorkeepers —a scrutiny which invited and received the complaints of every discharged or discontented official who chose to appear or to write—and yet such a scrutiny did not, so far as I can discover, disclose a single instance of peculation or fraud, nor was there any evidence or charge that illicit gains or corruption (except in the survival of the abuses of the old system as illustrated in the examples I have given) anywhere existed or were *by anybody believed to exist in the public service.* And I am unable to find any other explanation of a condition of things so striking, except selections and promotions based on merit, a tenure not disturbed for political reasons, retiring allowances, and the various methods to which I have adverted for promoting self-respect and respect for the government on

[1] Third Report 1873.  Answer 3176.

the part of those in its service.    It is only when we contemplate the full significance of such freedom from even the suspicion of corruption or dishonesty, and compare it with the pervading venality and malversation which had prevailed in earlier generations, that we are able to comprehend the scope and the blessing of administrative reform in Great Britain.    We then feel the force of the reasons which have called her greatest statesmen to the work and made it the pride and the safety of her people.

# CHAPTER XXV.

## THE EXECUTIVE INVESTIGATION OF 1874.

Relates to department details.—Better organization.—No change in the principles of the new system.—Restrictions removed.—Aristocratic division into two classes disapproved.—Open competition approved and extended.

THE reasons which gave Parliament the courage and independence needed to probe abuses in 1873 had a similar effect upon executive officers. Most of those who had secured places by their favor had received promotion before 1874, and such officers had no personal interest in screening those who had obtained places by open competition. No one, I think, can peruse the series of stern and searching examinations into the English Civil Service, made between 1860 and 1874, without feeling that a new and fearless spirit in harmony with the higher sentiment of the nation has come over official life. The inquiries made by the commission of 1874, unlike those before considered, were not ordered by Parliament, but by the executive. The commission consisted of nine persons (two being members of Parliament), of whom the Right Honorable Lyon Playfair (Postmaster-General in Mr. Gladstone's last cabinet) was chairman. The main aims of the investigation seemed to have been to review the method of selecting civil servants, especially in reference to its operation within the departments; to grade the service so as to make compensation and labor more equable; to provide a method of transfer of officers from one office to another, and to arrange for doing the lower grade of public work through less expensive clerks. The inquiry ranged over almost the whole field of civil service, and three elaborate reports were made. Even a summary of the topics and recommendations would carry me far beyond reasonable limits. It affords a still more striking illustration than any I have referred to of the extent to which the British Government has sought to secure efficiency and economy in the public service by introducing just and scientific methods.

It was not proposed to interfere with the principle of open competition or with any of the essential features of the *merit system;* and in fact they were not only strengthened and extended, but were relieved of the encumbering *débris* of the old system as well as of some needless restrictions. Nor, in the immense mass of testimony taken in 1874 and 1875, any more than in that taken in 1873, can I find *anything tending to show personal corruption on the part of any officer, or any feeling that such corruption existed in the public service.* There is no lack of complaint about inadequate salaries, too hard work, too exacting regulations, slow promotion, and unfair distribution of labor and of honors ; but everywhere faith in official integrity and pride in being connected with the public service. From the numerous topics that will be likely to command our attention, wherever we shall make a thorough study of the condition of good civil administration, I select but two as especially calling for notice here. The public opinion that broke through patronage and favoritism had been too radical and exacting, in its hour of victory, to impose wise conditions upon its great demand that all places should be won by merit tested in open competition. It was consequently insisted that he who should stand highest in the competition should have the first vacancy, if indeed the competition was not directly for a single vacancy. And such had been substantially the practice ; a practice that gave but the smallest discretion to the appointing power, and hence afforded less opportunity than was desirable for giving to those having a high average, yet varying qualifications, the particular places for which they, were best fitted. This was an inconvenient restriction needlessly imposed, and was not involved in the principle of competition. In some cases it too much curtailed a salutary official liberty of choice. Through the commission of 1874, this undue restriction was removed ; and provision was made that the appointments (always as heretofore to be made to the lowest grade) should be made from among several of those highest in the competition : the liberty of choice, as to the several officers,

always being large enough to allow the most appropriate talent
and attainments being chosen for the particular place to be
filled, but not so large as to give room for official favoritism.
It is plain that the fit range of choice, in this regard, may well
be greater for some places than for others, according to the
peculiarity of capacity needed, and that the subject is one for
detailed provision in the rules.   The other leading subject
dealt with by the committee was that of the aristocratic division of those in the public service into two classes.   The
principle of free, open competition is repugnant to that distinction.   The division was also as objectionable by reason of its
effect upon economy, convenience, and good feeling, in the
public service, as it was on the score of justice and principle.
Those of the first class had higher salaries, performed higher
work, and they claimed social precedence ; though they might
be morally and intellectually inferior to those of the second
class.   Jealousy and antagonism, and a sense of injustice on
the part of the lower class, were the natural results.   Haughty,
aristocratic officials favored Class I., and used their influence
to crowd the service with that class, and to depress Class II.,
whereby needless expense for salaries was incurred.   It was
made very difficult to get from the lower class to the higher.
When humble young men of worth had won their way to the
service, they found, to their disgust, that they were admitted
to hardly half of it, and that the lower half, on which a higher
grade looked down frowningly.   They were in the relation of
English attorneys to barristers, of Commons to Lords.   In
accordance with the scheme of the report of 1874, the line of
demarcation between the two classes has been substantially
opened to merit, and the division itself must soon, I think,
cease to exist.   But the idea of classes is too deep in the English mind to allow its speedy suppression in official circles,
and it will doubtless survive its application to practice.

There is another view of this series of investigations, from
1853 to 1876, well worthy of notice : as it indicates a continued
growth of the reforming sentiment.   With departments of
government as with individuals, it is far easier to criticise
others than to institute self-reform.   An officer who thoroughly
inquires into and exposes the defects allowed by himself has

taken one of the most difficult steps in public duty. The inquiry of 1853 was, in substance, an inquiry by the executive
into usurpations and shortcomings of members of Parliament ;
taking care to say only the least about the real object. The
intermediate investigations were made by Parliament into
executive administration ; while those ordered in 1874 were
made by the executive into the detailed abuses in its own administration. And by this time the independent sentiment of
the country had become so strong that I find no evidence that
the leaders of either party ventured to interpose any objections
to the most complete exposure of abuses, or to the large reduction of expenses effected. Indeed, the time seemed to be
past when either party could hope to gain as much through
the influence of its friends in subordinate stations as through a
reputation for favoring an honest and economical execution of
the laws.

# CHAPTER XXVI.

## THE RESULTS OF THE MERIT SYSTEM BASED ON OPEN COMPE-
## TITION IN BRITISH INDIA.

Official opinions between 1853 and 1875.—Law of 1860 requiring examinations before Civil Service Commission.—Full investigation ordered in 1875.
—The investigation made.—The new system approved.—Better men obtained.—Better administration.—Great difficulties overcome.—Open competition free to all British subjects, now the door of entrance to the Indian
service.

It has already been shown that, after many experiments,
with a view to render favoritism and patronage tolerable in
India, it had been found necessary to abolish both in 1853 and
to substitute the *Merit System* founded on open competition.
The changes being novel, were of course regarded as wholly
tentative, and they were carefully watched by both the friends
and enemies of the new system. The first official inquiry as to
its effects was made in 1863, with these results officially promulgated : " It is enough to observe that the general results
of the inquiry were in favor of the system, so far as it had
been then developed : and that this favorable judgment was
adopted and confirmed, somewhat later, by the Government
of India, in a dispatch dated May 5th, 1866.". . . The
results of the inquiry instituted by the Government of India
were thus summarized by the Governor-General, Lord Lawrence, one of the ablest administrators ever at the head of
Indian affairs, in a dispatch dated May 5th, 1866 : " We would
observe that, as the civil servants who were at first appointed
under the system of competitive examinations have not as yet
been ten years in India, and as consequently the great majority
of the servants so appointed are still holding very subordinate
positions in the service, it would, in our opinion, be prema-
ture to pronounce, conclusively, whether or not the civil ser-

vice has, on the whole, been improved by the present system. We are inclined, however, to believe that it has, and it may at least, we think, be confidently affirmed that the present system is effective to exclude great inefficiency, which undoubtedly was not excluded under the old system ; and also that the young men who enter the service under the present system are, as a rule, more highly educated than those who found admittance under the former system."[1] As these reports only relate to the practical effects of the new system *in* India, nothing is said in them of the check it put to the intrigue, and favoritism in connection with nominations which it arrested, in England. I need not enter into details on that subject ; for it is enough to say that the advantages of the new system were so early appreciated in England that in 1859–60 it was provided by statute[2] "that no candidate shall be admitted to the service in India . . . without a certificate from the Civil Service Commissioners of examination by them." . . . These examinations were competitive. It is declared in the before cited, Parliamentary Report made in 1860,[3] that the competitive examinations for the India service are entirely open and free. No one nominates those to be examined, but they propose themselves. The chairman of the Civil Service Commission uses this language : " The Minister for India has no knowledge with regard to these candidates until we return to him the list of those who have passed us, nor does he in any way interfere in regard to that competition."[4] The new system, therefore, completely excluded all patronage, favoritism, threats, and solicitation; success in competition alone giving a chance for a place in the service. He who wished to test his merits by competition could do so without asking permission from anybody. And this was not only true of all British subjects proper, but of the natives of India as well, of whatever race, caste, or religion they might be. All are allowed to compete alike. Among the 754 who first won places by competi-

---

[1] Report of Commission of Inquiry of 1874, as to selections, etc., for Civil Service of India, pp. 12, 19, and 20.

[2] 21st and 22d Vict., chap. 106, § 32.

[3] Report of 1860, p. 328.

[4] Ibid., p. 328.

tion, there were natives of France, Canada, Brazil, and of the
United States. How little the contest favored mere college
learning was shown by the fact that of the forty who won the
highest places, in the competition of 1874, thirty had gained
their education in the public schools. And in practice
open competition was made as republican and democratic as
it is in theory. It has been one of the significant results that
intelligent and docile Hindoos and Parsees have, to a great extent, crowded the stolid and domineering Moslems out of the
public service of India. Thus the experiment was continued
on trial until 1875, when it was thought that, as more than
twenty years had elapsed since it was commenced, it was time
for a thorough investigation of its general effects. It had encountered opposition not only from officers who had long been
accustomed to the old system, but also from those who have a
great love of unlimited, official authority. I have cited Mr.
Robert Lowe's testimony that such officials always oppose competition. It was also opposed by a few very cautious and conscientious persons, who feared the results of a change so
radical and unexampled. In 1875, the Secretary for India
ordered a thorough investigation of the Indian Civil Service.
Lord Northbrook (the late Viceroy) and Lord Napier were
among the eight eminent persons by whom it was conducted.
Their report was unanimous in its favor, and, with the evidence
taken, is contained in Parliamentary Blue Book, issued in 1876,
from which I shall quote. The Viceroy begins his opinion by
declaring that " there are few subjects, connected with the
Government of India, of more importance than the manner in
which candidates for the civil service should be selected and
the selected candidates should be trained for service in India."
In 1855, Lord Ellenborough declared, as President of the
India Board, " that the prosperity and peace of India depend
upon the characters of those who govern." This Blue Book
contains the elaborate opinions of one hundred and one of the
most experienced administrators in India, ranging from the distinguished Sir H. Maine down to those most worthy to be consulted in the lowest class of the service ; and those from officers
of position are marked by an ability and elevation of tone
which goes far to enable one to understand how it is possible

for so few, of a foreign race, to hold the millions of India in
peaceful subjection and to carry on such vast public works
with so much vigor and so little corruption. I should have to
go beyond all reasonable limits, if I should attempt more than
to state the conclusions reached upon the few decisive points
of the great experiment. All that relates to such questions as
the proper age for entering and leaving public service, to the
best subjects and methods of education, to retiring allowances,
to transfers and promotions in the service, to the best measure
of official discretion, to the peculiar duties of judges, fiscal
officers and governors, to the best plan of dealing with questions of caste, nationality, and others of similar kind, I must
therefore pass over without further notice, much as the study of
such details has improved the Indian service, and sadly as we
have neglected such matters. What then was the judgment
passed upon the merit system as a whole? Was the method
of selection by open competition and of promotion with reference to merit, which were the decisive issues, approved or
condemned? The report of the Commission of 1875 gives a
clear and decisive answer to these questions. The Commissioners not only had before them those one hundred and one elaborate written opinions—coming from every division and grade of
the service—presidents, governors, judges, fiscal officers, engineers, school and college officers, from Bengal, Madras,
Bombay, and every part of India, as well as from Assam,
Berar, and Ceylon, but they inspected records, conferred
with leading officers, and examined into the practical working of the administration. Their final and *unanimous* report, made in September, 1875, uses this language : " We
desire to call your lordship's particular attention to the ability
and good sense of the replies which we have received, and
which form the enclosures of this despatch. . . . With regard
to the general result of free competition for the Indian Civil
Service, we consider that the experience which has been
gained since the Government of India expressed their opinion,
in despatch No 25 (public), of the 5th of May, 1866 —that the
result was satisfactory—amply confirms the favorable judgment then expressed. In our opinion the civil service is filled by
officers of merit and ability, and we are confident that they will

be found fully competent to discharge the duties which they have to perform, and to *supply statesmen and administrators of high distinction* in the different branches of the administration. . . ."[1] In an official communication subsequently made to the Secretary for India, the Viceroy says : " As regards the maintenance of free competition, I do not perceive that it has been challenged by any high authority, and I do not think it necessary to discuss the subject. . . ."[2]

And as an illustration of the spirit in which open competition had been adopted, and as some evidence of the justness of the opinion I have expressed, that it is liberal and republican rather than royal or aristocratic in tendency, I may quote this further passage from the Viceroy's instructions :

" In the first place, I should regret that any man should be debarred from entrance to the Indian Civil Service who possessed such energy and ability as to enable him in a *humble* position of life to succeed at the competitive examination. Such a man it would be to the advantage of India that he should form one of the Civil Service. . . ."[3]

It is certainly significant of the great changes wrought in public opinion, that the head of the Government in India, the Viceroy of the most aristocratic monarchy in the world, should thus especially commend that effect of the new system which so favors the opportunities of humble life ;' nor does it take from this significance when Lord Salisbury, the head of Indian affairs in England, and among the most aristocratic of British noblemen, approves both the communication and the report. The explanation of course is that British statesmen have long since found that common justice and the exclusion of partisan tests, in selecting civil servants, are essential for securing those most useful, and they have had patriotism and independence enough to act upon their convictions of duty, even in a foreign province. These declarations appear not to have been mere professions, for in the final order, made in

---

[1] Report, p. 53.        [2] Ibid., p. 224.        [3] Ibid., p. 230.

[4] In the same spirit the late changes in the army have abolished the old custom of enlisting only high-caste Hindoos, and those of the *lowest* caste are rather preferred.

1876, for the permanent establishment of open competition, as the sole means of entry to the Indian Civil Service, it is provided that during the two years of special study, which are to follow success in the competition, the sum of $750 a year is to be paid to each successful competitor, thereby enabling the children of the poor to go on with their preparation for the public service.[1]

Lord Salisbury gave his opinion in his final instructions to the Viceroy and Council of India, in this language :[2]

" With respect to the principle of competition itself, the evidence you have collected sufficiently shows that it cannot be disturbed without injury to the public service. The expressions of opinion which I have received from competent judges in England led me to the same conclusion. Of its success, as a mode of selecting persons fit to serve in the Indian Civil Service, there seems to be no reasonable doubt."

Not only was the Commission of Inquiry unanimous, and those responsible for administration convinced that the merit system based on open competition was the best ever tried, but its avowed enemies become converted. A member of the Government of India, who had been hostile to competition, uses this language in his official opinion :

" It is needless to state views in regard to the competitive system, as compared with that of nomination, because it is clear, in the present state of public feeling, it is out of all probability that competition could be abandoned ; and, moreover, *I confess, after careful perusal of these papers*, I arrive at the conclusion that, on the whole, it has been more successful than I for one ever expected it to be. . . ."[3]

The conclusion of the whole matter was that in 1876, open competition, in which those of every race, religion, caste, color, or party could freely participate, on the same terms, became the established and sole means of entering the Civil Service of India. To this there is, of course, the exception of the Viceroy, and of any other officers who may be sent to guide the general policy of the Indian Government. Original admission is to the lower grade of the service, and the higher

[1] Lord Salisbury's Order, Report, p. 323.
[2] Report, p. 323.                    [3] Ibid., p. 318.

17

places (save the very few exceptions just noted) are filled by promotions based on merit and experience in the subordinate service. Special study for two years after selection by competition, and before entering upon practical duties, is made necessary by reason of the considerable knowledge of local laws, languages, and institutions which are indispensable in the public service of India. The same rule, in that respect, had existed when selections were made under the old system.

The world knows full well what oppression and extortion marked the early years of British rule in India. The original system was one of pillage and spoils. I have now given the merest outline of the failure of the partisan system (which succeeded the spoils system) and of the method of patronage in the hands of members of the Indian Board, supplemented by a college course, which stand between the old order of things and the new. We have reached the point where it is demonstrated, by the most ample experience, that the prosperity and safety of England and India alike require that places in the public service of the latter shall depend neither upon the favor of any party, any cabinet, any great officer, any board of control, nor upon anything other than the personal merit of the applicant, tested by a standard, public, uniform, and just. If I could afford the space, I might call attention to particular facts showing that competition had given not merely more bright men of learning, but men with physical systems as strong, with characters quite as high, with practical, administrative capacity not less, to say the least, than had come into the service under any other system. But no evidence I could present would perhaps be so satisfactory or conclusive as the official opinions already quoted.

Another aspect of the subject, however, may well arrest our attention for a moment. History, perhaps, affords no example so remarkable as that of British India of the efficiency and power of able and upright officers and good methods in administration to lead on a people in order and prosperity and to hold them in subjection while raising their civilization.[1] The

---

[1] "No thoughtful person can read what General Upton says of the firm but beneficent rule of England in India, without earnestly wishing to see that rule extended over all of Southern Asia."—*International Review*, July, 1878, p. 57.

civil servants of Great Britain in India are but a little band of a few thousands, scattered over a vast empire, holding in obedience nearly one hundred and ninety millions of people of different races, castes, and religions. These races are not wanting in ability or learning, and they are proud, bigoted, and warlike. They have many languages, and laws and customs older and more numerous and complicated than any other people. Nowhere is the peril or the responsibility of government greater. All the officers are remote from the seat of ultimate responsibility, and many of them are widely separated from each other ; so that discretion, firmness, practical resources, and high administrative ability are more than anywhere else indispensable and invaluable. It had been thought by many that even if competition would secure bright men and perhaps good theorists, it would fail to secure practical men, sagacious administrators, competent to command and to lead. It is worthy of notice, therefore, that its first great trial and success seems to demonstrate the incorrectness of that view. It is not any longer ability to lead an army and a body of civil tyrants, in enforcing measures of oppression and exaction, that is needed in India, but ability to collect and expend a revenue as large as that of any but a few of the greatest nations of the world ; ability to take supervision of the construction and management of railways, roads, public drainage, irrigation, hospitals, and other works of internal improvement of great magnitude ; ability to sustain a judicial administration demanding more learning, patience, and high sense of justice than any that ever existed in any other country. Nor should it be forgotten that whatever places the merit system has thus opened to worth and capacity have been taken from the perquisites and the spoils of office and politics. Where, before, governors, judges, directors, members of Parliament, heads of offices or great noblemen or party leaders, could, at their arbitrary will, say to one, you can enter, and to another, you cannot enter, the public service of India, they must now accept some one from among the most meritorious in the competition, even if he be the child of a Hindoo of the lowest caste, or the orphan of a British sailor. We may well believe, I think, that haughty Indian officers long accustomed to patronage and arbitrary power, that the leaders of politics and the great aristocratic families, who, for more than a century, had found the Indian service a convenient field for rewarding their relations and dependents, did not submit to such sacrifices as the new system called for, until the defence of the old was no longer possible and the safety of the empire was seen to be in peril. The first advocates of the new system were, in the eyes of such officials, not only theorists but meddlers. No five Senators or Territorial Governors, with us, have ever, altogether, had a patronage at all comparable with that formerly enjoyed by the Queen's chief officer in Madras, Bengal, or other great presidency, to say nothing of that of the Viceroy himself. There i. one of the many of dependent princes even who has a yearly revenue of $3.300,000. The official service and the public affairs of all our territories united are but small compared with those of a single presidency in India. In any view, the late changes there must be regarded as a remarkable and noble triumph of justice and patriotism over all that was selfish, venal, and partisan in official life. Like our late constitutional amendments, they established equality, justice, and liberty, irrespective of race, color, religion, or nativity. They gave to the humblest Hindoo and Parsee the same right, that they allowed to the favorite of the greatest family or of the strongest party, to enter the public service, both civil and military [1]— upon the basis of their character and capacity as men, whatever views of politics or religion they might hold a right not practically enjoyed in this generation in this boasted land of freedom. The contrast of the mild and fair spirit of this system, with the rapacity and injustice which marked the policy of Clive and Hastings, presents a significant illustration of the vast political changes of a century. If we are to look beyond patriotism for any part of the general support the reform has received in the high official circles of India, we might, perhaps, find it in the exemption it has brought from the wearisome solicitation of office-seekers, from the vexatious adjustments of the rival claims of patronage, from unjust

[1] Native officers of low caste have often been promoted, who were yet forced, when off duty, to give precedence to common soldiers of the Brahmin class.

charges of partiality, from the enmity of a hundred persons disappointed for every one gratified with an office—to all which the records bear evidence.

When we consider the many thousands of miles of railroads under government charge, the extensive public works for irrigation, for drainage, for land and water transportation, for sanitary improvement,[1] and for varied forms of utility or benevolence, on the security of which Englishmen have become the holders of bonds in the amount of more than $900,-000,000 ; when we take into account the educational system with its peculiar difficulties and the delicate and responsible relations of government to many religions ; when we consider the chances innumerable for fraud and peculation (if our army and Indian affairs are the units of comparison) that must exist in the equipment and supply, and in connection with hundreds of stations and posts, of an army of more than 250,-000 men distributed over a vast country of 190,000,000 of people ; as we calculate the opportunities of cheating and malversation (if tested by our experience) among the great army of officials required to collect and disburse an annual revenue (in great part internal) of $250,000,000, in a remote country and among an alien and notoriously cunning and deceptive race ; and when we find that both the most careful researches of British commissions and the common understanding of mankind agree in considering this stupendous administration not merely unsurpassed in justice and purity among all instances of foreign domination, but in itself in a high degree economical and honest, and generally just[2] (even as compared with the domestic administration of the leading States), we must, at least,

---

[1] The once filthy and pestilential city of Bombay, with all its natural disadvantages of people and situation, has, through good sanitary control, come to have a death-rate lower than that of Baltimore, Richmond, or New Orleans.

[2] That there is frequent injustice and sometimes corruption and oppression among those innumerable small officials, especially among the lowest classes of justices, mostly native, and whose sphere of duty is beyond the possibility of direct supervision by the better class of officers, cannot, I think, be doubted. Only education and Christianity can remove such evils. There are over 190,000,000 of natives directly under British rule, to which over 48,000,000, living in feudatory States, with an army of nearly 300,000 men, are to be added. India has only 121,147 persons of

I think, reach the conclusion that a great deal depends on the mode of appointment and discipline of those in the public service, and that Great Britain has not bestowed so much care upon the affairs of India without abundant reward.   Nor can we feel surprise at the just pride of British statesmen, in the presence of so noble an example of successful administration, or dispute them when they assert that " in the history of the world, no other State has shown how to govern territories so extended and remote, and races of men so diverse ; giving to her own kindred colonies the widest liberty, and ruling with enlightened equity dependencies unqualified for freedom." [1]

I am glad to be able to cite the opinions of a competent and impartial observer ; [2] and he has found that the merit system, enforced in the military service, has been as salutary as in the civil service.   " In no country," he says, " is the subordination of the military to the civil authority more clearly defined.   .  .  .   All the officers we met at Delhi and elsewhere, in India, showed a capacity and confidence above their rank.   .  .  .   The results attained in India are worthy our closest study.   .  .  .   No stranger free, from national prejudice can visit  .  .  .   India without rejoicing that England controls the destiny of 200,000,000 of people ; neither can he observe the great institutions which she has founded for their moral and physical amelioration, without hoping that, in the interests of humanity, she may continue her sway until she has made them worthy to become a free and enlightened nation."

non-Asiatic origin ; of which only 75,734 (besides 63,000 British soldiers) are of British origin ; while there are 190,000 native policemen alone in the public service, besides a native army also consisting of about 190,000 men.—*Westminster Review*, January, 1879.

[1] May's History, p. 546.

[2] General Upton, of the United States Army, lately sent by the Government to make observations from the military, as I have made them from the civil side of administration.—*Armies of Asia and of Europe*, 1879, p. 51, 67, 81 and 87.

# CHAPTER XXVII.

Great numbers who compete.—The new system in the British colonies.—
Promotions.—The census.—Comparison of old and new systems.—Further extensions of the new system.—Probation made more efficient.—
Publicity of appointments and promotions.—The new system becomes more popular and salutary.—The Civil Service Commission likely to be permanent.

WE are now to consider the operations of the new system, in that more perfect form into which the various investigations and improvements we have traced have finally brought it.

The report for 1875 shows that the whole number of persons who had been before the commission since its creation (in 1855) had been 142,423, of which 70,452 (and among them were 1622 for the military service) presented themselves within the four and a half years of open competition since July, 1870. In other words, during the fifteen years of limited competition, the official monopolists who selected the candidates only allowed an average of about 5000 persons a year to come forward for examination;[1] but under open competition more than 15,000 each year had freely presented themselves before the commission; from which it would seem to follow that members of Parliament and other officials must have deprived about 10,000 persons every year of their equal right to have their claims tested for a place in the public service. And there is the most decisive evidence that the 5000, which the official monopolists ticketed for examination, were by no means the more worthy portion of the 15,000 who wished to be examined. These excluded 10,000

[1] During several years, immediately preceding 1870, the number of persons presenting themselves for examination had exceeded 5000 annually; for open competition was to some extent allowed, the partisan system was rapidly decaying, and the official blockade was less rigid.

were generally, I think we may believe, either too humble to command influence or too manly and independent to ask favors. It is this official tyranny of exclusion which still exists in this country, but which, I am persuaded, could not be resumed in Great Britain without the utter overthrow of the party proposing it, if it could be without serious agitation.[1] This report also traces the progress, I have before noticed, which is being made in the British colonies and dependencies for taking their public service out of party politics and giving public honors to persons of merit. In August, 1874, examinations for admission to the civil service were introduced by the legislature of South Australia. They had been introduced into New Zealand in 1866; and the reports for 1873 and 1874 seem to show that such examinations had already been made more efficient and had been raised to a higher standard than ever has been the case in our own service, save in a limited sphere and for a short time under President Grant. Reference has before been made to reforms in the Canadian civil service.[2] From all which, we are, I think, at liberty to infer that the time is not remote when, if we do not very soon improve our system, the most partisan and the most illiterate civil service in any part of the world where the English language is spoken will be that of the United States. That part of the Anglo-Saxon race under republican government will then stand alone in its open toleration of the official coercion, intrigue, and corrupt bargaining in public honors and places which had their origin in the most despotic experience of the mother country. Of all those speaking our language, republicans alone would proclaim that partisan and official influence should be paramount in public affairs over all considerations of personal worth and capacity; a distinction, perhaps, not less likely to arrest the world's attention than the conspicuous position we so long occupied as a slave-holding republic.

The report of 1876 records the death of *Sir Edward Ryan*, who had presided over the Civil Service Commission during the whole twenty years of its existence. During the year

[1] See the letters of John Bright and Sir Charles Trevelyan in the Appendix, and also ch. 30.

[2] See last paragraph, chap. I.

(1875), 15,342 persons had appeared for examination; and some idea of the activity of the commission and of the public interest felt in its work may be gathered from the fact that the number of letters received and written during the year had been 147,350. This report contains an order for certain adaptations to be made in conformity with the recommendations already mentioned as resulting from the executive inquiry of 1874. Among other things, it provides for boy clerks, who are to secure their places through open competition. It further increases the authority of the Civil Service Commission, by providing that no promotions shall be made from a lower to a higher division in the service without a special certificate of qualification from that body; and it is further ordered that all appointments, promotions, and transfers from one office to another shall be notified to the commissioners for record in their office, and that they shall be, by them, published in the *London Gazette*. By such means, the publicity so much needed to prevent suspicion will be secured, and the office of the commission will contain a sort of official record of every person in the public service—a great convenience in making promotions for merit as well as a powerful stimulant of good conduct. This report also shows that, for some unexplained reason, the *General Registrar's* office (which has charge of taking the census) had not, in 1871, been brought under the provisions for open competition; although the official nominees for clerks (or census agents) were directed to go through a sort of pass examination before the Civil Service Commission.

The evidence taken on this subject in 1874 facilitates a significant comparison of the new system with the old. The head of the office gives a sad account of the motley imbeciles put upon him by members of Parliament for taking the census (they seem fully as bad, I think, as any similarly imposed upon Mr. Walker for taking our census); for example, " two were suffering from such offensive complaints that others could not associate with them, and I was forced to put them into separate rooms, . . . they were a heterogeneous mass from 14 to 60 years of age . . . who had tried many occupations and failed in all." When the Registrar was ordered to take the census in 1871, he says he supposed he was to be allowed to have better clerks, obtained through open competition, under the order of 1870, but he was deprived of them. "The Lords of the Treasury decided against me, . . . and their Lordships took to themselves the patronage, . . ." and divided it among members. "Their Lordships acting on the old system, and following the recommendation of influential adherents, nominated no fewer than 261 census clerks." He found that inquiry into their character and history "was productive of pain and confusion," and he gave it up. But he forced this miscellaneous herd of official favorites into a pass examination, before the commission, which *rejected fifty-seven per cent of them,* and with the residue the Registrar succeeded in taking the census of 1871, and wonders that he could do it. He says : " Nothing could be worse than the system of nomination of clerks by the Treasury : . . . their Lordships know only their names, and that they were recommended by influential peers or members of Parliament, supporters of the government of the day, . . . no inquiry being made as to their character and qualifications." [1] This is only one of the many examples (which together would cover nearly the whole field of administration) that might be presented, as showing how closely analogous—if I may not say how exactly alike— have been the abuses of official power and the opposition to reform in England and in this country. On certain points connected with the aristocratic element in the social life of England, and with the administrative subdivisions, there is a material difference ; but beyond those matters, the analogy is so close that you may read for hours in the British documents almost without a reflection that you are not going over abuses in the service of the United States. Had open competition been applied to the census clerks, those wishing to compete would have quietly joined in a public and manly contest, in the several places where the examinations would have been held, and the most competent would have been speedily ascertained and selected without the least political significance. But, by the method pursued, great noblemen and members of Parliament, political bodies and aspiring demagogues, the

[1] Report Investigation, 1874, vol. i., p. 383, etc.

Lords of the Treasury and the leaders of parties, were drawn into a demoralizing and ignominious scramble for patronage, reaching to hundreds of cities and villages, and affecting no one can tell how many elections, which finally resulted in 261 nominees so disgracefully incompetent that, in mere self-defence, the census officer was forced to subject the motley throng to a non-partisan examination before the Civil Service Commission, which excluded 57 out of each 100 as utterly incompetent. And it may well be doubted if ten per cent of them would have been left if he could have put them into open competition with such young men as would, if permitted, have voluntarily presented themselves for examination. This illustration is not the less interesting because the taking of a census is before us, in which our general rule is quite sure to work like this British exception.

In 1877, there were 14,362 persons before the commission, of which 1723 were for the military service, and 472 for India. Besides those rejected as too young or because of insufficient health or bad character, there were 3840 denied certificates as unqualified for the public work. It will be seen that the ratio of incompetents is far less, and hence the capacity of those applying is much higher, than when officials designated those to be examined. Examinations had already been so extended in the home, military service as to regulate admissions to *the Royal Military College, the Royal Military Academy, the Royal Marine Artillery*, and *the Royal Marine Light Infantry*. Promotion in the military is made to turn mainly upon attainments tested by examination. These several military institutions, I believe (owing to the fact that there is no military service in Great Britain corresponding to that of the States of our Union), are more than the equivalent, in our army and navy system, of the schools of West Point and Annapolis. When we consider how short has been the period since admission to those English military schools was as much dependent, as admission either to the school at West Point or at Annapolis now is, upon political influence or official favor, and especially when we recall the fact that up to 1871 commissions and promotions in the British military service were matters of open sale and purchase, we can better appreciate the strength of conviction, in favor of the new system, which has so rapidly extended it in all directions.[1]  Only the English State Church has withstood its advance.  Her official places are still made merchandise or bestowed by official favor.

It is provided (concerning new appointments) that "no clerk *shall remain more than one year in* any department, unless, at the end of that time, the head of the department shall certify in writing to the Civil Service Commissioners that the clerk is accepted by the department.  If he is not accepted, the department shall report to said commissioners *the reasons* for not accepting him."  On this rule probation now stands.  Promotions from lower to higher divisions[2] of the service are not to be made without a certificate from the Civil Service Commission, nor until after ten years of service.  All appointments, promotions, and transfers are to be recorded by the commission and published in the *London Gazette.*  This is a part of the procedure through which the records of the commission are made to contain a brief history of every one in the public service, and the secrecy that facilitates corruption and injustice are thus avoided.  The public is treated as having a right to be informed as to what is being done in the public service and of the reasons for it.  The same rule, it will be seen, that throws out an inefficient clerk after a year's trial also puts a

---

[1] The executive (adopting some of the suggestions of the report of the last Parliamentary Commission already considered), by an order in Council, made in February, 1876, provided for the selection, through open competition, of a less expensive class of men and boy clerks in the public service, the members of which are made liable to do work in any office, and to go from department to department, as convenience may require.  By reason of this provision, there will no longer be a need that every department and office shall have a force equal to the greatest demand that may be made upon it ; but this movable, clerical force of all work can be shifted from places where there is relatively least to be done, to places where there is most.  Men with such experience must soon become far more valuable in their sphere of duty than mere routine clerks, who often know little about administration beyond that small part that takes place at their own desks.  This supplementary order rather increases the stringency of the new system, and with the further orders of June and December, 1876, appears to extend it and to enlarge the authority of the Civil Service Commission.

[2] Division is not synonymous with our word grade or class.  There may be grades in a division.

check upon arbitrary rejections, by requiring the written reasons for non-approval to be preserved of record. Prior to August, 1877, the whole number who had sought to enter the public service through examinations had reached the vast aggregate of 172,127. Coming from, perhaps, as many homes, and from nearly every district, borough, village, and hamlet of the kingdom, where the fate of those examined has arrested attention, it is easy to see how naturally the public examinations have stimulated study, how broadly and usefully they have advertised the fact that character and attainments, and not influence or partisan activity, are honored by the government.

It is worthy of notice that not a charge of favoritism, of intentional injustice, or of interference in party politics, has ever been brought against the commission, nor has an instance of actual injustice, as the accepted result of an examination, been substantiated. The commission has steadily advanced in public estimation ; and now, in the twenty-fifth year of its growing work, with duties more extended than ever before, and unchallenged by any party or by any class of the people, it stands entrenched in public confidence, with guarantees of enduring usefulness hardly inferior to those which support the strongest agency of British government.

# CHAPTER XXVIII.

## CONCERNING PARTS OF THE OLD SPOILS SYSTEM EXCLUDED BY THE CONSTITUTION OF THE UNITED STATES.

What is so excluded.—Mr. Helps's theory of governing by religion and honors.—How titles and knighthood have been conferred.—For what they are now conferred.—The great "Orders" and their influence.—Enormous abuses in former times in granting pensions.—How they are now granted. —Relations of religion to politics.—Powers of the crown over church appointments.—Corruption in the official life of the church.—Use of the appointing power by archbishops.—Right to be a minister a matter of merchandise centuries ago and to this day.—Advowsons and presentations still openly advertised as for sale.—How far old checks on abuse of patronage worthy our adoption.—Patronage and proscription have failed to sustain the English Church.—They are now its opprobrium and its weakness.—Patronage in the Church of Scotland has dismembered it, and given birth to "the Free Church of Scotland."—How Englishmen and Americans regard each other's abuses.—Purchase in the British military system, —Its abolition.—Examinations for admission to the British military schools. —Favoritism abolished in the British army during the time it has grown in the army of the United States.—Illustrations from the laws applicable to the schools at Annapolis and West Point.

THE repugnancy of a spoils system of office to the Government of the United States is illustrated by the fact that some of the most pernicious and characteristic elements of the original system are made impossible by the constitution itself. The granting of titles of nobility, the requirement of religious tests, and laws respecting an establishment of religion, therein prohibited, were not only great bulwarks of that system, but they have shown themselves to be prolific sources of injustice and corruption, endowed with a vitality so tenacious that they have outlived almost every other part of the ancient abuses ; and, at this moment, a demoralizing method of church patronage and favoritism, in the spirit of mediaeval times, stands out conspicuously alongside the ruins of the old system in the domain of politics.

When Mr. Arthur Helps, whose attacks on competitive examinations the apologists of a republican spoils system are so much in the habit of quoting, in his " Thoughts on Government," approved the maxim of Buonaparte, which declares that " religion and honors are the two things by which mankind may be governed," and declared " that the British Constitution is the best that has yet been devised by man," he knew very well what he meant ; for, from his central place as the Secretary of the Privy Council, he had during many years looked down through the ranks of social life and all the grades of state-church officials, and knew how they were moved ; but he had no more sympathy with the Constitution of the United States than he had with the partisan manipulations and intrigue of those who so absurdly invoke and misconceive his words and the system he approved.

In a general way, the exercise of the powers of the government in matters of religion, and of those of the crown in conferring rank, pensions, and social distinction, in a proscriptive and corrupt spirit, have been already pointed out ; but some further explanations may both illustrate the great difficulties of overcoming the British spoils system and place in a clearer light the true character and tendencies of our own.

It is familiar knowledge that the power of conferring titles, orders, knighthoods, and social distinction in many ways, has been in past centuries an important source of strength on the part of the crown, and in later years on the part both of the crown and the ministry. The exercise of such a power concerns elements of hope and ambition, active and powerful under every form of government, but especially so in an old monarchy, where standards set up by itself have acquired something like the respect accorded to the dictates of natural justice. A true history of its exercise would be found to run parallel with that of the use of the appointing power, to which it has, in corrupt times, been little more than an adjunct in creating and dividing the spoils of politics. When

---

[1] Published in 1872.

James II. or Charles II. or Walpole used offices and places
as merchandise and bribes, they gave titles and decorations to vile women and corrupt men. In the reign of
Queen Anne twelve peers were created at one time in order
to secure a court majority. William Pitt caused peerages to
be freely created—one hundred and forty being created during
his administration—and he used them to reward his political
followers. The passage of the great Reform bill of 1832 hung
in doubt until the administration turned the scale by a threat
to create a large number of peers who would vote for it.
The scramble for peerages appears to have been as fierce and
troublesome as the scramble for office has ever been in a
republic. Mr. May says that every minister is obliged to resist the solicitation of not less than ten earnest claimants for
every peerage which he can bestow, and that recently a minister
found that in a single year upwards of thirty of his supporters
were ambitious of a peerage, as an acknowledgment of their
friendship toward himself and of their devotion to his party.
As a natural result, aided by the increase of population and
wealth, the House of Lords, which at the accession of George
III. consisted of one hundred and seventy-four members, had
by 1860 increased to four hundred and sixty members. George
III. abused the power of creating knights and baronets, as he
did all his other powers, for political and personal purposes.
During his reign four hundred and ninety-four baronetcies
were created; and he responded to congratulations on his
escaping assassination by conferring so many knighthoods that
the degradation of that order was long recognized, even if
it has ever regained its old distinction. If, in these times,
many men, with real claims to social eminence, in a republican
spirit decline royal aid to that end, it is yet true, I think, that
rank and social distinctions thus conferred by the crown are a
powerful influence for royalty. In 1860 there were eight
hundred and sixty baronets, as against about five hundred on
the accession of George III. Without attempting to trace the
history of the power of conferring titles, it must suffice to say
that it survives in great though in waning vigor; a royal and
aristocratic agency in government still holding its place in the
liberal currents of British politics by which it is being slowly

abraded.[1] The same causes which have compelled the use of the appointing power in the common interests of the people have enforced the exercise of nearly all kindred authority in the same spirit; and at this time titles and decorations are rarely conferred in a mere partisan spirit, nor does any suspicion of corruption appear to attach to their bestowal.

While the true republican theory in regard to this agency of government seems to be gaining strength, no one can look over the list of those honored by the favor of the crown, or listen to the prevailing views of Englishmen on the subject, without being deeply impressed with a sense of the vast influence thus exerted, and of the utter incompatibility in principle of this medieval prerogative with the new methods in British politics. The variety and prestige of the great orders —" Knights of the Garter," "Knights of the Thistle," "Knights of the Order of St. Patrick," "Knights of the Bath," with its many classes; "Order of St. Michael and St. George," "Order of the Star of India," with their numerous and distinguished membership, extending to foreign statesmen and princes and drawing within their seductive influence so many men of the highest capacity and station at home—present another forcible illustration of the adverse interests and the traditional privileges by which the reform of the civil service has been confronted and delayed in Great Britain.

Perhaps no part of this old authority of the crown is now exercised in closer analogy to the partisan use of the appointing power than that of conferring knighthood and baronetcies. "In acknowledgment of the *zeal* displayed by the city of London, on the occasion of the thanksgiving, a Baronetcy is to be conferred on the Lord Mayor; and Sheriffs Truscott and Bennett will obtain the honor of Knighthood,"[2] is a journal-

---

[1] "It is of the nature of the curious influence of rank to work much more on men singly than on men collectively;" it is an influence which most men —at least, most Englishmen—feel very much, but of which most Englishmen are somewhat ashamed. Each man is a little afraid that "his sneaking kindness for a lord," as Mr. Gladstone put it, be found out.—*Bagehot on The English Constitution*, pp. 24 and 25.

[2] *London Daily Telegraph*, March 1, 1872.

istic illustration of the use of this power, of which frequent examples are to be met with in the leading newspapers ; and yet, while non-partisan zeal for the Queen may be thus rewarded by royal favor, no administration, I think, would venture to advise its exercise on mere partisan grounds ; and it is but just to say that it is generally exercised for the purpose of rewarding exceptional capacity or devotion in the interest of science, literature, or philanthropy. Let the citizens of a republic, if they will, condemn the tame compliance with official wishes which such notices may be thought to prove, and find in the reward of mere zeal for royalty an unworthy use of executive power, but let them at the same time remember the pervading subserviency, of minor officials among themselves, to officers having the appointing power, and the fact that they have seen not individuals only, but conventions and legislatures obsequious before, not the head of an ancient line of princes, but the temporary officers of their own creation. If it is bad in a monarchy to give social precedence to those who are zealous for the crown and the nobility, for which the constitution provides, is it better in a republic to give offices and salaries as rewards for zeal for parties for which the constitution does not provide ?

Closely connected with the governmental agency just considered is another affording a similar illustration and equally repugnant to our system—that of pensions granted by the crown (formerly) or the administration in (the practice of) recent years. This authority, once as vast as it was pernicious, has in later times been reduced to small if not to harmless proportions. It is important that this power of pensioning should be apprehended as distinct from the authority of granting superannuating or retiring allowances in the public service, which I have already explained.[1] Those allowances are really a part of the compensation of the officer—of the conditions on which he entered the public service—and are not, therefore, given on any theory of a gratuity or of favor. Looked at from the side of the government, they are regarded as presenting an ingenious and just method of securing a good quality of

---

[1] See ante, pp. 141-144.

service at the most reasonable rates ; and from the side of the officer, as an inducement to greater economy, at the opening of official life, in order to secure, by reason of what he then forbears to receive, a certain provision for his declining years.

The pension proper (in civil life) is a different matter altogether ; being the bribe of the crown or administration for political effect, or its favor bestowed upon some person deemed fit for its charity or deserving of its honor, and often irrespective of such person being or having been in the public service. The history of giving pensions, like that of conferring offices and titles, may be easily traced back to the dark ages of corruption, and if possible the authority to grant them has been used more disgracefully and craftily than any other power of the government. I cannot spare the space needed to give anything like a history of this branch of executive authority, but a brief notice of it may be useful. It is well known that vast sums were squandered as pensions upon royal and court favorites—male and female—in the times of the Stuarts. In the earlier years of the House of Hanover, the extravagance was hardly less, if the moral tone was a little improved; and in later days, amounts not much smaller, though not technically called pensions, have been used in a respectable way to support the households of the members of the royal family. Now " the crown," says Mr. May,[1] " repudiates the indirect influences exercised in former reigns, and is free from imputations of corruption." That the crown is neither corrupt nor thought to be capable of corruption is, I believe, beyond question ; but in view of its broad bestowal of titles, and of the lavish votes of money to keep up the prestige and influence of the several members of the royal family, I fail to see how it can be said that " indirect influence" is repudiated.

It had been the practice and the conceded right of the crown, before the reign of Queen Anne, to charge pensions and annuities in perpetuity upon its hereditary revenues ; but on her accession, the right of making such charges was limited to the lifetime of the reigning king, but this restriction did not extend to Scotch or Irish revenues, nor did it cover all other

---

[1] Const. Hist., vol. i., p. 203.

revenues within the power of the crown. "From the period
of the revolution, places and pensions have been regarded as
the price of political dependence," and in 1705, persons enjoying a pension during the pleasure of the crown were by law
excluded from Parliament.[1] Even after the accession of
George III., when a fixed civil list was provided, there was
authority to charge pensions upon that list. Vast sums as
pensions and annuities were charged upon it or other property,
by that prince and his successors; and corruption and servility,
as a consequence, were serious evils. Mr. Burke made a great
effort for the reduction of the pension list to $3,000,000; and
under the Rockingham administration it was provided that
until it should be reduced to $4,500,000, no pension above
$1500 a year should be granted, and that the aggregate pen-
sions granted in one year should not exceed $3000. It was
further provided that pensions should be given only "as a
royal bounty to persons in distress or as a reward for desert."
But, notwithstanding these great reforms, large amounts of
revenue from Ireland and Scotland were available, and were
used for the purposes of political corruption and royal coercion. The Irish pension list of George III. was in 1793
$620,000, when important restrictions were imposed. In
Scotland the free use of pensions by the crown was tolerated
until 1810, when the pension list had reached $195,000.
There was an available pension fund apparently in the discretion of the crown for political purposes until 1830, when all
the pension lists were consolidated. And on the accession of
Queen Victoria to the throne, in 1837, the right of the crown
to grant pensions was limited to $6000 a year, and they can
only be granted in that amount "to such persons as have just
claims on the royal beneficence, or who, by their *personal
services to the crown*, by their performance of duties to the
public, or by their useful discoveries in science and attainments in literature and the arts, have merited the gracious
consideration of their sovereign and the gratitude of their
country."[2]   It will thus be seen that this vast power of cor-

1 May Const. Hist., p. 294.   4 Anne, chap. viii.
2 1 Vict., chap. ii.

ruption, under the form of pensions, has departed with the prostitution of the appointing power, and that the reasons for the use of $6000 a year in pensions are—if the principle of granting pensions at all is conceded—of a kind as fit to be approved by a republic as by a monarchy ; except in so far as the right of pensioning on political grounds may be covered by the phrase " personal services to the crown ;" and we may accept the declaration of Mr. May that " the names of those who receive the royal bounty are generally such as to command respect and sympathy." [1]

But of all the authority conferred by the British Constitution, in excess of what is allowed under the Constitution of the United States, that which has been the most grossly perverted for the purposes of coercion and injustice in administration is the authority over religion and a state church. It would require a volume to set forth the disastrous consequences which have flowed from the forced relation between religion and politics, as disclosed in British history. " In the sixteenth century the history of the church is the history of England. In the seventeenth century the relations of the church to the state and society contributed, with political causes, to convulse the kingdom with civil wars and revolutions." [2] Having already given adequate illustration of the great fact that authority in ecclesiastical affairs has been as unscrupulously prostituted as authority in civil affairs, there are only a few important considerations to be added in this connection. The British king, as the supreme head on earth of the Church of England, has been held to have not only the right to convene, prorogue, and regulate all ecclesiastical synods and conventions, but also the right of nomination to all vacant bishoprics ; and through that supreme power he has had a similar facility, for interference, intimidation, and control in regard to all subordinate nominations and all official action in the lower spheres of ecclesiastical life, to that possessed by a President of the United States, or by Senators and Governors in their own States, to meddle, without constitutional warrant, with every subordinate nomination down to that

---

[1] 1 Const. Hist., p. 214.     [2] 2 May's Constitutional History, p. 291.

of doorkeeper in a warehouse or a clerk in a convention ; and
I hardly need add, that this royal prerogative was formerly
used to its full measure. When we consider the superstitious
awe inspired by the head of the church, added to the pervading fear of the head of the state, in earlier ages, we can more
readily comprehend how crushing was the weight of a despotic,
spoils system which was supreme alike in the sphere of religion and in the sphere of politics. It should also be borne in
mind that several of these church officers had authority affecting property and persons in their secular relations united with
their spiritual and ecclesiastical powers, and that, for the support of the state church and the use of its officials, the tithes
of all lands and stock were set apart. Offices and places of
every grade—from that of the archbishop to that of the
beadle and the churchwarden—were given as bribes or sold
for money just as openly and as unscrupulously as were offices
and places in the state. Those miscellaneous kinds of venality
and corruption—for which our statutes have no aggregate
name, but which in English statutes are designated as " office
brokerage"—were early developed in connection with the offices
and patronage of the church. More than three centuries ago, it
had become an established custom, for example, that an archbishop, upon consecrating a bishop, might name a favorite of
his own to be called a clerk or chaplain, who was " to be provided for" [1] by the bishop ; just as republican officers, who now
have the power of appointment or confirmation, require those
toward whom they discharge a public duty " to provide for "
some of their dependants ; but, more openly and boldly, the old,
church spoils system allowed this venal imposition to be confirmed, by deed in due form of law, running to the archbishop, his executors and assigns. With such an example on
the part of the archbishop, we may well believe that the
bishops, the deans, the archdeacons, the deacons, and
every church official having any right of nomination or confirmation, had their favorites " to be provided for." This
right to be provided for was treated as a fit subject of trade

---

[1] This phrase, generally supposed to have been first used to mark a peculiar
form of corruption in our politics, is to be found applied in the modern sense,
in Blackstone's Com., vol. i. ch. ii., to high church officials.

and barter, and was known and protected in law under the name of the archbishop's " option."[1] In times which tolerated such dealings with the sacred offices of the church, it was natural that the rights of selection of rectors, parsons, curates and vicars—that is, the right to live in the parsonage house and to officiate as a minister of a parish—should become venal, mere matters of bargain, barter, and sale ; and under the names of "advowsons" and "presentations" they early became as much articles of merchandise, and as such were as openly a subject of negotiation and trade, and were as fully recognized by law, as land titles or cattle. Ownership of these rights of naming the next minister could be held by the crown, by individuals, by corporations, or even by military orders. It is no part of my purpose to here describe the scandals, dilapidation of church edifices, corruption in the care of church property, decay of spiritual life, or contempt for religious and sacred things, which flowed from such abuses.[2] This right of property in advowsons and presentations was as carefully protected by the law and the courts, and is by British lawwriters made the subject of as elaborate description, as any other kind of property whatever ; Blackstone, saying that " an advowson" (which he declares to be " synonymous with patronage," that is, it expresses the same relation to an office[3] of the church that "patronage" does to an office in the state) will more completely illustrate a particular kind of property than any example he can give. When church patronage had thus come

[1] I am not aware that any analogous right has ever been recognized under American law, much as we have acted on the same theory in politics. In morality and legal theory it is most suggestive of a stock-jobber's " put."

[2] See, on these points, ante, p. 47.

[3] Despite this high authority, I must think there is considerable difference between patronage as applied to the choice of a minister and patronage as applied to civil offices generally ; yet they have these most important elements in common : they make merchandise of places of trust, and they refuse to allow worth and capacity to determine the selections for office. But, beyond the special kind of church patronage here referred to, patronage, essentially the same as that which prevailed in politics, also extended to the selection and promotion of church officials ; and perhaps that form of it, known as *nepotism*, was even worse in the church than in the state. The making of his infant son Bishop of Osnaburgh, by George III., is an example.

to be valuable property, the monastic orders (among others) " begged and bought " as many advowsons as possible ; and having in that way got control of the income of a vast number of benefices or parishes—said to have been one third of those in England—they devoted it to their own establishments, to the great prejudice of the poor and of religion among the people.    But on the breaking up of these orders under Henry VIII. their advowsons were seized by the Crown, and were afterwards in large part given as favors or bribes in the ordinary course of the corrupt administration of the times : thus making the circuit of venality, from one private owner, through both ecclesiastical and civil officers, to another private owner.    " Lay patronage placed the greater part of the benefices at the disposal of the Crown, the barons, and the land-owners ;" [1] and hence we see a whole hemisphere of patronage, beyond any ever known in this country, in the control of the privileged classes and their friends — the party forever in power under a despotic government.    This ownership of patronage, both on the part of the crown and of individuals, seems to have continued, doubtless with great changes, until the present time.    The same causes which thus largely tended to make the sacred domain of the church a great arena for bargaining and pecuniary greed ; which developed a system of corruption which in many ways greatly increased the difficulty of reform in civil affairs ; which caused those who officiated in Christian pulpits to be looked upon and to be referred to in the laws, not so much as being unworldly guides and teachers in spiritual matters, but as purchasers and holders of "livings" for their own enjoyment—also caused holders of church offices to be treated as having a pecuniary right to their offices : "So that even parish clerks and sextons are also regarded, by the common law, as persons who have freeholds in their offices." [2]

The holder of an advowson in theory had no absolute right to have his man—called " a clerk "—made a minister, rector, pastor, or vicar, any more than a member of Parliament or of Congress, in the use of his patronage has, in theory, a

[1] 2 May's Const. Hist., p. 297.    [2] Blackstone's Com., vol. i. ch. ii.

right to have his man made a collector, bookkeeper, weigher, or inspector; but ancient bishops found resistance to be as difficult as secretaries and heads of offices have ever found it to be in later times. I have already explained the device of a "Patronage Secretary of the Treasury," and his duty of weighing and apportioning patronage as an indispensable restraint upon parliamentary importunity; and, for similar reasons, perhaps, barriers were set up between the pushing holders of patronage and the bishop, some of which would be very embarrassing if applied to our patronage holders in politics; for the bishop might reject a clerk if "an alien," in "want of learning," or when "under age"; but there were other conditions which modern partisans would not object to, for the bishop could not reject the clerk "for haunting taverns or playing unlawful games." His vice must be *malum in se*, or the clerk was held good enough for a minister. And may it not be true that the regularity, justice, and publicity which such provisions secured—that the open recognition of the rights of patronage and of the real influences which controlled appointments, however venal—are preferable to the secret intrigue, corruption, and uncertainty which disguise the iniquity of the transaction itself in our politics, without exposing either the obsequiousness of the official, or the unpatriotic importunity of the patronage-monger? If we are to endure much longer the evils of a civil patronage system, borrowed from Great Britain, why should we not also borrow the methods by which she mitigated its evils, and, like her, openly avow our venality and boldly practise in the light a corruption which, perhaps, to be arrested needs only to be seen? Until we can prevent legislators and party leaders foisting their unworthy dependants and henchmen upon the executive departments, why not have "a patronage secretary" and patronage itself apportioned and entered of record on the books of the Treasury like salaries, and the reasons for which a secretary may reject a nominee as distinctly stated as were the reasons for which a bishop might reject a clerk? We should then know, at least as between those who urged and those who accepted a bad nomination, where the responsibility rests, and how to direct the public censure.

If under any circumstances it be possible for a church—any more than for a party—to maintain its prestige and authority by favoritism and proscription, it would seem it should have been the case of the Church of England—the church of the king, the nobility, the rich and high-born classes—thus privileged and fortified in her vast patronage and her all-pervading ministrations. And she had yet other and not less powerful means of domination. For the Corporation Act of 1661 shut the gates of office against the Protestant nonconformists, and the Test Act, 1663, made the papists incompetent to hold any official position, high or low, national or municipal, civil or ecclesiastical ; and these laws, under which both the creed and the sacrament of the state church were made conditions of holding office—even though her highest dignitaries admitted a fear that they " had led, in too many instances, to the profanation of the most sacred offices of religion"—remained unrepealed for more than one hundred and fifty years—until 1828. It is hardly worth while to stop to inquire which, in point of justice, is the most indefeasible, or which in practice is most disastrous :—this old despotic system, under which, by permanent provision of law, mere opinions about religion were made grounds of exclusion from all offices ; or the modern, partisan system, which, going beyond law, and without the courage to declare mere opinions a ground of exclusion, yet accomplishes an equal amount of proscription by giving each party in turn the opportunity to expel and exclude its adversaries from office, for mere opinions about politics. But it may perhaps be useful for us to reflect upon the facts that, besides all the strength which a state church or a state church party could gain from all this patronage and proscription in its behalf, there was the still further advantage of having its creed taught in all the great institutions of learning, where it excluded those professing any other faith ;[1] of its having a monopoly of entrance at the

---

[1] It was not until 1871 that all religious tests were abolished for admission to offices and degrees in the Universities. The nonconformists had to pay rates for the benefit of the state church until 1868 ; and though something like justice is thus secured to the living, the dead are still made the subjects of state church restrictions before they can be laid for their final rest in the cemeteries.

gates of the great professions ; of its being proclaimed in the courts of law, in the halls of legislation, at the head of regiments, in the cabins of ships, in every office and in every place of honor, from the smallest fort or consulate to the palace and the throne ; but with what results ? Catholicism, toward which the state church itself has an ominous leaning, is growing more formidable in Great Britain. Among the dissenters are to be counted, probably, one half of the people and of the piety of England. Patronage and favoritism—upheld, doubtless, by their connection with the creed and the sacraments, in the sphere of religion after they have been crushed in the domain of politics—are at once the opprobrium of the Church of England [1] and the weakest point in her battlement, through which her enemies are making their most dangerous assaults ; while on this continent the old, state church faith, transplanted without its patronage and venality, has grown with an earnestness of spirit and a material prosperity which are the best of all refutations of the theory that a party based on religion, any more than a party based on politics, can prosper on the prostitution of its offices or the degradation of its principles.

---

[1] Speaking of these abuses, the Bishop of Gloucester and Bristol says : "In regard to the sale of benefices, and especially of next presentations, it must be admitted we are in the greatest possible difficulty. . . ."—*Nineteenth Century*, March, 1877, p. 58.

The dissenters of course stop with no such moderate language. "A more mournful and painful book (" Purchase in the Church, etc.") can scarcely be imagined. . . . It is impossible to question the accuracy of these instances, the aggregate of which—1400—is one tenth of the entire livings of the Church in the market for sale or barter at the same time. . . . The living of Trahaverock, in Cornwall, worth £180 a year, is advertised for sale. The advertisement states "*there is no cure of souls to perform, and no residence is required.*"—*British Quarterly Review*, Oct. 8, 1878.

The following are advertisements (similar to those to be found in any of the journals) cut from the London *Times* in September, 1870 :

"Advowson for Sale (a Rectory), situate close to a good town in an eastern county. Situation most healthy and pleasant. Good society. Income is about £250 a year, and there is a prospect of a very early possession, excellent vicarage house, grounds, etc. Address, J. B., 51 Hollywood Road, West Brompton."

"140 Preferments for Sale. *The Church Preferment Register*, for September (32 pages), contains all details of advowsons, presentations, Episcopal chapels, for sale by private treaty," etc., etc.

Advertisements and transactions of the kind mentioned in the note last referred to, which with us would undoubtedly be deemed in the last degree scandalous, have so long been common in Great Britain, that they attract little more attention there than the habitual bestowal of offices for mere partisan services, in disregard of personal fitness, attracts in the United States. Indeed, it is not easy to say which is the more astonished—an American when he first learns that a young clerk, the merest stranger from the other end of the empire, may, against the common wishes of the parish, buy his way into a pulpit of the English state church, or the Englishman when for the first time he learns that a mere politician, an inexperienced stranger from the hills, may be pushed by a clique of partisans into a collectorship over the heads of all those in the custom house, who alone are qualified for the office. If the British example of venality and injustice seem more disgraceful because in the sphere of sacred things, we must bear in mind that, before the clerk can enter his pulpit, he must have been approved by a bishop; while no moral standard can be applied to the politician—partisan services and prospects of services, by whatever means, being the grounds of his claim. And it would be unjust not to mention that the bishop's standard of acceptance has been raised higher and higher, that mercenary influence has been limited in various ways, so that, aided by the better public opinion which banished patronage from politics, and sustained, in later years, by a higher sentiment within the church itself,[1] a great part of the evils are now prevented which originally attended the church patronage system. But the system, with its inherent tendency toward venality and corruption, survives; and, much as its abuses have been mitigated, it has been a great obstruction to the reform of the civil service, of which the enemies of that reform have not scrupled to avail themselves.[2]

This system of purchase and sale of places in the Church—of

---

[1] "While loyalty to the crown has survived all the advances of democracy, the church has awakened from a long period of inaction, and by her zeal and good works have recovered much of her former influence."—*May's Democracy in Europe*, vol. ii. p. 501.

[2] See, for example, ante, p. 198.

" lay patronage," as it is called by the Scotch—has not been confined to the Church of England, but has demoralized and embroiled both the Episcopal and the Presbyterian churches in Scotland as well. John Knox opposed it from the beginning, but not successfully. It led even to scandalous acts of violence. But patronage was recognized by statute, and its spirit and example for centuries contributed to the venality, favoritism, and corruption of all official life in Scotland. Growing more obnoxious as the moral tone and independence of the nation rose, and largely drawing into the controversy about patronage the broader question of state interference in affairs of religion, it became in the first quarter of this century a cause of contentions in the Presbyterian Church so serious as to lead at last to its dismemberment. The party which resisted lay patronage, and claimed the right of the congregation to decide what minister it would have, led by Dr. Chalmers, finally, in 1834, secured a majority in General Assembly ; a result followed by long-continued litigation about the rights of patrons, in which both the Scotch and the English courts affirmed a right of private property in church patronage in Scotland (analogous to that existing in the English Church), which no congregation was allowed to defeat by rejecting the minister who had been tendered them by the patronage-owner. This was too much for the honesty and manhood of a great portion of the members of the (state) Church of Scotland, and they formally seceded and withdrew in 1843, Dr. Chalmers being still a leader. " The secession embraced more than a third of the clergy of the Church of Scotland, and afterwards received considerable accessions of strength. . . . Their once crowded churches were surrendered to others, while they went forth to preach on the hillsides, in tents, barns, and stables. But they relied, with just confidence, upon the sympathies and liberality of their flocks, and in a few years the spires of their free kirks were to be seen in most of the parishes of Scotland." [1] In eighteen years, more than $26,000,000 were contributed for the purposes of the new organization, and the devotion and earnestness of its

---

[1] 2 May's Const. Hist., p. 442.

members have not been less than its material prosperity ; results which the vigorous growth of the same faith in the United States, without State aid, patronage, or proscription, must have led all thoughtful minds to anticipate.  Here, therefore, in a rebellion against the ecclesiastical part of the old spoils system, we have the origin of "The Free Church of Scotland," as well as an illustration of the cost and the difficulties of removing some portions of that system which the principles of the Constitution practically made impossible in the United States.  The fate of so much of that despotic, old system as still lingers in the more worldly divisions of the Scotch Church and in the Church of England—whether anything less than disfranchisement can make an end of that system in Great Britain—whether it be destined to survive the longest among the state church Tories of the Old World in the domain of religion, or among the republican freemen of the New World in the domain of politics—these must remain interesting questions of the future.  Certainly, few things are more anomalous, in the public affairs of the English-speaking people, than the facts that the champions of the mediæval and despotic spirit on one side of the Atlantic should be defending whatever there remains of the old system of patronage, favoritism, and proscription in the avowed interests of royalty and a state church ; at the same time that the self-proclaimed champions of republican institutions, on the other side of the Atlantic, are defending whatever of the same old system there survives, in the pretended interest of democracy, liberty, and justice.  Nor is this contrast less significant when considered as illustrating the extent to which provision may be made against evils of the same kind, in one direction, while, with something like unconsciousness, the people allow them to flourish in full view in another direction ; for the people of Great Britain went on removing abuses in the civil administration without their sense of the enormity of such abuses in the affairs of the state church being very much increased ; and the people of the United States, on the other hand, look upon the provisions of the Constitution, which have protected them from these latter abuses, without much reflecting that its authors could never have imagined that like abuses would grow in the

civil administration.    Standing in the presence of church
patronage, which, if allowed, would speedily sink any religious
organization in the United States, Englishmen are filled with
horror at our political abuses, and grow loyal and patriotic
over the virtues of the civil administration of their country ;
while, standing amidst civil abuses that have been impossible,
for nearly half a century in Great Britain, Americans are
amazed that the offices of religion should there be in the market as merchandise, and that men should be able to buy their
places as ministers in the temples of divine worship.

There is another branch of public service in Great Britain
which, though not literally within the scope of this chapter,
or perhaps of the present work, yet affords striking illustrations of the spirit of the new system and of the obstacles it has
overcome ; nor is it without importance as showing the decay
of patronage and favoritism in Great Britain during the period
in which they have been growing in the United States.    We
have seen that under the despotic kings there was no distinction between civil and military officers as to the conditions of
their appointment, government, or removal ; that James II.
as unhesitatingly turned out colonels and generals as he did
collectors or heads of bureaus, for mere political or household
reasons ; that Walpole denied all grounds of distinction between civil and military officers as to removal ; that George
III. deprived General Conway, Colonel Barré, and other military officers of their commands for favoring the patriotic cause
in America, and that it was with great difficulty that the king
was induced to promise that military men should in the future
be treated as beyond removal for mere political reasons.    But
while the king forebore any extreme application of his proscriptive theory to military affairs, appointments in the army
and navy became a part of the patronage monopoly of members of Parliament. · There had also been growing up a system
under which the war offices of the nation, just like the ministerial places in the Church, were the subjects of open barter
and of bargain and sale for money.    This system spread until
under the name of "purchase" it appears to have embraced
almost the whole military (and no small part of the naval) service of the Empire.    Army purchase, like Church patronage,

was recognized and protected by law ; and when it was finally brought to an end (since the order for open competition in 1870, it was on the basis of an allowance or compensation in money for all commissions then held by purchase. While there was much in the spirit and exigencies of military life and in the high demands of national sentiment that put some check upon the grosser abuses to which so demoralizing a system tended, it is easy to see that it could hardly fail to bring many unworthy persons into military office, to be a serious obstacle to the introduction of the merit system into civil service, or to add greatly to all that was venal and suspicious in official life. No examinations were provided and no effective standard of qualifications applied as against the purchaser of the office. Everywhere there was only a gross competition of money and influence, in which personal worth had little favor and no aid in the methods of government. It was this military system which we had before us when our Constitution was formed ; but we also had before us the experience of the revolutionary war. Our statesmen had seen what caused them to feel the necessity of having military officers adequately instructed for the practical duties of their calling. It was this conviction which resulted in the establishment of the Military Academy at West Point in 1802, and in fixing a literary qualification for admission to it in 1812. In foresight and in patriotic disinterestedness, the American Congress was then far in advance of the British Parliament. The law creating this school provided for no patronage in nominating cadets on the part of members of Congress, for they were to be selected by the President ; and its whole spirit was hostile to making merchandise of military commissions. England had then no such school, and her military system was, during the first quarter of the century, on a low moral plane as compared with that of the United States. But a change was soon to appear in both countries, which has resulted in contrasts full of significance. It was not long before military instruction was provided for in Great Britain, and the claims of personal merit began to rise over Parliamentary patronage and the opportunities of wealth. The greater abuses of the purchase system were one after another remedied. Rigid examinations were provided for admission to the military schools; and at last Parliamentary patronage has been compelled to yield to open competition as the key that opens the gates of those institutions from whose graduates generally the army officers are selected. I need not here recount any of the facts to which I have already referred (or shall refer), showing that, in India and in the home service, members of Parliament have lost their patronage of nominating cadets for either the naval or the military schools, and that a fair public contest of merit—open competition before the Civil Service Commission—wins the cadetships and gives a better class of candidates for the regular army and navy. It would seem that the same method guards the official places in what we should call the militia service. Parliamentary patronage and purchase in the war service of the nation have thus died and been buried together. In the United States, however, the tendency has been in the other direction. The partisan spirit that created the spoils system was equally favorable to the disastrous growth of Congressional patronage. The first step toward Congressional control over cadet appointments was made in 1843, when it was provided that one cadet should be taken from each Congressional district. In violation of the provisions of the law which vested the nomination of cadets in the President, members of Congress took their selection to themselves, and they have since maintained that usurpation, though the statutes still provide that "they shall be appointed by the President."[1]

In the law providing for cadet appointments in the Naval School, enacted in 1862,[2] we find the claims of this growing Congressional patronage system more significantly expressed. The "number allowed at the Academy shall be *two for every member*" (of Congress), says the statute, and the President shall select two from the District of Columbia and ten at large, and "the President shall also be *allowed* three yearly appointments of midshipmen . . . to be selected from boys enlisted in the Navy. The Revised Statutes of 1875[3] require the Secretary of the Navy to notify the member of any vacancy

[1] See Revised Statutes U. S., § 1315.    [2] Laws 1862, chap. 183, § 11.
[3] § 1514.

in his district, and declare that "the nomination shall be made on the recommendation of the member," and permits the President to appoint one cadet from the District of Columbia and ten at large.

Here we see the advance of a system of legislative patronage unknown to our politics in the beginning of the century, and which was abandoned in Great Britain after long experience of its disastrous consequences; and a new spirit with a new claim has grown into such domineering tones and assumptions, that the small portion of the constitutional authority left to the President—the selection of eleven out of near four hundred cadets—is mentioned as being what is "allowed" to him, and the nomination by members is spoken of as if it were a perquisite and right as legitimate and as absolute as any claim of Parliamentary or State Church patronage ever set up by a member of Parliament in the most corrupt and proscriptive periods of British history. These and other encroachments of the Legislature upon the Executive have attracted the attention of thoughtful, foreign writers. "A legislative chamber is greedy and covetous; it acquires as much, it concedes as little as possible; . . . the law-making faculty, the most comprehensive of the imperial faculties, is its instrument; it will *take* the Administration if it can take it. Tried by their own aims, the founders of the United States Constitution were wise in excluding the Ministers from Congress." In the facts recited, we see, not merely how law-makers can "take" patronage, in flagrant violation of the fundamental principle of the government, which requires that the legislative and executive functions shall be kept distinct, but we also see regulations for apportionment, division, and enjoyment laid down as formally and with as little disguise as in any rules of a prize court for sharing the spoils of war, or in any customs of Newcastle's or Walpole's "Patronage Secretary of the Treasury" for sharing the spoils of peace.

It is interesting to note that here, as in Great Britain before

Bagehot's "English Constitution," pp. 92 and 93. It is Mr. Bagehot's view that Secretaries coming into Congress would increase the power of that body over the Executive; and he feels the necessity of not increasing that peril, much as, in the abstract, he favors their presence.

the new system became general, public opinion tends more and more to compel members to hand their cadetships over to open competition; and here as there it seems clear that such competition secures a superior class of students;[1] but it would carry me too far from my subject to present the proofs on these points, and they would but add another to the many examples of our repeating continually, for good or for evil, the experience of the older country.

[1] Twenty-two years ago, upon the first experiment of competition for the selection of military cadets, we find Mr. Mill (Representative Government, p. 110, edition 1857) saying : " I am credibly informed that in the military academy at Woolwich the competition-cadets are as superior to those admitted on the old system of nominations in these respects (bodily activity) as in all others." And the report of the U. S. Civil Service Commission, made in April, 1874, uses this language on the same subject : " So unsatisfactory had been all other methods of nomination that the official circulars from the Secretary of War, under which this courtesy is regularly extended, recognizing the precedents of disinterested members of Congress, now contain a notice that 'competitive examinations,' etc., have been introduced, ' with results satisfactory,' as the basis of these nominations ; and in the Naval School, also, the advantages of competitive examinations, induced by the example of such examinations under the civil service rules, have still further supplanted the old methods. The facts, which we find confirmed by the highest authority, are stated by the editor of a Washington journal as follows :

" ' The position of cadet-engineer being open to any youth of proper age and proficiency, the Secretary of the Navy received last summer a very large number of applications, and in order to secure the most efficient he made the examination competitive. The wisdom of this course has fully proved itself in the second class of cadet-engineers, now at the Academy, *which has been declared both mentally and physically superior to any* that preceded it.' "—*The Chronicle*, February 14, 1874.

# CHAPTER XXIX.

THE history of the growth of the reform sentiment and of
the new methods to which it has given birth has to a large extent explained their practical effect. That they have been a
victory of public virtue and intelligence over corruption and
incompetency, of common justice over special privileges and
feudal customs, of equal rights and opportunities over official
favoritism and partisan tyranny, and especially of the great
cause of elementary education over the exclusiveness and the
selfish hostility of the aristocratic classes,—are results almost
too plain for further comment. In one aspect, the reform in
its later stages may be looked upon as an illustration of a
great movement in the public conscience and thought, which
marks an epoch in British history ; finding kindred expression
in laws, of rare beneficence and wisdom, for the protection of
the poor and humble in mines, shops, and factories ; for the
suppression of vice and crime ; for the security of life, health,
and virtue ; for the acquisition of land, education, and common rights ; for the extension of suffrage, and the purity and
responsibility of public life in various ways. In another aspect, it presents itself as a remarkable concentration of public
intelligence and scrutiny upon a method for elevating the
standard of official duty and capacity, above what might be expected from the general condition of the people ; and, whereby political contests, no longer mere scrambles for office,

are made to turn upon great principles and good administration; so that the very processes of governing are made fountains of strength to the conservative forces of society. The early reformers naturally expected that popular instruction would be stimulated by their work, and this opinion was, we find, soon shared by practical statesmen at the head of the government. "I hope we shall give a great stimulus to primary education by holding out this large number of rewards . . . for those who excel in competition." [1] That hope was not disappointed. I have space for only the most meagre illustration of the marvellous strides [2] which have been made during the past few years in common-school education, so long shamefully neglected by the ruling class in Great Britain. It was in the same year (1870) when open competition was introduced, that school boards, sustained by local rates (which had been long resisted by the State Church and the privileged classes), were for the first time provided for in all the districts of the country.

Competent observers think the new school system to be in some respects unsurpassed, and no well informed person will deny that parts of its administration deserve our serious study. [3] The vigor with which popular education has advanced, since 1870, makes its own suggestion as to its being aided by some new and powerful cause—not so much, perhaps, by competition for the public service as the ultimate force, as by the new spirit which demanded both competition and schools—and which now stands behind and stimulates education. The election for the London School Board in the autumn of 1870 is said to have aroused more interest than

[1] Evidence of the Chancellor of Exchequer, Parl. Rep. 1873, p. 231, Vol. 3.

[2] "In your elementary schools you are in advance of us. . . . Ten years ago we were a long way behind, but we are improving rapidly, and if you intend to keep before us, you will have to work hard."—*Impressions of America, by Rev. R. W. Dale*, 1878, p. 163.

[3] Several able women have been elected members of the London School Board, and their services have been found invaluable—a kind of membership not so compatible with our partisan system. The new system of cumulative voting for school officers excludes the absolute domination of either party in school management.

any municipal election ever held in the metropolis. Between 1870 and 1875, that Board alone completed 53 school
houses, at a cost of nearly $3,500,000 ; and in 1875 it had 80
others in the course of construction, on which more than
$2,800,000 had been expended. Attendance in the schools is
compulsory. In 1874, there were 77,985 official notices served
to attend ; 4681 persons were convicted for neglect in that
regard, and 41,697 parents were required to appear and show
cause why their children were absent from school. A part of
the expenses of destitute children attending school are paid
from the public funds, so that their poverty may not prevent
their education.[1] The popular support of education advanced
so rapidly that, in 1876, compulsory attendance was made
general by act of Parliament. It appears[2] that the rapid
spread of elementary instruction among the people continues unabated. In England, the attendance upon the public schools
has increased sixty per cent in five years, and in Scotland forty-
two per cent in three years. In the city of Birmingham, it increased one hundred and thirty-eight per cent between 1871 and
1876. The success of the higher institutions of learning, in
testing capacity by examinations, would seem to have originally
suggested the practicability of such tests for the public service.
There can be no doubt, however, but the debt has been many
times repaid by the greater honor and profit which the action
of the government has conferred upon learning in every grade.
What elevates and widens the base of course raises and
strengthens the whole pyramid of knowledge. It has not
therefore been in the lower range of learning alone that examinations for the public service have given new vitality to popular education. The example helped to stimulate the higher
schools and even the universities to a more active life. Much
higher qualifications have also been required, within the last few
years, than formerly, for admission to the bar or to practice as
an attorney or solicitor. The right to practice as a doctor
or surgeon, or to carry on the business of an apothecary or
medical chemist, has, in the same period, been conditioned on higher attainments. In 1865, Oxford and Cambridge

[1] Firth's Municipal London, p. 442-457.
[2] Report U. S. Commissioner of Education, 1878, p. CLXIV.-CLXIX.

(which had before conducted local examinations for young men engaged in literary and scientific studies) extended them to young women, not with a view of admitting them as students, but of stimulating and rewarding home studies by public encouragement. Other institutions have followed these examples. In 1865, only 126 young women were candidates, but in 1875 examinations were held at fifty-six different places, and there were 1552 female candidates [1] examined. The growing spirit of justice and liberty, within the same period, has opened the public museums, libraries, and galleries freely to the people, and made the Kensington Museum the centre of a vast system of instruction in the practical arts now being given in numerous places throughout the British Islands.

It is a matter of common observation that the taking of the corrupt elements and the venal prizes out of party contests in Great Britain has in no sense weakened the wholesome public interest in elections. Parties have never stood more firmly by their principles or maintained more vigorous contests at the polls than since these contests have ceased to control nominations, appointments, promotions, or removals. Indeed, it has been during the same period, in which that service has been gradually raised above corruption and partisanship, that the English people have most vigorously and successfully contended for an enlarged suffrage and for the ballot. The same reforming spirit which abolished compulsory church rates in 1868, disestablished the Irish Church in 1869, opened the public service freely to merit in 1870, swept away religious tests for admissions to offices and degrees in the universities, and suppressed the sale of army commissions in 1871,—finally, in the last-named year, secured to the people the invaluable privilege of voting by ballot. So far from there being indifference to elections, the right of voting is now held and exercised by a larger proportion of the people of Great Britain than at any other period of her history.

It is a point of interest to know what effect the new methods for selecting executive officers have had upon the amount of

[1] Harvard University, among our own institutions, five years ago offered American women the benefit of such examinations upon the English principle, and they are being continued with increasing success.

crime and the administration of justice ; but I cannot spare space for more than the briefest illustration. The fact has been that crime and criminal arrests have been steadily decreasing in Great Britain, as corruption has disappeared from her politics. London is, perhaps, a fair example of the whole country ; and there a recent English writer asserts : [1] " It is satisfactory to notice that crime in the metropolis is on the decrease, not merely proportionally, but actually ;" but it is not satisfactory to us to be compelled also to notice that the number of crimes and criminal arrests in London are less in each year than they are in the city of New York, which has only about one-third the population of London.[2]

It would require too much space to give the facts necessary to illustrate in any general way the efficiency with which the laws are now executed in Great Britain. It must suffice to make a simple reference to sanitary administration, which, as much as any other, measures the ability and fidelity of officials. New York city has a health administration of unsurpassed efficiency in this country (considering the partisan abuses which cripple it and which demoralize the whole city government on which it depends) ; but the more favorable political conditions of London have, in later years, enabled its health officers—despite its slums of fearful vice and ignorance which have come down from generations that knew neither cleanliness nor schools—to reduce its ratio of disease and death below that of the city of New York ; and, by reason of able health officers, the death rate of Bombay—that ancient haunt and breeding-place of plagues, leprosies, and choleras—with its population of 650,000 of all races and religions under the sun—seems to have been reduced below that of Baltimore, Richmond, New Orleans, and other American cities. Perhaps the greatest sanitary reforms ever yet undertaken in the world are those which have been carried forward in Glasgow

---

[1] Firth's Municipal London, 1876, p. 431.

[2] The number of arrests in London in 1869 was 72,951. In 1870 it was 71,269, and has since decreased. In 1870 the number arrested in New York city was 75,692. In 1871 it was 84,514, and in 1875 it was 84,399. I have not the exact figures to make the comparison since, but the ratio has not materially varied.

and Edinburgh within the last twelve years. The artisans' and laborers' dwellings improvement acts of 1875 are being carried into effect with an official ability and fidelity worthy the spirit they embody : and the tenement house law (and all the other most efficient sanitary) statutes of New York city are in large part based on British precedents.[1]

It would require a whole chapter to do justice to the economical results of the new system. It is by no means easy to make due allowance for the different rates of wages in the two countries so as to show with exactness the relative cost of the merit and partisan systems. Besides, as the British officers have a graded salary, which increases with years of service, and is followed (after ten years of service) by a retiring allowance, the relative cost is not shown by a mere comparison of salaries. No argument, however, is needed to prove that, as the respectability and honor of the public service is raised, it becomes more attractive. Men will work for less compensation, when their tenure is secure during good behavior and their position commands public respect. It has already been shown that. by reason of securing a better class of officers, a much smaller number has been found adequate. Facts might be cited, could I give space for them, which would show a great saving in the cost of administration.[2] It must suffice, as illustrations, to state that the government clerks—clerks corresponding to those to whom we pay $900 a year, begin on a salary of from $400 to $450 a year, and that the police of London are paid salaries that are not much

[1] 38 and 39 Vict., chaps. 36 and 49. These are most comprehensive statutes, and in their elaborate provisions for securing sanitary protection to the homes of the poor, they go far beyond anything attempted in this country. And another act of the same year (38 and 39 Vict., chap. 55), which fills 152 pages of the statute—being a general public health law—in the variety, benevolence, and breadth of its provisions, probably transcends the united body of all our State and Congressional legislation on sanitary subjects. So wise and just provisions, in the special interest of the humble and the feeble, would not seem to be most fit to be monopolized by a monarchy ; and at a time when our legislators, State and national, are so anxiously debating sanitary subjects, in aspects that have long since entered into British administration, I venture to depart a little from my subject to draw attention to these matters of supreme importance.

[2] For some illustrations, see Chap. XII.. pp. 147–150.

more than one half those paid policemen in the city of New York.

The method of coming into the service upon the basis of merit has not *necessarily* anything to do with the tenure of office, though its spirit is of course utterly hostile to removals except for good cause, and for such removals the British system gives ample authority. The moment that open competition is made the door of entrance to the service, there is little pressure to put men out in order to get others in. It is far too uncertain who will win the place made vacant, to make the attack attractive to office-brokers or place-hunters. So long as every executive officer having the right of nomination is exposed to the menace of congressional influence, and all the gates of the public service stand wide open to the siege of partisan organizations, it will, I am persuaded, hardly be possible to establish any wise tenure of office ; but as soon as an effective test of merit can be placed at these gates, the vast army of interested politicians now so obstructive will no longer be able to foist their favorites upon the Treasury, and they will therefore no longer take the trouble to oppose a just and economical official tenure. It will be only after corrupt and partisan ways of getting into public places have been closed, that we shall be able to consider the subject disinterestedly and calmly, and thus be in a fair condition to decide for how long a time, or until what age, in the several branches of the service, it is for the public interest to retain an official. There does not seem, in view of British experience, to be any great promise of usefulness in giving much attention to that subject at present ; though if we could return to our original system, by repealing the laws which limit the term of collectors, post-masters, surveyors, and various other subordinates, to four years, we should get rid of many demoralizing contests, and should soon gain that experience that would enable us to decide upon some tenure more inviting to worthy persons, and hence more economical for the government—upon some tenure that would not bring on a new contest for existence, by the time an officer has gained experience enough to know his duties.

No one can go over the British investigations on the subject, or come in contact with British officials, without being

impressed with the need and the importance of some fixed
rules as to the age most fit and advantageous for entering and
leaving the public service—and hence, as to the proper tenure
of a subordinate, executive officer. The question is one which
equally concerns public economy and official morality. So
long as the absurd theory of "rotation in office"—a change
for the sake of a change—a theory that could not bring about
the justice to which it appeals, even if official tenure was for
only a single day—or the partisan theory of appointment and
removals—move the majority, it is in vain to expect any practical result from inquiring what a proper regard for efficiency,
economy, or official fidelity demand. I have no space to adequately present the reasoning on the subject to be found in
British documents, and yet I am not willing to dismiss them in
silence. What can be plainer than this—that when an officer or
clerk has no assurance that great capacity or industry in his place
will either prevent his removal, ensure his promotion, or even
protect him from assessments, he is deprived of the strongest
motives to usefulness, and is naturally filled with a sense of the
injustice of his government? To be most efficient he needs to
study the duties of his position ; but why should he labor beyond the needs of to-day, when to-morrow he may be sent
home in disgrace, without cause and without trial, or be
humiliated by seeing an official or partisan favorite, every
way inferior to himself, put over his head? He has not even
the motives to good conduct which the government of all the
more enlightened States throw around the inmates of their
prisons, who are allowed by good conduct to reduce their term
of confinement. This precariousness—the constant sense of
uncertainty and peril which it produces—is, I am persuaded,
in two ways the cause of great pecuniary expense to the government ; first, by compelling it to pay higher salaries, as an
inducement to competent persons to enter so uninviting a service, and next, by compelling it to employ a greater number
of officials, because those it has are without the higher inducements to exertion, and are distracted by efforts to protect
themselves against dismissals, and to secure promotions by
influence. It hardly need be added that such utter uncertainty of tenure—the general conviction it produces that when

a place in the service is forfeited nothing stable or reliable is lost—tend to weaken the inducements to honesty and fidelity. When a public officer or clerk feels that, if he be faithful, he can hold his place, with an increasing salary, so long as he is competent, and that if he is especially efficient, he will be promoted, it is almost too plain for observation that he is bound to honesty and fidelity by ties far stronger than the man can feel who has before him nothing but a dreary, dead level of uncertainty—a hold of his place utterly frail and precarious —liable on any day to be broken by an order which arrests his income, and—if it does not suggest his incompetency or infidelity—for that very reason must proclaim the arbitrary injustice of his country. No one, I think, can become acquainted with the very different feelings cherished by those in the civil service, toward the government, under these contrasted systems, without a strong conviction that the pride of place and the sense of justice and gratitude which the one develops and the other destroys, are subjects well worthy the attention of statesmen ; and I shall take occasion to more adequately present the significant fact that, in Great Britain, those in the subordinate service hold their places and serve the government with pride, always certain that a knowledge of their employment by the government will advance rather than prejudice their standing in public estimation.

It should be mentioned that, under British laws, no limit but incompetency—and hence no tenure expressed in terms of years—applies to those in the civil service ; but the superannuation laws cease to make additional allowances after forty years' of service ; and perhaps the great question for us, on this subject, is not that of fixing any tenure of office, but that of deciding upon some age or period of service before which an officer may feel safe if worthy, and after which, if his capacity is impaired, he may feel it is wise to retire lest he be requested to do so.

[1] See ante, pp. 142–3.

# CHAPTER XXX.

## THE MERIT SYSTEM IN THE GREAT DEPARTMENTS.

Internal revenue administration.—Examinations.—Promotions.—Discipline.—Exclusion of politics.—Removals.—Extent of delinquency.—Customs service.—Examinations.—Removals.—Neither patronage nor politics.—Stringent regulations.—Extent of delinquency.—Method of appointments and promotions compared with that of United States.—The Treasury.—Open competition for clerks.—Promotions.—Statement of Mr. Gladstone.—Post Office Department.—Classes of postmasters.—How clerks are examined and appointed.—Appointment of postmasters.—Open competition in large offices.—Severe rules of discipline.—No electioneering in offices or interference with elections.—Mr. Mundella's statement.—State Department and Consular and Diplomatic Service.—How far politics excluded.—Examinations for clerks and consuls.—Regulations.—Members of Parliament without patronage.—Clerks of the two Houses of Parliament.—Not removed for political reasons.—Members relieved from solicitation.

*The Inland Revenue Department* is in charge of a board of five commissioners, appointed by the Crown, and they continue in office during good behavior. More than two thirds of the income of the British Government comes from its inland revenue. The amount thus collected in 1876 was $225,730,180. The number of officials in the service was 7093, besides employés. Of the revenue collected, more than $75,000,000 comes from spirits, and more than $38,000,000 from malt. In addition to what is covered by our internal revenue collections, the system of land taxation, of income taxes, of house duties, and of game and dog licenses, are administered by this board. It hardly need be said that in the number of agents, in the magnitude and complexity of the business transacted, and in the opportunities of cheating which a lax discipline would afford, British internal revenue administration greatly transcends that of the United States. The taxation it controls, in variety and difficulty, approximates what would

be the condition with us if State taxation were added to the
internal revenue administration of the Federal Government.
By reason of the stability of its tenure, the long experience it
secures, and its independence of elections and politics, the
board is able to pursue a firm and consistent policy and to enforce a rigid discipline.[1]

With very slight exceptions, all entrance to the service is
to the lowest grade, and by the way of open competition, before the Civil Service Board. Corrupt or partisan influence
and official favoritism are thus effectually excluded. The exceptions referred to are in the lowest grade of the service,
being mere messengers in some of the local offices, as to which
the right of nomination seems to have survived. But even
these nominated messengers are examined under the board.
And from messengers and porters up to the heads of bureaus,
no one can be removed, except for cause, and no one is removed without being given a proper hearing or opportunity
for explanation in his own defense. Appointments for political reasons are, I hardly need add, excluded by competition.

The board has the right of promotion and authority for discipline without interference from any other quarter, but cannot increase salaries or expenses. Promotions are for merit.
In certain parts of the service, they are based on examinations,
and in other parts on official records kept in the offices, and,
almost without exception, all the higher places are filled from
those below. Personal records of the conduct of all officers are
kept by the board. The right of discipline, in its application,
ranges from a mere caution to a dismissal, and includes the
right to reduce both rank and pay. It would seem plain that
there can be little or no opportunity for politics in this branch
of the service. Neither the dominant party nor those controlling local elections are allowed chances for patronage or coercion anywhere in the vast network of official places through
which, in all parts of the empire, such enormous internal revenues are collected. Year after year, through elections follow-

---

[1] For example, each clerk has to sign, every morning and evening, his
name in a book which shows the hour and minute of his arrival and depart-
ure, and this record must be daily signed by a supervising officer. Fines
are rigidly imposed for tardiness.

ing elections, during one administration and then into the
next, without change of method or members, the work of the
department advances steadily upon business principles ; not a
clerk with a fear of losing, not a politician with a chance of
gaining, an office by any result in the field of politics. The
best information I could get as to the character[1] of the administration is to this effect : It is universally believed to be
efficient and without corruption or political bias. I could hear
of no reports that revenues were not properly collected or
accounted for. There is no public rumor or belief (so far as I
have been able to learn) that in any way corresponds to the
current views in this country in regard to whiskey frauds and
official delinquency in connection with internal revenue administration. Such seems to be the conclusion of an American
gentleman, than whom, probably, no one is better informed
on the subject ; "Great Britain," he says, "has for many
years had an internal, income tax which, . . . with her trained
officials, is assessed and collected with as much of accuracy as
any such tax probably can be."[2] I have high authority[3] for
stating that "peculation amounts to nothing. . . . I do not
think there is an average of three cases a year. . . . The
revenue seldom loses anything from such cases." Referring
to collecting officers, it is said, "I think there have *not been
more than half a dozen defaults in twenty-four years . . . in
no case has the revenue lost anything.* The estimated losses
by fraud and default for the year 1877-8 amount to £400
out of a collection of £46,000,000 . . . amongst the collectors
of land tax and inhabited house duty . . . five defaults have
occurred since 1874." It would require far more space than
I can spare to set forth the carefully matured methods of
supervision and precaution by which such fidelity has been
secured. Next after the exclusion of politics and favoritism,
in the selections of those who enter the service, the stability,
vigor, and sense of responsibility, which a permanent Board
is able to impart, are the most important elements.

[1] In the appendix will be found several letters bearing upon this point.
[2] David A. Wells, in *International Review*, April, 1878.
[3] Letter from one of the Internal Revenue Commissioners to the author
Nov. 17, 1877.

*The Customs Service.* The foreign (or customs) duties of Great Britain in 1876 amounted to $96,446,000, and hence fall below our own in a ratio approximating that in which her inland duties exceed ours. The whole number of established clerks in the customs service in 1876 was 4626, but these do not include messengers, porters, or mere employés. This branch of her fiscal affairs is administered by a board of four commissioners, the members of which are appointed by the Crown, and they continue in office during good behavior. There has been such a board for over a hundred years. To them and their subordinates, what I have just said (in connection with internal revenue administration) as to the exclusion of politics and favoritism, and as to authority and discipline, also applies. As illustrating the discipline and system that prevails, I may mention that the board makes an annual report, which not only sets forth every fact necessary to disclose the character of the administration, in the ordinary sense, but states, in apt medical phrase, the several diseases which have caused sickness, and for how long a time, and to how many persons, among those in the customs service, at the larger ports.[1]

The hours of duty of the indoor branch of the service are from ten to four, and of the *outdoor* branch from nine to four. Every ordinary clerk has, each day, to sign a record when he reaches and again when he leaves his office, which fixes his daily service even to the minute. The head of the office must put his initials daily at the foot of the page. Fines are regularly imposed for tardiness or absence, and no salary can be paid when any fine is in arrears. These signed "appearance sheets" are laid before the board weekly, and if fines often occur, other consequences beside their payment follow. There is a system of supervision of official conduct by officers having that duty (and the same in other departments), which is analogous to the duty imposed on roundsmen in a police force, and the instructions declare that "the board rely on their zeal and discretion in taking every necessary means for ascertaining, not merely the official conduct and character,

---

[1] The names are not given.

but the habits and pursuits of every individual under their control." Full records are kept in every office of the official conduct of those who serve there; and it is on such evidence, on the official opinions of the leading officers formally taken, and and on appropriate examinations, and not on politics or influence, that promotions are based. It would seem plain there can be but small opportunity for neglecting public business in order to attend to politics, and I have thought such details not unimportant, in view of the notorious laxity which has prevailed in so many of our custom houses.

There are one hundred and forty ports of entry in the United Kingdom, and they are all under the jurisdiction of the same board. Like the Inland Revenue Board, it has a full authority of appointment, promotion, and removal as well as of discipline. I hardly need to point out that a permanent Board, having charge of all the custom houses, has great facilities for securing uniformity of administration and for bringing the expenses of each into comparison with the others, in a way which largely contributes to responsibility and economy; but I have no space for details. If I should merely say that this authority is really independent of both general and local politics—that a custom house is no more a party or a political agency in Great Britain than a college is with us, and that a collector is no more a political manager than is one of our college presidents—I fear I should hardly be believed in thus declaring the simple truth. I must, therefore, give some further facts. The clerks, at all these ports, and in all the offices, are appointed according to well-known rules, from among those who were first in the competitive examinations before the Civil Service Commission. No influence can secure a clerkship,[1] and no officer or politician can decide who shall compete for one. The clerks are, therefore, neither politicians by trade nor insolvents for want of ability to trade, but young men whose character and capacity have stood a severe

---

[1] There are a few messengers, boatmen, and porters below the grade of clerks, who, through a curious survivorship of a fragment of the old system, are yet nominated by the Treasury for only a pass examination. But that examination is exacting, and when once in service, they are only removed for cause after an opportunity of explanation.

20

public test, and whose places have been gained by their
own merits.  They must serve at least six months on
probation, and then if approved they are appointed ; and
they can only be removed for cause, and after a hearing before the board.  They may be fined or reduced in rank
for bad conduct.  Such public servants as housekeepers, doorkeepers, watchmen, etc., have  in addition to place on file
evidence both of character and of " the course of life they
have led."  The rules are of many years' standing which require such officers as searchers, landing waiters, and gaugers
" to go under a course of instruction three months without
pay."  The higher places, including collectorships, are filled
by promotions, which are based on merit ; and full and careful records are kept in order that a just judgment may be
formed.  The board annually inspects the administration
at each port, and a careful record of the cost and character of the administration of each is made.  In the
outdoor service, where the board has less personal acquaint-
ance with the officers, one half of the promotions are
secured by competition among the clerks.  The office of collector at Liverpool, London, or other large ports is only
filled by a person who has been collector at some port where
he has supervised every branch of port service.  Our practice
of placing inexperienced men at the head of even a small port
is as utterly unknown as is the practice of considering party
politics in making such appointments.  Nothing can be in
wider contrast than our toleration of miscellaneous influence
for effecting appointments and promotions and the British system which excludes them.

" It has long been the practice in the Customs to require the chief
officers of each branch to make a report in writing to the Board of
Commissioners as to the character and qualifications of the officers
coming forward for promotion, and to name the persons whom they
consider most competent and deserving.  It is usual in the more
important cases to summon the surveyors general and inspectors
general to the board room, and take their opinions separately on the
subject.  And, as a further security against improper selections, the
board is required to transmit a formal report to the Lords of the
Treasury, stating all the circumstances, and requesting their Lordships'

confirmation of the appointment. . . The circumstances of all promotions stand recorded in the official books, and may be referre l to in the event of any complaint or inquiry being made into the matter." [1]

Regulations long in force contain these provisions :

" In any case in which an officer would be entitled to promotion on his own merits, application made in his favor . . . affords grounds for suspicion that the selection of the officer has been influenced in some degree by private considerations . . . and private applications from officers themselves, or from others, on their behalf, addressed to individual members of the board, are interdicted ; and the same will not only have the effect of retarding the promotion of the parties, but subject them to the board's severe displeasure. The board . . . will consider any private application for promotion to have emanated from the party in whose behalf the same shall be made . . . unless he shall satisfy the board that he had no knowledge thereof, directly or indirectly. Beyond recording your vote, if you shall be so entitled, you are not in any way to interfere in the elections for members of Parliament."

These facts must be sufficient to show how radically different are the systems prevailing in the customs service of the two countries. Promotions constantly tendered on such conditions would seem to be a powerful stimulant to good conduct, and such, I am convinced, is the fact. They also cause those in the service to give earnest attention to the relative merits of each other and to the manner in which the members of the board apply the principle of advancement to which they are thus publicly pledged. A few facts bearing upon the discipline, honesty, and efficiency of this branch of the service will be found interesting. There has been an average number of fifteen a year, during the past five years, dismissed from the service for bad conduct.[2] During those five years there has

---

[1] Civil Service Papers, p. 337, printed in 1855.

[2] The Board being independent of party politics, the rules as to dismissals are rigid, and are, I think, fearlessly applied. As an illustration of the precautions against abuses—and perhaps of their infrequency as well, I may mention that the standing instructions require that even an " anonymous complaint" shall be publicly investigated on public notice, the complainant being called on in such notice to appear ; but if he does not appear, " a second notice is to be published," and the charge investigated, pursuant thereto.

been only a *single case* of defalcation in the customs service proper, and that was for only £3 5s. But, even in this case, a jury failed to find the officer guilty, though the board dismissed him. " There have been eleven cases in five years of pilfering small quantities of goods. The government, however, finally lost nothing. During those years, there were also two cases of defalcation in collection of money belonging to the corporation of Trinity House, but which is collected by the Customs Department," the amount being £4225 6s. 5d., a part of which was lost.[1]

It is not for me to attempt to describe the different effects upon public business, public morality, and political affairs—a difference almost indescribable, and not easy to imagine even—between such a customs system, based on personal character and capacity, and independent of partisan politics and corrupt influence, and a system under which coercions and favor make and unmake officers, and every custom house on the borders is the centre of a feverish, costly and useless partisan activity, if of nothing more pernicious. What can be more widely contrasted or more significant than the different methods pursued, in the two countries, for the common object of selecting that mere business officer called a collector of a port? In the one, he is quietly taken by the administrative board, through a well-known process, based on merit, and without political significance, from some lower place of duty where his public record of efficiency and economy has brought his capacity to the notice of his superiors. Once in office, he remains, like a judge, during good behavior. In the other, the selection raises an exciting contest of partisan strategy and influence, certainly in the district, and very likely in the State, if not in Congress and the whole nation; with intrigues and embroilments which bring all the vicious machinery of political management into action, convert every custom house clerk into a factionist compelled to fight for his salary and his place, absorb the activity of every grade of officials from doorkeepers and porters to Senators and Cabinet Secretaries, disgust the merchants and all the best citizens with the very name of

[1] Letter Secretary Customs Board to the author, Dec. 11, 1877.

politics and office ; and all with the result, perhaps, of a collector utterly unacquainted with his duties, but bound fast in demoralizing pledges to remove a third of his best subordinates in order to meet the promises which are likely to compel him to be an active partisan leader, but a poor collector of a port, during the four years or less which may intervene before another battle of the same kind must be fought. By one method, the selection is so made that it stimulates and honors capacity and integrity in every grade of the service ; by the other, such qualifications are spurned, and the nation is made to declare its preference for political intrigue and management—to practically say to every clerk, No matter how devoted and capable you may be, you have no chance of becoming a collector—no chance of escaping dependence upon a politician put over you—unless you become a politician yourself.

In general terms, I ought to say that public confidence in the customs service in Great Britain—in its honesty, its freedom from political partiality, its economy and efficiency—appears to be very nearly if not quite universal.[1]

*The Treasury.* The two great revenue divisions already described include the bulk of the administration in the British Treasury Department. And this fact illustrates a very important difference between the revenue system of Great Britain and that of the United States. There, as with us, the Treasury is, to a certain extent, a political office ; and those at its head are expected to carry out the financial policy of the dominant party. This duty requires a right of giving general instructions to those legally at the head of the revenue departments, to the extent that such policy is involved ; but it is not concerned with the discipline or the political opinions of subordinates, or with the miscellaneous details of the public work, which needs to be the same whatever party is in power. And on this theory, the two great Revenue Boards I have described, the heads of which remain unaffected by political changes in the cabinet or in Parliament, have charge of all the offices, officials, and the work connected with revenue collection, subject only to such instructions and to certain rights of appeal

---

[1] Here again I refer to the letters in the appendix.

in connection with the higher grades of promotions and a few
other issues of paramount importance. The Treasury does
not interfere with revenue officers or affairs directly, but only
by general instructions communicated through the proper revenue boards. It is apparent that such an arrangement must
largely contribute to make revenue administration independent
of both local and general politics. The British system as-
sumes that it does not follow, because the head of the Treasury
is a statesman, competent to guide a national policy, that he
is at once endued with the local and personal information
needed to pass upon innumerable appeals for office and multi-
farious claims for promotion ; or that he has suddenly mas-
tered the manifold questions of skill, science, routine, and
method which it is the labor of an ordinary official life to
understand ; nor, on the other hand, does that system suggest
that it is wise to have the head of the Treasury daily besieged
by office-seekers and schemers pushing for advantage under a
vast body of complicated laws and regulations, with which he
is perhaps little familiar, and which questions of national interest give him no time to study.

I have before stated that the head of the Treasury itself
is a board, which now has seven members, of which the
First Lord (or member) is Prime Minister, and the Chancellor of the Exchequer is also a member, and he is generally
the leader of the ruling party in the House of Commons.
These seven members are political officers, and go out with
each administration. But there is also a permanent Secretary of the Treasury who has charge of the administrative
work, and is unaffected by political changes. The clerks in
the Treasury gain their places by open, competitive examinations before the Civil Service Commission. They enter at the
lowest grade ; and the higher places (except membership of
the board) are filled by promotion from below. Neither
partisan politics nor official favoritism can secure appointments
in the Treasury Department of Great Britain. And, therefore,
when Mr. Gladstone said [1] that, " as to the clerkships in my
office—the office of the Treasury—every one of you has just as

---

[1] In his speech to the electors of Greenwich in 1871.

much power over their disposal as I have. . . . In order that
the public service might be, indeed, the public service ; in
order that we might not have among the civil officers of the
State that which we had complained of in the army, namely,
that the service was not the property of the nation, but of
the officers, we have now been enabled to remove the barriers
of nomination, patronage, jobbery, favoritism, in whatever
form ; and every man belonging to the people of England, if
he so please to fit his children for competing for places in the
public service, may do it entirely irrespective of the question,
what is his condition in life. . . ." when Mr. Gladstone
proclaimed this noble triumph of common justice and common
honesty over all that had been aristocratic, venal, and partisan
in British administration, I am convinced he not only said
what was literally true of himself, but what, in principle, was
true of every member of the Cabinet and of Parliament.

*The Postal Service.* It is not necessary, after what I have
said of the revenue service, to enter much into detail as to the
application of the merit system to the postal service. Its reputation is familiar to all well-informed Americans. Though
legally under the control of the Postmaster-General, (who is
a member of the Cabinet, and hence a political officer,) the
postal service is practically managed by a permanent, non-
political secretary. All subordinate officers serve during
good behavior, and they can be removed only for cause. The
reason for any removal of a clerk must be stated in the records. With reference to the appointment of postmasters and
the clerical force, the department may be considered as in four
divisions :

1. There are the very small offices in which an aggregate
sum is paid for carrying on each office, and not much scrutiny
is extended to the clerical force, if indeed there is any, provided the business is well cared for.

2. In offices larger than the last named, but with an income
not above £120 in England and £100 in Ireland and Scotland,
the clerks are nominated by the postmasters and are examined
upon a uniform method by the Civil Service Commission.[1]

---

[1] I find myself unable to state that such examinations extend to all offices
of this grade, but I believe such to be the fact.

The clerks being few in so small offices, each may be well known to the postmaster, and the form of competition is hardly necessary, and has not been applied. The postmasters, in this class of offices, are selected by the Treasury, but are only to be removed for cause.

3. In offices where the income is larger than the amount last named, the postmasters are selected from the entire service as a recognition of their efficiency. They are appointed by the Postmaster-General, and are removable only for cause. How effectually these appointments are severed from legislative dictation, is illustrated by the fact that the official notices of the vacancy declare that applications through "members of Parliament are calculated to defeat rather than promote the object in view," and no candidate is allowed to apply save through his superior officer.[1] The clerks are examined as last mentioned.

4. In the great offices of London, Edinburgh, and Dublin, the clerks all secure their places by open, competitive examinations before the Civil Service Commission.

Removals are nowhere made for political reasons, but only for causes connected with their efficiency or character. The Postmaster of Liverpool has held his place since 1841, and the Postmaster of London his place since 1834. Careful examinations are held for sorters, carriers, distributors, and telegraph operators, etc., in the postal service.

It would require too much detail to make any adequate comparison between British and American postal administration. But by way of illustration, I may mention that in the city of New York the long experience and rare executive ability of the postmaster,[2] aided by a clerical force improved (so far as our system would permit) by examinations and competitions like those thus practised in Great Britain, have brought the postal service to a degree of efficiency I think never before reached in this country ; yet, as compared with that of London, it stands as follows : London, 12 daily deliveries in a portion of the city, 11 in other portions, and 6 in the suburban districts : New York, 7 daily deliveries in a portion of the city, 5 in other portions, and 3 in the rest of the city : and

[1] Report Com. Inq. 1873, App. F, p. 78.          [2] Thomas L. James, Esq.

the superior efficiency of the British service is, I think, hardly more marked in London than in the other cities and in the villages and rural districts.[1]

It is well known that the money order system prevailed in the postal service of Great Britain for a considerable time before we applied it. The telegraph system and the issuing of revenue licenses are now a part of her postal service, and there are also attached to it between 5000 and 6000 post-office savings banks, which cause a complexity and responsibility in the postal administration unknown in the United States. Over 25,000 separate deposits of money have been made in the postal banks in a single day, and open accounts are kept with more than 1,700,000 depositors. Postal savings banks (which have been adopted in France and Belgium, on a large scale) are regarded as a great aid to economy and saving on the part of the poor ; but the duties they impose, and the sending of more than 24,000,000 of telegraph messages and the issuing of nearly a million of revenue licenses each year, I hardly need say, call for rare capacity and discipline in the officers of the postal service, and for an amount of experience and trained skill to which our partisan system of appointments and removals is fatal. I may say, generally, that the discipline is as strict in the Post Office Department in every particular as in the others to which I have referred. For example, " An officer who borrows money of his subordinate or lends money to his superior is liable to dismissal ;" and it is also a cause for dismissal " for any letter-carrier or rural messenger to borrow money from any person residing on his walks." In many of the larger offices, the clerks are organized and trained as fire brigades ; and general efficiency and discipline have been increased by the supervision of medical officers in the postal service, who report on the cause and kind of sickness, and take care that absences for alleged ill health are not too easily obtained. But it is more important to mention that every post-

---

[1] Mr. James' competitive tests have, perhaps, raised the ability of his force nearly or quite to that of the same number in London, but the higher public standard of administration in that city would not be satisfied with what it is possible to do with a force of sorters and carriers so inadequate as that allowed in New York. Mr. James is about extending open competition to the selection of all the clerks in his office.

master and deputy, and " every person employed by or under him or them," are prohibited[1] from *exerting their influence* either for or against any particular candidates" (except they may vote themselves), and from by " word, message, or writing, or in any manner whatever, endeavoring to persuade any elector to give or dissuade any elector from giving his vote.
. . Canvassing within a post office is not permitted," and postmasters are instructed, when permission to canvas is requested, " to refuse it absolutely."[2]

It is, I presume, quite impossible to imagine the astonishment with which an officer in charge of a British post-office would receive a proposition from a partisan assessment collector to go among his clerks and make a levy of political blackmail. There are no politics in a British post office, no partisan contentions over its officials, no political management within its walls, no reliance by any party on the vote of its clerks, or on exactions from their salaries. In the light of such facts, we can see the significance of the words of Mr. Mundella,[3] when he said : " I stand before you the representative of the largest constituency in England, and yet have not the power to control the appointment of the lowest excise officer :" for what he states is not only true as to excise offices, but as to all other offices in whatever department ; and the broad fact he meant to illustrate was not that technically he could not appoint, but that, as a member of Parliament, he had no opportunity to control, and that the public opinion and administrative methods of his country would not permit him to control any official appointment in her service.

*Department of State and Consular and Diplomatic Service.*
There is no other part of the public service so difficult to bring under rigid rules, none in which so peculiar information is required, none wherein partisan and personal favoritism is more disgraceful and disastrous. It would, however, require too much space to enter fully into the particulars ; but I can, in a general way, state the methods through which the Gov-

---

[1] This part of the regulation is based on the statute 9 Anne, chap. 10, § 44, already referred to.
[2] Instructions to Head Postmasters, 1873, pp. 24, 31, and 32.
[3] Speech in New York city.

ernment of Great Britain has pretty effectually taken these branches of administration out of patronage and politics. The mere exigencies of her supremacy and safety in so many quarters of the globe where she rules, together with the demonstrated conditions of success in that vast foreign commerce which is vital to her prosperity as a nation, have long since impressed upon her statesmen, merchants, and manufacturers a deep sense of the paramount importance of honesty and capacity in her consular and diplomatic service.[1] This conviction alone has become a powerful influence (far stronger, I must think, than any existing in this country) in restraint of solicitation and political pressure brought to bear on the foreign service. The conviction is not less general and decided that essential efficiency in either branch cannot be attained without much experience in the service. With such support from public opinion, official duty is not so difficult, and demands for removals are more easily resisted.

While there is a right of exception, not often applied in practice, it is the rule and course of administration that the higher places are filled from the lower[2] (perhaps with considerable reference to seniority of service, but) mainly with a view of rewarding and securing merit. This is beyond question a great stimulus to fidelity and learning in the line of duty. Competition has been resorted to in making selections for promotions. The clerical places in the Foreign Office (corresponding to that of our Secretary of State) are filled from the best qualified on a list of persons sent by the Secretary to compete together in an examination before the Civil Service Commissioners. It is quite easy for the Secretary to have personal information concerning each of the small body of clerks in his office, and the fact that state secrets are so open to them is

---

[1] We may note its strength, in the fact that the present, Conservative administration has just appointed Lord Dufferin (a Liberal, and lately Governor-General of Canada) to be Ambassador at St. Petersburg.

[2] Perhaps there is sometimes too much regard for seniority, which may have been allowed to exclude larger ability from the more important posts ; but the Secretary is always at liberty to take the best. This is a deep and many-sided question, I will not assume to express any opinion about, and is not to be decided by instances, but by the general effect upon the whole service.

hardly consistent with allowing any person not known to him to come into that branch of the service by competition or otherwise than on his personal information. Persons seeking clerical places under the foreign legations, or elsewhere in the diplomatic service, are examined in the same way, and their examinations appear to be thorough and exacting.[1]

The rules require attachés to serve in the Foreign Office six months before going on foreign duty, and they are under probation for two years. Applicants for consular appointments must also be examined before the Civil Service Commission; but the nature of the service hardly allows competition.[2]

The spirit of the rules for the examination of those who apply for consulates may be inferred from the following: They must be able to speak French as well as English; "and they must have a sufficient knowledge of the current language, so far as commerce is concerned, of the port at which they are appointed to reside, to enable them to communicate directly with the authorities;" or, in other words, they are not allowed to depart in a condition of ignorance that leaves them utterly unable even to communicate understandingly in regard to duties which are sent to perform. They must "also have a sufficient knowledge of the British mercantile and commercial law to enable them to deal with questions arising between British shipowners, shipmasters, and seamen." It does not seem to be thought wise to send persons destitute of all knowledge of the legal principles, or of the intricate commercial codes they are to administer, to be the protectors of the commerce and subjects of a great nation in a foreign country. And, in addition, where it is not impracticable, those going for the first time to a foreign consulate are required to attend three months at the Foreign Office, in order that they may become more competent for their duties.

It does not fall within my plan to consider the great difference in the consular systems of the two countries in regard to

---

[1] The examinations would seem to show that the knowledge required of the history of the United States even is greater than has, sometimes at least, been found to suffice for getting into our own service.

[2] In cases where the appointees are abroad or the exigency of the service requires it, examinations may be deferred, or even dispensed with. Where foreign merchants are made consuls the rules of examination do not apply.

fees and the payment of expenses. The English system makes the character and capacity of its official representatives, the great interests of its commerce, the certain protection of its citizens, and the preservation of the national prestige and honor, paramount objects. All the world knows the character and capacity of the British Consular Service. And, I hardly need add, in view of the explanations given, that political pressure and personal solicitation for appointments, in the foreign service of Great Britain, appear to be as much less than they are in our own as the standards of her qualifications for such service are higher than those we enforce.

*Parliament.* After the explanations already made, it is hardly necessary to say that members of Parliament have, practically, ceased to possess patronage. They must, in their election contests, make their appeal for support on the principles of their party and their own worth as men. Officers, places, or promotions in the public service can no more be bartered for votes or peddled for influence. Parliamentary patronage—that prolific and degrading element, for a hundred and fifty years one of the great curses of British politics—is substantially no more, and no one mourns its loss or denies its corruption.

The same influences which have raised executive appointments above the corruption of Parliamentary traffic have, in the same spirit, made themselves felt within the doors of the two Houses. We might easily go back to the time when the appointment of the subordinate officers and clerks of Parliament was attended with personal contests as desperate, with management as lamentable, with a subordination of worth and experience to partisan interests and ambition as much to be deplored, as any which have ever been witnessed in our legislative bodies. Only a faint remnant of such abuses has survived the later reforms in Great Britain. As a rule, these clerks and officers of Parliament go on from session to session in the orderly and satisfactory discharge of their functions, which are in no proper sense political. They are required to pass an examination before the Civil Service Commission, which is sufficiently stringent to secure an order of capacity quite beyond what a mere partisan struggle is competent to supply, say nothing of the saving of time, temper, and dignity.

In the House of Lords, an officer (the Clerk of Parliaments) with a tenure, which in practice continues during good behavior, selects the persons to be examined for clerkships, and in the House of Commons the selection is made by the Librarian, who holds his place by the same tenure. These clerkships, I am assured by high authority, are looked upon by members as without political significance, and the discharge of their duties is not regarded as affected by partisan considerations. The dignity of legislative functions is no longer degraded either by petty wrangles about readers, engrossers, and messengers, or by general contests in the interest of local patronage, rival factions, or ambitious leaders.

I have already so fully called attention to the demoralizing influences which an interest, on the part of the members of the legislature, in appointments, promotions, removals, and salaries in executive departments, has been found to exert upon their independence and their disposition toward reforms, that nothing need be added in this connection.[2] If any changes from the old system could be greater, in the relations of members of Parliament, than those which I have already pointed out, it would be their present, happy exemption from the harassing and exasperating importunities of office-seekers and demagogues, by which their predecessors had been tormented during more than a century and a half. I ought to add, as a part of the reform brought about in Parliament, that contested election cases have been practically removed from the forum of the party majority to the decision of the judicial tribunals, which would seem to have caused great relief to Parliament and great gains to justice.

It must not be understood, because my illustrations extend no further, that the new method is confined to the great depart-

---

[1] I may mention, by way of illustration, that the present Clerk of the House of Commons is Sir Thomas Erskine May, the accomplished author of the " Constitutional History of England," so often quoted in these pages ; and also of " Democracy in Europe," with which he evidently has liberal sympathies.

[2] Questions upon the enactment of laws were continually complicated by questions of Parliamentary patronage.—Report on Civil Service, 1860.

ments. On the contrary, it is in force in nearly all the executive offices. Legislative officers are the representatives of political opinions and private interests, of whose qualifications the people judge for themselves; and, from the very nature of their duties, such officers must be guided by views of politics and theories of policy. To their selection, therefore, the popular judgment must put the only conditions. The judges are so few in number that it is quite practicable that every appointment should be made upon the personal knowledge of the executive; and public observation, in every case of their selection, is too great and discriminating to allow that secrecy which elsewhere, under the old system, so facilitated the victory of favoritism and partisanship. It has been no more needful than it is practicable, therefore, to extend the new methods, in the legislative and judicial departments, beyond their clerical force.

I need not enter into details, which would be tedious, concerning the selections and promotions in the many subordinate offices. But it should be borne in mind that national offices and affairs are by no means as restricted in Great Britain as in the United States. They include nearly all those parts of civil administration which with us fall to the several States, and a great deal which with us falls to municipalities. The officers of some of the prisons, of the national asylums, of the Board of Public Works (carrying on a large part of the municipal work in London), of the Poor Law administration, of a great part of the sanitary administration (being all that carried on by the nation), of the British Museum, of the Kensington Museum, of the national galleries, of the University of London, of the Charity Commission, of the Education Office, of the Public Record Office, of the Emigration Office, of the Stationery Office, of the Board of Trade, and of the Lighthouse and of the Life-Saving Stations, are among those appointed, promoted, and removed under the national civil service regulations, and on the basis of examinations and competitions.[1]

It is to be noticed, however, that neither these rules nor any

---

[1] There are a very few of these officers to whom competition, for special reasons, does not apply.

modern reforms have in any respect centralized administration
or made it national ; but, the principles of the reform having
been found salutary in the great departments, have, for that
reason, been extended to the places mentioned, which were
before a part of the national jurisdiction.  I must also add
that although it seems a contradiction in terms to include
officers of the army and navy as a part of the " civil service")
when those in the civil service are spoken of as descriptive
of the extent of the application of examinations and competition, they must be understood as extending to admissions to
the military and naval schools (which stand at the gates of office
in the army and navy), and also as extending, with, I think,
some exceptions, to the officers of that part of the military
force which most nearly corresponds to our militia.  From
these explanations, it must be apparent how wide and varied,
in Great Britain and India, is the field of official life, political
activity, and personal ambition and jealousy, which is now
dominated by the reform methods.  They extend to all but a
very few of the highest places for the exercise of the appointing power of the Crown.  They are supreme through almost
the whole vast range of what was, for generations, the patronage of the Treasury and of members of Parliament ; a patronage which was as much greater than that of our heads of
departments and members of Congress, as their authority
would be greater if the entire legislative and executive power
of the States was made a part of the Federal jurisdiction.
The merit system, therefore, with its tests of character and
capacity, and its claims of justice and principle against favoritism and partisanship, has achieved a victory over patronage
as seductive and universal—has suppressed opportunities of
intrigue and corruption as varied and numerous—has overthrown a tyranny of partisan and official influence as pervading
and powerful, as would be involved in this country in a struggle which should draw to itself every selfish and partisan
element—all the offices and gains—all the intrigue and influence—all the hopes and fears—of a Presidential campaign, of
Senatorial contests, and of elections for governors, united into
one grand issue dependent upon a single national vote at the
polls.

# CHAPTER XXXI.

## SOCIAL, MORAL, AND INTERNATIONAL BEARINGS OF THE NEW SYSTEM.

Women brought into the public service.—The social position of the Civil Service raised.—Service of the public regarded as evidence of fitness for private service.—Examinations and competitions applied by banks, corporations, and business houses.—How the public opinion of government is affected by good administration.—The character of the persons brought into office by the old system, and by the new.—What the people see honored and rewarded in the practical working of the new system.— Its moral and educational influence.—Effect on patriotism, national prestige and prosperity.—Relations of revolutionary tendencies, from 1830 to 1848, to Civil Service reform.—Influence of the United States then at its *maximum*.—British statesmen seeking to strengthen monarchy and exclude republicanism by good administration.—Their success.—The European view of our system.—Tendency to republicanism has declined.— Character of republicanism in France.—The Holy Alliance and the position of the United States in 1815.—Civil Service reform in Sweden.—In Prussia.—Americans humiliated in Europe.—Monarchists declare our partisan system inherent in republicanism.—Our system really favorable to rewarding merit.

I. THERE are other effects of the new system, or at least of the influences sustaining it, which ought not to be overlooked. They are social and moral as well as political, and some of them are in a sense international.

The principle that appointments should be made on the basis of character and capacity as tested by examinations, was utterly inconsistent with the further exclusion of women from the public service merely by reason of their sex. And, as a consequence—in a country where women had been depressed by legal restrictions and by a popular sentiment,[1] far

---

[1] This spirit found expression as late as 1873, in a regulation of the Returned Letter Office, which forbade women being entrusted to open any letters with valuables. They were to be opened and the valuables taken out by male clerks, on the presumption, apparently, that women are not by nature

more unjust than have ever prevailed in the United States,
— the new system gave them, on principle, that opportunity
to take part in the public work which has been in great
measure allowed them here, rather on the score of gallantry,
or by reason of calamities in the war from which they had
suffered. The number of women employed in public positions in Great Britain is steadily increasing. They may now
be seen in the exclusive charge of offices in the postal and
telegraph service, which they have won by open competition
and manage with success ; and these new opportunities of
usefulness must, I think, be counted as among the principal
causes which have helped on the great improvement in the
education and in the intellectual and benevolent activity of
women (especially of the middle classes) in Great Britain during the last few years.[1] The marked executive ability, the

as honest as men. And the head of the office expresses great surprise that
the experiment of employing women had been " a perfect success"—which
" completely surpassed my expectation." But the women have steadily
won their way, vindicating their honesty and showing there is no need of
matrons. So great was the distrust and hostility on the first employment of
women, that the men were " jealous" of the innovation, and it was thought
necessary to employ " a matron" to take special charge of the female clerks.
—Report C. S. Inq. Com., 1873–5, Vol. I., p. 146.

[1] In view of the great and manifest advantages to women of having a
means of access to such kinds of public employment as are appropriate for
them, far removed from the dirty highway of partisan politics, and in all particulars compatible with their modesty and self-respect, it seems almost incredible that any sane women, however eccentric, should be found justifying the spoils system on principle, after men, who by reason of some knowledge of politics are more discreet, have prudently abandoned all attempts at
such justification. But it is a curious fact that an abnormal class of women
seem to have been the last to practise the abuses of a system which they
may as consistently, perhaps, be the last to defend. History has preserved
the name of Miss Alice Perrers as among the foremost in political corruption in the thirteenth century, and she seems to have been as bold and successful as Mrs. Jenks. The shameful part acted in court politics by a class
of women under the Stuart princes is familiar history. " Walpole," says
Mr. Bagehot, " declared he would pay no attention to the Queen's daughters" (those " girls," as he called them), " but would rely exclusively on
Madame de Walmoden, the King's mistress." The Duchess of Kendall
under George I., Mrs. Clark and Mrs. Cary under George III., the Marchioness of Conyngham under George IV., appear to have been among the last to
practise the forms of political corruption for which they were notorious.
Mr. Bagehot quotes a writer under George IV. as saying, "The King is in

the fidelity and decorum illustrated in the official conduct of women, not merely in the local offices and central departments, but in the London School Board and in many positions of high responsibility, have done much to change an unjust public opinion and to utilize, for the benefit of society, the capacity and moral worth of the female sex, which that opinion had before so largely excluded from opportunities of usefulness. The memorable work of Florence Nightingale in the Crimea was as much a duty of public administration as of Christianity—as much in the interest of economy as of humanity—and, in the schools, in the poor law boards, in the prisons, in the public asylums and hospitals, in sanitary administration, and in many other ways, the beneficent results of the new opportunities opened to women have been felt.

While, for reasons sufficiently indicated, we may well fear that the honor and dignity of office in the abstract, and the respect in which the people hold their public servants, have been falling during the last forty years in the United States, it would seem to have been quite otherwise in Great Britain.[1] We have seen that it has been little more than a century since

our favor, and, what is more to the purpose, the Marchioness of Conyngham is so too." But such instances, I am persuaded, only show the extravagances of exceptional characters when out of their sphere, and are in wide contrast with the almost universal feeling and recognized interest of the sex on the subject of civil service reform. I cannot think that the many gifted and well-instructed women who, to the great advantage of society and of themselves, are more and more turning their attention to the moral and social problems of the day, will long omit to bring their powerful influence to bear in behalf of a system which stimulates and rewards virtue and education on the part of their children, and opens to women a respectable and honorable way of reaching the public service ; while it repudiates those coarse and corrupt methods in politics from which so many worthy women suffer, and which every true woman abhors. But even exceptional and unfortunate women ought to welcome the new system, which has opened to them a new way of hope and consolation. For, of the first trial of examinations and competitions for school teachers, it is said "that the females have been so far advanced in mental power and influence as to have been lost to the service by matrimonial engagements obtained with exceeding rapidity. To avoid these losses, plainer candidates were selected for training, but they too have attained preferences as wives to a perplexing extent."—Civil Service Papers, p. 139.

[1] For facts bearing on these points, see Appendices A and B.

the subordinates in her civil service were without legal recognition—the mere hirelings of superior officers—and, until a
very recent period, they appear to have had comparatively little
social consideration or self-respect.   And how could it be otherwise, when the consciousness of servility and dependence, and
the scandalous repute of patronage and favoritism, through
which places in the public service were gained, were at once a
humiliation and a taint?   But as soon as those places became
the rewards of personal merit, so that an official position was,
in itself, evidence of good reputation and good capacity—of
attainments that had not been surpassed in an open competition—of a character that could not be impeached by a rival
in a public contest—it was natural that the estimation of the
civil service should rise with its real worth.   There was no
longer any reason why its members should not take rank
with the officers of the army and navy in sharing the social
honors of the people.   And such appears to be now the fact
in Great Britain.[1]   With a manly pride, an officer in that
service, whether at home or abroad, sends his card, with
the words, "*Of her Majesty's Civil Service,*" upon its face,
with a certainty that, everywhere among his own countrymen,
and in every quarter of the globe where the reputation of that
service is known, it will be at once accepted as a certificate of
character and an aid to social attention.   The same thing,
and for like reasons, may be said of our officers of the
army and navy; and I know of no single fact that so strikingly and so painfully marks that silent but severe, popular
judgment, according to which the methods of gaining the
official places of peace and industry consign those who fill them
to an inferior rank in the scale of social life.   How long
would officers of our army or navy hold their social prestige
or retain their claims upon public confidence, if they reached
their positions through methods as partisan and as regardless
of capacity and attainments as those which have secured most
of the places in our civil service?   To give to the civil officers
of the nation, of corresponding grade, a social rank equal to
that of officers in the army or the navy—a rank which, if

---

[1] See on these points, the letter of Sir Charles Trevelyan, in Appendix A.

selected by means considered equally pure and honorable, they would surely take—involves the whole problem of civil service reform ; and in the discrimination now made we may see both the proof and the measure of the public estimate of corruption in our politics.

In 1854, an English officer of great experience used this language : " I am assured that the fact of previous service in the government offices has, in reality, operated as a powerful objection to candidates for employment in commercial houses. . . . It would be practicable to reverse the present general condition of the civil service, and to make the fact of service in a public office a recommendation not only for any social standing, . . . but for efficiency." [1] And after six years' experience of competition, another officer made this prediction : " I have no doubt that private persons will find it for their interest by and by to institute competitions of this kind in order that they may get the best clerks ; indeed, very large numbers of public and private persons, merchants, bankers, directors of railroads, and managers of public companies, have signed a declaration approving of the scheme of examination. . . ." [2]

These anticipations have already been fully realized. Not only has the government been much troubled by reason of private persons and corporations endeavoring to get away the superior men and women which the new system has brought into the public service, but the Civil Service Commission has been compelled to refuse the applications of persons who for private ends have sought the honor and advantage of an examination before it. Nor is this all : for large corporations, whose employés are too numerous for intelligent, personal selection, have adopted the methods of examination and competition, which the success of the government has commended to their attention.

For example, the great London printing house of Spottiswoode instituted examinations [3] for its clerks as early as 1854. The Bank of England has not only established a system of examinations for clerkships, but it has found its advantage in a

---

[1] Civil Service Papers, 1854, p. 138.

[2] Report on Civil Service Appointment, 1860, p. 288.

[3] Civil Service Papers, p. 14.

gradual increase of salary and in a superannuation allowance on retirement, according to fixed regulations, in close analogy to those which prevail in the public service. The Railway Clearing House, employing nearly fifteen hundred clerks, has examinations for their admission (so rigid that sometimes fourteen out of fifteen applicants have been rejected at a single trial) and a system of competition for promotion to the higher grades; and to these it has added a superannuation fund and a savings bank, in aid of both economy and efficiency in its clerical force. The London and Westminster Bank, employing about four hundred and fifty clerks, has adopted competition for admission to its employment; and, abandoning favoritism, it has also established a regular system of promotion for merit; and, like many other great establishments, it has found its profit in graded salaries and retiring allowances.[1]

II. The silent effect of administration, everywhere carried on before the eyes of the people, by officers who have secured their positions by reason of personal worth, tested by open and honorable means, is, I am persuaded, both great and salutary. Into whatever offices you may enter, whether they be those of the light-house or life-saving stations along the shores, of the custom-house service in the commercial cities, of the postal or inland revenue administration anywhere in the interior, of the vast departments of London or of India —you do not find servile officers and clerks who have gained their places either by the influence of members of Parliament or by the importunity of great politicians, but men of self-reliance, who have succeeded, through public competitions, in which they established the highest capacity and character. And for these reasons they are no man's men—no party's agents—no officer's dependents—but self-respecting, competent public servants, standing on their own worth, taking an honest pride in their record, and commanding the respect of their fellows and of the community. It is only necessary to compare the social and political elements thus brought into the public service, with those which find representation there under a system of spoils and favoritism, in order to get a clear view of the

[1] See First Rep. of Civil Service Inq. Com., 1875, pp. 179 to 181, 204 and 205, and 230 to 232.

very different effects which the two methods exert upon
political action and public morality. Even under that vicious
system, there are unquestionably many worthy persons appointed, and they are, of course, indispensable ; but how great a portion of all to be met, in passing through public offices, filled
under that system, have reached their places for reasons or by
means that would not bear publicity ? Here are those whose presence marks the corrupt victory of a local faction or the vicious
influence of unscrupulous party managers ; there are the men
whose appointments prevented an exposure by a great officer or
hushed the just complaints about a local office ; at these desks are
the men who did immoral work in the last election, and at those
the men who are expected to do such work in the next election ;
this man's fraud gave one member his seat, and the appointment of that incompetent clerk secured from another member his vote ; in this bureau is the bankrupt cousin of a
governor, and in that the unworthy dependent of a secretary. The natural influences from such examples in the
great departments pervade every part of the country, and
are felt in every political meeting and at every family fireside,
moulding the common opinion of politics, tainting the air in
official places, lowering the popular estimate of public life,
degrading government in the eyes of the people. The old
spoils system, which Great Britain has destroyed, said to young
men seeking office : " Politics is a game of intrigue and
influence ; court the great politicians who can force your
nomination ; be submissive to corrupt officials and excuse
their sins ; attack no popular abuse which may deprive you of
influence." The new system says to him : " Official life is
a place of duty and responsibility ; preserve a character so
pure that no rival can attack it if you compete with him ;
make yourself so well informed that you cannot be defeated
in the examinations ; stand manfully for principles and fear not
to expose abuses ; condemn all intrigue and manipulation for
deceiving or coercing the people."

I am convinced that the salutary effect of the new system
has been felt not only in every part of the empire, but in
every grade of life. Mr. May declares that the authority of the
crown, formerly wielded haughtily as a power, is now " held

in trust as it were for the benefit of the people." Every place which the son of a farmer or sailor has been able to win through competition, has been lost both to the arbitrary discretion of the crown and to the class interest of the nobility ; and it has not the less been taken from the vicious capital of the demagogues and the pawnbrokers of politics—from the prizes to be won by manipulation, intrigue, and corruption. "I am not indifferent" (says a distinguished leader of the British Parliament) "to the consideration that these offices have become the patrimony of the poorer part of the middle class, or even perhaps of the working class."[1] "I consider that public office is a *solemn trust*, and that one of the most important conditions is to choose the best possible men for the different places."[2]

Such is the spirit of the new power in British politics, and the tendency of the reform, which the people support with a genuine enthusiasm. The consequences have been not merely that royal and aristocratic authority, as well as intrigue and venal influence, have been limited ; that education has been encouraged ; that common justice has been promoted ; that partisan tyranny has been arrested ; that corrupt elements have been taken out of elections ;[3] but government itself has been presented to the people as having a purer character and nobler ends—as based on principles and recognizing duties, and not merely as a merciless and selfish power always yielding to the greater influence, however vicious, and forever ready to turn to advantage the services of agents, however corrupt. The people are enabled to see the government everywhere seeking and honoring the best capacity and character among them, everywhere repudiating servility and manipulation, everywhere defeating partisan intrigue and official prostitution, everywhere affirming that fidelity to principles and to public interests is an obligation paramount to all the selfish claims of individuals and of parties. They take notice that skilful methods have been elaborated, and that they are carefully applied, for the purpose of separating the worthy

---

[1] Evid. Chancellor of the Exchequer, Parlia. Report, 1873-4, p. 231.
[2] Report Investigation Committee, 1874-5, Vol. II., p. 103.
[3] See Letters of John Bright and Sir Charles Trevelyan, Appendix A.

from the unworthy, among the thousands who press for places
under the government.   They find that if their sons or their
daughters would gain public places, what is most essential is not
that they should be servile to great officials, or great lords, or
great partisan managers, but that their private lives should be so
unspotted that they cannot be assailed by rivals, and that their
attainments should be so respectable that they cannot be
thrown out in competition.   They see in the great army of
sixty thousand civil servants, not a body of men and women,
the greater portion of whom high officials and political cliques
have pushed into their places for ends of their own, and
whose stay there depends more on their servility than on their
merits, but they see a body, each member of which secured
his place through personal qualities which are as honorable
to their possessor as they are useful to the nation.   They
take notice that the new system—which, by making elections
turn on principles and not on patronage, invites worthy men
not seeking office to take part in politics—has, at the same
time, removed the larger part of these elements which most
attract the vicious and the corrupt, and most disgust the pure
and the patriotic.   In short, they see the vast machinery of
government itself—the most potent of all human influences
for raising or lowering the character and prosperity of a nation—no longer, as formerly, a prolific source of fraud and
immorality—no longer in alliance with the most venal elements of politics ; but a mighty force in the interest of education, justice, and public virtue — a discriminating power
that embodies and appeals to the higher intelligence and the
nobler sentiments of the nation.   Such an influence and example, when continued for a considerable period in Great
Britain, will, I am persuaded, disclose beneficent consequences of which the whole civilized world will take yet more
emphatic notice.   The rapid growth of her prestige and commerce, and the great capacity for government displayed by
her within recent years in so many parts of the world, are,
I am compelled to believe, closely connected with the character of her consular[1] and diplomatic service, and are by no

---

[1] For a comparison between American and British consular service, see
Appendices A and B.

means independent of the worth and capacity that pervade every part, and not in the least degree the higher part, of her domestic administration. Ability and experience in the lower official grades invite and can be controlled only by ability and experience in the higher grades. The public service, instead of being longer a source of corruption, which flows out upon private life, has become a sphere of manly and conservative virtues which are a strength to the State and an inspiration to patriotism. And, how else can we explain the anomaly that, through all these later years, in which views and methods, thus wholly democratic and republican in their tendency, have been rapidly growing before the eyes of the British people, the old spirit of loyalty to the crown—fervent devotion to the constitution—an honest and pervading belief that no system of administration is so pure, so efficient, or so abiding as the British system—and a sturdy purpose to maintain and defend them all—have survived with a vigor and a universality unsurpassed in the national sentiment of modern times? How else, but upon the merits of her administrative methods, and the capacity and integrity of her officials, of all grades, in her many dependencies, and under such diverse conditions, can we explain the unrivalled growth of the power and influence of Great Britain? And can any one doubt, if the old system of George III. or any system of partisan spoils and official favoritism had been continued, that British patriotism and loyalty would have decayed, that India would have been lost, that the Constitution would have fallen into universal weakness and decay, or that despotism would have triumphed over liberty and law?

III. It is worthy of notice that the broader effects of the reform, which, transcending all mere questions of economy and internal method, have deepened the fountains of patriotism and made monarchy itself dearer to the British people, were not wholly unanticipated at the opening of the great work in 1853; nor was that work began merely to remove administrative abuses; but it was expected to strengthen the very bulwarks of the government and to aid in averting the grave perils which, between 1830 and 1848, had threatened the thrones of all the leading nations of Europe. Sir Charles

Trevelyan (who with the present Chancellor of the Exchequer[1] first set forth the merit system in their celebrated report of 1853) puts the sense of peril very clearly when he says, " the revoluntionary period of 1848 *gave us a shake and created a disposition to put our house in order*, and one of the consequences was a remarkable series of investigations into public offices which lasted for five years, culminating in the . . . report."[2] Speaking for a different class of society, at about the same date, Matthew Arnold says: " The growing power in Europe is democracy. . . . Our society is destined to become much more democratic. . . . The time has arrived when it is becoming impossible for the aristocracy of England to conduct and wield the English nation any longer."[3]

Before 1848, the constitutional system of the United States and its administration had probably reached the maximum of their effect in Europe in favor of republican institutions. Until near that date, our administration had generally been worthy of our principles ; and the savage partisanship and official corruption with which we were then first becoming familiar— and which marked the extent of our fall from that high standard which European statesmen had recognized in our public affairs—were little known in Europe ; so that our political system had no drawbacks, and stood commended in foreign countries by the great attractions of equality, liberty, and justice upon which it rests. That influence was then pervading and considerable in every enlightened community on the continent ; and in the profession of republican principles at the great centers of thought, and in revolution or in tendencies to revolution in many quarters, was to be seen the measure of its peril to feudal institutions and arbitrary government. If the " shake" which such fears of disturbance gave in England was less violent, it was not less significant, than on the continent. Between 1840 and 1848 many monster meetings were held in Great Britain, by which the public peace was threatened and serious anxiety was caused. Responding to armed revolution on the continent for popular rights in 1848, the

---

[1] Sir Stafford Northcote.    [2] Civil Service Inq., 1873., Vol. II., p. 100.
[3] Mixed Essays, pp. 7, 14 and 27.

"Chartists" organizations and other republican sympathizers, with their demand of "universal suffrage, the ballot and annual parliaments," alarmed all England by their lawless and revolutionary action. A petition, said to bear the signatures of five millions of people, was backed by such a host, resolved to attend its presentation to Parliament, that 170,000 special constables, to aid an army with artillery, were sworn in for keeping the peace of London. It was under such a state of affairs that British statesmen, sustained by the better public sentiment, carried forward five years of investigations into the methods of government, with a view of "putting their house in order." A peril was upon the nation, and thoughtful men felt its gravity. "On what action may we rely to prevent the English people from becoming *Americanized?* . . . I answer on the action of the state.[1] . . . They could not radically change the British constitution. But they could make reforms that would ensure pure, economical, and efficient administration. They could suggest to the crown, and they could compel the members of Parliament, to surrender their power of making partisan and selfish nominations. They could by honest and equitable methods open the public service to the whole body of the people, so that the most deserving should get the offices. They could, perhaps, thus, under the forms of a monarchy, secure to the people nearly all the practical blessings which a real republic could promise. In this way they could, perchance, be more republican than the great republic itself; and through such means present monarchy to the people—as enforcing the highest possible standard of official duty—as having more regard for equality, liberty of opinion, and respectability of private character, than a republic had ever exhibited. What, therefore, was, in form, only a salutary method of administration, was in intention, and in broad effect, a conservative force in government—a barrier against republicanism by actually conferring blessings which republics had given only in theory—an antidote against revolutions by putting in practice the equality and justice which revolutions

---

[1] Bagehot's English Constitution, p. 23.

demanded.    " The salutary reforms of this active period averted revolution.'

It is interesting to note how soon after 1848 the sad effects of our then recently developed, partisan system were presented before Europe.   In a volume published by the British Government in 1855 (which quotes *continental* authority for its statements), the very worst abuses of British administration are said to have " the prominent features of the *general* as well as local administration of the United States.   These features are : absence of any special qualifications for any administrative service unless it be that of subserviency  .  .  .  removability  .  .  .  upon every change of party,  .  .  . an increasing distaste to public office, and the consequent exclusion from it of the most accomplished persons in society ; the lowering of the efficiency and the respectability of public administration : the retardation of its progress relatively to the general progress of society ; and a tendency to increasing corruption concurrently with increased party feeling."[2]   "The whole issue is based on a single election—on the choice of a president. . . .  The managers of the contest have the greatest possible facility for using what I may call patronage bribery, . . . and the efficiency of promised offices as a means of corruption, is augmented, because the victor can give what he likes to whom he likes."[3]

Such is the character of our administrative methods as they have been understood by the reading people of Europe for a quarter of a century.   While Great Britain (accompanied by all the leading European States, as I shall more fully explain) has been carrying forward administrative reform, in a truly republican spirit, and we have fallen from the better precedents of our history down upon the partisan spoils system of her less civilized times, can it be any matter of surprise that this country—that republican institutions as we represent them among the nations—have lost a great part of their influence as an example ?  Is it strange that republicanism has, on the other side of the water, become, to a sad degree, iden-

---

[1] Democracy in Europe, by May, vol. ii. p. 495.

[2] Civil Service Papers, p. 150–2.

[3] Bagehot's English Constitution, 1873, p. 264.

tified with extreme partisanship, a low standard of official capacity and integrity, perpetual agitation about petty offices, and management and manipulation, where statesmanship is essential?' It is Mr. May's judgment that there is far less republicanism and democracy in England (and such, I believe, is the general opinion among the best informed) than there was thirty-five years ago.[2] " Freedom and good government, a generous policy, and the devotion of rulers to the welfare of the people have been met with general confidence, loyalty, and contentment. . . . The constitution . . . *has gained on democracy.*"[3] The United States is judged as a nation not so much by the noble principles of its constitution as by the measure of purity, economy, and capacity to be found in its official life, and by the style of men who fill those high places where experienced statesmen and unselfish patriots are needed.

" Outside of Switzerland or France[4] there can hardly be

---

[1] See Appendix B for considerations bearing on these points.

[2] The advance of democracy referred to relates rather to its tendency to attack the monarchical form of government, than to the spirit and principles of democracy itself; for they have advanced continually, and in no way more strikingly, than in the reformed methods in the civil service, which have been explained in this volume.

[3] 2 May's Const. Hist., p. 576.

[4] The great republican principles of equality, liberty and justice have not, of course, lost their attraction ; and in establishing them, France has not adopted our partisan system, but retains the admirable administrative methods which, based on examinations and not allowing arbitrary removals, have aided her in so many fearful crises. In the profound changes lately brought about, but few removals have been made, and those only in cases where vital principles were involved—less in all, probably, than the number we should make upon a change in the party majority, upon the election of a mayor in a city of 50,000 people. Had the republican leaders of France understood that a change to a republic would involve the substitution of our partisan-spoils system for her merit system, I venture to think France would not have become even in form a republic. And it is not without significance that the relation of her cabinet to parties, to Parliament, and to the civil service, is more analogous to that of Great Britain than to that of the United States. Indeed, English writers seem to claim the new French régime as a reflection of the British system : " The Premier, as we should call him," is nominated and removed by the vote of the National Assembly ; the experiment of government in France, the position of M. Thiers, is " singularly illustrative of the English Constitution."—(Bagehot's English Constitution, p. 45.) The example of France, in becoming a republic, is all

said to be, in any country of Europe, a strong popular movement towards a republic, . . . and, unhappily, the United States have utterly lost, in Europe, that influence for republican institutions which was so potent in the first half of the century." [1] And while partisan and corrupt administration has so damaged us abroad, are we sure it has been less destructive of patriotism and confidence at home? [2] What, but the too frequent elections and the corrupt administration which a partisan system produces and requires, has raised the ominous question " Whether popular suffrage is a failure?" What, if not the perpetual struggle for patronage and the absorption of the valuable time of Congress and of legislatures—required by the great affairs of the States and the nation—in demoralizing wrangles over clerkships, postmasterships, collectorships, and the many petty offices, has done so much to impair the just and ancient prestige of our legislative bodies? What is it, forever before our eyes as most humiliating and disastrous in our public life, but those bargains, intrigues, prostitutions and frauds in connection with getting office and holding office, which we have seen that a merit system is able to correct? Is it because liberty and equality are less prized by the people as their intelligence rises—because the great principles of our constitution are distrusted the more they are known—that republicanism as we practise it has lost ground in Europe? Or is it by reason of a bad system of administration, which, in perfect harmony with those principles, we are at liberty to reform?

IV. In 1815, when the leading sovereigns of Europe, in

the more instructive and encouraging, because she has become such through a conviction of the beneficence of republican principles, and not through the seductions of a partisan-spoils system of office; and, perhaps, it is a part of her mission to teach the United States, from which those principles were borrowed, how they may be applied in practical affairs, without being soiled and enfeebled by the corruptions of that base system which France has spurned. For some facts bearing on the *Merit System*, as enforced in France, especially in her consular service, see Appendix B.

[1] *Princeton Review*, May, 1878, p. 737.
[2] For facts bearing on these points, see Appendix B, and John Bright's letter in Appendix A.

the " Holy Alliance," declared themselves " delegated by
Providence to govern," and that they " looked upon themselves, with regard to their subjects and their armies, as
fathers of a family." Great Britain—which alone declined to
join—was the only leading monarchy in which the people had
an effective voice in the government ; and of the secondary
class of monarchies, Sweden—in which for more than a century ability to read and write had been a condition of the full
privileges of citizenship—was the only one in which there was
a constitutional government, giving a representation of popular interests. Since that date, the old theory of a divine right
to rule—absolutism and clerical domination—the supremacy of
class interests and the monopoly of official places by those of
noble birth—have yielded to the claim of equal rights, and to
the paramount need of capacity and moral worth in the service of the government ; but in this advance of justice and
liberty, Great Britain and, in some degree, Sweden have
maintained their old precedence. And it is interesting to
find that in Sweden the reform of the civil service—though
not sufficiently excluding opportunities of bureaucratic
and aristocratic influence, perhaps—has been attended by
results closely analogous to those of which we have taken
notice in Great Britain. I have already alluded to the fact
that the principal continental states, including Sweden, have
greatly reformed their civil service in later years,[1] but some
further facts more especially relating to Sweden (and Norway
being under the same king) will not be without interest.[2]
That government, many years ago, provided for the examination of candidates for office. The standard of attainment,
which (like that first fixed in the British service) somewhat
reflects the influence of an aristocratic class, appears to be
higher than in Great Britain, and may perhaps be fairly
objected to as tending to give a needless monopoly to highly
educated persons. As the democratic spirit shall gain
strength, the standard will doubtless be lowered, in the

[1] See ante p. 10.
[2] The facts are to be found in a letter of Mr. Andrews, our Minister to
Sweden, dated October 11, 1876, and in " Foreign Relations United States,
1876," p. 553–563.

interest of humble life, so as to include only the qualifications essential to the public service. The king has patriotically surrendered his arbitrary right of appointment, for the sake of obtaining the worthiest men for the service of the state. And, without interference from the members of the legislature, he uses the appointing power for selecting the best from among those examined. The severe tests of character and capacity for admissions gives the service a social rank which makes it attractive and honorable. The tenure of office is much the same as in Great Britain, and there is an analogous system providing for an increase of pay based on length of service and for retiring allowances. And Mr. Andrews says : " There is no doubt but the high respectability and rank of the civil service in Sweden tend much to induce people to enter it." He thinks this has been sometimes allowed to draw in supernumeraries ; and it, of course, causes places to be accepted at a lower grade of salary than would attract young men into a disreputable service. " For a member of the legislative branch of the government, as such, to recommend or urge the appointment of persons in the civil service would be considered intrusive, and would have no weight, certainly, in excluding a more meritorious officer. Anything like patronage does not obtain. . . . While the subordinates have the free enjoyment of their political convictions and can express their opinions and vote against the government, it is never their practice to seek to propagate the political views of the government among the people. . . . Such attempt, whether for or against the government, would probably excite the same feeling that would be excited in our country if an officer of the regular army or of the navy should undertake to play the party politician. It is, therefore, considered, here, *rather of slight importance to the government whether civil service men are included among its political supporters or not.*" And here, therefore, as in Great Britain, we are shown that, if the government will not compel its officers to fight, in every campaign, for their places, they will not interfere with the freedom of elections or waste their time on partisan politics. The abuses we suffer in those regards are the legitimate outcome of our partisan and demoralizing methods. Coming to the effects

22

of this system upon the moral tone of official life and the
safety of the public moneys. Mr. Andrews shows that defalca-
tions are extremely rare : " only about *four* cases of defalcation a year on an average ;" and that the government almost
never lose any money. " It is very seldom that a subordinate
officer is . . . *even charged* with lesser misdemeanors, notwithstanding the Rigsdag appoints and pays *its own* special Attor-
ney-General (under the constitution) to see that persons in the
public service fulfil their duties, and to accuse them before
the courts of justice if they fail to do so." It hardly need be
pointed out how widely different is the attitude of the members of the Swedish, from that of the members of the American
Congress toward efficiency and integrity in official life. In
the one case, their power and influence are used to push personal and partisan favorites into the public service, and to keep
them there ; in the other, no such selfish and demoralizing
use of authority stands in the way of justice to the public
interests ; but, on the contrary, a special officer of the legislature
has a duty to prosecute in its behalf every unfaithful servant ;
and there is neither any party nor patron pledged or specially interested to screen the guilty. With such a system,
we see how natural it is that defaults should so rarely occur,
and are prepared for the stern dealing with official delin-
quents of which Mr. Andrews gives examples. One of the
latest is that of a whole board of directors of a charity institution at Stockholm—" all prominent citizens"—sentenced to
pay thirty thousand crowns, the amount lost " for lack of
proper watchfulness" in the custody of a key ; each of two
directors having, " without wrong intention," left his key
with the same third officer, during an absence from the city,
who by the use of the three keys was able to embezzle that
amount of money.

It would take me too far from my subject to separately
point out how, in all the more enlightened European states,
since 1815, and more especially during the last generation, the
old claims of royalty and aristocracy, of church and class interests, of favoritism and patronage, the social prestige of centuries, and the old theory of government itself, have yielded
to the paramount need of high character and capacity in the
public service, and to the just and equal right of each citizen,

according to his fitness, and irrespective of his birth or party affiliations, to tender his claim upon that service and have its merits impartially considered. And it is worthy of notice that on the continent, as in Great Britain, improvements in the civil service have everywhere been attended with a great advance in popular education, and in legislation for the protection of humble life ; so that several of the more enlightened monarchies now enforce a more general attendance and provide for and secure a more thorough instruction in the public schools than has yet been attained in the United States. The statistics are too familiar to be repeated ; but the concrete significance of the main fact cannot be too much insisted on— the great fact that the leading monarchies have, in this generation, made the common education of the people, in the interest of patriotism, justice, and general prosperity, more beneficent and universal than it has ever yet been in any republic except Switzerland.

V. I can refer to only a single other example of improved civil administration on the continent—that of Prussia. Reference has been made to the civil service system of France, as embodying the better methods ; but the capacity of her military officers in later years had not been properly attended to. The opinion has been general that the superior capacity of the military officers of their enemy caused the defeat of Austria and France in the late wars with Prussia ; but careful observers also tell us that " Prussia, whose soil and physical resources are third rate in quality as compared with those of the United States, while in magnitude they bear but slight comparison with ours, owes it very much to the high order of efficiency which has been introduced into her *civil* service, that she has risen to be one of the first powers in the world."[1]

Another competent observer says, " Our civil service should be above temptation and beyond suspicion. Prussia has such a service. The pay is, indeed, not large ; but it is graduated on the economical habits of the people. The service is honorable, and brings certain social consideration ; it admits of promotion as the reward of merit, and it ensures a pension for the decline of life."[2]

[1] " Foreign Relations of the United States, 1876," p. 553.
[2] " The United States as a Nation," by Rev. J. P. Thompson, 1877. p. 261.

In a government in which so strong elements of aristocracy and royalty survive as in Prussia, we are not surprised to observe that a phase of bureaucracy and a tendency to favor high, literary attainments find expression in the examinations and perhaps in the selections for the civil service; but despite this lingering of the old spirit, which may yet do some injustice to humble life, the service is lifted high above the corruptions and intrigues of partisan politics, and men of capacity and moral worth everywhere stand in the official places of the nation, and were the leaders in the great events which have given Germany the first place on the continent.

If considered in the light of the past, the example of Prussia, as an illustration of the effects of educating the people and of bringing the most meritorious of them rather than mere partisans and schemers into official leadership, is all the more significant. The United States were conspicuous among the nations, not only for the general intelligence of their citizens, but for a pure and able civil service, and for a common-school system in the interest of all their children, when, in 1815, Prussia, far behind in the education of her people—with a great part of them in a condition hardly above serfdom—was a blind and arrogant champion of the " Holy Alliance," of the divine right of kings and despotic administration, with as little regard for the education as for the equal rights of her subjects. But the sober reflections caused by her humiliation by Napoleon developed in the minds of her rulers a new political philosophy; and her king, or the great statesman Stein, who spoke through the king, avowed his purpose to " rehabilitate the nation by devoting the most earnest attention to the education of the masses of my people." That work was promptly undertaken and has been firmly pursued; and the great results are well known: perhaps the best educated people in the world—a foremost place in science, art, and letters—the military leadership of the continent—a civil administration of unsurpassed purity and ability.[1] Stein, like William III.

[1] It is not my purpose to commend the Prussian Government as a model of justice or wisdom, and in various particulars it exhibits not a little of the old spirit. But it has been the beneficent methods referred to which have produced so great results, despite all drawbacks that have existed.

(of England), was the first, under the government he had in charge, to appreciate the vital importance of good methods in administration ; and each of them gave the subject a prominence which in later years it has never lost.  The German statesman secured the gratitude, and, in large measure, the greatness, of his country by three great measures of administrative reform—the reorganization of the army, improved municipal government, and the " constitution of the supreme administrative departments"—and by his emancipation of the serfs. It has been by such means—by surrendering the monopoly of office, which had been supposed to be essential to the existence of a crown and a privileged class—by educating the common people, which had been claimed to be the peculiar virtue of a republic—by freely bringing into the official places of the nation capacity and moral worth wherever found among the people—by legislating kindly for their protection—that royal and aristocratic governments have in large measure averted the hostility that threatened them, and, at the end of two generations of great advance in liberty and justice, find themselves, perhaps, stronger in the confidence and patriotism of their subjects than they were in the beginning.  In 1833 we find Mr. Macaulay saying, " I see nothing before us but a frantic conflict between extreme opinions, . . . . a tremendous crash of the funds, the church, the peerage, and the throne. It is enough to make the most strenuous royalist *lean a little to republicanism* to think that the whole question between safety and general destruction may probably . . . depend on a single man, whom the accident of his birth has placed in a situation to which certainly his own virtues or abilities would never have raised him ;" and he even predicted that the House of Peers would soon have to give place to an elective chamber.[1]  I think it may be safely said that no Englishman of Macaulay's character at this time leans even " a little toward republicanism ;" but, on the contrary, there are Americans who, disgusted by the magnitude and frequency of our administrative abuses, and not comprehending that they are only a neglected excrescence upon the abiding virtues of republican

[1] " Life and Letters of Macaulay," chaps. v. and viii.

institutions, incline to lean a little to monarchy. Of that
class of thoughtless or unpatriotic sympathizers with the
showy and exclusive features of aristocratic governments, I
have nothing to say ; but not a few sensible and patriotic
republicans—some from their experience at home, others from
their observations and discussions abroad—have had, if not
their faith and patriotism, at least their pride, not a little
disturbed.'

Having detected the point at which republicans may be put
to a disadvantage, the active supporters of monarchy have been
so successful in giving prominence to the evils of our civil
service as to attract the attention of our foreign ministers,
who have brought the fact to the notice of the President.²
Prudent monarchists no longer deny the justice and beauty of
republican principles, theoretically considered. But when a
government is established, they say that all the good that can
be got out of it is to be found in the effects of its administration. Administration is the only thing practical or of current
interest. All else is theory and sentiment. What is the
advantage, they ask, of proclaiming universal liberty and
equality in the constitution, if a monarchy really provides the
best education for the children, the best and cheapest courts of
justice for the parents, the best poor-law and sanitary admin-

---

'The humiliation which patriotic Americans have suffered abroad, by
reason of administrative abuses at home (which I can all the better appreciate from having spent three of the last eight years in Europe), is well
illustrated in a volume already cited, "The United States as a Nation,"
Preface, p. vii.): "When I announced a course of lectures" (in 1876, at
the time of the Whiskey Ring and District of Columbia frauds), . . .
"to be given in the hearing of Europeans, some of my countrymen were of
the opinion that, in the painful aspect of public affairs at home, it were
better that Americans should do nothing to call attention to their country,
already the subject of so much adverse criticism." I ought to add that Dr.
Thompson did not follow their advice, but that he stood manfully and patriotically in vindication of the sound principles of his government ; and he
would seem to believe, as I believe, that when our people come to adequately
understand the causes of the abuses which exist, they will be found to possess the wisdom and virtue needed for their removal.

² "Believing most sincerely that the United States have much to gain in
prosperity at home and in *reputation abroad* by a reform of their civil service,
and as the subject now *occupies much attention there*," etc.—"Foreign Relations U. S., 1876," p. 553.

istration for the sick and the destitute. What, they inquire, is the advantage of a republican senator who corruptly worked his way to an election through a partisan caucus, over an aristocratic lord who reached his seat through the birthright of an ancient family, especially, if in the first case the government permits the promises made to be discharged by the prostitution of offices, and in the last, no such prostitution is allowed? If a monarchy, having educated the children, then opens alike all the offices and places, high and low, domestic and foreign, freely to public and manly competition by any and every citizen, so that character and capacity have an unobstructed way to reach the positions where they can be most useful and honorable to the nation—what more, the monarchist demands, can a republic offer—what more can a republican patriot ask?[1]

But the enemies of our institutions do not stop with these questions. They challenge a comparison between our government and theirs. "The practical choice of first-rate nations is between the presidential government and the parliamentary, . . . and nothing, therefore, can be more important than to compare the two, and to decide upon the testimony of experience, and by facts, which of them is the better."[2] They point to the debasing, partisan intrigues through which so many

---

[1] Of course, there are the exceptions of the king or emperor and of the hereditary members of the legislature. And I may add that I am not comparing the general merits of the two kinds of government, but only accounting for the state of European opinion, and for the loss in later years of republican prestige and of influence on the part of th United States. If it were any part of my purpose to make such comparison, or to set forth the unjust and depressing effects of an hereditary class upon humble life, many other facts would of course need be stated. I am not unmindful that I may be denounced as unpatriotic in bringing forward facts, not creditable to my own country; but it is enough for me, that these facts ought to be understood by the American people, and that they cannot, without dishonor, follow those pseudo-patriots, who, like Turks and Mexicans, having substituted conceit for patriotism and vanity for virtue, remain blind, and reckless of the world about them, while claiming for their countrymen all wisdom and perfection, at the very moment that other nations are gaining in the race of civilization and liberty. The facts presented, I have hoped, may help to recall the true friends of the republic to their duty and to encourage the work of reform which shall make our administration worthy of our principles.

[2] Bagehot's English Constitution, pp. 66 and 67.

unworthy persons gain office ; to the many removals made for
political reason, which are fatal to the stability and experience
essential in the public service ; to the constant and acri-
monious contests about places, which exert a demoralizing
influence upon elections ; to the frequent condemnations of
our whole partisan system, and the exposure of its scandals, to
be found in our literature, in the debates in Congress, in
the resolutions of national conventions ; and with these in
hand, and in presence of the fact that the evils, which the
better public opinion so fully condemns, yet go on unchanged
from decade to decade—they argue that the people are better than their government, and that the continued existence of
the evils is proof of the inherent imbecility and peril of
republican government, and that they should be accepted as
a good cause for a return to monarchical institutions.    They
declare, as a fact, that better administration in Europe than in
America has arrested the progress of republicanism, and maintained the prestige of royalty.    " All evidence, therefore, con-
tradicts the assertion that loyalty has declined in England.    It
is well known that republican speculations have occasionally
been ventured upon, but they have found no favor with any
considerable class of society ; they have not been addressed to
a single constituency ; they have not even been whispered in
Parliament ; and they are repelled by the general sentiment"
of the country.[1]

These facts and arguments have not been reproduced, I
hardly need say, because they are agreeable to me or because
I am indifferent to the patriotic feelings of the reader, which
they may tend to disturb.    But republican institutions—their
honor, their prospects, their hope and glory in the world—are
under our patronage, as the leading republican State ; and it
is not only our duty to make them most beneficent at home,
but to take care that they be not needlessly distrusted or
placed at a disadvantage abroad.    To these ends, we need to
look the facts, however disagreeable, fully in the face, and we
must not allow any misapprehension or false pride to bias our
judgment.    For the very reason that a republic rests, less than

---

[1] Democracy in Europe, by May, vol. ii. p. 501.

any other form of government, upon birthright, selfish interests, or class distinctions— for the very reason of its disinterestedness, which proclaims liberty, equality, and justice for all alike —it needs, more than any other kind of government, to exclude every form of monopoly and proscription in bestowing office, and to strengthen and adorn itself, by bringing into its service the highest worth and capacity to be found among its citizens. A failure to bring about such results is both infidelity to the principles of a republic and a peril to its safety ; while, on the contrary, their accomplishment by a monarchy is really to rise above its essential principles—to elevate the masses at the expense of the nobility and the crown : a consequence which we have seen the enemies of reform advance as good reasons for opposing the merit system.[1] I am profoundly convinced that a republic, being without hereditary officers, without a privileged class, without a state church, without feudal traditions, without any form of authorized restraint upon equality, liberty, and common justice, is, of all forms of government, in principle and opportunity, the most favorable for bringing its best citizenship into its places of public duty, and that our failure, in that regard, is largely to be explained by the fact that no sense of peril—until within a few years—has prevented our being blinded by our marvellous growth and prosperity, or disturbed our neglect of growing abuses in the administration ; so that the subject, not in any other way much pressed upon public attention, has never yet taken its appropriate place in the reflections of the citizen or the action of the government. When, at no remote day, such shall be the case, it need not, I think, be doubted that the honor and the safety of the people will alike be seen to demand, or that their unmistakable voice will require—that, in the advancing stages of civilization, the official places in the republic shall be filled, and its honor, dignity, and rights shall be upheld, at home and abroad, by men in experience, education, and moral worth, not inferior to those who may hold corresponding places in the foremost monarchy in the world.

[1] See ante, pp. 196–197, and 202.

# CHAPTER XXXII.

## A SUMMARY AND THE SIGNIFICANCE OF THE REFORM MOVEMENT.

The original spoils system.—The first appearance of partisan methods.
—The origin of parties.—The beginning of the partisan system.—
Source of parliamentary patronage.—A partisan spoils system developed.—Checks upon that system by legislation and public opinion.—The
system of George III.—Reforms after the American Revolution.—A
higher and bolder public opinion.—When examination first introduced.
—Limited competition.—Fear of revolution.—Civil Service commission
created in 1853.—Only limited competition required.—Unpopularity and
decay of parliamentary patronage.—The leaders of both parties find the
partisan system a failure.—Open competition in India.—Open competition made general in 1870.—The significance of Civil Service reform.—It is
not a mere method or process.—It involves great principles, and the
morality and the stability of government.—The general results reached
in Great Britain.

THE decisive influences, and the more important measures,
in civil administration during the long course of history which
we have followed, can now be presented within narrow limits.

I. In the feudal times, upon which we first entered, government represented neither the wishes nor interests of the
people, nor were its objects the protection of common rights
or the promotion of common justice. A hereditary king,
the source of all office, the nobility, forever in office, and their
subordinates, true to the feudal spirit, recognized neither equality nor liberty nor responsibility, but claimed a divine right to
rule and insisted on an absolute duty of the people to obey.
The modern rule of duty, that laws should be framed and executed in the common interests and on the basis of the equal
rights of the people, and the theory that the power to appoint
and remove public officers is one of trust and strict responsibility, to be exercised only for the general welfare, were not
recognized, and they were repugnant alike to the theory
of the government and the spirit of the age. Power was the

only limit of official action, and fear the only reliance of the government. The mass of the people were in gross ignorance, and many of them were in slavery. The authority to make laws and to appoint and remove officers, like the power to confer titles, to give pensions, to grant pardons, to extort taxes, to enforce service in the army, to excuse compliance with statutes and judgments, were alike used to advance the interests of the king, the officers, and the privileged classes, who made up the one party forever in power. In no other sense was there any party ; nor had the people the necessary intelligence or liberty to form a party, in the modern sense, until centuries later. A spoils system of office was wrought into the very structure of government and society. Nearly all kinds of official abuses known in modern times—from the open sale of offices by the head of a nation down to petty pillage by a baggage-searcher at the docks, from bribery on the highest seats of justice to extortion by constables and robbery by collectors— were developed in all their manifold forms. They were not confined to politics, but extended to the church, to the army, and to the conditions of privilege and precedence in social life. If the salaries of petty officers were not pillaged by great officials under the pretence of party assessments, it was because there was no party but the members of the privileged class, some of whom had sold the offices and got a larger price by reason of their being delivered free of taxation ; if there was no invasion of the appointing power by members of Parliament, and almost no bribery at their election, it was because that body had but little power and its members were as dependent upon the king and the great lords as clerks now are upon members of Congress. We need only to read the history of these times, to expose the unpatriotic slanders by which modern partisans and demagogues have sought their own justification, in representing that the abuses they practise are the peculiar and inevitable drawbacks of republican institutions. Our spoils system is only that portion of these old, royal abuses which we have foisted upon our republican institutions.

II. A despotic spoils system was an essential part of the power of the crown and of the bulwarks of the nobility and the church ; and there was neither the sense of duty, the justice, the liberty, nor the intelligence, that made even its fit discussion possible ; nor could there be until centuries of a rising civilization had not only raised the conscience, the education, and the freedom of the people, but modified the very structure of government and society.   If, as in the age of Wyckliffe, a great uprising of the manhood and the moral sense of the nation gave birth to a civil-service reform statute, as much in advance of the age as any thing he said or did, it was yet true that, in religion and politics alike, such glimpses of better things were but lights on the dark way of progress, and that real reform was far in the future.   As it had been under the Plantagenets, so, substantially, it continued under the Tudors and the Stuarts, until the time of Cromwell.   There was no public opinion sufficiently enlightened to grasp the idea that there is no more right to use the appointing power than there is to use the public money for selfish and corrupt purposes—if indeed there could be said to be any that comprehended the idea of official responsibility to the people in any sense.   It would have required a bold man, ready to peril his life, to assert such principles before the king.   To question the selfish use of the appointing power—which now only subjects a reformer to the ostracism of a party, was then treason against a king, if not rebellion against the divine order in the state.   Until near the time of Cromwell, the idea of true political reform as a right or a duty, in the sense of modern times, hardly existed in England.   There had, indeed, begun to be a public opinion that, in a general way, claimed rights and responsibility in connection with government, and there was some co-operation to secure them ; but public thought rested on principles without reaching the definite conception of methods in administration—results only to be reached in the next century.   Parliament still remained too feeble to usurp any part of the appointing power, and the clerks in the departments were not public servants at all, but were the mere hirelings of the great officers at their head.

III.  In the time of Cromwell, there were combinations in the nature of parties, and that which supported him had a well-defined policy, and principles—as much religious as political—which in many ways raised the administration above

the selfish interests of persons and classes. He recognized a
sort of responsibility to his party for the use of the appointing
power, and in that regard made the first great advance toward
administering the government in the interest of common justice. At this period, we find the character of the administration beginning to attract the attention of statesmen ; and
Marvel, Eliot, and Vane may be regarded as the first of the
illustrious patriots who began to comprehend the great work
of administrative reform ; and the republican, Algernon Sidney, declared the new doctrine, "that magistrates are set up
for the good of the nation, not nations for the honor or glory
of magistrates."

IV. Cromwell had done nothing toward the establishment
of a better method than mere official favor for making
selections for the public service, if indeed the times were
not too violent and ignorant for a reform based on character
and justice. Under Charles II., therefore, the old spoils
system was restored with the crown ; and in the form of pensions, titles, and bribes he increased all the former elements of
corruption in ways which his profligacy and recklessness suggested. The appointing power was as much an article of
merchandise as the crops on the royal estates. Parliamentary
corruption increased with the power of Parliament, and nearly
every officer was open to bribes, from the king, who set the
example to the keeper of the dog-kennels, who followed it.
Under James II. it was not better, but worse. Religious as
much as political opinions continued to be tests for office in
the army and in civil life, as well as in the church. Districts
were *gerrymandered*, Parliament was packed with placemen,
members followed the precedent of the king in accepting
bribes and in bribing others. Proscription extended to the
judiciary, and Jeffreys expressed the savage spirit it breathed.
Officers were removed by reason of their opinions, as ruthlessly
as they have ever been by any republican president, governor,
or mayor in later times. Official life became a source of corruption, which poisoned and debased every thing in connection
with government, and helped to arouse the wrath of the people,
which drove James from the country. But outside of official
life, and despite the demoralizing influence of politics, a better

public opinion, a larger and bolder sense of right and duty, were growing among the people, and taking more and more notice of public administration.

V. William III. was the first English king who brought a reforming spirit to the throne, and the first who appreciated the importance of good administration; and he soon discovered that without reforms he could not carry forward his great enterprises, if indeed he could retain the throne. He did little for better methods, but much for a better spirit, and more efficiency and responsibility. He became his own Secretary of Foreign Affairs, and day after day he personally investigated abuses in the other departments. Laws were passed for the protection of the freedom of elections, judges were made secure in their offices during good behavior, placemen were excluded from seats in Parliament. But a desperate spirit of faction prevailed. The nation was unaccustomed to the responsibilities of freedom and without experience in the management of parties. The power of Parliament had greatly increased, but with more power had come more bribery and more factious activity. The king created a select cabinet of advisers, the beginning of the present British Cabinet, and the model on which that of the United States is closely framed. The members were all taken from the dominant party in Parliament, and they were to go out (unless the Parliament should be prorogued) whenever, on any important measure, they should fail of carrying a majority in that body. This system gave to the Parliamentary majority the great prize of guiding the administration and of controlling all appointments; and very soon and very naturally drew its members and their constituents into two great parties. Here was the origin of parties and of party government, as understood in British history. The majority could before make all laws; but now, through the cabinet, it could also control all national policy, name all officers, direct all subordinate officials in the line of their duty. It was the greatest prize ever offered to the victors in a party contest. Party government, thus introduced under William III., has continued, with no fundamental change, to this day. It made no provision as to the mode of the appointment or removal of subordinate officials; and it was quite consistent with its theory that their selection should be based on their personal qualifications, irrespective of political opinions. In that particular, the condition was the same as it is under the Constitution of the United States. So great a regard for character and so non-partisan a spirit were, however, too much for the political virtue and general intelligence of the times of William III. Despite the failure of party government to rise above a partisan, spoils system, and its continued inability to make reforms that kept administration up to the level of the rising plane of public intelligence and morality, its introduction was in itself no small improvement. To a great extent, it took administration out of the secret intrigues of the court, and opened it to the members of a party or at least to its leaders. If it did not give the offices to the people, it in principle gave them to such of the people as belonged to the ruling party—though in practice it only gave them to official favorites and partisan manipulators. The leaders of the dominant party insisted on proscription, and made opinions the test of nominations. Members of Parliament demanded patronage, and very soon began their long-continued encroachment on the appointing power of the executive. They demanded places as a condition of helping fellow-members to seats in the cabinet; and here was one great source of their control of appointments. There were not at this time (nor has there since been, except for very brief periods) any general practice of removals without cause; but the dominant party continued to grasp larger and larger patronage, and more and more, it came under the control of members of Parliament. And party politics strongly tended to venality. Here we have the introduction of the partisan system of appointments —of the practice of parties looking to their patronage, rather than to their principles and their good administration, for the sources of their strength among the people. This usurpation of the appointing power by members of Parliament and the introduction of a partisan system of appointments, at the very beginning of party government, made indispensable that long contest, in which members were finally compelled to surrender their spoils.

VI. From Anne to George III. was the period of the first great trial of party government. It did not fail, nor has it since failed, within its true sphere. But having descended to partisan methods, it proved that by such methods public administration cannot be raised, or the just demands of an intelligent nation be satisfied. The partisan system of appointments and promotions aggravated the evils of Parliamentary patronage, made administration costly and feeble, spread corruption from the department to cities, boroughs, and elections, while it disgusted the better class of citizens, alarmed statesmen, and exasperated and debased all political contests. At the same time that every thing within the domain of administration and politics was becoming more and more demoralized, until the lowest depths of corruption were reached under Walpole, Newcastle, and Pelham—while statesmanship tended to sink into the mere management and manipulation of parties and elections, and those at the head of public affairs became the leaders of a servile class seeking places, pensions, and titles—a higher and bolder public opinion was being developed outside political circles, which demanded more purity and patriotism in politics, and more zeal and spirituality in religion—an opinion which found noble utterance by Chatham and Burke in Parliament and by Wesley and Whitefield in the pulpit. Political writers became more bold, and the reforming spirit found a more enlightened and vigorous expression. Still reformers were ridiculed as *doctrinaires* and sentimentalists,—were denounced as canting hypocrites, seeking office,—were branded as enemies of the party who threatened its safety. Nevertheless the reforming spirit steadily gained strength, and more and more the inherent evils of Parliamentary patronage and the partisan system were demonstrated. Even in Queen Anne's time, the interference of officials with the freedom of elections became intolerable ; and in that ninth year of her reign those in the postal service were by statute prohibited using their influence to affect the vote of any elector. This statute is, I think, the first of that series of enactments which enforce a more just and wholesome restraint than we have yet imposed on official interference with the freedom of elections.

Still members of Parliament insisted on their patronage and used it basely. Inexorable partisan tests in the departments were reinforced by proscriptive appointments and promotions in the church, by corrupt pensions, by titles that rewarded venality, by promotions that insulted merit, by a corrupt borough-system, and by fearful bribery at the elections. The abuse of partisan removals was not as great as it has been with us, though the Tories attempted to introduce universal proscription.

VII. George III. added new elements of debasement to the evils of the partisan system which he inherited. He arbitrarily interfered with the details of administration and rivalled members of Parliament in bribery and coercion. His policy, especially, during the administration of Lord Bute, was as proscriptive as that of our most partisan Presidents, and immeasurably more corrupt. Pensions, titles, decorations, court favors, social influence, espionage, open bribes at elections, bribes of members, threats, were used to carry the projects of the king and to punish his enemies. Members of Parliament, high officials and party leaders, generally, were little above the morality of the court. The king tried to rule through a party based on patronage, official influence, and corruption ; and he failed as sadly as any party has ever failed in the use of the same means. Lord Bute ignominiously surrendered on the failure of that system. The higher sentiments and the nobler minds of the nation exhibited a growing power. But the war with America—to the support of which the king brought all the corrupt resources of the spoils system, and which that system unquestionably protracted—silenced for a time the voice of reform. At the conclusion of the war, an administration distinctly pledged to reform came, for the first time in English history, into the possession of the government.[1]

Independence for America, administrative reform, freedom of elections, exclusion of placemen from Parliament—these were its pledges, to which it was faithful. The triumph of the spirit of Burke and Chatham—victory for those who had stood

[1] The first Rockingham Ministry was certainly friendly to reform.

for America and for reform—gave significance to the change
of ministry.   If there was delay and occasional reaction, the
higher sentiments, whose victory these events record, never
again surrendered to patronage or partisanship.   We very
soon come upon the time when British legislation, in a long
series of statutes against bribery and office brokerage, passed
during the reign of George III. and since perfected, was made
far more effective against the prostitution of the appointing
power and the abuse of official authority generally, than our
laws have ever been.   If there was not enough public virtue
or wisdom to remove the causes which induced subordinate
officials to interfere with elections, there was at least a patriotic
public opinion bold enough, in the last half of the reign of
George III. to crush out that evil by disfranchising those
officers ; a disability that continued until 1868, when the merit
system had removed the cause of the great evil at which disfranchisement had been aimed.   And before his reign came
to an end, the system of superannuation allowances, ever since
enforced, had been well developed, and there were several
other laws intended to advance the self-respect and social position of those in the public service.

These statutes, by making official prostitution more perilous, by holding up a higher standard of public duty before
the people, by encouraging the criticism of the better public
opinion, have largely contributed to the purification of political life and to the upbuilding of that more exacting popular
demand which has imposed a wholesome sense of responsibility
upon British officers of every grade and in every part of the
empire.

VIII.  Before 1820, when George IV. became king, the
better public sentiment had nearly driven corruption out of the
partisan system, while the system remained ;  but its inherent
viciousness had only become the more conspicuous in the
light of a higher civilization.   Bribery of members of Parliament was at an end, and removals for mere political reasons
were very rarely made.   But members of Parliament were by
their patronage disarmed for some of the higher duties of
legislation ; they forced incompetent favorites into the service ; the departments were crowded with supernumeraries ;

elections were debased, and the whole atmosphere of politics was poisoned by the evils of patronage and favoritism. These evils had become known to the more intelligent part of the people, and there was a far more discriminating condemnation of parliamentary interference with appointments than ever before ; but for a time the great reform measure of 1832 absorbed public attention.

As early as 1834, however, pass examinations for admission to the service were begun in a small way, and before 1850 they had been greatly extended. In 1854 they were adopted in the United States. But in their very nature, they were inadequate, and more efficient examinations were called for. Patronage in all its forms, by reason of the good effects of examinations, encountered more and more powerful opposition. Statesmen clearly perceived, that a partisan system is as unnecessary to the vigorous life of a party as it is disastrous to the higher interest of a nation. Under the influence of such convictions, patronage and proscription were put under more effective limitations, and examinations were extended and made more efficient by limited competition in some of the offices. The great party leaders on both sides comprehended that neither parliamentary patronage nor the partisan system itself could long survive. Even as early as 1820, the patronage of promotion in the customs service had been surrendered by the head of the treasury in favor of promotions for merit ; and the results not a little aided the cause of reform by increasing the efficiency of that branch of the service. To the other influences, which led to the radical movement of 1853, must be added the fact that pass examinations—inherently defective as they are—everywhere, in a perceptible measure, both limited the abuses of parliamentary patronage and brought better men into the public service. It was no longer possible for politicians to prevent the question of better administrative methods coming into the foreground as a great measure of executive policy ; and it became distinctly such before 1853. It was not, in form, ever a party issue ; for, in its nature, it divided not party from party, but what was higher from what was lower in each party ; and not even the more partisan managers of either party

thought it safe  any more than they have in the United
States in later years  to avow hostility to the duty or principle of reform, however much they might sneer and secretly
oppose.

IX. This brings us to the radical reform measures of 1853.
In large part by reason of the statutes I have referred to,
the general character of official life had so risen, between 1780
and 1853, that, at the latter date, it was, I think, decidedly less
partisan and less venal in Great Britain than in the United
States ; though patronage in the hands of members of Parliament—the main source of the abuses in the civil service—was
still as arbitrary and pernicious as it has at any time been in
the hands of members of Congress.  The moral planes of
official life in the two countries -the one ascending and the
other descending—had crossed each other in the period between those dates.   The nearest correspondence between the
use of the appointing power by an English king and an American president was the practice in the earlier part of the reign
of George III. and that which began under President Jackson ;
though George III. added to merciless partisanship, pecuniary
bribery, an offence of which President Jackson was never
guilty.

If the character of administration had, in a degree, risen
with the intelligence and moral tone of society since party
government began, it had neither risen as rapidly as the
demand for reform, nor reached the efficiency and purity
which the statesmen of both parties felt that the exigency of
the empire demanded.   They saw that the waning partisan
system was capable of nothing better than what it had given,
that the reform sentiment was steadily gaining strength, that
parliamentary patronage must from its very nature be fruitful
of evil continually, and was incapable of defense on any sound
principles.[1]  And they felt that the revolutionary tendencies in
England and throughout Europe, since 1830, and especially
since 1848, were a warning not only against any elements of
feebleness, but against every abuse that might impair the

[1] "Some years have now elapsed since Lord Althorp declared in the
House of Commons that the time for a system of government by patronage
was gone by."—Speech of Earl Granville in House of Lords, 1854.

patriotism of the people. Though we have high authority for saying that on a secret vote a reform policy would have been suppressed by overwhelming numbers, the great party leaders dared not longer oppose it on principle. " If the clubs had been polled, there would have been ninety-nine out of a hundred against us." [1]

The strength of the minority was not in numbers, but in the influence of high character and capacity, and of deep, moral earnestness—a force in public affairs which politicians are very apt to underestimate. It was then, as it had been long before, and has continually since been, a part of the conviction of all English statesmen that the good administration of the laws is a matter of serious concern, to which they ought to give their best efforts. " Every eminent statesman has since [2] shown that the true policy of a government was in appealing to the good sense and intelligence of the large classes of the community." Such was the condition, in 1853, when the government ordered Sir Charles Trevelyan and Sir Stafford Northcote to make their celebrated investigation and report. It was not a movement by members of Parliament toward the surrender of their usurped patronage, nor did that body, at first, co-operate beyond voting money to pay expenses ; but it was an exercise of the long-dormant authority of the executive, in its own sphere of duty, to see that the laws are faithfully executed—sustained by the better public opinion. Members of Parliament, with few exceptions—each grasping firmly his little parcel—persistently claimed as a right that portion of the appointing power which they had originally gained as a usurpation ; nor can they ever be credited with surrendering it—until a frowning public opinion enforced that duty. [3]

X. The investigation made by those gentlemen showed that pass examinations had been useful ; that limited competition between those nominated by members of Parliament and the Treasury—though applied only within very narrow limits—

---

[1] Evid. Sir Charles Trevelyan, C. S. Inquiry, 1873, vol. ii., p. 102.

[2] The date referred to is 1854, and this language is from Earl Granville's speech cited in the last note.

[3] See Appendix A, Letter Sir Charles Trevelyan.

had been still more useful. It also developed good reasons for believing that open competition, under which any one applying could be examined without permission of any official, would be far more salutary ; and it hardly need be added that it would exclude the evil of parliamentary patronage. Open competition was therefore recommended ; and also a general *Civil Service Commission* for supervising and giving harmony to examinations throughout all the departments and offices. Open competition was the application of a new and higher standard in official life ; for, it was a proclamation that worth and capacity have higher claims upon office than official favor or partisan services. Partisans and official monopolists were naturally enough alarmed, and became hostile. Denunciation, sarcasm, ridicule, gross exaggerations of the probable expenses and of the difficulties in enforcing the new system, bold prophecies of its futility, and of its pretended centralizing tendencies, were urged with a skill and persistency which were not surpassed when a similar measure of reform was initiated in the United States. But Lord Palmerston—remarkable alike for courage and practical experience—and his cabinet supported the report and had the commission promptly appointed. It was thought prudent, while allowing open competition, to only require limited competition, as a first experiment—which did not prevent a monopoly of nominations by members of Parliament—lest a too sudden change from the long-prevailing system should arouse a dangerous opposition. Open competition was about the same time applied to the administration of British India, under the immediate supervision of Mr. Macaulay. The practical effect, in both countries, was to exclude the worst nominees, to give places to the best men nominated, to improve the moral tone and the capacity of the public service, to speedily make parliamentary patronage ridiculous and odious, by publicly exposing and rejecting the class of incompetent favorites and disreputable henchmen which members had been, for more than a century, in the habit of foisting upon the public treasury in the interest of their purses and their elections. It was soon plainly seen that open competition, which would alike promote common justice and general education, was all that was needed to exterminate vicious patronage, to destroy the old official monopoly, and to give to the intelligence and manhood of the nation free access to present their paramount claims upon places under the government. Public opinion rapidly grew stronger for the reform. Parliament, which in 1855 had condemned the new merit system (as our Congress condemned it under President Grant), had in 1856 grown wiser, and by a small majority commended it ; and, rising with public opinion, it unanimously, in 1857, not only approved what had been done, but suggested that open competition be established as the sole test for entering the public service. Patronage so rapidly lost its attractions and its respectability, and the *Civil Service Commission* so early demonstrated its usefulness, that in 1859 Parliament refused all retiring allowances to those who should get into the service without an examination before the commission. The machinery of the new system had worked so easily, its expenses were so small, and the certainty of obtaining the best men by examinations was so overwhelmingly demonstrated, that criticism was silenced and the enemies of reform were confounded. The charge of centralization was seen to be absurd ; for the unconstitutional share of the appointing power (before centralized in members of Parliament) did not, practically, revert to the executive, but was in practice distributed to the persons, of character and capacity among the people, who should win their way into the public service by an open competition, which left the executive nothing like the arbitrary caprice of appointment which had belonged to every English king from the origin of the monarchy. The reform, therefore, was as democratic and republican in its operation, as it was moral and educational in its origin and influence. The same method which broke up that centralization of power in the hands of the members of the legislature which impaired the counterpoise of the Constitution, also enlarged the liberties of the people by giving to personal worth an open way to office.

The victory of the merit system was thus complete, and the disposition to oppose or argue was over, in five years from the time it was first officially proposed. The nation was proud of guarantees for a better official life ; the cause of education and common justice was advanced ; members of Parliament were glad to be relieved of the degrading and exasperating solicitation for office ; elections began to turn more on character and capacity, and not so much on hopes of patronage and salaries ; parties were found to be not less vigorous and wholesome when the main issues were those of policy and principles without embroilment with questions about all sorts of offices and places. The time had come when hopes of personal gain, adroit management, and official manipulation were seen to be forces in politics far inferior to honest and open appeals to the judgment, honor, and patriotism of the people. Those seeking office turned for support from the place-brokers and partisan speculators of politics, whose business was broken up, to the independent and honest citizenship of the country, whose influence was increased.

X. In the presence of such effects, it was only natural that the series of thorough investigations, already explained, should be made into all the old abuses of the departments—that open competition, free to every British subject, with no possibility of limitation or obstruction by any member or any executive officer, should be introduced in 1870, and since continued with a satisfaction that has never diminished ; that popular education should receive a marked impetus ; that the general efficiency of the administration and the character and social standing of those who execute the laws should be elevated with the standard for admission to the public service. Open competition, which had, much longer and in a more extensive way, been on trial in India, had given results not less salutary ; and these examples caused the new system to be extended to the army and navy, to the jurisdictions of the royal governors, to Australia, Tasmania, and, to some extent, to Canada ; so that, in every quarter of the world where the English language is spoken (except in the United States) the wholesome influence of the new system was early felt, and the foundation was laid for a public service based on personal worth and capacity. Thus, we see an ancient government, of imperial proportions, with all its dependencies—a monarchy in form and historical development—which has been generally supposed to find its strength in royal and official favoritism and in selfish and class interests, going forward with a reform, in principle founded on equal rights and common opportunity for sharing its honors and salaries—a reform which in practice (with a few exceptions) takes from parties all chances of trading in public franchises, surrenders the gracious privileges of the crown to a stern rule of justice, deprives every officer of the power of granting favors, and holds officials to a responsibility more democratic and republican in spirit, and to a moral standard of duty more severely exacting and sternly in the common interests of the people, than any ever yet been enforced in a republic.

The whole advance—the result of the efforts of patriots and statesmen for good administration during six centuries—is expressed in this simple fact: In the beginning, a man was in the public service because a corrupt and arbitrary king wished him there; at the end, he was in that service because a fair test of his worth gave him the place, as the best man to fill it.

But consider what an immense advance in justice and liberty, in the standard of official duty and the rights of simple manhood, this change illustrates! In the beginning, and for centuries, all offices, salaries, and places, all authority exerted in ways innumerable in every grade of official influence, all the prestige, profits, and spoils of carrying on the vast affairs of government from the hamlet to the throne, were the perquisites, the privileges, the monopoly, or the spoils of kings, nobles, or bishops and their favorites; into a participation of which no man as a man, or because the ablest and best of men, could come, except upon conditions almost certain to be a compromise of manhood or a prostitution of public interests. But at the end the great principle has become established, that the personal character and capacity which fit a man for public duty are in themselves *the highest claim upon office*; and to ascertain, select, and appoint the men thus fitted for the public service are affirmed to be duties paramount to all royal policy, to all aristocratic interests, to all state church ambition, to all partisan exigencies: and thus, high exalted over every other reason of preference and every other interest, stand the simple claims of personal worth, and the interest and right of the people to leave them regarded in making selections for office. It is plain, then, that the reform of the civil service in Great Britain has not been, and that nowhere should it be looked upon as being a mere device in procedure, a mere method in public business, or a mere collection of rules in the departments: but that it involves all this besides

a test and expression of the justice and moral tone of a nation's politics; a decision between the relative claims of worth and manhood, as weighed against official favoritism, and selfish interests, upon public confidence and respect; a theory of the true sphere of parties and of their best means of gaining the support of a free and intelligent people; a principle of duty and responsibility in official life; the character of political leadership—whether it should be by statesmen making their appeal upon principles and good administration, or by manipulators relying on patronage and management; the question whether it be better to encourage selfish and partisan activity by selecting officers on the bid of cliques and caucuses, or to encourage education and manliness by selecting them through examinations and competitions; the relations of the legislature to the executive departments, and therefore the construction of the constitution and the counterpoise and stability of government itself. It was because civil service reform—or, what is the same thing, administrative reform, as embracing the essential conditions of good administration—was apprehended in this higher spirit and broader range—as being a great and permanent question of principle and duty—as presenting a perpetual issue between the higher and lower elements—in politics, that, more than a century ago, it began to receive, and has ever since received, the attention of the foremost of British statesmen. The first germs of it are in the declaration of Algernon Sidney, that magistrates are created for the benefit of the state, and not the state for magistrates. Eliot and Vane comprehended it in that spirit when they staked their lives upon a reform policy. It was understood, in that spirit, by Lord Chatham when he refused the spoils of office, and declared—of a Parliament steeped in patronage and corruption—that if it was not speedily reformed from within, it would be reformed with a vengeance from without; by William Pitt when he brought in reform bills and, while living on a narrow income, renounced the great sinecure salary which the partisan system tendered him; by Edmund Burke, when he " bent the whole force of his mind " upon those great measures of reform with which his name will be forever associated; by Lord Grey and Sir Robert Peel when, giving their best efforts to reform in various ways; by Lord Liverpool, when, a generation ago, he surrendered the patronage of promotion in favor of merit in the Customs service; by Lord Palmerston, when as Prime Minister he confronted the selfishness of members of Parliament who opposed the great reform of 1853; by Lord Granville when, as we have seen, he declined the patronage of various appointments " in order to make them available for the purpose of encouraging education ;" by Mr. Gladstone, in the steady and vigorous support he has given to administrative reform during his whole official life; by John Bright [1] and Lord Derby, when, representing the opposite parties, they devoted so much labor to the great civil-service investigations to which I have referred; by the eminent statesmen examined on those investigations, whose convictions find expression in such words as these : ' all persons have an *equal right* to be candidates if they are fit,'" [2] " this is the *critical* part of our national institutions, namely, the selection of candidates for the public service : " [3] by the honest, intelligent people generally, of every class, by ministers representing all parties, and, finally, even by members of Parliament themselves, who have co-operated in advancing the new system at home, in India, and every dependency of the British Empire. And can we believe it to have been understood in any narrower sense by the leading nations of Europe, which, in the common interest of good administration and national safety, have one after another destroyed the official, patronage system, and the class monopoly of offices, upon which monarchies were originally based, and opened them, with but few exceptions, to the intelligence and worth of the people irrespective of their birth or their political opinions ?

---

[1] See Letter of Mr. Bright in Appendix A.          [2] See ante, p. 227.

[3] Report Com., 1873, vol. i., p. 133.

What is the lesson, of such a history and of such results, for the United States?  How far are such reforms compatible with our constitution and social life?  What, if any thing, may we wisely do to improve our administration, in the light of such an experience?  Are not these questions vital enough for the reflections of an intelligent people, large enough for the action of statesmen in a great republic?

# CHAPTER XXXIII.

## THE BEARING OF BRITISH EXPERIENCE UPON CIVIL SERVICE REFORM IN THE UNITED STATES.

Caution in accepting foreign experience.—The theory of the framers of our constitution on the subject.—A summary of the principles and conclusions reached in British administration.—The question of a long term of office and its relations to the *merit system.*—Who are certain to oppose the new system.—Reasons for more confidence in its support.—The world's experience on its side.—Who are the theorists and the *doctrinaires?*—Who the statesmen?—Examinations and competitions supported by an irresistible public opinion in Great Britain.—Lord Beaconsfield rebuked by it.—Various principles and methods of the new system considered in reference to our institutions.—The right to claim and the duty to bestow office.—The extent to which patronage has been surrendered by the Crown, by noblemen, and officials in Great Britain.—Have our officers equal patriotism?—Our subordinate officials made feudal dependents.—Whether patronage is essential to the utility and prosperity of parties.—Do republics awaken less patriotism than monarchies?—Parties would gain more than they would lose by abandoning the spoils system.—Practical effects of adopting the merit system.—It would destroy a vicious monopoly over office-getting.—Effects on the Presidential elections.—Promotes self-reliance, good character, and education.—How members of Congress would be affected.—Effects on custom-houses and other local offices.—Consequences of bringing persons of worth and capacity into subordinate positions.—Promotions for merit.—The merit system would give new dignity to office and government.—Means by which the reform may be advanced.—How far and what kinds of legislation useful or practicable.—Political assessments.—The reform a question for the people, and its need in State and municipal offices as well as in Federal offices.—Whether we have the public virtue to carry it forward and are as unselfish and patriotic as the people of Great Britain.—Competition a general law of progress.—The permanent nature of the reform issue.

THE undertaking to point out the bearing of the reform measures of Great Britain upon administrative questions in the United States has, the author trusts, been in large part performed as the work has proceeded ; and perhaps few suggestions can now be made which have not already occurred to the reader.

The mere fact that any given principles or methods of political action have been found salutary in one country, is by no means a sufficient reason for introducing them into another; nor is it often that corresponding relations among officers, or between the officials and the people, will be found practicable in any two countries. But the probability that they may be naturally increases with all that is in common in race, language and religion, in laws, institutions, and civilization. And, therefore, notwithstanding the people of Great Britain have so much more than any other people in common with ourselves, the mere success of her reform measures within her own borders has not been accepted as a reason why we should find them equally salutary; and hence their influence has been considered in its bearings upon liberty, common justice, general education, public morality, and the complicated and essential relations of great parties in a free State. In the opening chapter, attention was called to the extent to which our fathers incorporated into their new structure the principles of the British constitution. It is worthy of our notice that the question now presented is not so much a question about adopting processes and methods as it is about approving certain great principles which embody a theory of political morality, of official obligation, of equal rights and common justice in government. It was the principle, rather than the mere methods, of the division of government into three great departments, of the independence of the judiciary, of free, parliamentary debate, of representative institutions, of trial by jury, of the *habeas corpus*, of the common law, of personal rights, of the subordination of the military to the civil power, which we adopted in our original constitution. The question now before us is, whether the nation which has maintained, as faithfully as we have, all these great foundations of liberty, still equally fundamental in the two countries, may not now be able to tender us other principles worthy of our adoption, which she has developed in perfecting the vast and complicated operations in her civil affairs during the period in which—absorbed by the interests of new States and territories and by the many matters peculiar to a young nation—we have given little thought to the practical working of government? Our fathers did not borrow so much from the mother country because the two peoples had kindred blood, spoke the same language and gathered inspiration from the same literature, but because England, being at that time the freest and most enlightened of the old nations, and her higher precedents having been forged in the furnace fires of liberty and sanctioned by its saints and martyrs, were best adapted to our needs and most naturally commanded the confidence of our early statesmen. Now, as then, the two great English-speaking nations maintain their original precedence in freedom and justice. For what great nation, besides Great Britain and the United States, even yet allows a true freedom of debate and of the press—makes the military really subordinate to the civil power—affords a safe asylum for the victims of despotism—or secures an efficient protection to every citizen without the aid of bayonets or the menace of policemen bearing deadly weapons? Still, after all such general reflections have had there true weight, there remain the direct questions: Has the new system been adequately tested? Is it adapted to our constitutions and social life? Is it republican in spirit and consistent with the practical administration of government under our institutions? Have we the public intelligence and virtue which warrant the attempt to carry forward such a reform?

Some of these questions, I must think, have been sufficiently answered, if indeed it were possible to hesitate as to the answer to be given; and the others can be more intelligently considered if we have distinctly before our minds the principles and conclusions which have become accepted in the later experience of Great Britain. They may be briefly stated as follows:

1. Public office creates a relation of trust and duty of a kind which requires all authority and influence partaining to it to be exercised with the same absolute conformity to moral standards, to the spirit of the constitution and the laws, and to the common interests of the people, which may be insisted upon in the use of public money or any other common prop-

erty of the people ; and, therefore, whatever difficulty may attend the practical application of the rule of duty, it is identically the same whether it be applied to property or to official discretion. There can in principle be no official discretion to disregard common interests or to grant official favors to persons or to parties.

2. So far as any right is involved, in filling offices, it is the right of the people to have the worthiest citizens in the public service for the general welfare ; and the privilege of sharing the honors and profits of holding office appertains equally to every citizen, in proportion to his measure of character and capacity which qualify him for such service.[1]

4. The ability, attainments, and character requisite for the fit discharge of official duties of any kind,—in other words, the personal merits of the candidate—are *in themselves the highest claim* upon an office.[2]

5. Party government and the salutary activity of parties are not superseded, but they are made purer and more efficient, by the *merit system* of office,[3] which brings larger capacity and higher character to their support.

6. Government by parties is enfeebled and debased by reliance upon a partisan system of appointments and re-

---

[1] I do not here refer to cases of offices conferred, or other rewards given as compensation for patriotic efforts or sacrifices, by the act of the people, who, in voting, are a law unto themselves ; or to elections by the people ; but to the exercise of power by an officer, whether in respect to the nomination, confirmation, or removal of some other officer, or otherwise in his discretion. Patronage and favoritism, in connection with the exercise of official power, are therefore in their very nature abuses—repugnant to the nature of the official trust—actual violations of the duty which the officer owes to the people—just as reprehensible as it would be to use official authority to deprive a citizen of his equal right to send his children to the public schools, or to prevent his vote being cast for the candidate he prefers —wrongs upon every ground upon which it would be wrong to give a part of the public money or of the public lands to a person not having a good claim to it.

[2] Subject of course to the limitations mentioned in the last note ; and therefore to ascertain such merits and to decide upon competing claims arising thereunder are important parts of the duties of a government, and are equally essential for doing justice and for obtaining good officers.

[3] For the meaning of the phrases, the "partisan system" and the "merit system," as here used, see *ante* pages, 77 to 81 and 161, note.

movals ; and, for its most vigorous life and salutary influence, it is only needful for the party majority to select, as the
representative of its views and the executors of its policy, the
few high officers with whom rests the power to direct the national affairs, and to instruct and keep in the line of their duty
the whole body of their subordinates[1] through whose administrative work that policy is to be carried into effect.

7. Patronage in the hands of members of the legislature,
which originated in a usurpation of executive functions, increases the expenses of administration, is degrading and demoralizing to those who possess it, is disastrous to legislation,
tends to impair the counterpoise and stability of the government ; and it cannot withstand the criticism of an intelligent
people when they fairly comprehend its character and consequences.[2]

8. Examinations (in connection with investigations of character) may be so conducted as to ascertain, with far greater certainty than by any other means, the persons who are the most
fit for the public service ; and the worthiest thus disclosed may
be selected for the public service by a just and non-partisan
method, which the most enlightened public opinion will
heartily approve.

9. Open competition presents at once the most just and practicable means of supplying fit persons for appointment. It is
proved to have given the best public servants ; it makes an
end of patronage ; and, besides being based on equal rights
and common justice, it has been found to be the surest safeguard against both partisan coercion and official favoritism.

10. Such methods, which leave to parties and party government their true functions in unimpaired vigor, tend to reduce
manipulation, intrigue, and every form of corruption in poli-

---

[1] Where the line between the two classes of officers should be drawn
in the United States—between those political officers who command all the
others and who should go out with each administration, and those administrative officers whose duty it is to obey their superiors—it is not my purpose
to attempt to point out. The first class, in Great Britain, we have seen,
includes only from 34 to 50 officials. We cannot draw the line in the
United States until after we have adopted the principle by which it is to be
guided. See ante, pp. 80 to 83 and 161.

[2] See chap. 14.

ties to their smallest proportions. They also reward learning, give more importance to character and principles and make political life more attractive to all worthy citizens.

11. Regarded as a whole, the new system has raised the ambition and advanced both the self-respect and the popular estimation of those in the public service, while it has encouraged general education, arrested demoralizing solicitation for office, and promoted economy, efficiency, and fidelity in public affairs.[1]

12. A system is entirely practicable under which official salaries shall increase during the more active years of life, and through which a retiring allowance is retained to be paid upon the officer leaving the public service ; and such a system appears to contribute to economy and fidelity in administration.

13. Open competition is as fatal to all the conditions of a beaurocracy, as it is to patronage, nepotism and every form of favoritism, in the public service.

14. The merit system, by raising the character and capacity of the subordinate service, and by accustoming the people to consider personal worth and sound principles, rather than selfish interest and adroit management, as the controlling elements of success in politics, has also invigorated national patriotism, raised the standard of statesmanship, and caused political leaders to look more to the better sentiments and the higher intelligence for support.

II. Such are the principles and conclusions which have obtained almost universal acceptance in British administration—and perhaps, I may add, in the administration of every nation of the old world, to the extent that its government has been liberal enough to tolerate them. Objections are most likely to arise against whatever —like graded salaries and retiring or superannuation allowances—may be thought to favor a long tenure of office. It is certainly desirable to have clear views upon these points. They have before come under our notice in some of their aspects ; and I must leave the less important questions of the effects of graded salaries and retiring allow-

---

[1] See Letter Sir Charles Trevelyan, Appendix A ; and in Appendix C will be found the results of a short trial, within narrow limits, of the merit system in the United States.

ances to the observations already submitted.[1] But the bearing
of the merit system upon the tenure of office perhaps requires some further notice. That system and the partisan-
spoils system, considered in relation to their influence within
the service, might be treated under three separate heads :
(1) what relates to bringing persons into the public service,
(2) what relates to their government and duty while there ;
(3) what relates to the determination of service. It would be
seen that the question of duration of tenure would fall wholly
under the last head. But, under the partisan-spoils system,
the question of removals stands in close relations with the
question of appointments ; for by far the greater number of
removals are urged, not because there is a good reason for putting the officer out, but because there is a purpose to put
some other person in his place. All serious abuse from removals without good cause will disappear the moment it becomes necessary to fill the vacancy by open competition. In
deciding, therefore, how long an officer should be allowed to remain in his place—or, in other words, for what reason he
should be removed—we must look beyond the effects upon
himself or upon the office he fills, to the general influence upon
the whole question of proscription and of partisan intermeddling in administration. But as all these collateral influences
make in favor of an extended term of office, which would diminish the number of opportunities for corrupt appointments,
we may dismiss them, and confine our attention to the more
direct relations between tenure of office and the new system.
It needs but a moment of reflection to make it plain that
neither the qualifications demanded for entering an office, nor
the influences or conditions that control the nomination or
confirmation, have, intrinsically anything to do with the time
during which the office is to be held. Nor need the authorized
causes of removal have any intrinsic relation to the length of
tenure, unless the fact of having been in office a designated
number of years or up to a certain age be made in itself a
ground of removal. Every other part of the merit system
could be put in practice, and no small share of its salutary
influences might be secured, though the present tenure of

[1] See ante pp. 141 to 143 and pp. 294 to 297.

office should be left unchanged; however repugnant to the
spirit of that system removals without good cause may be.  The
most rigid competitions may be set up at the door of every office
in the republic, civil, military, and naval   years of careful study
may be exacted to fit applicants for their special duties—and yet
the tenure of office be left utterly indefinite and precarious,
if such we think to be the part of statesmanship or justice.
Like officers in the old Italian republics, our civil servants
may be allowed a tenure of only one, three, or six months,
and, like the Athenian generals, our military and naval officers
may be allowed to command for only a single day, if we think
that the part of wisdom.  What does the public interest
require in that regard? is the decisive question.   Neither
nominations nor competitions have changed the tenure of office
in Great Britain or in India.   It must be clear, I think, that
the question of the proper tenure of office may be treated separately and upon its own merits, though the spirit and suggestion of the new system are utterly hostile to removals for
political reasons.  And if the principle should be accepted that
the best qualified person has the strongest claims to office, and
that no incompetent person should be appointed, no matter
what the influence in his favor, there is little ground for
doubt that experienced and worthy officers will be retained as
long as they shall properly discharge their duties and the public shall have need of their services.

There is really no question presented, as to having a permanent body of officers, but only the questions as to each class of
officers—or more accurately, as to each officer: What tenure
does the public interest require?  How long a tenure should
the laws and the administrative rules therefore encourage?
Should officers be exposed to arbitrary and capricious removals?
These are the only questions.  With these questions, Great
Britain has dealt by laying down certain general principles,
but not by actually fixing any tenure of office, in the civil service.  Much less has she made the fact of having been in
office a certain number of years in itself a cause for removal or
for resignation.   If we think that having been in the service
one year or ten years is a good cause for going out—if we
feel that we have too much trained skill and experience

in our administration—we can place those reasons among the grounds of removal " for cause." It is not my purpose to consider the general question of the proper tenure of office in the civil service. We have only to go back to our early laws and usages to find a system far more in harmony, than the spoils system, with our constitution and the general welfare. The tenure of these properly constituting the civil service—at least as the constitution was understood in the earlier and less partisan period of our history—was, in theory and practice, like the tenure of our judiciary, the same as the British Civil Service tenure, as I have defined it. The laws limiting the official terms of collectors, naval officers, post-masters, or other subordinates, to four years or other fixed periods, are, like the practice of making removals to satisfy the greed of parties and the clamors of favorites and henchmen, the fruits of the proscriptive spirit which began to be so powerful and reckless in the last generation. They were opposed by our greatest statesmen, and they respond to partisan greed rather than to public interests. What we need in this regard is not what is new, but a return to the rule and the practice of the fathers of the constitution. These laws, I venture to think, and the question of the most salutary tenure of office in all its forms, national, state, and municipal—as to which the discordant and fluctuating official terms indicate a lamentable absence of a matured public opinion—will not long hence be recognized as worthy the most serious consideration because they concern the morality of politics and the economy and integrity of official life.

It is not, of course, to be expected that methods of administration which tend to diminish the spoils of party managers and the arbitrary patronage of officials, in the same ratio that they increase the just opportunities for office of every man and woman of worth and capacity, will in this country, any more than they did in Great Britain, escape the persistent and unscrupulous hostility of those whose occupation and profits they threaten. With many of this latter class, reason is of little avail, and they may be left to repeat the sneers and the sarcasms, the falsehoods and the fallacies, long so familiar, but for a quarter of a century abandoned as stale and unavailing, in British politics. We have doubtless a class of extreme partisans ready to listen and to laugh at their reiteration; ignorant enough, perhaps, even to believe they have reason and experience on their side; prejudiced enough to reject whatever is denounced as of foreign origin. It will only be another example of the repetition of English history, if we shall find aspiring party-leaders and a certain stamp of officials becoming more and more widely separated from the most unselfish and patriotic portion of the people, and more and more making their appeal to a highly organized body of servile followers, who substitute manipulation for statesmanship and convert politics into a trade. So long as faith in patronage retains its influence, and the spoils of victory attract and reward the politicians, why, in the light of reason any more than in the light of history, should we be surprised at those later and ominous phases of our politics, wherein we see partisan contests losing none of their fierceness, when all real differences of avowed principles have ceased to exist, and both parties, in theory, joining in reprobation of the identical abuses which both alike practise? It is further worthy of notice that the increasing divergence and repugnance, in recent years, between the independent voters and the partisan politicians, are quite as much due to the more vigorous reforming spirit of the former as to any growing servility and intrigue of the latter. Here, as was the case in Great Britain, that divergence and repugnance must go on increasing until the reforming elements shall obtain the mastery, unless, indeed, we are to fall under the hopeless bondage of the spoils system.

III. But has not the time arrived when the friends of reform are justified in using a more decided and confident language—when they ought to make prominent the great fact that the system of administration which they commend is as well founded in experience as it is in sound and just principles? The *merit system* now presents itself, not merely as a fine theory or as a high, ideal conception of purity and justice in politics, but as an embodiment of principles and methods matured during a century, in which the foremost statesmen have bent their minds upon good administration as never before—as a system of practical arrangements and safeguards which at every stage of develop-

ment have gone on from victory to victory, under the eyes of
the most practical of administrators, in the most practical and
utilitarian of nations—as conclusions and results reached not
on the British Islands alone, but in colonies and provinces
variously governed, and in all quarters of the globe (except in
the United States), where the English language is spoken—
as principles and methods tested and confirmed, so far as
the form of government has been liberal enough for such confirmation, by the administrative experience of all the nations
which lead the world in commerce, arms, and industry, in education, morality, and religion. Nor can the better or even the
longer part of the experience of the United States be cited
against it. Our first generations sustained administrative
methods quite in the spirit of these later reforms. And
for every candid person who really approves our partisan-spoils
system of later years, there are scores of worthier men (having views of a remedy, perhaps rather obscure) with whom
that system is an abhorrence and a despair. Outside of the
American Union, that spoils system has not the support of a
single State above the moral level of Mexico, Turkey, and
the factious Spanish-American republics which our backsliding
example has helped to demoralize. It is not, therefore, the
friends of the *merit system*—not the reformers—who are theorists, and who insist on measures not yet justified by good results in practice. It is rather the partisans, the party leaders
claiming to be statesmen—all those who insist on applying the
partisan spoils theory, after all the higher public opinion of
their own country and the judgment of all enlightened mankind beyond their own country have condemned it—who are
the theorists. It is they who have got a favorite method —unknown to our fathers, novel in our history—of managing parties and of getting into and holding office, which they enforce
with the passion of enthuiasists and the recklessness of theorists.
In another sense, indeed, they are not theorists, but plant
their feet on ancient usage, inviting us to go back on the
road of civilization and again put in force the methods of
James II., of Walpole, Newcastle, and George III. ; claiming, as they did, that an administration cannot be kept in
power without proscription, that patronage is a fit perquisite

of members of legislature, that offices and places are the just and essential spoils of party victory. If he be not a theorist or an enthusiast, how shall we describe the man who calls upon us to shut our eyes, both to the degradation of our spoils system and to the beneficent experience of all the rest of the world under the merit system, to allow our officers to appropriate the perquisites and employ language of feudal lords of the middle ages, to deny ourselves the right and opportunity of gaining office by reason of our own merits, or otherwise than upon the consent of patronage monopolists and partisan manipulators? What is a *doctrinaire* but one "who rigidly applies to political or practical concerns the absolute principles of his own system," without due regard to past experience and practical consequences? And who are such doctrinaires? The men who urge the partisan spoils system upon the people of the United States, without being able to show that there, or in any quarter of the world, it has produced any good results, or the men who urge the *merit system*, because they find it in practice in every other enlightened nation, and are able to show that, in every instance where, in any degree, it has superseded the spoils system, it has in that degree checked abuses and raised political life to a higher plane? And who is the statesman, the man who scorns the higher sentiments, who defies the broader experience, who bends his energies upon manipulating his party, who puts his faith in the selfish instincts, in patronage and in spoils, who lives on the adulation of servile politicians and forfeits the respect of nobler minds; or the man who has faith in the virtue and intelligence of the people, who considers the great questions of his country in the light of its permanent interests, who recognizes moral forces and obligations in politics, who, rising above narrow prejudices and selfish interests, gives due weight, in all his judgments, to the experience and wisdom of the great nations who share in the leadership of human affairs?[1]

The *merit system* comes before us not only sanctioned by this long, this diversified, this almost universal experience, but

---

[1] "A belief in the perfection of their own systems could only exist among a people who knew nothing of any other systems."—A History of Our Own Times, 1879, by McCarthy, vol. i., chap. 8.

supported by a matured and enlightened public opinion, which seems to secure for it the same elements of permanency which are the safeguards of our dearest constitutional provisions. A pervading sense of its justice and the intelligent conviction of the British people that it is essential to their well-being entrench it in the popular judgment. There can be no doubt that they have deliberately accepted these three principles as axioms in their politics : (1) that the true and highest claims upon office are the character and capacity that best qualify a person to discharge its duties ; (2) that common justice requires the application of a fair public test for ascertaining these qualifications ; and (3) that he who thus presents the highest evidence of fitness has morally, and should have legally, a *right* to receive the office. They ceased to reason upon these maxims years ago. The public conviction has become so decided and outspoken that no law seemed necessary to insure obedience to them, and none has ever been enacted[1] which requires it, or even examinations and competitions for the civil service ; these latter resting, so far as any coercive element is concerned, on the orders in Council, the demands of public opinion, and the conditions of retiring allowances. From the very outset, proceedings under the new system have been regarded by British statesmen as an agency of higher education in public affairs. It has been treated as but an act of justice to the people that they should be kept informed of the manner in which the appointing power is exercised. "The examinations should not only be rightly conducted, but they should be shown to the whole country to be rightly conducted ; and every amount of publicity should be given to them."[2] "I think it would be very advantageous that every thing in the matter of appointment and promotion or transfers should be known to the public."[3] That publicity has been attained ; and clear and ample reports and the records of the Civil Service Commission leave no use of the appointing power,

---

[1] Except for British India.

[2] 2 Report Committee 1873 and '4, pp. 105 and 106. Evidence Sir Charles Trevelyan.

[3] Report 1873 and '4, vol. i. p. 133. Evidence Chancellor of the Exchequer.

and no reasons upon which it has proceeded, concealed
from the knowledge or the criticism of the people.    Those
exercises of official authority are treated as no more party
or official secrets than the use made of the seats in the
public schools or of the moneys in the national treasury.    This opening of the public mind to a knowledge of
the morals and the logic of administration, while overawing
official favoritism within the departments, has educated the
people up to a higher sense of their rights and their duties.
And may we not well ask ourselves whether this salutary
publicity—this new educational and purifying influence in
politics—is possible only where the executive wears a crown,
where the senate is hereditary, where privileged classes and a
state church are tolerated?  In a republic, must all such affairs
be shrouded in mystery, in order that they may the more easily
be made subservient to partisan interests?  Must they be
planned in secrecy, and be carried into effect with defiance, as
a part of the irresponsible discretion and privileges of republican officials?    However that may be, I repeat that this publicity in Great Britain has developed a public opinion so discriminating and stern that examinations and competitions
stand unchallenged and impregnable within the ramparts of its
high sanction alone.    No minister or party would now dare
affront that opinion.    Indeed, a party might almost as safely
discriminate on political grounds in levying taxes, or a ministry in collecting them, awarding contracts, or allowing suffrage,
as to make nominations or removals in the civil service for
partisan reasons or in violation of reform principles or methods.
There have been striking examples of the power of that
opinion to bring ministers and cabinets to obedience, in which
members of Parliament, once so hostile, appear to have made
haste to speak for the new and popular system.    When, for
example, a few years since, Mr. Layard was thought to have
been appointed Minister to Spain in violation of the civil service system, the cabinet was speedily forced to vindicate the
regularity of its action before Parliament.    In the late promotion of a Mr. Pigott to a very subordinate place, Lord
Beaconsfield was believed to have departed from the spirit of the
civil service rules.    So vigorous was the protest, so fierce

was the assault of the press, so many of his own party refused to sustain him, that his administration suffered its first defeat. A vote of censure was carried against him upon the question raised, in a House in which his party had a majority of from sixty to a hundred votes. So intense was the feeling that "the House of Commons was deserted, and the members flocked to hear what their former colleague could say in the House of Lords." It was only by a frank and elaborate speech, in self vindication, showing that the charge was unwarranted, that the prime minister saved himself from the necessity of resignation. A well-informed American, long resident in England, referring to this event, says that "the point for us is that civil service reform is so much a reality in this country that one of the strongest governments that England has ever seen suffered a defeat in the house, because it was supposed, in a single instance, to have overriden the settled principle which now controls appointments to office—the principle that fitness for office, and not need of office nor party service, shall be considered in the nomination of public servants."[1] In these facts we may not only see how soon, by proper means of education, a debauched public opinion may be elevated into a conservative moral power, but we may be reminded that, in our own country also, the time has been when offices could not be used as partisan spoils, without an equal shock to the public sense of duty and justice. For "when the Democratic party came into power with Mr. Jefferson, the removals were few—so few that single cases excited a sense of wrong through a whole State."[2] "Then, the dismissal of a few inconsiderable officers, on party grounds as was supposed, was followed by a general burst of indignation; but now the dismissal of thousands, when it is openly avowed that the public offices are the spoils of the victors, produces scarcely a sensation."[3] *These facts show us that the moral tone of politics, to which the British people have risen, is only that of our last generation, from which we have fallen.*

The evidence of the permanency of the new system appears to be not less decisive than that of its popularity. Sir

[1] Letter of Mr. Smalley, New York *Tribune*, August 4, 1877.
[2] Woolsey's Political Science, vol. ii., p. 561.
[3] Speech J. C. Calhoun in U. S. Senate in 1835.

Charles Trevelyan,[1] —now enjoying public respect in his retirement, and who, I believe, is justly thought to have exhibited more practical statesmanship than the whole body of parliamentary monopolists and partisan manipulators who sneered at and obstructed the new system in its earlier stages—says, "You cannot lay too much stress upon the fact that the making of public appointments by open competition has been accepted by all our political parties, and there is no sign of any movement against it from any quarter."[2]    In the fact of his holding the high positions of head of the British Treasury and leader of the Conservatives in the House of Commons, (where he faithfully carries into effect his own reform methods), Sir Stafford Northcote illustrates not less the abiding nature of the reform toward which he has so much contributed than he does the feeling of the people toward its authors.    The declaration of John Bright, who may speak for the Liberals, to the effect that "it would be impossible to go back to the old system,"[3] has already been quoted.    But there are assurances of the stability of the reform methods far beyond what can be shown by examples or on the authority of great names.    They are to be found in the sentiment, now pervading every class of respectable society, that patronage-mongering by members of Parliament is ignominious and disgraceful ; that bartering in nominations and prostituting the appointing power for selfish or partisan purposes is a reprehensible breach of official trust ; that it is not less an act of justice than of wisdom to give the offices to those shown in a fair contest to be best qualified to hold them.    While parties have ceased to look to patronage or spoils as sources of strength, and no man or woman of respectability can be found to defend the old system, all the young men and women who have so much as a common-school education—all honest persons of the rising generation who have the capacity and attainments which justify a hope of reaching even the lowest appointments—recognizing no party issue in the subject, stand to-

[1] Already mentioned as having, with Sir Stafford Northcote, first presented the merit system in a formal report in 1854.
[2] See his second letter in Appendix A.
[3] See his letter in Appendix A.

gether for a system which has conferred new honors upon
learning and a higher dignity upon simple manhood.    They
now comprehend that every office, which has been bestowed as
patronage or spoils, was so much pillaged from the just inheritance of good citizens and so much capital added to the corruption fund of partisan politics.    These facts are not without
an important bearing upon our affairs.    Those worthy citizens who have so little faith in public virtue and intelligence
that they fear a reform can never gain strength enough to withstand its natural enemies, unless it be first made a part of the
constitution itself—who excuse themselves and their party for
not beginning it from a fear that the other party coming
into power would overthrow it[1]—may perhaps find encouragement in such results, and be able to see that justice and wisdom are not without power even in politics.    They may begin to comprehend that the great principles involved in administrative reform, when fairly presented, take a strong hold
of the public mind (without the support of laws or of constitutions), because they have inherent powers of vitality
which appeal alike to the general sense of justice and to
every individual's conception of his own personal rights.
Efficiently, therefore, as a party might support these principles,
the conditions of their success are in no small degree independent of the action of parties or the sympathy of legislators.
Indeed, that is one of the most significant and encouraging

---

[1] What measure is there at issue between the parties against the adoption
of which such a reason would not with equal force apply ?  Each party is
ready to reverse any measures of its adversary if the public will sustain it
in doing so.   But here again the experience of Great Britain is instructive ;
and in the triumph of the merit system there, over both parties, we find evidence that such want of faith in the intelligence and virtue of the people is
without warrant ; unless indeed we believe that those qualities are higher
in Great Britain than in the United States.   In the light of that experience,
is there much reason to doubt that—when, in 1874 members of Congress
betrayed the reform policy to which they and the party in power were committed—if the President had stood firmly for it, and had withstood the
patronage-mongers and partisans who beset him as stubbornly as he withstood his enemies on the battle-field, he would have prevented its temporary
abandonment, and might, by adhering to its principles, have averted a great
loss of support by the dominant party, and have established additional
claims to the gratitude of his country ?

lessons of British experience which shows the power of these principles, when once in the mind of the intelligent and independent voters, to arrest the arrogance of politicians and to bring members of Parliament to their duty. " Large as were the numbers who profited by the former system, . . . those left out . . . were still larger and included some of the best classes of our population : . . . professional persons of every kind, lawyers, ministers of religion of every persuasion, schoolmasters, farmers, shopkeepers, etc., . . . who rapidly took the idea of the new institution . . . as a valuable privilege. . . . Whatever may have been the individual sentiments of members of the House of Commons, they received such pressing letters from their constituents as *obliged them to vote straight.*" [1] Patronage became odious from the moment it was exposed, and fell mortally wounded by its first defeat.

IV. If, from these considerations relating to the stability and trustworthiness of the new system, we turn to the principles and methods upon which it proceeds, interesting questions at once present themselves as to their adaptation to our social condition and form of government. It would be little less than an insult to the intelligence of the reader to gravely argue that a policy, which would bring into places of public trust the moral character and the intelligence needed for the proper discharge of their duties, is at least as appropriate and needful in a republic as in a monarchy. Is a monarchy with a state church creed at the door of every office, with an hereditary executive which is the source of all office, with its Upper House of Parliament whose members take their seats as an inheritance, with birthright and property as the basis of political and social privileges, with its vast and imposing system of ranks, honors, and decorations—the natural friend and supporter of such a policy? And is a republic—which proclaims justice, personal equality, and common rights as its cardinal principles, which, discarding property and birthright, makes virtue, liberty, and intelligence its chief reliance—a sort of natural enemy which should look upon that policy with dis-

[1] Letter Sir Charles Trevelyan, Appendix A.

trust, if not with dread? If any among ourselves are so partisan or so prejudiced as not to be able to see that every step which monarchies have taken in the way of that policy is repugnant to the main principles of their original form of government, while it is, on the other hand, in complete harmony with our institutions, English statesmen at least are not so blind. They comprehend the fitness of the merit system for the reformation of our abuses. " I have long been struck by the singular suitableness of our new but well-tried institution, of making public appointments by open competition, for the correction of some of the worst results of the United States political system." [1] We have already seen that the merit system, as established in Great Britain, has been built upon the fundamental principles of common right, individual worth, and universal justice. " All persons have an *equal right* to be candidates if they are fit; . . . we consider the *right* of competing should be open to all persons of a given age; . . . if you do not concede that right, and make it accessible, you do *injustice*, first to the public service and then to Her Majesty's subjects generally," [2] is the language of the British statesmen who devised and put that system in practice, and the view of the people who sustain it. Are these principles—are such ideas of right and justice—safe and appropriate to be carried into practice in a monarchy, but repugnant and dangerous in a republic? After they have achieved a victory in the mother country over so many centuries of official despotism and aristocratic monopoly—while they are now being applied in every quarter of the globe where English-speaking people are under a royal flag—is it fit and natural that they should be distrusted and denied—that, in the true feudal spirit, patronage and spoils should still be allowed as the perquisites of officials— in the leading republic of the world? The standard of official duty, in the light of which these ideas of justice and right are to be carried into effect, is, according to these statesmen, this : " Public office is a solemn trust, and one of its most important conditions is to choose the best possible men for the different places." Shall we look upon this as an obligation of

---

[1] Letter Sir Charles Trevelyan, Appendix A.

[2] See ante, pp. 190 and 227.

official life fit to be observed in a monarchy, but which officers
in a republic should be at liberty to disregard as inconsistent
with the constitution of their country or too high for the
spirit of its politics and the morals of its administration.[1]
Looking to the ultimate aims of the new system, we find
them not to rest in mere economy or efficiency or in anything
within the circles of administration, but to comprehend the prosperity and the elevation of the people at large. "I am not
indifferent to the consideration that offices have become the
patrimony of the *poorer part* of the middle class, or even, perhaps, of the working class," says a British statesman at the
head of his party in Parliament.[2] "I should regret that any
man should be debarred . . . who possessed energy and
ability enough to enable him, *in a humble position of life*, to
succeed at the competitive examinations," says the Viceroy of
India,[3] while commending the new system in that dominion.
Are these national aims and sympathies appropriate to be encouraged in the theories and the very processes of royal administration, but such as a republic may wisely discard for the
greater blessings of favoritism, patronage, and spoils—for a
system which thrusts back or crushes every poor and humble
applicant for an office or a place under the government, however high his character or ample his capacity, unless he promises servility, has voters at his back or influence at his bidding?

We have seen members of the British Cabinet refusing
patronage in order that the places which they would be enabled to hand over to competition might become the prizes of
popular education. Eminent statesmen have sustained the new
system the more heartily because it was seen to be favorable to
the general instruction of the people, "to which it has given
a marvellous stimulus."[4] It would be an affront to the
reader's intelligence to ask the question whether the encour-

[1] Whatever answer politicians may give, the Supreme Court of the United
States has declared that "the theory of our government is that all public
stations are trusts, and that those clothed with them are to be animated in
the discharge of their duties solely by considerations of right, justice, and
the public good."—Trist *v.* Child, 21 Wallace R. 450.

[2] Ante, p. 324.                        [3] Ante, p. 252.

[4] See pp. 190, 201, 214, *note*, and see Sir Charles Trevelyan's letter, Ap
pendix A.

agement of popular education is in the spirit of republican institutions. But may we not well pause and consider · in presence of the fact that Great Britain is gaining upon us, and that several monarchies have already surpassed us, in the education of the people, and of the further fact that the ratio of well-educated persons in official life has been growing less in the United States under our partisan spoils system— whether we can longer afford to hand over the offices, as the prizes of partisan contests and the perquisites of officials? And especially can we do this at a time when foreign States, giving new vigor to the means by which they have distanced us in the race, are, through superior officers and a growing commerce, more and more placing us at a disadvantage, and enhancing the distinction and the dignity of the kind of government which they represent, in every quarter of the globe?

To execute that "solemn trust" of official life, to select the best men for public places in the light of the highest tests of fitness, to secure humble citizenship its equal right to office according to its capacity, to thus make the orderly processes of administration in themselves a daily example before the eyes of the people of the justice and integrity of the government and a powerful force in aid of education and morality, it was first necessary that the king should surrender, or at least forbear, the exercise of that haughty and absolute prerogative of selecting officers at his pleasure which every English sovereign had wielded from the foundation of the monarchy ; that dukes, and noblemen of every class, should waive that vast influence over minor appointments which for ages had been in great part the patrimony of their children and the strength and prestige of their order in the State ; that members of Parliament should surrender a patronage, won in contests not wholly foreign to the progress of liberty, which for more than a century had been held as the unchallenged perquisite of their predecessors. And now that all this has been done—that the old feudal and class barriers have been broken down, so that simple manhood and womanhood, unobstructed by monopolists, stand with all the liberty and equality of their just and natural relations before the law in the mother country and in all her provinces—now that her

25

politics have risen practically to the principles upon which our fathers framed our constitution — is it for us, upon a new construction of that instrument and a degrading theory foisted into our administration, to take the lead in presenting republicanism before the world as the only kind of government, accepted by a leading nation, whose administration is held together by spoils, and whose officers require patronage as a condition of serving their country? I am unable to find any reason, in the sentiment of our people or the nature of our government, why the members of the American Congress, any more than the members of the British Parliament, need patronage and spoils, or can justify the use of them, to bring about their elections, to inspire their patriotism, or to reward their fidelity. But if it be too much to hope that congressmen will ever lead in a reform, the fundamental conditions of which are that they surrender the patronage they have usurped and no longer violate the Constitution by leaving their own sphere to invade the Executive—may we not at least believe that they will not again refuse appropriations? May we not expect that, not less patriotic than members of the British Parliament, they will give a free field, and vote the necessary moneys for that systematic reform in administration which seems in this country to be, as plainly as in Great Britain, within the province of the Executive to inaugurate? Another of the great and salutary principles of the new system, which, if in any way dependent upon the form of government, would seem to be peculiarly congenial to the more liberal institutions, is that which it applies to promotions in the public service. It requires that they shall not be regardless of capacity and well tested fidelity. They must not depend on partisan services, or the ambition of high officials, or the interests of patronage monopolists or of politicians of any sort. When, in the great report of 1860, a distinguished parliamentary committee (of which such men as the present Chancellor of the Exchequer, Robert Lowe, John Bright, Lord Houghton, and Lord Derby were members) declared it to be one of the great purposes of their appointment " to encourage industry and foster merit by teaching all public servants to look forward to promotion according to their desert, and to expect the highest prizes in the service if they can qualify themselves for them," they touched upon a subject of profound importance, which vitally affects fidelity, efficiency, and economy in the public service. I have no space for pointing out the salutary effects which such a rule faithfully executed in our service would be sure to produce. What industry, and consequently what economy, would it not encourage? What worthy ambition would it not inspire and crown with honor? What imbecility and indolence would it not rebuke? What injustice and favoritism, in superiors, would it not arrest? What new life and aspiration would it not breathe into the dreary, servile atmosphere which pervades offices and departments, precisely in the ratio that merit is without recognized claims to a reward, that the reasons for advancement are shrouded in mystery, that official favoritism and partisan interests are believed to determine the position and consequently the salaries of every officer in the service. More than fifty years have elapsed since the head of the British Treasury set the example,[2] still followed, of surrendering patronage in the interest of merit, in the matter of promotions, in that vast department. It has been a little longer, perhaps, since an American Secretary of the Treasury for the first time violated the rights of merit, in the interest of patronage and spoils, in his great office. It is a part of the issue for the people to decide, whether we are to continue the downward, or resume the upward road, in the future? Whether those holding official places under a republic are to have their manhood respected and their merits rewarded as justly and surely as they would be under every enlightened monarchy in the world, or are to be exposed every moment to the perils of caprice and the humiliations of unregulated and irresponsible authority? Whether every hour they are to be liable to be taxed without limit, and removed without hearing and without cause? Whether, in short, those in our public service are to enjoy the rights due to merit and the liberty of speech due to freemen, or their relations are to have more of the character

---

[1] See ante, p. 220.　　　　[2] See p. 156.

which belonged to feudal dependents centuries ago than of
that which befits the representatives of the justice and intelligence of the foremost republic of the globe ?  I cannot think
that any principle or interest of our government stands in the
way of promotions being so regulated that, in our service, as in
the British service and in that of all the leading States, they
shall be the encouragement and the reward of the highest virtues of official life.'

There is but one other great principle involved in the reform methods to which reference need be made.  It is that
which declares the patronage and spoils, which a partisan system places at the disposal of parties, are not essential to their
greatest usefulness, but rather tend to degrade and enfeeble
them.  It should be no matter of surprise if, in a generation
reared under that system and little accustomed to consider
the attitude and influence of great parties when acting
independently of spoils, there should be found not a few
candid persons who hesitate over that principle, and do not
see their way to its adoption.  An adequate presentation
of the subject would require a whole chapter, and it is not
within the scope of this work to comment upon our own
party history.  Let it be borne in mind that the merit system does not interfere with the freedom of choice on party
ground in any popular election ; that it leaves unimpaired
the power of the party majority to control the enactment
of all laws ; that the officers its majorities have elected will
have the right of instruction and control—according to
law, and for the purpose of executing its policy—of the
great body of civil servants by whom the laws are carried
into effect.  The system thus gives to parties the broadest
field of discretion and responsibility.  It enables the will of
the people to be carried into effect everywhere from the highest centres of political action—from the Cabinet and Con-

---

¹ If it be said that quite as many of those in our public service violate
official propriety and diginity, by excessive partisan speech and action, as
by servility and hypocrisy, the answer is that both forms of abuse, are the
result of the same enslaving system, producing opposite effects upon different natures.  A tenure dependent upon merit would equally remedy both
forms of the evil.

gress, through every grade of office and every form of juri-
diction—to the humblest public servant and the remotest territory. Whatever parties can now do to uphold and carry
into effect a sound national policy, to develop and express
the sentiments of the people upon any question of politics,
to invite or honorably reward patriotic service in the interest
of good government, to secure true and honest suffrage, to elect
worthy men to office, to rebuke treachery or to reform abuses—
all these things they can do as freely and far more certainly
under the merit system of administration. But the prostitution of the functions and honors of the State for partisan ends,
bribery by the promise of offices, the huckstering of employment on the public works for votes, feudal tyranny and
pillage in the form of arbitrary taxation of official salaries,
despotic patronage in the hands of legislators, all the forms
of partisan interference with the internal affairs of departments by which discipline is impaired, economy made impossible, promotions are degraded into favoritism, and unworthy
henchmen are foisted upon the public treasury—these abuses,
one and all—that system, faithfully enforced, would in great
measure bring to an end. The good effects of this theory
of parties and of such principles in the execution of the laws,
not only within the departments, but upon the people and
upon parties themselves, have been demonstrated in Great
Britain by an amount of evidence which has there placed the
subject beyond discussion. The question is, whether there is
any reason why similar effects would not flow from the same
principles applied to our politics? In other words, is it not
practicable for great parties in a republic to express the will
of the people in regard to public affairs and to serve the nation, as justly and efficiently as in a monarchy, without any
more reliance upon corruption, patronage, and spoils? The
same history which has shown us that rulers and parties, in
an old monarchy, long ago devised and put in practice, in
forms more aggravated than we have ever allowed, the varied
kinds of proscriptions, frauds, and prostitution known in our
politics, and others yet more flagitious—which has shown us
how parties and the partisan system began and the uses to
which every variety of spoils and patronage may be put—has

also shows the inherent inability of these devices of corruption to sustain a party or to meet the requirements of the higher sentiment in a free State. It has further shown us how such cases fell before the rising intelligence of an enlightened people. Upon a broad, historical review of the course of British affairs, Hallam declares that "government may safely rely on the reputation justly due to it;" and from the deepest experience of practical politics, Lord Granville declared in Parliament, in 1854, "that the time for a system of government by patronage was gone by." He also laid down the rule "that the true policy of a government was in appealing to the good sense and intelligence of the large classes of the community." [1] The appeal here meant was an appeal to the people to come forward and show themselves qualified for office without resorting to partisan coercions to compel its bestowal. Is not this appeal based on a faith and a policy upon which a republic as consistently and safely as a monarchy may act? Were not these the theories of our early statesmen, and are they not in the spirit of our constitution and our social life? When, in royal old England, feudalism and patronage and privilege have been laid so low, by the people's demand of common justice at the gates of office, that no man without the prescribed qualifications can pass those gates, though having in his veins the blood of all the Howards and at his back the influence of the whole bench of bishops and all the coronets that glitter on the heads of noblemen,—is that the time for this young nation of republican freemen to make a privileged class of its politicians, and feudal lords of its officials and partisan leaders, without whose consent, no man, however meritorious, can enter the public service of his country? Are we not as competent to make a reform, in the spirit of our institutions and according to the better precedents of our history, as the English people were

---

[1] "The recent utterances of leading statesmen and thinkers in England regarding the submission of questions of fundamental policy to a fairly educated people, as compared with the submissions of such questions simply to the most highly educated classes, are very striking." Address of Hon. Andrew D. White on Education and Political Science. February, 1879.

to make the same reform, which took away privileges as old as civilization in Great Britain and undermined theories and classes which every former generation had cherished? Consider further what is involved in the assumption that it is easier under a monarchy than under a republic—more in harmony with the political relations of the subjects of a king—for a party to forbear the use of proscription and corruption in carrying forward its policy. These may be accepted as the principal reasons why men act together in parties: 1. Patriotic devotion to the form of government or to the general welfare, which the party is believed to promote. 2. Interest in the success of a particular measure or policy. 3. Personal ambition for office or power. 4. Subserviency to the dominant public opinion. 5. Love of contention, excitement, and mere pride of victory. 6. Selfish expectation of direct personal gains. It is plain that it is only the latter and lower class of motives for acting with a party which would be weakened by the diminution of the bribes which it can hold out and the spoils which it can distribute. If it be true, therefore, that the application of the principle we are considering would impair the support given to parties in a republic more than it would in a monarchy, it must be because the corrupt elements are relatively stronger and the patriotic elements relatively weaker in the former than in the latter. Royalty, class distinction, aristocratic privileges must, consequently, be greater inspirations to patriotism and self-sacrifice than liberty, equality, common rights, or any thing upon which republican institutions are founded. If we hold such views, we may, with some consistency, fear that our parties will fall to pieces, and that citizens of a republic will refuse to serve their country, unless party managers are at liberty to pillage the officials in order to supply their treasuries, and to practice proscription and make merchandise of office in order to reward their henchmen. But, in that event, let us cease our grandiloquent talk about "the oppressed and downtrodden masses in the effete monarchies of the Old World," and about the people's glorious love of freedom and equality on our happy shores. Let us frankly admit that monarchy is the government most loved

and best served by the people—the government which alone
develops a truly self-sacrificing patriotism—while a republic
can command the services of its citizens only to the extent
that they are bribed and paid by offices and spoils.   If such
views are well founded, let us also be prepared for the gradual
decadence of republican States.   For, what is more certain, in
the great international rivalry of governments and institutions,
than that those will triumph which most attract to their support the virtues and higher sentiments of the people.   It can
only be in a world surrendered to chance, or under a civilization hastening to decay, that a political system which makes
its appeal to the baser motives of men can win the foremost
places in the competition of nations.

I have no space for more than an allusion to the fact that,
if the taking of the bribery and corruption fund out of party
politics should result in the more venal and rowdyish voters
keeping away from the polls—if a class of mercenary manipulators should not be so much busied in caucusses and conventions—British experience shows us that worthier citizens, which
a corrupt system repels, will more than fill any places left
vacant.   It also shows us that such citizens, for which a contest of principles has attractions, will give more virtue and
ability to political leadership than can ever be secured under
the system we tolerate.

V.  Dismissing the questions of principle involved in the
new system, we come to the practical effects which would be
likely to attend its adoption.   It not being within the scope of
this work to set forth the abuses in our administration, no attempt will be made to do more than indicate, in broad outline,
the changes the new system would bring about.   They have
been largely suggested already, and most of them are so plainly
deducible from the explanations made concerning the British
departments, that not much need be added.   Civil service
reform, though in its indirect effects a powerful aid to education, has for its more direct object the utilization, more effectively for the public good, of the virtue and intelligence
already existing.   But, with whatever success this may be

¹ See especially Chap. 30.

done, we may well believe that need will always exist in our politics for giving the utmost efficiency to all influences which directly mould character for higher ends. If faith in the better sentiments is an element in all true statesmanship, anticipations of any sudden or absolute purification of politics are evidences of weakness and inexperience. Great reforms are the slow growth of years.

The most important change which the merit system would at once bring about would be the breaking up of a pervading and pernicious monopoly, now held by party managers, by jobbers in politics, and by office-holders possessing (or usurping) the appointing power, which everywhere obtrudes itself between the people and all nominations for office and all public employment. This monopoly everywhere, in the departments and offices of the cities, of the States, and of the nation alike, imposes conditions in the interests of personal gain or partisan supremacy— and largely irrespective of personal worth—upon nearly every applicant for a public position. All the ways to offices and places, under the partisan spoils system, are through the narrow gates held by this vast monopoly, at which there is a degrading, secret, and corrupt competition of influence, to which these gates are opened. The surrender of independence and of liberty to serve the people faithfully are the toll. Free, public examinations, directed to subjects of essential knowledge for the public work, and open competitions of merit, to which no officer, party, or monopolist could prescribe the conditions of entry, would break up both this monopoly and the great trade in patronage and spoils. They would allow citizens a real freedom and equality in presenting their claims for office. They would deprive intrigue and partisan influence of their controlling power in politics. Better still, they would exhibit the methods of exercising the appointing power before the minds of the people in an aspect of justice and purity which would command their confidence and respect. No longer affiliated with intrigue, manipulation, and mere influence, that power would stand in alliance with industry, education and personal worth. It would be exercised without concealment. It would appear to the people as based on principle, as intended to reward capacity and character, as making ability to

discharge the duties of an office an essential condition of securing it. Where now there is secrecy, intrigue, uncertainty, and
consequently suspicion, distrust and ignorance, pervading and
darkening all the approaches and purlieus of office, and a dis-
orderly contention, in large measure only between the venal and
unscrupulous forces of politics, there would be openness of procedure and complete publicity of method. In place of the
secret contests of influence, there would be a public competition and a rivalry in presenting in the highest degree those
qualifications needed in official places—character that could not
be impeached—attainments that are in themselves evidence of
virtuous industry. The final decision of the appointing officers—which under the spoils system is based, so generally, on
the secret preponderance of menace and persuasion in the
interest of a motley throng of applicants—would, under the
new system, be required to be made as between only a few of
the more worthy persons to whom competition had reduced
the many applicants. And that decision would necessarily
have to stand upon public records, in writing, concerning the
character and capacity of each successful competitor, which
would remain as abiding evidence of the justice or injustice
of the final selection.[1]

As a natural consequence of arresting partisan control of
nominations and of subordinate administration generally, the
main causes would cease to exist which now hold together so
many active and mercenary cliques and " rings " in our politics. Without the power and the profit of such nominations
and control, and without the ability to collect party assessments any longer, their business and means of support would
come to an end together. They do not exist by reason of any
patriotic interest in public affairs, nor do they contribute to
any healthy activity or to the public enlightenment. It is
these combinations, managed by men of low moral tone and
mercenary aims, and their domineering influence upon elections which have driven worthy men from the polls and

---

[1] For example, the record of each of the hundreds of thousands of applicants who have been examined under the British Civil Service Commission,
has been preserved ; and the justice of every appointment made from among
them could be verified to-day as well as at the date of the examination.

brought politics into disgrace. When they are broken up, we shall have left only that legitimate popular action which directly concerns officers elected by the people and the principles by which the great parties may be divided.

In presidential elections, the introduction of the merit system would bring about changes too manifold and profound for description here. These elections would become true national contests, in which little beyond the personal worth of candidates and the principles and the policies of the rival parties would be involved. The filling of a very few high places would depend on the result : but the innumerable side issues of self-seeking and partisanship could no longer be made to trail the whole canvass in corruption. Those within the departments and offices would have the full liberty of citizens to express their opinions and to vote. They would not be forced, by fears of arbitrary removal, to prostitute their authority, or waste time needed in the public service, upon the servile work of partisan politics. They would no longer be compelled to invade the freedom of elections as a condition of holding their own places. Among the people at large, every question of principle, the devotion inspired by patriotism, the earnestness prompted by a cause believed to be righteous, whatever zeal comes from a true party spirit, and every honest interest that can be involved in political contests, would have a fair and open field. Such motives of action would be all the more effective in giving vigor to speech and drawing honest voters to the polls, because innumerable issues of corruption would have disappeared. They would be all the more powerful for good, because the expectations and intrigues of a million of claimants for a hundred thousand offices and places would not be involved, and the people would feel that the great question to be settled was not which party should capture the offices, but what policy should guide the nation.

The same causes which, by giving official places to merit, would deprive officers and party leaders of their irresponsible control of selections and appointments, would also make political leadership and official life less attractive to self-seeking and corrupt men. Those causes would also make public affairs more attractive to all patriotic and high-minded citizens. It has been one of the most lamentable tendencies of our spoils system to hand over political leadership and office to a class of persons quite inferior to the men who held such positions in the earlier years of the government. As a natural result, we have seen a class of politicians become powerful in high places, who have not taken (and who by nature are not qualified to take) any large part in the social and educational life of the people. Politics have tended more and more to become a trade, or separate occupation. High character and capacity have become disassociated from public life in the popular mind. We see small bands of trained partisans, who, while servile to officials, yet domineer over the great parties. British experience warrants the belief that rigid tests of merit, enforced against every applicant for office, will aid powerfully in restoring the old sympathy and union between the politics and the ability and worth of the nation. How can we expect political morality to improve under a system which makes the higher officers the most interested in preserving existing abuses at the same time that it surrenders to them ample power for continuing these abuses at their pleasure?

It requires some effort of the imagination to get a clear idea of the manifold effects in detail—of the profound influences upon the relations of citizens to parties and to office—of the stimulus to education and to independent, manly thought, speech, and action—which such an exchange of systems would cause. Where now we see all thought, all hope, all influence, all effort, concentrated upon partisan cliques, upon jobbers in influence, upon official and unofficial patronage-mongers, upon what good-natured citizens may be unduly persuaded to recommend in aid of an unworthy office-seeker, henchman, or dependent—we should see exertions to educate one's self up to the standards needed for official duty, concern to keep one's character above danger of attack at a public competition, encouragement to independence in politics, study of whatever would contribute to the acquirement of a just distinction for ability and efficiency in the discharge of official duty, upon which all promotion would depend. With the greater ability and higher character which such improved methods would bring into the public service, its self-respect and its public estimation could not fail to be enhanced.[1] Our politics would tend to rise from the degradation in which vicious and corrupt methods have involved them, and to take the position befitting a science which deals with the greatest affairs of a nation and the profoundest human interest of a people.

Some brief explanations will give definiteness to these general statements and to the practical methods of the new system. The secretaries, the foreign ministers, the judges, and some other high officers will, it may be assumed, always be appointed without examination or competition. In dealing with this limited number of conspicuous places, it would be practicable for the President to become well informed of the qualifications of the candidates, and for the people to take notice of his action in each case. And therefore examinations would be no more necessary than they would be appropriate for such selections. At the other end of the official scale, there would be the small postmasters, numerous isolated officials, and the clerks in various small offices, as to which there would probably be no examinations, or only those of a general character, conducted in a less formal manner and without competition.[2] Between these extremes, there would be the great body of the subordinate officers, from 50,-000 to 60,000, perhaps, in all, to whom examinations and (generally) competition would extend. It is the persons who fill these offices who would be brought within the range of appropriate tests of qualification and rules of procedure. It is in connection with efforts to obtain these offices that the greater part of the deception, the official and partisan intrigue, the fraud and corruption of our politics take place. The hopes and the profits of success are sufficient to keep in a state of feverish and mercenary activity innumerable bodies of politicians who render no real service to the people, and who, but

---

[1] See Letter of Sir Charles Trevelyan on this point, Appendix A.

[2] It is very plain that the need of competition in any office or department depends, in large measure, upon the number of clerks being too great for the head of the office to know the merits of each applicant for appointment and promotion, and upon the amount of partisan and other corrupt pressure applied for foisting unworthy persons into its official places.

for chance of corrupt gain, would never take any active part in public affairs.

A general Civil Service Board would supervise the examinations, to be conducted in convenient parts of the Union upon a uniform plan. These competitors found worthy would be certified to local officers and to the great departments at Washington, so as at all times to enable selections to be made for appointments with due reference both to the just claims of every section and to the needs of every office.[1] From the persons thus shown to be qualified, the President and the heads of departments at Washington, as well as officers having the right of nomination in local offices, would readily make their selections without interference from politicians, without agitation of the community, and without disturbance of the business of congress or of legislatures. The whole duty and responsibility would in practice, as they do in the theory of the constitution, rest with the executive department to which they relate. That department would therefore be relieved of the demoralizing necessity of surrendering to, or of deciding between, any of the rival claims of factions or of favorites; and it would no longer be besieged by an army of importunate office-seekers, backed by high officials and influential politicians of every sort. The executive would be, for the first time in this generation, at liberty to give the attention needed for the proper working of the departments. It would also be possible to separate executive affairs from those legislative questions with which congressional patronage has so disastrously embroiled them.

Examinations and competitions would not only supply worthy persons from whom appointments could at all times be readily and safely made, but would be a part of a system which would exclude appointments from persons not thus shown to be competent. It would therefore have as salutary an effect upon the legislative department as upon the executive. Those candidates for Congress who might be capable of such a pros-

---

[1] The practicability of this method was being tested with success, when Congress deserted the reform policy under President Grant; and it has been found satisfactory, after a trial of more than twenty-five years, in Great Britain.

titution, having no longer power to give places in custom-houses or other public offices, could no more pledge and barter them with effect for votes, speeches, or influence, in aid of their elections. They would have to go before the people on the policy of their party and their own worth as men. Many great fountains of corruption would thus be closed. The most unscrupulous candidates would no longer be able to gain advantages over the best, in the ratio of the numbers they bribed or deceived by corrupt promises of offices and places. Nor would the effects be less salutary after members of congress had reached Washington. For there, also, they would be without power to barter in patronage, and without opportunity for fawning or threatening successfully in the departments, in aid of their supporters or themselves. But they would be left free, in the dignity of their high stations, and able, in a manly and independent manner, to discharge their only function—the high function of making laws for a great nation. They might find time for acting upon the thousands of bills that year after year remain upon their tables, and for dealing thoughtfully with the great interests of the nation which are now neglected. No longer liable to be charged, however unjustly, with prostituting duty to patronage, they would be exalted in the respect and confidence of the people and of each other.

It ought, however, to be clearly perceived that it does not follow (because the members of the legislature are to give up their usurped patronage and lose their corrupt influence), that the executive would be aggrandized under the new system. Such would not be the fact. Good citizens would be the only gainers. The executive would be rather limited in its arbitrary discretion—curtailed in opportunities to act selfishly. For it would be required to appoint only from the most worthy among the people, as shown by the examinations. It would, therefore, be only justice and the sanctions of official fidelity, which would be made stronger, and only a selfish and capricious favoritism which would be made weaker. Justice would advance upon official discretion to do wrong and limit its range. The President, not less than members of Congress and other high officials, would be compelled to surrender his secret and unpatriotic favoritism. The new system is decentralizing. It is democratic and discriminating to the last degree. It not only says to every official, it is your duty to appoint the fittest man, but, in a measure, it compels him to do so. It not only takes away the opportunity of selecting the unworthy, but it enables the people, by their own acts, to determine the conditions of a proper choice from among those most competent. In other words, the examinations, by showing who are the most worthy, put limits to the arbitrary discretion of nominating the unworthy. To that extent, the people themselves would aid the executive in doing its duty.

British statesmen speak of the position of members of Parliament under the old system as "a double bondage from which they were at once liberated when the junior appointments were opened to competition;"[1] and there is abundant evidence that such a relief would not be less welcome to all high-toned members of Congress than it was to all high-toned members of Parliament.[2] It is but justice to believe that most members of Congress, who consent to perform the ignominious and demoralizing work of office brokers and patronage-mongers, do so only because, not having studied the methods by which the legislators of other great nations have risen above such servility, they have accepted an inherited usage as a public necessity. They would, undoubt-

---

[1] See Appendix A, Letter Sir Charles Trevelyan.

[2] In a debate in the House, in 1869, a Representative declared that " it is no more a part of a Representative's duty to seek and dispose of executive offices than to solicit pardons for traitors or condemned criminals. . . . If, as a matter of personal or political favor, he goes to the State Department to beg a consulate, or perhaps something higher, . . . he is made to feel . . . that he surrenders his independence when he accepts the gift;" and in a debate in 1870, another member used this language : " I appeal to the members of the House, if it is not one of the greatest curses of the position of a member of Congress that there are continual demands made on his time and patience by persons whom it is utterly impossible for him to satisfy, who demand that he shall secure office for them. The enemies we make are disappointed office-seekers almost exclusively." Report U. S. Civil Service Commission, April, 1874, pp. 17 and 18. Still, the people will, doubtless, be more impressed with the injustice of burdens thus cruelly put upon members of Congress, if they shall more generally manifest their courage and patriotism by speaking out plainly against them, and by vigorous efforts to throw them off.

edly, welcome a reform which would as much enlarge their own freedom as it would their ability to serve the people with advantage. And if there shall be members deaf to the calls of duty and patriotism, they have only to act on the lessons of partisan selfishness. In 1871, Vice-President Wilson declared in the Senate (having reference to the patronage of representatives), that "looking over the country this year, and I have taken some little pains to learn the facts, I believe that a large majority of the districts lost to the administration party in the House of Representatives, were lost on account of bad appointments made in the districts, and by the disappointment of men who were turned out of office or wanted to get into office."[1]

We may also see in these facts how such changes would contribute not less to keeping the great departments within their constitutional spheres of duty—and therefore to the counterpoise and stability of the government itself—than they would to the dignity and manhood of official life and to the chances of men of a scrupulous sense of honor at the elections.

I have no space to explain—if it be not too clear for explanation—that the same methods and principles are as applicable to governors and members of the legislature, and to mayors and aldermen of cities, in the exercise of the appointing power, as they are to the President and to members of Congress. It needs but little reflection to comprehend what a mass of corruption and intrigue would be suppressed, and what superior officers, State and municipal, might be secured, by enforcing examinations for fitness and by selecting, for the subordinate officials of the States and the cities, only those who should win in competition. And what encouragement would not be given to fidelity and efficiency by providing that all but the very highest positions should be filled by promotions from the lower places? The first city that shall put in practice rigid and honest examinations and competitions of character and qualifications for admission to its clerkships, and require the higher places (below that of mayor and perhaps two or three other officers) to be filled by competitive promotions from among the subordinates, will make an era in

---

[1] Report U. S. Civil Service Commission, April, 1874, p. 74.

26

city affairs. It will be equally salutary in reducing expenses, in suppressing a demoralizing and partisan intermeddling, and in giving respectability and efficiency to municipal administration. Who can estimate the advantage of suppressing the useless and pernicious partisan machinery now operated in our municipalities, for the purpose of controlling local nominations and officials in the interest of patronage and spoils? And can it be doubted that open competition would cause that suppression? That municipal government in Great Britain is more efficient and less affected by official corruption than in the United States, is well known. We have only to refer to facts already cited to learn the salutary effect of such methods of reform in her cities.[1]

In the light of these explanations, it is hardly necessary to point out how naturally and inevitably the administration of our custom-houses and post-offices would rise above servility to partisan interests, upon the enforcement of a merit system of office. The bands of manipulators, who so generally dominate them, would lose their control of nominations, removals, and promotions, and with it the power to levy party assessment. Their occupation and their income would be gone. Appointments, promotions, and removals would cease to be mere appendages to popular elections, and would go on as a part of an orderly procedure, managed within the offices and not in the partisan caucuses or cliques. Neither senators nor representatives, neither governors nor other State officers, would be disturbed by the ordinary administrative duties, or be able to meddle effectively with their due performance. Unless the experience of all other nations should be belied, better administration and economy would soon give the new system a strong hold upon the confidence of the people.[2] I am convinced there is no need that the places in our revenue or postal administration should be the prizes of partisan politics, or that the public buildings should be the fortresses of the dominant party. For a whole generation, there has been little more politics in a British custom-house, or in the cus-

---

[1] See ante, pp. 157 and 158.
[2] See Letter Sir Charles Trevelyan. Appendix A.

tom-houses of any leading nation in Europe, than in court-
or colleges. And it is very plain that no political principles
and no conditions appropriate for the interference of parties
are involved in the ministerial business of collecting the revenues according to law and the instructions of the Secretary.
The duty and the discretion are the same, to whatever party
the collector belongs. He has, in the view of the constitution,
and should have in fact, no control over the policy of the administration. It is only our partisan spoils system, the like of
which has not been tolerated by any other great nation for a
century, which has prostituted the revenue and postal services
and made them the sources of scandals which are the shame and
the peril of our people at home and their opprobrium in foreign countries. It is that system which, in a single year, has
brought more partisan and mercenary intrigue, more incompetency, more extravagance, scandal, and corruption into the
New York Custom House alone, than have existed, in a whole
decade, in both the Customs and Inland Revenue Services
of Great Britain united.

Another evil from which the adoption of the merit system
would indirectly, but not less surely, bring great relief, is that
of too numerous elections and too short terms on the part of
elected officers, especially of an inferior grade. Nothing has
more significantly illustrated the growth and predominance of
partisan theories and habits in this country, during this generation, than the many officers originally appointable which are
now elective. It was natural that the people should think
their direct choice would secure better officers than the spoils
system of appointment. It was natural that when political
management became a sort of trade, of which offices, places,
and promotions were the capital stock, and the elections
supplied the profits, there should arise a class of politicians
directly interested in increasing the number of those elections.
Laws and constitutions were changed in the interest of frequent elections until most of the judicial and administrative
places in the States and municipalities, and not a few mere
clerkships, were not only made elective, but the terms were
made so short that adequate experience was impossible. It
has even been seriously proposed to throw the choice of the

many thousands of postmasters into the turmoil of elections which now burden and disgust the people. The many evils which have been the consequences of these measures, I need not stop to point out. The confusion, the vast expense, the corrupt partisan activity, the inability to judge of the merits of candidates, the refusals to vote, the disgust and despair (especially in cities) which have been thus caused are well known. No nation not tolerating a partisan spoils system has been thus tormented or has thus departed from all sound principles. It cannot, I think, be doubted that the people would never have made such radical changes, had it not been for the prostitution of the appointing power.[1] Nor need we doubt that the proper measures of relief would speedily follow the elevation of that power. It was not more elections which the people wanted, but more certainty that worthy men would be made officers. So rash and expensive a proceeding—bringing into play the whole machinery of caucus nominations—as that of calling upon a community to ballot for town, village, and city postmasters, would probably never be proposed to any people not made desperate by a corrupt and partisan system of appointments.

One other effect of the merit system is too important not to be noticed—the indirect effect of bringing able and self-reliant young men and women, who have stood highest in competitions, into the departments and local offices. They would soon create an atmosphere of intelligence, thoughtfulness, and independence, which, in itself, would make it very difficult to treat such offices as the asylums, or the citadels of partisan politics. They would come in on their own merits, and would owe fealty and incline to be servile to no one. They would be more ready to expose abuses, and more inclined to assert and defend the rights and manhood of those who serve the public, than the dependent appointees of patronage monopolists ever

---

[1] Allusion has already been made to the fact that the people are becoming tired of these short terms of office. New York has lately extended the term of her governor to three years, that of some of her police justices to eight years, and that of her judges from eight to fourteen years. Several States have not only extended the tenure of various officers, but have made the sessions of their legislatures biennial.

can be. The people would rejoice to see their government befriending education and honoring worth and capacity in the selection of its agents. Their pride and patriotism would be all the greater, when in every official place they beheld a man or a woman whose very presence proclaimed, not the success of official or partisan influence in secret ways, but the victory of personal merit, won by its own strength in open and manly contest with all who chose to compete. Office would rise in public respect; and government itself would have a higher dignity in the eyes of those who saw it spurning servility, while seeking the service of the ablest and worthiest among its citizens. With better and abler men in the subordinate places, mere politicians—mere strangers to its business, of any sort—would have a hard time indeed, when foisted over such subordinates to the head of a great office. They would be contemptible even in their own estimation. The bare fact that there were many able men in the lower grades would make it certain that the higher places would soon be filled from the lower. No people can withhold their respect from a body of men who have gained their places by demonstrating their superior fitness to perform the duties which such places impose. Every successful competitor would begin to share that respect the moment he won a place by his own merits. If no self-seeking patron could claim a right to disturb his career, the friendly sympathy of the circle or the village where his honors were won would attend his progress. Feebly developed as the public feeling now is on such points, I venture to think that an officer would call down upon himself no slight criticism who, after a competition under civil service rules, should reject the victor, in order to give an office to a favorite dunce at the foot of the list, or to an office-seeking partisan so ignorant that he dared not enter the contest.

VI. We can hardly take leave of our subject without some reflections as to the best policy to be pursued by the friends of reform, and the lines along which they can act most effectively.

1. The demand for better administration and the spirit that supports reform are extending, and have been rapidly gaining strength. But how the spoils system may be most

effectually attacked, and what should be substituted in its place are points by no means clear in the public mind. Many of the friends of reform are only in the stage of disgust, denunciation, and general discontent with our administration. They have not those definite views needed for devising or even for giving effective support to better methods. While there are bad methods that must be done away with, the main work is constructive—the framing and putting into practice of a new system which will open a free field to merit—a system strong enough to withstand the assaults of the old monopolist and the constant pressure of hostile interests. We need clear views and a wise and generally accepted theory of action, as a prerequisite to the thorough performance of that work. The natural enemies of reform—whether they be the baser spirits in parties acting in the party name, or selfish individuals, each seeking his own gain—stand together. They will make a common attack and defence. They have on their side the familiar usages, and the distrust of non-partisan methods, which have grown up during more than a generation of partisan supremacy. Many worthy people will, probably, even against the weight of reason, for a time allow their influence to go with these enemies—at least they will adhere to the partisan theory—from mere want of knowledge of better methods, and consequently from lack of faith in their sufficiency. These facts show the need of a dissemination of clearer views concerning the merit system and the improvement it would bring about. That system is not yet clearly in the public mind. To understand it is the first, if not the only argument needed to make a supporter. To bring its just principles and its simple, practical methods distinctly before the intelligent classes, is therefore a patriotic and paramount duty. Perhaps nothing would contribute more to this end than its application, before the eyes of the people, in any public office —national, State, or municipal. The examples of the New York City Post Office and of the Department of the Interior have been educating the people on the subject. But we need a didactic literature which shall show what can be done to improve administration, and how to do it. A literature of complaint and denunciation will not suffice. It is only barren and disintegrating. The people are in a mood to listen to those who will properly present the issue between the two systems—the question whether the merit system or the partisan spoils system is the better, the most in harmony with our institutions, the safest with which to trust the fate of this great country. The subject has a direct bearing upon every man of property, upon every pupil in the schools, upon every man and woman in office or who seek office, upon every parent whose children hope for public employment, upon the action of parties and the prospective gains of partisans, as well as upon all the more unselfish interests which find their support in the higher sentiments of the nation.

We cannot expect to change the moral tone or the political theories of a generation at once. The new system, therefore, must be gradually introduced and allowed to aid its own progress through its good effects, and its educational influence, as was the case in Great Britain. Its enemies will contest not only the theory and principles of reform, but will resist its application to every department, every city, every office, every nomination and promotion. Hence, its friends must regard every separate contest as having some importance and as worthy their attention. There is no greater delusion than the theory held by some worthy but inexperienced and sanguine reformers who, scorning deliberate and educational processes, expect the removal of all our abuses to be brought about, suddenly, in a grand reform campaign, which shall drive all bad men from office and inaugurate an era of purity and patriotism. A great and salutary victory of reform principles at the polls may doubtless be expected very soon. The great parties should be forced to take well-defined positions upon the reform issue. But the bases of a permanent reform are to be sought only in public enlightenment, and in those practical methods of administration, which, by steadily vindicating their own utility and disproving the need of partisan officials, will educate the people up to a higher standard of official life and a clearer conception of their own rights and duties.[1] Our spoils system is the natural result of the combined and perennial forces

---

[1] See on this point, ante, p. 205 to 207.

of individual selfishness and partisan zeal, left free to work their ends in political life. And however stayed for a time by spasmodic efforts, they can be permanently arrested only by salutary methods in daily administration, which the public intelligence can accept as founded in natural justice and as conducive to the general welfare. The friends of reform must not despise the day of small things. It must be seen that the issue, the opportunity, and the duty are at their own doors. They are, in a degree, involved in every local appointment or promotion, as well as in the great departments at Washington and in the presidential elections. The man, who signs an undeserved recommendation, or goes before a mayor or an alderman, to get his relatives or his dependents into office, through favoritism, is in spirit as much an enemy of good administration as the great manipulator who brings the whole power of his party to bear in the interest of partisan appointments, or the high official who prostitutes his authority by the use of patronage for his own ends. Faithful citizens all over the country, in every narrow as well as every broad sphere, must stand up for the right and interest of the people to have worthy men and women in office. It is not enough to make a loud complaint because the President and Congress do not bring a great reform complete to our doors. We need a definite, resolute, public opinion that will cause both the President and Congress to do their duty whenever they neglect it, and not merely miscellaneous protests and indefinite indignation. A cause, which is that of the patriotic and disinterested classes against all partisan monopolists and schemers against all corrupt officials and all jobbers in politics against all the immoral interests of society,—necessarily demands effort, self-sacrifice, and public enlightenment. A free people, in the long range, have as good administration as they deserve. If we fold our hands while other nations advance, we must suffer the loss and the disgrace. Whatever can be done to bring home to the people a more vivid sense of the true dignity and duty of office, and to make them comprehend how taxes are made higher, how immorality and crime are increased, how the country is dishonored and law and politics are brought into contempt, by incompetent and corrupt officials, are among the most efficient means of advancing the cause of civil service reform. Here, I think, is a field but little cultivated. And are not the people in the towns, villages, cities, and counties prepared to listen with interest to a candid and courageous statement of the facts on these points which affect their local affairs? Wherever there is a corrupt officer, wherever public money is lost or administration is inefficient, by reason of official incompetency or partisan dictation, there is a need for civil service reform, and a place where good citizens have a duty.

2. But public opinion, as already developed, demands that more vigorous and extended reform measures be carried forward, especially by the national government. There is, however, a question whether their more direct support should be sought in a law of Congress or in the action of the executive under existing laws. A similar question arose in Great Britain, and, in considering it, the reasons have been given[1] which clearly show that the duty of initiating and guiding a reform policy belongs to the executive. These reasons suggest that, inasmuch as the first effect would be to deprive members of their patronage, Congress is little likely to take the lead in devising regulations for a reform; but they further show how that adverse interest and the hostility it produces may be overcome.[2] These reasons also present grave objections to encouraging legislative interference with executive functions. They show how very inconvenient, if not disastrous, it would be, were rigid provisions laid down by statute for conducting the detailed work of administration in the tentative stages of reform. So far as the executive might be without adequate authority under the Constitution, the co-operation of Congress would, of course, be essential. But that lack of authority has been, in the main, supplied by the act of March 3d, 1871 now Revised Statutes, § 1753), which is as follows: "The President is authorized to prescribe such regulations for the admission of persons into the Civil Service of the United States as may best promote efficiency, and ascertain the fitness of each can-

[1] See ante, pp. 185 to 189, and also pp. 211 and 212.
[2] See ante, pp. 211 to 213.

didate, in respect to age, health, character, knowledge, and ability, for the branch of the service he seeks to enter ; and for this purpose he may employ suitable persons to conduct such inquiries and may prescribe their duties ; and establish regulations for the conduct of persons who may receive appointments in the Civil Service."

It will be perceived that this is a very comprehensive enactment, covering three important points : (1) Regulations fixing the conditions of admission to the service ; (2) The employment of suitable persons to conduct the examinations ; and (3) Regulations for the conduct of those in the service.[1]

The authority given by this law is ample to enable the executive to do much, directly, in behalf of good administration;[2] and also to go forward with the work of reform on a large scale, whenever Congress can be induced to vote a moderate appropriation of, say, $25,000 each year. That amount is needed to meet the necessary expenses attending examinations in various quarters of the Union and to provide for the proper supervision of the new system as a whole. *Upon these points, it is important that the full force of public opinion should be brought to bear.*

It is desirable to so amend this statute as to provide that the chief examiners (who should constitute a civil service commission) shall hold their places by a tenure similar to that of judges. Their duties would seem to be essentially judicial in their nature. It is important that their appointment and tenure should be as far removed as possible from any peril or suspicion of partisan influence.[3] No argument is needed to make it plain that the examinations and the regulations, as well as their interpretation and enforcement, should proceed upon a

---

[1] It would be more satisfactory perhaps if the law had provided that those who have charge of the examinations should have a general duty of supervising the execution of the regulations ; but the regulations themselves and the inherent authority of the executive may be made to cover that duty, and thus the necessary vigor and uniformity may be given to the whole system.

[2] The executive order of June 22d, 1877, against federal officers taking part in the management of local politics is only an example of what may be done under this authority without the co-operation of Congress.

[3] See ante, p. 255.

uniform principle and method in all the departments and in every quarter of the Union.    Diverse and independent rules and Boards of Examiners in each separate department or great office, applying one standard in one department or in one local office, and a very different one in another    allowing regulations to be enforced now as understood by one board and then as understood by some other board—would only lead to confusion, feebleness, and injustice.[1]    The result would be suspicion and hostility, highly prejudicial to the public interests, and perhaps, for the time, fatal to the new system.

3.    There is another class of legislation, practicable both on the part of Congress and of the State legislatures, which might be made to reinforce the cause of reform.    The instructive British precedents have been already pointed out,[2] and they cannot be too carefully studied.    It cannot, I think, be doubted that, to clearly lay down the rules of official duty in the exercise of the appointing power, to give them the prestige of law, and to enable their violation to be made the basis of investigation and punishment, would as greatly strengthen the reform sentiment in this country as it did in England.    The alleged violation of the New York Statute of 1877, referred to in the last note, has already been made the subject of a legislative investigation.    Upon what theory, which does not also embrace the exercise of the appointing power, can partiality, favoritism, or any form of corruption in a judge or a collector be made a ground for inquiry and punishment?    Is it less a crime against morality or public safety to wilfully bestow the office of collector, judge, or commissioner upon a person known to be unfit—who may do injustice and cause loss in a hundred instances—than it is to give a single corrupt decision or appropriate a few dollars of the public money, for which we promptly send officers to prison?    Can there be any good cause why the reasons upon which public officers act in making appointments should not be investigated whenever

---

[1] Harmony of action could be secured by providing that one member of the general Board of Examiners should act as a member of the several local Boards for Examinations.

[2] Chap. xi., pp. 85, 130 to 143, and p. 33, note 3.

there is *present their* evidence that they have used their authority for indefensible purposes ?[1]

Has a collector, a postmaster, or a mayor any more right, with
the intention of serving his party or his friends, to foist upon
the public treasury sinecurists, or clerks known to be incompetent to earn their salaries (when efficient persons are applicants),
whereby the Government suffers a loss of money, than he has
to use as much of the public money for personal or partisan purposes ? In morals or in reason, how much worse is
it for a member of Congress to secretly sell a nomination to the
military or naval academy or to a civil department, than it is to
gain the votes and the commendation of many families and
cliques, on the deceptive promise of the same nomination,
which after the election he gives to a cousin or a favorite ?
Yet, for one class of these offences, the wrong-doer is subject
to criminal indictment, while for the other the law leaves him
untouched. A half developed public opinion hesitates and
doubts, and perhaps hints a judgment by calling him a politician.[2] But still we fail to see either our own inconsistency

[1] There is a late New York statute providing for summary investigations
which is in principle perhaps a precedent, even in this country, for such an
inquiry. See Laws of New York, 1873, p. 514, Chap. 335, Sec. 109.

[2] If it be asked whether the suggestion be that every exercise of the appointing power should be liable to be inquired into—perhaps by a hostile
member of an opposing party—the answer is, that whenever there may be
adequate proof of a corrupt or otherwise indefensible use of that power, it is
as fit a subject of investigation and punishment as would be a case of the corrupt or indefensible use of public property appearing upon like proof. There
would be no more danger of too frequent or unreasonable investigations of
one kind than of the other. It is only because we have been accustomed to
allow the appointing power to be exercised in a feudal and partisan spirit, and
to look upon it as an irresponsible power, that it seems strange to us to have
it brought within the same rules of duty and responsibility which we enforce
in cases analogous. In the same inconsiderate manner, it may, very likely,
be said that it would be hardly possible to decide whether the officer made
an appointment either for a personal or a partisan purpose, or only for an
honest public purpose. But the least reflection will show that question to
be far less difficult than those which are presented in every criminal and
most civil cases, viz. : whether there be " premeditated malice," " felonious
purpose," " disregard of human life," " an intent to appropriate to one's
own use," " gross negligence," " ability to distinguish right and wrong ;"
questions which, though much more metaphysical and much further removed from the outward sphere of facts, are every day made decisive, not

or the force of those British precedents to which our partisan theories have so nearly blinded us.

Need it be doubted that here, as in Great Britain, the branding of a prostitution of the appointing power as a criminal offence would not only greatly limit the abuse itself, but would arouse a strong public opinion against it? Duelling, gambling, and lottery selling soon become infamous under the condemnation of the statutes.

The theory, that the reasons for an appointment are the secrets of the officers or the party leaders, is only a part of the system which treats the appointments themselves as the perquisites of the officer, and the gains to be made of them as the spoils of his party. It is not enough that we denounce this system and pass resolutions condemning it. We must do as the English did a century ago—make official action, in its spirit, criminal in the view of the statutes and the courts.

4. In close connection with the British statutes restraining the corrupt use of the appointing power, are the laws forbidding public officers interfering with the freedom of elections and the political equality of the people in private life. The most characteristic of them is the statute of Anne,[1] to which special reference has already been made. The salutary effects of laws like this cannot be questioned. They are not less effective in keeping officers to the discharge of their duties than they are in protecting the people against official coercion and in preventing pernicious combinations, between public servants and partisan managers, for the purposes of political intrigue and dishonest gains. I cannot doubt that a comprehensive law, in the spirit of that last referred to, which should cover the whole field of official life, would be of great public utility. It must be regarded as one of the greatest anomalies of our politics (especially in view of the fact that Great Britain has not only enforced that statute, but from the same cause for several generations utterly disfranchised her subordinate officials' that we have had no pervading public opinion which has fixed

simply of a continuance of public favor, but of property, character, and life itself.

[1] See ante, p. 85 and 309 to 313.

any well-defined limits to the use of official authority for
political or even for partisan ends.   Nothing more strikingly illustrates the demoralizing influence of a partisan-spoil-
system, administered by the omnipotent party majority, in
degrading the sense of individual rights and official responsibility, than the fact that, in this republic, we tolerate an official
intermeddling with the political freedom of the citizen, which
has been unknown in the mother country for three generations, and which is only surpassed by the more despotic of
the continental governments.

5.  Another much needed law is one which shall be adequate to suppress the demoralizing and despotic practice of
levying political assessment upon the subordinates in the civil
service.   Had we not grown up in familiarity with this abuse,
elsewhere unknown among the enlightened nations, we should
probably look with something like contempt upon a government without the ability, the sense of justice or of its own
dignity, required to protect the salaries of its faithful servants
from public pillage under orders of confiscation from the camps
of politics.   I have no space for setting forth the manifold
evils which flow from this abuse.   How can we expect zeal in
the public service, or a high sense of honor, or a manly independence of thought or action, on the part of a body of
men and women every moment exposed to unlimited extortion at the hands of those whose favor gave them their places
and whose frown threatens their removal?   We have no
reason to expect a clerk to be honest to whom the nation
is not just.   Until we are ready to protect an officer in what he
has earned and to give him a tenure fairly reliable, we have
no right to complain if he takes time for his own defence and
makes leagues with robbers to whose mercy we leave him.
How can we hope to reduce the excessive and mercenary
activity in our politics within reasonable limits, so long as we
permit the partisan treasuries to be filled by freely intercepting
the public money between the pay offices of the people and
the pockets of the officials?   How can we expect to reduce
salaries to reasonable amounts, so long as their excessive rates
not only increase the chances of gain, on the part of every
corrupt politician and every partisan clique, but are in them-

selves a sort of justification of the levies by which the expenses of the great parties are paid?

It has been explained how it happened that this kind of extortion is almost the only abuse in our politics which did not, at an early day, exist in a more aggravated form in the mother country.[1] But it has also been shown that more than two and a half centuries ago there were legal prohibitions in Great Britain incompatible with introduction of that abuse.[2] Public officers, like other citizens, should of course be allowed to freely make contributions in aid of their own views of politics or religion. But all solicitation, whether by agents or by circulars, in any department or office, should be prevented by law. Every officer should be forbidden to take any part in reference to such collections. Every person in the public service—whether officer or workman—should be made to clearly comprehend that he is under no more constraint to part with the fruits of his toil for political purposes, and is in no more danger of losing his place if he refuses to do so, than any laborer upon a farm or any clerk in a private workshop. Such legal protection is essential to true liberty, manhood, or justice in public life. These views are gaining strength, even beyond the more non-partisan[3] circles. But they will never be vindicated in practice until the people give strong expression to their will on the subject. The principle of such a law is covered by existing statutes. One act prohibits officers, clerks and employés soliciting contributions for gifts, or making gifts to their official superiors, and such superiors are forbidden to receive gifts from their subordinates.[4] These provisions, however, are utterly inadequate in scope to put much restraint upon the great evil which they recognize. Relating only to officers in a line of subordination, they leave unchecked both the despotic use of the appointing power and the proscriptive influence of parties, by which payments are exacted under threats of removal and bribes of promo-

---

[1] See ante, p. 43.          [2] See ante, p. 43, 50 to 52, and 310.

[3] "No official or officeholder should be subject to political or partisan assessments,  .  .  .  and plain laws should punish all attempts  .  .  . to enforce such assessments  .  .  .  or to abridge absolute freedom in political action."—Resolutions of Republican Convention of New York, of September, 1877.          [4] U. S. Revised Statutes, § 1784.

tion.' Another statute[2] affirms the same principle somewhat more broadly, by prohibiting all executive officers and employés of the United States from requesting, giving to, or receiving from any other officer or employé of the government, any money, property, or other thing of value[3] for political purposes ; but with the exception that the prohibition shall not apply to officers " appointed by the President *with the advice and consent of the Senate !*" If that lamentable and significant exception came from the Senate itself, it would make the difference between its disinterestedness and that of the House of Lords still more conspicuous. It would certainly go far to confirm the popular belief that patronage and partisan interests are nowhere so strongly entrenched and so unblushingly defended as in the highest legislative body of the nation. In any event, the import and suggestion of this exception are of painful significance. The officers confirmed by the Senate are of the higher class, of whom many have an authority of nomination or a right to recommend promotions and removals. Their power and influence overawe the tens of thousands of officers who fill the grades below. Upon what principle of justice or policy can official tyranny and partisan coercion be prohibited, as between officers of nearly equal grade, and yet be allowed (if not by plain suggestion invited) on the part of those high officials whose caprice can be enforced and whose bad example is most demoralizing ? This statute is also sadly defective in affording clerks and employees no protection against partisan tax-gatherers who are not in the public service. An officer, *simply because he has been confirmed by the Senate,* is at liberty, under this statute, to use his influence for the removal of any poor, worthy clerk, if he refuses to pay the contributions which such tax-gatherers may choose to demand.[4] In the

---

[1] They do not even seem to have prevented a member of the Cabinet being himself the head of a political bureau of extortion.

[2] U. S. Laws, 1876, chap. 287, § 6.

[3] Is an office " a thing of value " within the meaning of this law ? Why not use the comprehensive prohibitions of British statutes, if the true intent be to stop bribery by promises of office and promotion?

A bill is now pending (46th Cong., 1st Session, H. R. 226) which prohibits, in very general terms, the demanding or paying of money for political purposes, by officers, clerks, or employees of the government. The prohibitions extend to superior officers permitting the collection of such

whole range of British and American legislation, during the last quarter of a century, I am aware of no contrast so striking, or to an American so painful, as that afforded by these statutes when compared with the action of the British Parliament in sustaining open competition over twenty years ago.[1] Is it too much to hope that this exception, in the interest of servility and proscription, will not long be allowed to dishonor the national laws? If but a single senator would present it in its true light before the people, he would arouse a sentiment which would make its early repeal inevitable.

6. On one other point there is a necessity of appealing to Congress. It is in regard to the laws, already referred to, limiting the tenure of collectors, postmasters, naval officers, and various other officials to four years. We have seen that these statutes came in with the causes of the spoils system, which they greatly strengthen; if indeed they may not be said to have paved the way for that system. They ought to be repealed. They suggest that such officers should come in and go out with each administration, and they cause many changes just when officers have been long enough in their places to become efficient. They cause uncertainty and perpetual agitation in all the lower circles of official life. They are utterly destructive of that experience, consistency, and steadiness of policy without which no good administration is possible. So short a term dissuades the worthier men from taking these offices. It forces those who hold them into constant efforts of a pernicious kind to strengthen their influence in aid of a reappointment. These short terms also add greatly to the disastrous effects which the present method of senatorial confirmations exerts upon the public service, and to the facility with which partisan manipulators can make their demoralizing influence felt within the departments. The mischievous tendency of these short terms of office, unknown under our original system, which the law of 1820 introduced, was so manifest even without trial, as to arouse the gravest fears of the great statesmen of that day.[2] In the humiliating abuses which we suffer, in connection with so frequent appointments

moneys, and, on certain conditions, to government contractors. The bill embodies very salutary principles.

[1] See ante, p. 213.  [2] Webster, Benton and Calhoun, especially.

and confirmations, we may see the fulfilment of their gloomy predictions,¹ which I regret want of space does not permit me to cite.

These may perhaps be accepted as the more important, practical issues to be made, and upon which public opinion may with advantage be concentrated. But there is another serious obstacle to a thorough reform, upon which British experience sheds no light. I mean the manner in which the Senate exercises the power of confirmation. To discuss that subject is quite beyond the scope of this work. It is well known this power is not used, as the Constitution contemplated it would be, merely as a check upon bad nominations by the executive. It has been so magnified as in great measure to supersede executive authority, and to confer upon the Senators from each State (or the Senator of the dominant party) a sort of feudal lordship over nominations for officers who are to serve within the State. The interference of the Senate, with executive functions, has not been limited to the matter of appointments. Since 1867, it has even been carried to the extent of assuming to restrain and regulate the discharge of the executive duty of removal for cause. This has been done by making the consent of the Senate essential to the removal, during his term of office, of an officer confirmed by that body. In this way the influence of the Senate has been greatly increased and the constitutional functions of the executive have been in a corresponding degree impaired.² The demoralizing influence of this system upon legislation, upon State politics, upon discipline, economy, and fidelity in the departments, and upon the dignity and usefulness of the Senate itself, is notorious and hardly disputed.³ The very counterpoise of the

---

¹ Speaking of the proscription to which the Law of 1820 so greatly contributed, Mr. Webster used this language in a speech delivered in Worcester, in 1832 : "Mr. President, so far as I know, there is no civilized country on earth in which, on a change of rulers, there is such an inquisition for spoils as we have witnessed in this free republic. When, Sir, did any British minister, Whig or Tory, ever make such an inquest? When did he ever take away the daily bread of weighers and gaugers and measurers? Sir, a British Minister who should do this, and should afterwards show his head in the British House of Commons, would be received by a universal hiss." ² U. S. Rev. Stat., 1767 to 1771.

³ It was declared in debate in the Senate, in December, 1869, that " nominally, appointments are so made [in the constitutional mode], but in reality

government has been disturbed by an invasion of the executive from the legislative department. This is no place for considering a remedy. But it is plain that whatever shall tend to weaken the spoils system in other quarters, whatever shall tend to fill the departments with young men and women of worth and capacity, whatever shall tend to restore to the executive its true and constitutional functions in other particulars, whatever shall bring the aggression and monopoly of the Senate more prominently before the people, will also tend to make such usurpation obnoxious and intolerable. It is only an aroused public sentiment that can open the way for bringing the exercise of the power of confirmation into harmony with the interests and rights of the people. That power extends to but a moderate portion of the officers. The Senate could not long resist a powerfully expressed, public censure, concentrated upon the narrow field of its monopoly. And it is only just to expect that Senators of the United States will be ready to yield to changes that may be shown to be essential for the public welfare.[1] They will not venture to defend an usurpation through which they have taken to themselves feudal prerogatives. They will never try to justify a monopoly of the appointing power which the public opinion of Great Britain more than a generation since took from members of the House of Lords. They now act upon precedents, the inherent evils of which long practice has deprived of half their hatefulness. If it be too much (and I do not think it is too much) to expect that the Senators of a republic will be found to have the pat-

they are dictated and controlled, in a vast majority of cases, by an influence unknown to the Constitution or laws. Every Senator, and every Representative in the other House, knows that appointments in most cases are dictated by them ;" and in a debate in the House in 1870, that " under the present custom in the Senate, it is almost impossible for a united House-delegation to get a good man confirmed if the Senators from the State prefer a bad one : in other words, Senators secure the rejection of those that the President has constitutionally nominated, not because *they are not fit for the place in question*, but because they do not themselves recommend them." Report U. S. Civil Service Commission, April, 1874, p. 18.

[1] In his message of December 5th, 1870, President Grant says : There is no duty which so much embarrasses the executive and heads of departments as that of appointments, nor is there any such arduous and thankless labor imposed on Senators and Representatives as that of finding places for constituents."

riotism needed to follow the examples of British noblemen—
of Chatham, Liverpool, and Granville many years ago—in voluntarily surrendering patronage, surely it is not too much to
expect that (like the majority of the members of both houses
of the British Parliament in the last decade), the members of
the Senate will make a virtue of necessity, by yielding grace-
fully to a frowning public opinion, without driving the people
to a constitutional amendment for the suppression of official
feudalism under the most democratic government of the
world.    Politics certainly exhibit many inconsistencies; but
thoughtful Senators are not likely to believe, because for a
time they have been allowed through usurpation to become
feudal lords of patronage, that the people will very long tolerate so anomalous and degrading a despotism.[1]

7.  In a late case before the Supreme Court of the United
States, in which that tribunal made a salutary application of
British law to some of our abuses, it is declared that " no people can have a higher public interest, except the preservation
of their liberties, than integrity in the administration of their
government in all its branches."[2]  If this volume proves that
vital truth not to have been so fully comprehended by the
American people as by the people of some other countries,
there has certainly been much to excuse their failure ; and the
future promises a better appreciation.   The American constitutional system was by far the most original and the grandest
political achievement ever yet made by one generation.
Our early administration was placed upon a basis of justice and purity far in advance of any which elsewhere existed.   It was but natural that the brilliant success of the great
experiment should dazzle the public mind.   It led the way
to a general conviction that a government founded in sound
principles held within itself preserving virtues so efficient that
it might be safely handed over to such voluntary combinations among the people as should be pleased to take an interest
in carrying it on.   The many questions incident to the creation

---

[1] " The democratic nations which have introduced freedom into their political constitutions, at the very time that *they were augmenting the despotism
of their administrative constitutions* have been led into strange paradoxes."
Democracy in America, by De Tocqueville, vol. 2, p. 395.

[2] Trist *v.* Child, 21 Wallace R., 450.

of a new government, to the developing industri.. of a new
continent, and to their relation to foreign States, absorbed
public attention. Exciting and novel theories, which naturally developed the most intense political activity, in connection with the interpretation and enforcement of the new constitution and laws, strongly tended to withdraw thought from
administrative methods and from all the internal relations of
the government. No state of facts, among a people in the
condition of our fathers, could be more favorable to the steady
growth of intensely partisan and vicious methods in administration or more effectually tend to blind the people to their bad
effects. A few sagacious statesmen comprehended the nature
and magnitude of the evil from the outset. But before any considerable portion of the people understood the situation, the
spoils system was not only developed but entrenched. In the
meantime, we had gone so far and were so shaken on the
stormy seas which carried us into the great civil conflict,
that little thoughtful attention could be secured for any questions relating to the more internal operations of the government. It hardly need be pointed out that the period which
immediately followed the civil war was in every way unfavorable to introspection, candid deliberation, or reform of any
kind. But, in the later years, a change has been coming over
the public mind. "The era of buoyant youth is coming to a
close ; ripe and sober manhood is to take its place."[1] Fourth-
of-July orations are no longer given to political boasting.
There is a feeling of soberness for giving some thought
to the fact that it is not enough to have a government
based on just principles. It must be administered by pure
and able men, or the people cannot prosper. Attention
rests more than ever before upon the facts that, though
the original questions which divided parties have nearly
disappeared, though the supreme, national peril which appalled
a whole generation has been taken out of our politics, though
principles less than ever before divide the great parties, yet
party struggles are not less intense. The vicious and excessive activity of partisans has rather increased than diminished. The people are more than ever before taking notice

---

[1] Preface, Von Holst's Const. History United States, p. i.

that the party issues tend to gather about the means of getting it to power and the possession and division of patronage, offices, and spoils. They begin to see that the questions which are permanently absorbing and important are administrative questions. They are as never before alive to the facts how seriously these questions concern economy and taxation, the efficiency with which the laws are executed, the safety of life and property, the morals of politics, the purity and freedom of elections— in short, the prosperity and safety not only of the nation as a whole, but of every State, county, city, town, and citizen which it contains. They are alarmed at the many cases of official infidelity. They begin to comprehend that to get good men into office is one of the paramount needs of all government— one of the supreme conditions of all prosperity. This riper and sounder temper of the national mind has, in the last decade, several times forced partisan organization to denounce the spoils system, and to make pledges of administrative reform ; but with what sincerity, in some cases, need not be here considered. And it has finally, for the first time in our history, made the question of such reform a distinct and leading issue in a national canvass. The experience of Great Britain shows us that when that question has been once raised in the forum of politics, it is sure to more and more arrest public attention. The reform elements, there, rapidly gained strength until their final triumph. Is there any reason to doubt that our experience will be the same?

The question whether the partisan-spoils system or the merit system shall prevail in our politics is really the question whether the self-respecting, intelligent manhood and womanhood of the whole nation may compete for the honor of holding official places, or a profession of dominant opinions and servility to the partisan majority of the hour shall fix the class and the boundary beyond which no selection shall be made— whether the caucus, the " rings," and the secret arts of the politicians, or the studious and industrious homes and workshops, the schools, the seminaries and the colleges, shall mould the character which is to serve and guide the nation? Is it possible that a method of selection based on equal opportunities and common rights for all can be overborne, in a great republic, by a system of proscription and privilege—of feudal and official favoritism? Are the United States to permanently stand before the world as the only great nation which foregoes the best methods of bringing into its high service the worthiest of its citizens—as the only nation which allows its officials to be plundered by its parties, and its parties to make merchandise of its offices?

Free public competition in the selection of nominees for the public service is the most essential feature of the merit system. It is at once the most democratic and the most just and salutary agency of good government which has been developed in the political experience of modern times. It is, in fact, no mere method in administration or politics. It embodies a great principle of justice and progress, which finds illustration alike in the rivalry of nations, in the competition of races, in the providential order of the universe itself. Wherever there is life and growth, there is a competition, in which the development and the survival of the fittest are the conditions of superiority and progress, if not of continued existence. For the improvement of every species and every breed, the best of the kind must be selected and cared for; nor does the rule fail when we come to the growth of communities, and the prosperity of nations. To secure the best men for officers and leaders is, next to the creation of government itself, the most difficult problem of statesmanship—the greatest achievement which political wisdom can make. The conditions of prosperity with every people are involved in the extent to which they bring their purest and wisest minds into positions of honor and control.[1] No nation however strong, no race however vigorous, could long preserve its relative prestige and prosperity in the world, if it should disregard these conditions. The need, in

---

[1] I am not unmindful that the officers directly selected through competition cannot be said to be "leaders," and are not at once given control. But I repeat that, as soon as non-partisan, self-reliant men of worth and capacity shall have filled the lower grades, the higher places (except a few of the very highest) will certainly be filled by promotions from those below; and upon that being the case, not only will it be seen to be incongruous and really impracticable to put into those controlling positions mere politicians or inferior men of any kind, but the theories and the morals of politics will be so improved that incompetent, self-seeking men will no more be accepted as leaders in civil administration than they now are in arms or in education.

every nation, of being served by its ablest and best men in the
great contests of arms and diplomacy, and even in the higher
places in its internal affairs, was not, of course, left for modern
times to discover.    It was, however, left to these times to comprehend, or if not to comprehend, at least to act upon, the
theory that it is of essential importance to have all the subordinate as well as the higher) official places, both at home and
abroad, filled with persons of sufficient ability and character.
The leading nations have treated this question of official competency as so vital as to require not only persistent national
efforts to that end, but the surrender of the privileges of
royalty and class, the theories of birthright and aristocracy,
upon which all the older governments had been founded.
The practice of sending mere favorites or influential partisans—after the fashion of the old colonial period—even to
the humblest offices in colonies or foreign ports, has ceased
on the part of every European nation.    That vicious old
practice survives only in the unnatural form in which it has
been grafted upon our institutions.    Not only have the older
governments placed better men in office, but they have
brought them under sterner rules of discipline and duty.
They "hold their subordinate officers under stricter control,
and invent new methods for guiding them more closely, and
for inspecting them with less trouble." . . . "They do everything with more order, more celerity, and at less expense."[1]
It is only in the light of such considerations that we can
take in the full significance of the efforts and methods
through which, in later years, the older nations have
invigorated and armed themselves for the grand international
competition of races and States for the commerce and domination of the world.    Some of the practical effects of this new
policy have been pointed out, and I cannot enlarge upon
them.    It is for us to consider whether we can maintain our
prestige and the honor of republican institutions by continuing to draw our official force only from the hotbeds of partisan influence, and only by the selfish and secret methods
of patronage and favoritism ; while every other leading nation
plants itself upon common justice and invites, by its competitions, and rewards by selections for its service, the highest

---

[1] "Democracy in America," by De Tocqueville, vol. ii., pp. 378, 379.

capacity and character in its citizenship. The facilities of modern communications are so great that the competitions of nations living on different continents are almost as direct and rapid, in all the inland towns and along every shore of the ocean, as they were in earlier times between rival villages of the same district. Who can doubt that the question of better ministers, consuls, and commercial agents has become as decisive of the industries as it certainly has of the prestige and the honor of rival nations ?[1]

But however great the need of reform, our attempts must be proportioned to the virtue and intelligence which we have for their support. To attempt too much may be for a time as unfortunate as to attempt too little. The moral tone of the American people, as compared with that of the British people, and their relative patriotism, intelligence, and readiness to make efforts for the general welfare, are not only intrinsically very interesting, but they have a direct bearing upon the applicability of British precedents in the United States. I have no space for their discussion. While it is unquestionable that public opinion demands higher qualifications for office and has secured greater purity of administration in Great Britain than in this country, I am by no means convinced that the moral standard or intelligence, averaged over the whole field of life, is higher there than here. The explanation of this apparent contradiction seems to be this : More attention to the subject of administration and the enforcement of better methods for a series of years, in Great Britain, have made public opinion more exacting and critical and raised all official life to a relatively higher plane. Whereas in this country, the neglect of administration by our Statesmen, and the use of corrupting methods by the partisan class which has controlled the government, have caused the character of official life to fall below the general average of morality in other matters. In other words, in Great Britain the public service and official life generally are so pure as to be more in danger from without than from any source of corruption within themselves ; while with us corruption is most developed in official circles and tends to flow out from politics and official life upon private life. That the

[1] See *Appendix B.*

partisan and office-holding class is generally the more demoralized and distrusted class of our people, of corresponding intelligence, will, I think, hardly be questioned. That the facts are quite otherwise in Great Britain could be made very clear, but I can do no more than allude to a few facts bearing on the subject.

The purchase of commissions in the British army, as it prevailed until 1871, spoke as significantly from one plane of life as the buying and selling of Church "livings" still speak from another plane of life.[1] It has been shown that fewer crimes are committed in Great Britain than in this country. But the fact of a lower rate of criminality among a people may perhaps be equally explainable on the theory of less disposition to break the laws or of more certainty and a prompter justice in the imposition of punishment. Now, nothing in British administration is more admirable than the purity, dignity, and ability to be found in her courts of justice of every grade ; and her most thoughtful writers have borne testimony to the law-abiding spirit of the American people. " Even in America, the most law-loving of countries," . . . there is " a regard for law, such as no great people have yet evinced, and infinitely surpassing ours."[2] And what higher evidence can there be of the relative moral tone of two peoples than their comparative disposition to obey the laws which their own representatives have made? It would seem, therefore, that good administration has reduced criminality to a ratio below that of the United States, even among a people more inclined than Americans to set the laws at defiance. These conclusions, and more especially the inference that good methods of administration in Great Britain have raised the morality of public life above that of private life, may, however, be directly supported by British writers. " As we have seen, it (private corruption) has worn its slimy way from the Butler to the Broker class. Almost every man who has patronage has also his price. . . . Shall we now attempt by legislative enactment to stamp it out and brand the briber and bribed with infamy, or shall we wait yet longer, until physicians, the bar, *our Judges, our civil servants at home, in*

[1] See ante, p. 278 to 281.
[2] Bagehot on the English Constitution, pp. 52 and 289.

*India, and the Colonies, government inspectors of mines and factories, our very ministers of State, are tampered with!*[1]

I cannot think it would occur to an American writer to thus represent the stream of corruption, in his own country, as having its springs in the regions of private business, and as flowing thence to taint pervading virtues in official life and poison a pure domain in politics. He would regard the stream as flowing the other way. If in these facts we may find consoling evidence of the elevating influence of our institutions and social life, in their aggregate effect, ought we to be the less rebuked by the consideration that, with at least equally good material out of which to construct a pure and vigorous administration, and with far less obstacles to be overcome, our neglect has been so great that we have fallen far short of the achievements of the older country? The comparison will not have its true significance, if we fail to remember that, by going back about the space of a single human life, we come upon a condition the very reverse in the administrative affairs of the two countries—upon a time when, in this country, respected and capable men filled all the public places, and distrust of officers was little known —upon a time when, in Great Britain, there was official corruption and a prostitution of authority such as our demagogues now hardly venture even to suggest against their partisan opponents.

To the other considerations which give importance to administrative abuses this must be added : that they are the most permanent known to politics. Having their ultimate source in the selfishness of human nature, they grow wherever ambition, the love of gain, or partisan zeal are not effectively restrained. Favored by the imperfections of all human governments and incidents of their daily operation, they are, in their causes, as abiding as government itself. It is in the struggles for office, and the opportunities for gain in the exercise of official power, that selfishness, deception, and partisan zeal have their everlasting contest with virtue, patriotism, and duty. It is in that contest that statesmen and demagogues, patriots and intriguers, the good citizen and the venal office-seeker, all the high and all the low influences of political life, meet face to face, and by the balance of power, for good

[1] *Westminster Review*, article on Illicit Commissions, July, 1877.

or for evil, give character to politics and determine the morality of nations. The questions raised by that contest, and the methods by which politicians seek their solution, are much the same and are equally vital under every form of representative government. From generation to generation, from century to century, partisans and self-seeking and corrupt men of all sorts employ much the same means to make office-getting and administration serve their ends. If we go back over the administration of a century, in any enlightened State, we find the abuses with which statesmen and patriots have struggled, if a little different in form, yet in substance much the same. Whether a president or a king be at the head of the government, whether the higher branch of the legislature be elective or hereditary, make little difference in the administrative abuses or in their perilous tendency. Our civil service abuses, as I have already explained, are in substance but a repetition of those of the other enlightened nations. As a people, we have cherished no more complete and disastrous delusion than that which has led us to think that the just principles of our constitution and social life have relieved us from dangers growing out of corrupt administration. Human nature has not been changed by republican institutions. Good government does not come from neglect, from conceit, or from party zeal, even in a republic.

If, from the inveterate permanency and peril of administrative abuses, we turn to the other great questions of politics, we see that every generation, every decade, almost every year, has had its peculiar policy, its temporary interests, its absorbing issues, domestic or foreign. The highway of progress is marked by the ever changing procession of subjects each thought to be paramount in its day. Even from our short history, a long list of forgotten questions, each most absorbing for a time, could be gathered. But at all times and everywhere, the questions—How to bring honest and capable men into office, high and low? How to secure economy and fidelity in administration? How to prevent official authority from being prostituted to partisan and selfish ends?—have been subjects of serious and increasing difficulty. Whether considered in that light or not, they have really been problems than which none have at once so constantly and so vitally concerned the prosperity and the morality of the nation. What other questions, among all those which have arisen in our politics, have so steadily grown in importance? What question to-day presents issues more difficult of solution, or which are the source of more anxiety to patriotic and thoughtful citizens, than this? How can we so administer the government that its daily operations shall not develop infidelity and corruption, fatal alike to all the virtues of official and private life?

However the past may be excused, we can hardly find in the future a justification for a continued neglect of the science of administration which, as we have seen, the statesmen of every other enlightened nation have made one of the the paramount studies of politics. For surely it is not the increase of wealth, the growth of great cities, or the advance of population that will purify the fountains of virtue or make the problems of government easier. When, perhaps in the lifetime of persons now living, the residents of Washington holding places in the public service shall exceed her present population; when the country shall contain three hundred millions of people, of which the names of half a million shall be upon the national pay-rolls; when the commerce and population of San Francisco shall far exceed the present population and commerce of New York; when the national revenues shall be tenfold their present amount, and consuls and commercial agents shall discharge their duties in Central Africa and in cities upon the upper waters of the Amazon— can we expect, if our neglect shall continue, that the perils of a spoils system of office will be less, or that the difficulties of its removal will be diminished?

But it is not merely such natural increase and expansion which will continue to make that science more profound and its neglect more disastrous. It is in the order of a growing civilization that the functions of official life must become more and more various, delicate, and difficult. "The authority of government has not only spread throughout the sphere of all existing powers, . . . but it goes further and invades the domain heretofore reserved to private independence. A multitude of actions, which were formerly be-

yond the control of public administration, have been subjected to that control in our time, and the number of them is
constantly increasing." [1]    A larger and still larger number of
officers are required, and their neglect and incompetency more
and more tend to become evils of serious magnitude.   The
railroad, the steamship, and the telegraph ; the system of
national banks and the new departments of agriculture, education, and public health ; the life-saving and the Marine Hospital service ; the money order system, and the light-house, the
internal revenue and the postal administration, greatly extended
—are but illustrations of the growth of administrative functions created or enlarged during the present generation.   In
the cities [2] and in the States, this growth has hardly been less
than under the Federal Government ; nor has it been less in
other countries than in our own. [3]   Year by year, the prosperity
and morality of every enlightened people become, in a still
greater degree, dependent upon the character and capacity of
those who fill their places of public trust.   In no country is
this more true than in the United States, where the very
structure of the government frequently produces a complication of official duties, by reason of the division of authority
over great subjects between the nation and the States. [4]

With so great evils upon us from the neglect of administration in the past, and still greater evils thus threatening us if that
neglect shall continue in the future, it would hardly seem possible that the subject should long fail to take its proper place
in the serious reflections of American statesmen.   How, indeed, can a man be called a statesman who is not well versed
in the world's wisdom as to the best means of carrying for-

[1] "Democracy in America," vol. 2 p. 376.

[2] Popular education and sanitary laws vastly extended ; parks, gas-works,
and water-works ; the more complete supervision of prisons, of charity
and workshops in the interests of health and safety, are familiar examples.

[3] "I assert that there is no country in Europe in which the public administration has not become . . . more inquisitive and minute ; . . it
regulates more undertakings and gains a firmer footing every day about,
above, and around all persons, to assist, to advise, and to coerce them.—
"Democracy in America," vol. 2, p. 377.

[4] At this moment, the embarrassments connected with the subjects of the
public health and elections present significant examples.   In no country is
there so great a need of a superior class of officers to deal with these subjects.

ward with steadiness and fidelity the vast administration of
his country, upon which the happiness and prosperity of its
people so greatly depend?  For self-seeking politicians—for
men with whom statesmanship means the manipulation of
parties—for any citizen without faith in public virtue and the
courage needed to stand for duty and the general welfare
against the ignorance and the blind majority of the hour, the
subject can have few attractions.  But those thoughtful citizens
whose hearts are warmed by a true love of their country,
who are humiliated as they see that country failing to rise to
its true dignity before the world, who comprehend that,
under better methods, worth and ability of a higher order
could be made to elevate politics and official life—will be
drawn to the subject by all the strength of interest, patriotic
duty, and national pride.  They feel that the United States
stand before the world as the original and the noblest embodiment of the republican ideal in government.  As the oldest
and the most powerful republican nation—as the example to
which young republics turn for wisdom and experience—the
character of public administration in the United States does
not concern merely the growing millions of her own people,
but the republican cause and the fate of free institutions in
every quarter of the globe now and for ages to come.
Need we fear that this generation of Americans will supply
patriots who will worthily lead in the reform of the civil service of their country?  Are not great masses of the people
ready to turn away from the politicians and to follow such
leaders?  Can it be doubted that, if the true methods of
reform were once brought clearly before the American people,
they would give those methods a support as vigorous and
enlightened as that extended to them by the people of Great
Britain?  Surely we are not to be permanently known as
" the people who boast most over their form of government,
and groan most over the abuses of their administration."[1]
We are not degenerate sons without the patriotism or the
courage of our fathers.  This generation, which has made the
greatest sacrifices for liberty and justice recorded in human
annals, must surely have the moral elevation needed for the
removal of any abuses that can be developed in administering

[1] *The Saturday Review.*

the government whose righteousness and honor it has greatly exalted. We are justly proud of the stability of a government, which has been less changed in the past century, and bids fair to be less changed in the next century, than any government in Europe. Its safety now depends upon the virtue and wisdom of its daily administration. While nearly every European country is agitated by hopes and fears, threatening the very framework of the State, no expectation of a change of structure colors our estimate of the future. Our fate must turn upon our capacity to administer institutions which we do not wish to abandon, and which we cannot expect, by any radical change, to improve. We are for those reasons all the more free, and we have resting upon us a duty all the more serious, to speedily solve our great problem—that of making our administration worthy of our constitution and our social life. If the present generation is too poorly instructed in the true methods of government to act upon the higher experience of the leading European States, then it is the duty of all who teach—in whatever grade, from the school to the university—to take care that the next generation be wiser in the knowledge of what so deeply concerns the character and stability of the nation—to make it appear that republics are not hostile to statesmanship, to education, or to official virtue. No other knowledge will compensate for ignorance as to the best means of securing capacity and fidelity in public administration. No amount of scholarship will cover the disgrace to republican institutions of allowing the world to believe that republics must fall below monarchies in bringing high character and ability into places of public trust. In no other way can the prestige and influence of such institutions be so much advanced in the world as by the United States making it manifest to the nations that a great republic seeks and secures, quite as surely as the most enlightened monarchy, the full measure of official worth and ability which good administration requires. To attain such results is, I repeat, the great problem of American politics—the paramount duty of American patriots. And I trust I may be pardoned for adding that the hope of contributing, in some small measure, to their accomplishment, has given me the courage to submit this volume to the public judgment.

# APPENDIX A.

I HAVE not wished that any important conclusion reached in
this volume should, to any needless extent, rest upon my own
opinion alone, and some of the points involved are of such
a nature that the opinions of competent observers are, perhaps, the highest authority that can be offered. Both these
considerations have induced me to present in this form the
views of several gentlemen—some of them Englishmen and
some of them Americans—some representing official life in
various grades and some of them only distinguished in private
life ; but each of them has had exceptional opportunities of
forming correct conclusions, and their views will probably be
thought entitled to weight. The portion of any letter which

28

has been here omitted is immaterial to the purpose of this Appendix, and neither in such portion nor in any other letter received, but not here referred to, were any views expressed contrary to those herein set forth. I give at length the letter of Sir Charles Trevelyan (formerly " The Permanent Secretary of the Treasury," and one of the two persons selected by the British Government in 1853 to report upon the best method of reform, because of its great historical interest.

## I. Letter from Sir Charles Trevelyan :

BRAEMORE, August 20, 1877.

DEAR SIR : Your letter of the 14th has reached me at this remote place, and I much regret that I cannot at present personally confer with you, for I have long been struck by the singular suitableness of our new but well-tried institution of making public appointments by open competition, for the correction of some of the worst results of the United States political system, and would gladly help to place you in possession of the mature fruit of our experience. . . .

Considering the practical nature of the English character, which abhors theoretical innovations based upon *à priori* reasoning, and reluctantly accepts even those changes which have been proved by experience to be desirable, a remarkable proof of the success of the system is to be found in the fact that all real opposition to it has long since died away, and, step by step, it has been extended to almost every branch of the service in its most advanced and only efficient form of perfectly open competition.

It may be useful to the President to know one feature of its early history : the change was made by persons conversant with public affairs from a practical perception of its necessity, but these early supporters of it *might be counted upon the fingers*, and if the matter had been put to the vote in London society, or the clubs, or even in Parliament itself *by secret voting*, the new system would have been rejected by an overwhelming majority. Nevertheless, whenever adverse motions were made in the House of Commons we always had a majority in favor of the plan. This at first caused us some surprise ; but on investigation the case turned out to be thus : Large as the number of persons who profited by the former system of patronage were, those who were left out in the cold were still larger, and these included some of the best classes of our population—busy professional persons of every kind, lawyers, ministers of religion of every persuasion, schoolmasters, farmers, shopkeepers, etc.  These rapidly took in the idea of the new institution, and they gladly accepted it as a valuable additional privilege.  We were especially interested and amused at the sudden popularity which the system acquired in Ireland, where " *the* competition," as they called it, was regarded as a very preferable alternative to the old jobbery.  You will now understand that, whatever may have been the individual sentiments of members of the House of Commons, they received such pressing letters from their constituents as obliged them *to vote straight.*

But all the best members soon felt that, by the abolition of patronage, they had been relieved from a degrading yoke.  While it was customary to place situations in the revenue and other departments at their disposal for distribution among their constituents, they were obliged, in self-defence, to dance attendance on the Patronage Secretary of the Treasury, besides having to carry on a large and annoying correspondence with their constituents.  From this double bondage they were at once liberated when the junior appointments were opened to competition ; and as all members were placed on the same footing, they were under no disadvantage in their elections in consequence of the change.

The most searching and vital improvement arising from the abolition of patronage is that it has purified the constituencies and increased the independence and public feeling of members of Parliament.  Every borough and county, except a few of the largest, had its local manager on either side—a banker, brewer, or solicitor—who purchased the vote and support of the leading men by a judicious application of the loaves and fishes.  The corruption so engendered was more constant and general than the bribery carried on by means of money, and it was also more influential, in the degree in which a provision for life for a son or some other person in whom a voter was interested was more valuable than the customary five-pound note. Both constituents and members now have to look, not to what they can get, but to what it is their duty to do.  At any rate, they must now seek to promote their interests in some larger and more public way than by obtaining appointments for themselves or their friends.

As regards the effect of the change upon the efficiency of the administrative service, the ordinary practice was to place the fool of the family in the civil, and the wild, idle, unmanageable youth in the military, service, for the plain reason that while this was a provision for life for them, they were not so fit as their brothers to compete with others in the open professions.  The promotion within the civil service was, for the most part, conducted on the same principle of patronage, and in the military service on a mixed principle of purchase and patronage. The civil service also was held in low estimation by the public, who regarded it as a *corpus vile* for political jobbers; and this reacted in an injurious manner upon the *esprit de corps* of the civil servants. Now both civil and military officers are appointed on the ground of superior ability and attainment, with an indirect guarantee for good moral qualities (inasmuch as superior cultivation and attainments is to be acquired only by industry, self-denial, and a preference of the future for the present), besides direct evidence to moral character from the persons best able to testify to it. As the persons appointed have no party connections, and are generally unknown to the political chiefs, there is now nothing to prevent their being promoted according to qualification and merit, which is the key to administrative efficiency. Lastly, the reproach of a corrupt origin has been removed from the civil service, and the members of it have been elevated in the estimation of themselves and others.

The same change which has increased the efficiency of the civil and military services has given a marvellous stimulus to education. Formerly boys intended for any branch of the public service had no motive to exert themselves, because, however idle they might be, they were certain to get an appointment. Now, from their earliest years, boys know that their future depends upon themselves, and a new spirit of activity has supervened. The opening of the civil and military services, in its influence upon national education, is equivalent to a hundred thousand scholarships and exhibitions of the most valuable kind—because, unlike such rewards in general, they are for life—offered for the encouragement of youthful learning and good conduct in every class of the community.

All this has led to a great improvement in the efficiency of the administrative service. That such is the case is proved by the general acceptance of the new national institution, so that no sane person has any idea of abrogating it and reviving the former state of things, but, on the contrary, there is a constant movement towards extending it in its entirety to the few remaining branches of the service to which it has not yet been fully applied. . . .

You ask as to the effect of the change upon " official morality." Official corruption was not one of the faults of the old system.[1]

---

[1] The " old system," as here referred to, is not the " old system" as the phrase is generally used in this volume, where it refers to the state of things

Trustworthiness mainly depends upon a secure tenure of office, and that has long been abundantly provided for. The rule that the first appearance of official delinquency should be thoroughly investigated and adequately dealt with, has been and still is fully enforced. The plan now acted upon is to have fewer of the higher class of civil servants, and to pay them better from the first, getting the copying, care of papers, and other less intellectual work done by a cheaper and more ordinarily educated class, which has a tendency both to promote economy and to encourage fidelity and exertion on the part of the most trusted servants by making their appointments more valuable to them. . . .

　　　　　Believe me, very truly yours,　　　　Ch. TREVELYAN.
D. B. EATON, Esq., etc., etc.

In a subsequent letter to the author Sir Charles Trevelyan says :

"You cannot lay too much stress upon the fact that the making of public appointments by open competition has been accepted by all our political parties, and that there is no sign of any movement against it from any quarter."

---

II. Letter from John Bright :

　　　　　　　　　　　　　　　LONDON, April 29, 1874.

DEAR SIR : I am sorry I have been so long in replying to your letter, and now I do not feel that I can say much that will be of use to you.

The opening of our civil service has met with general approval, and after the experience of some years it would *be impossible* to go back to the old system. The present plan is one which is felt to be more just to all classes, and it is calculated to supply more capable men for the various departments of the public service.

You are doubtless aware that appointments with us are to a large extent of a permanent character. No changes in persons employed in government offices, in the customs, excise, post-office, and telegraph departments, take place on a change of government, and thus we avoid a vast source of disturbance and corruption which would be opened if the contrary plan were adopted.

prior to 1800 or 1820. Sir Charles Trevelyan means by the old system only that which immediately preceded 1853, which was in large part removed at that time, and which was abolished in 1870.

In these days, when so much is done by governments, and so many persons are employed by them, it seems absolutely necessary to take precautions against the selection of incompetent men, and against the corruption which under the purest administration is always a menacing evil.

Your proposed reform is a great undertaking. I hope the good sense of your people will enable you to complete it. *All the friends of your country* in other nations will congratulate you in your success. I have directed to be forwarded to you some of our Parliamentary publications, that you may know the latest facts connected with what is doing here in the matter of our civil service.

I am, with great respect, yours very sincerely,

JOHN BRIGHT.

D. B. EATON, Esq., etc., etc.

III. Mr. Fairchild, then United States Consul at Liverpool, wrote the author, under date of October 8th, 1877, as follows:

"I do not hesitate to say that the civil service of this country is held in very high estimation by the people here. . . . There is a pervading feeling of confidence in and satisfaction with the civil service as a whole, and I am decidedly of the opinion that such confidence and satisfaction are well founded. . . . Not that it is considered by all as an entirely perfect system and incapable of improvement, but that it is held to be so perfect in its workings and results as to give great satisfaction to the people. During my residence here I do not now remember to have heard of but *three cases* where men in the service have been found guilty of financial dishonesty. . . . The service being non-partisan, they were treated just exactly the same as any other criminal would have been, . . . and the crimes of the individuals were not charged to either of the great political parties. . . ."

IV. General Badeau, the United States Consul-General in Great Britain, under date of November 1st, 1877, wrote the author as follows:

". . . That the general opinion in England—and I believe the facts carry out such belief—is that the inland revenue service, the customs service, and post-office department are efficient, and that every confidence is placed in the administration of those services; and in very few instances is that confidence ever abused. If an abuse of the confidence of the Government has sometimes occurred, it has been and is among the inferior officers of the postal departments, such as letter-carriers and sorters ; but in the very large number of these offices the percentage of crime is very small. I know of no scandals in these departments that are spoken of at all, and I am decidedly of opinion that one of the greatest causes of the absence of scandals and of the honesty of officials is the fact that after a short series of years each officer becomes entitled to a pension which continues for life and increases in proportion to the number of years of service and the efficiency of the officer. . . ."

V. Mr. Moran, now United States Minister at Lisbon, but for many years the Secretary of Legation in Great Britain, uses this language, in a letter to the author dated January 26th, 1878 : " I fully share your views of the efficiency of the revenue and postal services of Great Britain and their freedom from corruption. These views of mine are based upon the observation of years. The causes are not far to seek. Men are selected for these services because of their fitness, are fairly paid, are only removable for cause, and can always look forward to a pension when incapacitated by labor or old age.' Both services are thoroughly efficient, and there have been no great scandals attached to either service in my time. Delinquencies occasionally occur among the post-office officials of minor grades, but these are invariably punished. On the whole, the civil service of Great Britain is, in my opinion, the best in the world, and worthy of imitation."

VI. Mr. Hoppin, who succeeded Mr. Moran as Secretary of Legation in Great Britain, says, in a letter to the author, that " During the whole period of my stay here I do not remember to have seen in the papers any charge of peculation or improprieties of any sort against any permanent official. I presume the more closely I should inquire, the more unanimous I should find the sentiment in favor of the rules of the civil service as they exist here at present."

' The pensions here referred to are the superannuation allowances already explained, which are little more than another name for a part of the salary reserved for declining years.

VII. Letter from Edwards Pierrepont :

LEGATION OF THE UNITED STATES,
LONDON, October 14, 1877.

MY DEAR SIR   Yours of September 18th is received.   You rightly state that you understood me to say that I had very often asked men of different grades of life in England their views about the honesty of the administration of their imperial and their municipal governments, and that I invariably found that they believed, or professed to believe, in the purity of such administration.

Since my interview with you last summer, I have had increased opportunities to make further and more minute inquiries upon this subject, of which I have carefully availed myself, both in England and Scotland ; and I have never found a person who did not profess to believe in the strict honesty of the administration in all departments, so far as relates to the expenditure of money.   What the facts may be I have no means of knowing, but the belief, or expressed belief, among all classes is universal, that serious corruption does not exist either in the imperial or municipal administration, and I have no reason to question the correctness of this general opinion.

I am, very truly yours,        EDWARDS PIERREPONT.[1]
Hon. D. B. EATON.

---

VIII. The two following letters present the subject from the standpoint of private citizens of the United States, who also have had rare opportunities of forming a correct judgment :

NEW YORK, November 7, 1877.

DEAR SIR : I have received your favor of the 19th, asking me whether, in my opinion, it was the general belief of the English people, if not their almost universal conviction, that the civil-service administration of England, at least in the customs service, in the inland revenue service, and the post-office department, is efficient, and, as a rule, free from corruption.

To this inquiry I do not hesitate to give an affirmative answer. Not that there is no scandal and no abuse.   These evils, no doubt, exist in every country to a greater or less extent ; but that there is in England, generally speaking, a pervading fidelity and efficiency, with a corresponding feeling of confidence and satisfaction on the part of the people generally, there can, I think, be no question ; and, so far as my observation extends, that confidence is, as a rule, well

[1] At that time Mr. Pierrepont was United States Minister.

deserved. If I were to particularize any service it would be that of the post-office, for the working of that branch comes more nearly under my observation; and I do not hesitate to say that it is managed with singular efficiency and regard for public convenience, and, so far as I have known, with that freedom from public scandal which is proverbial in the English service.

Yours faithfully, J. S. MORGAN.[1]

D. B. EATON, Esq.

---

NEW YORK, October 25, 1877.

DEAR SIR : In reply to your letter of the 19th ult. addressed to me in London, I do not hesitate to say that the opinion I have formed of the administration of the civil service of Great Britain is a very favorable one. I consider it vastly superior in all important respects to that of the United States. It could hardly fail to be so, inasmuch as, while in that country the party in power may, and doubtless does, in getting offices give a preference [2] to its friends, no removals are made on political grounds. With a change of ministry changes take place in a few high offices, but minor offices in all departments of the government are held by their incumbents as long as the duties thereof are properly performed. On what grounds public offices in the United States are filled and vacated is understood by all who have paid any attention to the administration of our civil service. I have spent the most of the time since November, 1870, in London, and I do not think that I have *ever heard charges of corruption or complaints of inefficiency against the service in Great Britain.* There is undoubtedly, in some departments, too much of routine and of adherence to ancient modes of transacting business; but I am quite sure that the general administration of the civil services in Great Britain is approved by the intelligent and fair-minded men of both parties, Liberals and Conservatives.

Very truly yours, H. McCULLOCH.[3]

D. B. EATON, Esq.

[1] The well-known American banker, formerly member of the house of George Peabody & Co., and now the head of the banking house of J. S. Morgan & Co., of London.

[2] This preference, of course, can only take place within those very narrow limits where open competition has not wholly excluded favoritism—probably not extending to five per cent of the clerkships, and only in a qualified form even to those.

[3] Late United States Secretary of the Treasury, but for some years past the head of the London banking house of McCulloch & Co.

# APPENDIX B.

## SOME CONFIRMATION OF VIEWS EXPRESSED.

American opinions of British administration —Mr. Hewitt on consular systems.—American and British consuls in China.—Our territorial governments contrasted with the British.—Examples of the infidelity of both the great parties to reform.—How patriotism and public spirit are impaired.

PERHAPS the views most likely to be challenged of any expressed in this volume are those to the following effect:

(1) That the superiority of British administration is so manifest as to be readily seen and admitted by competent and candid observers.

(2) That our partisan spoils system, no longer a mere defect in administration, has really undermined patriotism at home and arrested the growth of republicanism abroad.

(3) That civil service reform is not merely a mode of procedure and an economy, but has become a vital question of principle and public morality, involving the counterpoise and in no small degree the stability of the government itself.

Upon the first point, perhaps, any thing beyond which is contained in Appendix A. is superfluous. A whole chapter might easily be filled with citations in support of the second and third propositions.

From the mass of evidence, I cite a few opinions from persons representing all parties, which seem to go quite beyond any statements in this volume.

I. "The thorough reform of our civil service would sweep away nearly the whole brood of evils which have *so dishonored the government at home and abroad* within the last generation; and our party leaders, and not the masses, have made that service a disgusting system of political prostitution."—*International Review*, Jan., 1879.

II. "In the British service, candidates (for consulships) must be examined for admission, and in all cases must understand French and the language of the country to which they are assigned for duty. . . Promotions are made for merit and length of service. . . They are never removed for political causes ; nor is it ever intimated, on a change of administration, that they are expected to make room for hungry politicians. They devote themselves for life to the promotion of British trade and commerce. They seek out new avenues for enterprise. . . If time permitted, I could furnish volumes of evidence of the zeal and energy of these missionaries in the cause of British trade. Their reports and the reports of the attachés of the British legations are models of patient labor and treasuries of valuable commercial knowledge. . . I need not waste any time in describing how our consuls are appointed, and, with some creditable exceptions, what manner of men they are apt to be. Appointed as a rule for subordinate and often discreditable political services, they usually have no qualifications for the position. They have no permanence of tenure, and hence are often removed just as they have acquired the experience to be useful. The result is that it may almost be affirmed that our consular system as now organized and administered, with its code, offers *an impediment rather than an aid to commerce*."

Mr. Hewitt also sketches a plan for reform almost identical with the consular system of Great Britain, France, and Germany—that system which France, in becoming a republic, shows no disposition to abandon. Of the French system Mr. Hewitt says :

" A most elaborate scheme of examination is laid down for admission to the permanent consular and diplomatic service. . ." " They must understand two modern languages besides their own." " The examinations include . . international law, diplomatic history, statistics, political economy, geography, and the languages." " Promotion is made from the lower grades of the entire foreign service." This system he declares has been found so efficient that it has remained unchanged for nearly half a century.

<hr />

¹ Speech Hon. A. S. Hewitt, H. Rep., 11th March, 1878.

III. Speaking of the dissatisfaction of American merchants in China with our consular system, a writer who is personally familiar with the facts says : " They contrast, for instance, that of Great Britain, which makes the service so *honorable and attractive* that entrance thereto is eagerly sought by an excellent class of specially fitted men. . . This system they contrast with one which makes it possible to send a man to perform commercial, judicial, and almost diplomatic functions among an ancient, formal, oriental people, because he has been an efficient ' worker ' in the primaries of Oshkosh or Yuba Dam. . . Yet our system does not save us money ; for satisfactory establishments at the leading ports, where alone they are needed, would cost less than the present aggregate. . . Our consular system is something ' to make the very gods of solemnity laugh.' " [1]

Surely it is not a matter for argument or doubt, whether the contrast of our political, ill-instructed, shifting consuls, with the experienced and highly-educated officials of the leading monarchical states, in all the commercial ports of the world —whether their relative influence upon national commerce, reputation, and honor are or not favorable to our trade, to republican institutions, or to American patriotism ? Or, looking to the contrasts presented in the State Departments at home— the one system tendering high standards of capacity and attainments, the other balancing the pressure of factions and the interests of partisan politics—is the suggestion and the influence any more favorable to American pride or patriotism ? If our foreign relations—whether the part pertaining to commerce or the part pertaining to the other great subjects of national jealousy and ambition—upon either of the continents presented any thing like the complications and difficulties with which the British Foreign Office has to deal, our Secretary of State would, I venture to think, find it absolutely impossible to give the amount of time and thought now wasted upon the miserable negotiations, bargainings, and balancings that attend the selections and appointments of a great portion of the consuls and not a few of the lower grade of diplomatic repre-

---

[1] *International Review,* April, 1879, pp. 357-359.

sentatives. He is compelled to listen to importunity, to weigh partisan influence, and to calculate and provide for political consequences every year in connection with the candidacy of hundreds of persons for these places, nearly every one of whom would be excluded by the non-partisan tests which are applied by Great Britain, and by every other great and enlightened nation of the world—tests of capacity and fitness which are as essential to advance the commerce as they are to maintain the honor of the country and the prestige of republican institutions.

IV. It would carry me too far—and it is quite superfluous—to cite authority as to administration at our own doors; but, by way of bringing into comparison the British and American systems, as applied to dependencies or territories, as to which the facts are perhaps not so familiar to the reader, I cite the following statement from a late article written by the Chief-Justice of the Territory of Montana,[1] who certainly must be familiar with our Territorial system; and, as a high judicial official, he may be assumed to be candid:

"Good men are often removed without cause or provocation, to make room for others whose claims are thought to be superior by reason of their services to the party in power, or whose importunity becomes unendurable. . . A swarm of office-seekers besiege the 'White House,' supported by a thousand and one pretended claims and influences; charges are made against the distant officer, and he is removed without notice or warning; the result is that Federal officials are constantly arriving in the Territories and departing from them, until the terms 'pilgrim' and 'carpet-bagger,' by which names they are generally known and designated among the people, become natural and appropriate. . . An officer, by the purity of his life and official conduct, becomes popular with the people. The embryo Senators and members of Congress see danger in the distance. Their rival must be humbled, and the word of one man upon an ex-parte hearing can cause his removal and degradation. This feeling is the parent of many an unjust charge and accusation, whereby the Territories may be kept in a constant broil."

[1] *International Review*, March, 1879. p. 303.

It is hardly necessary to say that abuses of this character, from the very nature of the British system, cannot happen anywhere in the vast chain of her dependencies, from imperial India down to the smallest island under her flag. And how long do we think her rule could be maintained—how many years could we hold India, the Dominion of Canada, the great Australian colonies, Tasmania, or even such second-class dependencies as Jamaica, New Zealand, Cape Colony, or Ceylon – under such a system as we tolerate? Even the smallest of these secondary dependencies has a population greater, I believe, than the entire white population of all the Territories of the United States combined.[1]

V. As bearing upon the last of the three points, I cite from a report lately submitted to Congress by a committee,[2] representing one of the great parties, which has just been making extensive investigations :

" At the end of each four years the entire Federal patronage (amounting to one hundred and ten thousand offices) is collected in one lot, and the people divide themselves into two parties, struggling in name to choose a President, but in fact to control this enormous patronage, which the President, when elected, is compelled to distribute to his party because he was elected to so distribute it. The temptation to fraud, to usurpation, and to corruption, thus created, is beyond calculation. A prize so great, an influence so powerful, thus centralized and put up at short periods, *would jeopard the peace and safety of any nation. . . No nation can withstand a strife among its own people, so general, so intense, and so demoralizing. No contrivance so effectual to embarrass government, to disturb the public peace, to destroy political honesty, and to endanger the common security, was ever before invented.*"

And yet, since that report was adopted, a deliberate removal has been made by that party of officers of the national Senate for political reasons alone—one of the most extreme, indefensible, and unprecedented acts of partisan proscription to be

[1] Their population is about as follows : Ceylon, 2,500,000; Jamaica, 506,000 ; Cape Colony, 700,000 ; New Zealand, 800,000.

[2] Report made by Mr. Potter from the Committee on Alleged Frauds in the late Presidential Election, p. 64, March 3, 1879.

found in the whole history of the government.[1]   In presence
of such declarations and such acts, does patriotism, and faith in
official life, remain unimpaired?

Over against these acts of one party, impartial history must
set acts of the other party hardly less discreditable and disastrous.[2]

Acting upon a reform policy recommended in 1870 by a
President of its choice, that party in the most formal manner
pledged itself to reform the civil service, and holding up
that pledge before the people, it carried a national election.
The work of reform was entered upon, but while it was going
forward, with the good effects set forth in Appendix C., it
was suppressed by the party which had started it through a
refusal to vote money to carry it forward, although an appropriation was requested by a special message of the President,
April 18th, 1874.   Such examples might well be discouraging
if the reform sentiment had not, after every betrayal, risen
yet more powerful to rebuke the folly of those who insulted
it, and to thrust aside those who attempted to trample upon it.

If I have cited these instances of infidelity to pledges and
professions, in support of views before expressed, they are not
less instructive as showing that here, as has been the fact in
England, there is more hope of reform from the Executive than
from Congress, and perhaps from the joint influence of the
best men of both parties than from either party acting alone.

In Appendix A. we can learn how little an Englishman
finds to place the administration of his country in a repulsive
or humiliating attitude before his eyes.   But how different is
it with us!   What I have cited is but here and there a line
from the vast volume of indignation, complaint, lamentation,
and disgust, in connection with our administrative methods,

---

[1] If only the claim of the principal officer removed were involved, I should
think that the extreme partisan work in which he so unbecomingly engaged
fully justified his removal.

[2] Having no party ends to save by this volume, and believing that civil
service reform is a great cause and interest of the people, which they must
carry forward against what is most selfish, corrupt, and partisan in official life and in each of the great parties, it is no part of my purpose to screen
either party, or to point out which party has rendered most service to that
cause, or from which it has most to hope in the future.

which comes from every quarter of the Union, from every grade of life, from every sphere of political action. The villages, the cities, the army posts, the special agencies, the custom-houses, the mayors, the governors, the consulates, the revenue officers, the president in short, public affairs of every nature and officers of every class—are involved in distrust and are degraded in popular estimation, by reason of the opportunities afforded by a partisan-spoils system of office and the use that is made, or is believed to be made, of these opportunities. In the formal papers of the President, in the resolutions of conventions, State and National, in debates in the Senate and the House, in reports of committees and of subordinate officers, in our periodical literature, in the speeches and sermons of our thoughtful men, in the press and in common speech of the people, in forms and at times innumerable, we see our administrative system, for such reasons, denounced, and the character, and motives of those who administer it arraigned and brought under suspicion. This goes on from month to month, from year to year, from administration to administration. Can any one undertake to estimate how much it has done to impair confidence in our institutions, to cast suspicion over all official life, to disgust the people with the very name of politics, to drive good men from the polls, to bring republicanism into disrepute both at home and abroad? And it is because these abuses are known, bringing joy to our enemies and sorrow to our friends in other countries, that we find John Bright using this language in 1874, *at the very moment the then dominant was strangling its own reform:* " Your proposed reform is a great undertaking. I hope the good sense of your people will enable you to complete it. All the friends of your country in other nations will congratulate you on your success." [1] Thus far, only the politicians and not the people have dealt with the reform. When the people shall have it fairly before them, need we doubt that Mr. Bright's hopes will be realized?

[1] See his letter of April, 1874, in Appendix A.

# APPENDIX C.

CIVIL SERVICE REFORM UNDER PRESIDENT GRANT.

The practical results of that experiment:—The good effects of the merit system established.—Its defeat caused by patronage monopolists in Congress.
—Analogous to the first experience in Great Britain.

It is a matter of general information, that under President
Grant a trial, beginning January 1st, 1872, was made of the
*merit system* in a limited way; the regulations, competitions
and examinations being closely analogous to those so long in
practice in Great Britain. I hardly need recall the well-
known facts that, by reason of the imperfect support given
the reform, of open hostility in various official quarters, and
of the damaging examples of official infidelity on the part of
some of those connected with the Administration, the new
system was placed at a great disadvantage; but it is important
not to forget that, despite all these drawbacks, its good effects
clearly appeared, and that they are established by authority so
high and direct as not to be open to question. From the report of the Civil Service Commission, submitted to President
Grant in April, 1874,[1] it appears that, upon the basis of their
own experience and of the reports of their subordinates, the
heads of departments—the members of the Cabinet—approved the language of the report, which stated the following
as the results of the trial of the new system—that is, of the
rules then in force:

(1) " They have, on an average, where examinations apply,
given persons of superior capacity and character to the service of the government, and have tended to exclude unworthy
applicants.

(2) " They have developed more energy in the discharge

---

[1] Report, p. 42.

29

of duty, and more ambition to acquire information connected with official functions, on the part of those in the service.

(3) "They have diminished the unreasonable solicitation and pressure which numerous applicants and their friends, competing for appointments, have before brought to bear upon the departments in the direction of favoritism.

(4) "They have, especially where competition applies, relieved the heads of departments and of bureaus, to a large extent, of the necessity of devoting, to persons soliciting places for themselves or for others, time which was needed for official duties.

(5) "They have made it more practicable to dismiss from the service those who came in under the civil service examinations, when not found worthy, than it was, or is, to dismiss the like unworthy persons who had been introduced into the service through favor or dictation.

(6) "They have diminished the intrigue and pressure, before too frequent, for causing the removal of worthy persons for the mere purpose of bringing other, perhaps inferior, persons into the service."

And the Commissioners, at the close of the report, make these statements as to the practical working of the new methods :

1. "The practicability of fairly conducting examinations as to the qualities to be tested, and of fairly rating the results of competition, and of preserving reliable evidence of the same, has been established.

2. "It has been demonstrated that competitive examinations for entrance to the public service will, besides diminishing evil influences in our politics generally, bring a better class of persons into that service and insure more efficiency in administration.

3. "In regard to promotions, it has been shown that the method of competition may be so united with the exercise of the proper authority of heads of offices or bureaus as to prevent the favoritism and discouragements too frequent under the old method of making promotions, and secure more fidelity and intelligence in the service.

6. "To carry on the reform for another year, there is needed an appropriation of $25,000. . . ."

There is no need, nor can the space be spared, to present here even an outline of the decisive evidence by which the utility of the new system was demonstrated in that report. It is enough to say that on the 18th April, 1874, President Grant sent the report to Congress with a special message in which he says :

" Herewith I transmit the report of the Civil Service Commission. If sustained by Congress, I have no doubt the rules can, after experience gained, be so improved and enforced as to still more materially benefit the public service and relieve the Executive, members of Congress, and the heads of departments from influences prejudicial to good administration. The rules, as they have hitherto been enforced, have resulted beneficially, *as is shown by the opinions of the members of the Cabinet and their subordinates in the Departments, and in that opinion I concur.*"

The message concluded by asking for the same appropriation for the next year that had been made for the previous year. President Grant repeated these views in his annual message of December 7th, 1874, in which he again appealed to Congress for an appropriation. Not even such unquestioned evidence, reinforced by the request of the President, could avail in that Congress. Its members lacked faith in the higher sentiments of the people as much as they desired patronage in their own hands. Party managers clamored for spoils. There was a lamentable absence of foresight and statesmanship. The pledges of the past and the promise of the future were sacrificed by a refusal to make the least appropriation, and by treating with contempt an experiment for which the party and administrative power were responsible. For a time this refusal in a large measure suppressed the reform methods.[1] That it did not arrest the reform sentiment, is very clearly shown by the fact that it was an element which

---

[1] I say for a time and in large measure, because, though the rules appear to have been formally suspended in some departments, they have hardly anywhere lost their influence, and various public officers have since shown so much respect for the public interests—notably Secretary Schurz and Postmas-

exerted a greater influence in the next Presidential election than it had ever exerted upon any previous national canvass.

With the members of that Congress directly, but not solely, must rest the responsibility of deserting and arresting a reform to which they were pledged, and of losing, without the least gain, a powerful hold upon the confidence of the nation. In noticing this lamentable triumph of personal and partisan selfishness over statesmanship and public faith, we cannot fail to recall the fact that, at near the same time after the first introduction of the merit system into Great Britain, Parliament condemned it by an adverse vote, but its members never (like the members of this Congress [1]) refused an appropriation requested by the Executive to carry it on.

From these facts, we can see that the *merit system* is just as practicable, and that it bids fair to be as salutary, in this country, as it has been found to be in Great Britain and the other leading nations : and that its strongest enemies are patronage monopolists in Congress. It is, perhaps, vain to expect that these monopolists or that partisan managers will voluntarily surrender their spoils, or in any way begin a reform ; but is it unreasonable to expect that the people will not much longer tolerate abuses the removal of which is thus proved to be entirely practicable, and which it only needs a firm and clear expression of their wishes to bring about ?

ter James of New York—that they have again put them in force, with the sanction of President Hayes : and within the last few days they have been, in the same spirit, applied in the Custom-House and in the Naval Office at the City of New York.

[1] It was stated in the public journals at the time, that *fifty-one* of them, soon after the 4th of March, urged their personal claims for office upon the President, to say nothing of claims innumerable made on behalf of their favorites and henchmen.

# INDEX.

## ERRATA.

Page 11, line 5 from bottom, for "is," read "are."

" 42, line 2 from top, omit "State."

" 237. Note 3 should be marked as a quotation.

" 305, line 15 from bottom, for "system," read "administration."

Stereotyped by S. W. Green's Son.

WORKS TREATING ON

# ENGLISH HISTORY.

## Published by HARPER & BROTHERS, N. Y.

☞ HARPER & BROTHERS *will send any of the following works by mail, postage prepaid, to any part of the United States or Canada, on receipt of the price.*

☞ HARPER'S NEW AND ENLARGED CATALOGUE, *with* COMPLETE ANALYTICAL INDEX, *sent by mail, on receipt of nine cents.*

MACAULAY'S HISTORY OF ENGLAND. The History of England from the Accession of James II. By Lord MACAULAY. 5 vols., 8vo, Cloth, $10 00; Sheep, $12 50; Half Calf, $21 25. 12mo, Cloth, $4 00; Sheep, $6 00; Half Calf, $12 75. New Edition from new Electrotype Plates, 8vo, Cloth, Gilt Tops, Five Volumes in a box, $10 00 per set. Sold only in sets.

MACAULAY'S ESSAYS. [32mo, Paper.]

JOHN MILTON. — LORD BYRON. 25 cents.
JOHN HAMPDEN.—LORD BURLEIGH. 25 cents.
THE EARL OF CHATHAM. 25 cents.
WILLIAM PITT. 25 cents.
SAMUEL JOHNSON, LL.D. 25 cents.
FREDERIC THE GREAT. 25 cents.
LORD CLIVE. 25 cents.
WARREN HASTINGS. 25 cents.

THE LIFE AND WRITINGS OF ADDISON. 25 cents.
SIR WILLIAM TEMPLE. 25 cents.
MACHIAVELLI.—HORACE WALPOLE. 25 cents.
GOLDSMITH.—BUNYAN.—MADAME D'ARBLAY. 25 cents.
LORD BACON. 25 cents.
HISTORY. HALLAM'S CONSTITUTIONAL HISTORY. 25 cents.

In Cloth, 40 cents per volume.

MACAULAY'S LIFE AND LETTERS. The Life and Letters of Lord Macaulay. By his Nephew, G. OTTO TREVELYAN, M.P. With Portrait on Steel. Complete in 2 vols. 8vo, Cloth, Uncut Edges and Gilt Tops, $5 00; Sheep, $6 00; Half Morocco, $9 50; Tree Calf, $15 00. Popular Edition, 1 vol., 12mo, Cloth, $1 75.

HUME'S HISTORY OF ENGLAND. History of England, from the Invasion of Julius Cæsar to the Abdication of James II., 1688. By DAVID HUME. 6 vols., 12mo, Cloth, $4 80; Sheep, $7 20; Half Calf, $15 30. New Edition from new Electrotype Plates, 8vo, Cloth, Gilt Tops, 6 volumes, $12 00.

GREEN'S HISTORY OF THE ENGLISH PEOPLE. History of the English People. By JOHN RICHARD GREEN, M.A. 4 vols. With Maps. 8vo, Cloth, $2 50 per vol. (3 vols. ready.)

GREEN'S SHORT HISTORY OF THE ENGLISH PEOPLE. A Short History of the English People. By JOHN RICHARD GREEN, M.A. With Tables and Colored Maps. 8vo, Cloth, $1 52.

ALISON'S HISTORY OF EUROPE. History of Europe. FIRST SERIES: from the Commencement of the French Revolution, in 1789, to the Restoration of the Bourbons, in 1815. In addition to the Notes on Chapter LXXVI., which correct the errors of the original work concerning the United States, a copious Analytical Index has been appended to this American Edition. SECOND SERIES: from the Fall of Napoleon, in 1815, to the Accession of Louis Napoleon, in 1852. By SIR ARCHIBALD ALISON. 8 vols., 8vo, Cloth, $16 00; Sheep, $20 00; Half Morocco, $34 00.

BELL'S LIFE OF CANNING. Life of the Rt. Hon. George Canning. By R. BELL. 12mo, Cloth, $1 00.

BROUGHAM'S AUTOBIOGRAPHY. The Life and Times of Henry, Lord Brougham. Written by Himself. 3 vols., 12mo, Cloth, in box, $6 00.

BULWER'S ENGLAND AND THE ENGLISH. England and the English. By Earl LYTTON. 12mo, Cloth, $1 50.

CARLYLE'S OLIVER CROMWELL. Letters and Speeches of Oliver Cromwell, including the Supplement to the First Edition. With Elucidations. By THOMAS CARLYLE. 2 vols., 12mo, Cloth, $3 50; Sheep, $4 30; Half Calf, $7 00.

CARLYLE'S PAST AND PRESENT. Past and Present, Chartism, and Sartor Resartus. By THOMAS CARLYLE. 12mo, Cloth, $1 75; Sheep, $2 15; Half Calf, $3 50.

COBDEN'S BIOGRAPHY. Richard Cobden, the Apostle of Free Trade: his Political Career and Public Services. A Biography. By JOHN M'GILCHRIST. Illustrated. 16mo, Cloth, $1 50.

CUSHING'S TREATY OF WASHINGTON. The Treaty of Washington; Its Negotiation, Execution, and the Discussions relating thereto. By CALEB CUSHING. Crown 8vo, Cloth, $2 00.

FORSTER'S DEAN SWIFT. The Early Life of Jonathan Swift. 1667-1711. By JOHN FORSTER. With Portrait and Fac-similes. 8vo, Cloth, $2 50.

FORSTER'S BRITISH STATESMEN. The Statesmen of the Commonwealth of England; with a Treatise on the Popular Progress in English History. By JOHN FORSTER. Edited by Rev. J. O. CHOULES. Portraits. 8vo, Cloth, $2 25; Sheep, $2 75; Half Calf, $4 50.

FOX BOURNE'S LIFE OF LOCKE. The Life of John Locke. By H. R. FOX BOURNE. In Two Volumes. 8vo, Cloth, Uncut Edges and Gilt Tops, $5 00.

GOLDWIN SMITH'S THREE ENGLISH STATESMEN. Three English Statesmen: Pym, Cromwell, and Pitt. A Course of Lectures on the Political History of England. By GOLDWIN SMITH. 12mo, Cloth, $1 50.

HALLAM'S MIDDLE AGES. View of the State of Europe during the Middle Ages. By HENRY HALLAM, LL.D., F.R.A.S. 8vo, Cloth, $2 00; Sheep, $2 50.

THE STUDENT'S MIDDLE AGES, incorporating in the Text the Author's Latest Researches, with Additions from Recent Writers, and Adapted to the Use of Students. Edited by WILLIAM SMITH, D.C.L., LL.D. 12mo, Cloth, $1 46.

HALLAM'S CONSTITUTIONAL HISTORY. The Constitutional History of England, from the Accession of Henry VII. to the Death of George II. By HENRY HALLAM, LL.D., F.R.A.S. 8vo, Cloth, $2 00; Sheep, $2 50.

THE STUDENT'S CONSTITUTIONAL HISTORY OF ENGLAND, incorporating the Author's Latest Additions and Corrections, and Adapted to the Use of Students. Edited by WILLIAM SMITH, D.C.L., LL.D. 12mo, Cloth, $1 46.

KAY'S SOCIAL CONDITION OF THE ENGLISH. The Social Condition and Education of the People in England. By JOSEPH KAY, M.A., Trinity College, Cambridge, Barrister-at-Law, and late Travelling Bachelor of the University of Cambridge. 12mo, Cloth, $1 50.

KEIGHTLEY'S HISTORY OF ENGLAND. The History of England, from the Earliest Period to 1839. By THOMAS KEIGHTLEY. With Notes, &c., by the American Editor. 5 vols., 18mo, Cloth, $3 75.

KNATCHBULL-HUGESSEN'S CROMWELL. Life, Times, and Character of Oliver Cromwell. By E. H. KNATCHBULL-HUGESSEN, M.P. 32mo, Paper, 20 cents.

MACKINTOSH'S HISTORY OF ENGLAND. A History of England to the Seventeenth Century. By Sir JAMES MACKINTOSH. 3 vols., 12mo, Cloth, $3 00.

M'CARTHY'S HISTORY OF OUR OWN TIMES. A History of Our Own Times. From the Accession of Queen Victoria to the Berlin Congress. By JUSTIN M'CARTHY. Vols. I. and II. in one number. 4to, Paper, 20 cents.

PERRY'S HISTORY OF THE CHURCH OF ENGLAND. A History of the English Church, from the Accession of Henry VIII. to the Silencing of Convocation in the Eighteenth Century. By G. G. PERRY, M.A., Canon of Lincoln and Rector of Waddington. With an Appendix, containing a Sketch of the History of the Protestant Episcopal Church in the United States of America. By J. A. SPENCER, S.T.D. Crown 8vo, Cloth, $2 50.

PHILLIPS'S CURRAN. Curran and his Contemporaries. By CHARLES PHILLIPS. 12mo, Cloth, $1 50.

RUSSELL'S MODERN EUROPE. History of Modern Europe; with a View of the Progress of Society from the Rise of Modern Kingdoms to the Peace of Paris in 1763. By W. RUSSELL. With a Continuance of the History by WILLIAM JONES. 3 vols., 8vo, Cloth, $6 00; Sheep, $7 50; Half Calf, $12 75.

RUSSELL'S OLIVER CROMWELL. Life of Oliver Cromwell. By M. RUSSELL, LL.D. 2 vols., 18mo, Cloth, $1 50.

STRICKLAND'S QUEENS OF ENGLAND. Lives of the Queens of England, from the Norman Conquest. By AGNES STRICKLAND. Abridged by the Author. Revised and Edited by CAROLINE G. PARKER. 12mo, Cloth, $1 46.

STRICKLAND'S QUEENS OF SCOTLAND. Lives of the Queens of Scotland and English Princesses connected with the Regal Succession of Great Britain. By AGNES STRICKLAND. Complete in 8 vols., 12mo, Cloth, $12 00; Half Calf, $26 00.

THACKERAY'S FOUR GEORGES. The Four Georges: Sketches of Manners, Morals, Court and Town Life. By W. M. THACKERAY. 32mo, Paper, 25 cents; Cloth, 40 cents.

THACKERAY'S LECTURES. Containing the English Humorists, and the Four Georges. By W. M. THACKERAY. Complete in One Volume. 12mo, Cloth, $1 25.

THE STUDENT'S HUME. A History of England, from the Earliest Times to the Revolution in 1688. By DAVID HUME. Abridged. Incorporating the Corrections and Researches of Recent Historians, and continuing down to the Year 1858. Illustrated. 12mo, Cloth, $1 46.